Please Select Your Gender

Please Select Your Gender

From the Invention of Hysteria to the Democratizing of Transgenderism

Patricia Gherovici

Routledge
Taylor & Francis Group
New York London

Routledge
Taylor & Francis Group
711 Third Avenue
New York, NY 10017

Routledge
Taylor & Francis Group
2 Park Square, Milton Park
Abingdon, Oxon OX14 4RN

© 2010 by Taylor and Francis Group, LLC
Routledge is an imprint of Taylor & Francis Group, an Informa business

International Standard Book Number: 978-0-415-80615-2 (Hardback) 978-0-415-80616-9 (Paperback)

For permission to photocopy or use material electronically from this work, please access www.copyright.com (http://www.copyright.com/) or contact the Copyright Clearance Center, Inc. (CCC), 222 Rosewood Drive, Danvers, MA 01923, 978-750-8400. CCC is a not-for-profit organization that provides licenses and registration for a variety of users. For organizations that have been granted a photocopy license by the CCC, a separate system of payment has been arranged.

Trademark Notice: Product or corporate names may be trademarks or registered trademarks, and are used only for identification and explanation without intent to infringe.

Library of Congress Cataloging-in-Publication Data

Gherovici, Patricia.
  Please select your gender : from the invention of hysteria to the democratizing of transgenderism / Patricia Gherovici. -- 1st ed.
    p. cm.
  Includes bibliographical references and index.
  ISBN 978-0-415-80615-2 (hardcover : alk. paper) -- ISBN 978-0-415-80616-9 (pbk. : alk. paper) -- ISBN 978-0-203-87222-2 (e-book : alk. paper)
  1. Transgender people. 2. Sex (Psychology) I. Title.

HQ77.9.G43 2010
306.76'8--dc22   2009024937

Visit the Taylor & Francis Web site at
http://www.taylorandfrancis.com

and the Routledge Web site at
http://www.routledgementalhealth.com

Contents

Acknowledgments vii
Author ix
Introduction xi

1 The imperative of choice 1

2 The democratizing of transgenderism 23

3 Genealogy of hysteria 41

4 Freud's sex change 65

5 Falling into sex like falling in love 91

6 Gender and sex as performance 113

7 Boy girl boy 131

8 Lacan's transsexuals 151

9 Hysteria and transsexualism 185

10 Writing the *sinthome:* The transsexual body as a written body 215

Conclusion	245
References	249
Index	271

Acknowledgments

This book took shape with the help of many people. For confidentiality reasons, I cannot name my patients, but I want to thank them for all that I learned with them. I feel grateful to Russell Grigg for his guidance, encouragement, and intellectual support. His contributions have helped me take this project off the ground and complete it. Special thanks are also due to Diana S. Rabinovich, whose help was instrumental in launching my explorations on hysteria and transgenderism. My discussions with Deborah A. Luepnitz and Charlie Shepherdson proved inspirational in the early stages of this book. Many thanks to Renata Salecl, Dany Nobus, and Paul Verhaeque for their interest in my research and for their intellectual advice. I have greatly benefited from the generous invitations of Paola Mieli to present my work in progress in the various seminars I gave at Après-Coup New York. I am grateful to Colette Soler for inviting me several times to participate in the English-Speaking Seminar in Paris of the Formations Cliniques du Champ Lacanien, where I was able to test a number of my hypotheses. I extend my deepest thanks to Judith Feher Gurewich for asking me to share panels in psychoanalytic meetings, where I was able to present and discuss the clinical material that shaped the work in this book. I feel fortunate for the unwavering support of Nestor Braunstein; I am inspired by the example of his own work. Several conversations with Jean Allouch proved invaluable in the development of certain of my ideas. I extend special thanks to Kareen Malone, at West Georgia University; Kenneth Gergen at Swarthmore College; Liliane Weissberg at the University of Pennsylvania; and Santanu Biswas at Jadavpur University, Calcutta, for offering me the opportunity to test and discuss with their students many of the ideas presented in this book. I have greatly benefited from the stimulating discussion and vibrant atmosphere in the Philadelphia Lacan Study Group and Seminar. The participants remain invaluable interlocutors. They asked searching questions and made useful objections.

The manuscript was reviewed by Gwyn Driskill, who provided many comments, suggestions, and skillful edits. Her help is greatly appreciated.

For their assistance in gathering the archival images reproduced in this book, I am gratefully indebted to Catherine Johnson-Roehr, Shawn C. Wilson, and Liana Zhou at the library at The Kinsey Institute for Research in Sex, Gender, and Reproduction; and Joan McKenzie and Brandon Zimmerman, at the Library of the College of Physicians of Philadelphia. I owe a special debt of gratitude to artists Lisa Kereski, George Ruhe, and Nina Poon for allowing me to reproduce their photographs here. They have been swift and generous. Many thanks to Lisa Ratmansky, my accomplice in an investigation of tango's unconscious roots and therapeutic effects.

I want to acknowledge the many friends and colleagues who offered help, suggestions, and criticism during the various stages of this project: Susana Bullrich, Thomas Bartlett, Claudia Gilman, Raquel Romberg, Gustavo Klurfan, Richard Sieburth, Mavis Himes, Carmen Lamas, Wilfried VerEecke, Claude-Noëlle Pickman, Christopher Lane, Betsy Mossiman, Pablo Kovalosky, Bruce Fink, Jamieson Webster, Edward Kazarian, Adriana Passini, Radu Turcanu, Jonathan Eburne.

Bernard Stehle took substantial time from his own work to improve mine, exercising his abundant editorial talents. Immense gratitude is due to other members of the Smedley Writers Group, who provided crucial commentaries and suggestions on excerpts and chapters: Justine Gudenas, Tom Purdon, Mona Doyle, Laurence McCarty, Daphne Herbert, Larry MacKenzie, Randall Couch, Ave Maria Merritt, Aldona Middlesworth.

For their support, complicity, and understanding, I thank my editors at Routledge, Kate Hawes and Kristopher Spring.

I am grateful to Beba and Marius Gherovici for their indefatigable help and especially for their immense love, which has been an important source of support. Special thanks to Araceli Gomez.

Jean-Michel Rabaté, my best reader and editor, has offered me unending encouragement and support and deserves far more thanks than I can express. All my heartfelt gratitude to Sofía Milena Rabaté, without her severely tested patience and humorous forgiveness, this book could have not been completed.

An earlier version of a section of Chapter 5 was originally published as "Falling on the Wrong Side of the Tracks: Sidonie and Female Homosexuality," *The Journal of the Centre for Freudian Analysis and Research*, 18, 13–42, 2008; sections of Chapter 2 appeared in "The Analytic Waver and the Democratization of Transgenderism," *The Ethics of the Analytic Treatment*, Formations du Champ Lacanien, Paris, 2007. Both have been extensively revised for inclusion in this book. I thank the editors of these publications for permission to use this material.

Author

Patricia Gherovici, PhD, is an analyst in private practice. She has published in numerous journals and collections, including the foreword to *Erotic Anger: A User's Manual* (University of Minnesota Press, 2001) and, most recently, *The Puerto Rican Syndrome* (Other Press, 2003), winner of the Gradiva Award and the Boyer Prize.

Introduction

Ask any Argentinean tango dancer about the origins of this rhythmic, glamorous, sensuous dance. First, he or she will tell you that tango is not just a dance but a feeling, that even before the music was created, tango already existed as the expression of the need to embrace felt by a man and a woman. Quite often *tangueros* (tango dancers) will wax lyrical that tango is not a dance but an emotion, that tango is syncopated love, that tango is an attitude. And, they will invoke the same passion to deny all the evidence in regard to tango's gender bending and class crossing. Tango was born in the late 19th century and results from a mixture of cultures. It appeared in the cafes, gambling houses, and waiting rooms of the brothels of the poorest *barrios* of Buenos Aires, where immigrant and local men began to tango with other men. A few women followed suit, dancing tango dressed as men with other women in drag.

With its increasing international popularity, the dance soon became a contagious passion and moved across class boundaries—from poor neighborhoods to high-society ballrooms, everyone fell under the spell of tango. Tango became more acceptable, and the tango music's lyrics, which at first were full of sexual double entendres, became more restrained. "Decent" women joined in the dance. Tango, however, remained a predominantly male activity. Groups of men gathered for hours to practice the steps and create new moves, supposedly to improve their dancing and look more attractive to women … and to other men.

Tango is a dancing melting pot. Rich and poor alike partake, all succumbing to the energy of tango that manages to combine paradoxical images: a luxurious Parisian ballroom and a poor Buenos Aires port bar, intimate seductions and formal ballroom performances, close physical contact and highly ritualized social interaction, two men dancing a dance of love with earthy qualities, swirling away next to two women in drag while embracing following a two-by-four beat.

My *tanguero* friends and even my cousin, a tango instructor, swear that tango's origins were heterosexual, that this electrifying, sensuous, amorous embrace practiced among men or women in drag was just a rehearsal for a strictly male–female activity in which men led and women followed. If I can pretend to be convinced by this preposterous or, at least, highly exaggerated claim, it is because I have done my own share of "passing." I lived the first 22 years of my life in Argentina. As a Jew, one of my first cultural shocks in the United States was the ease with which American Jews openly announced their religion. I was used to keeping such things quiet. I had a last name that sounded Italian, and I reserved the revelation of my ethnicity only to those with whom I felt safe. Not only was Argentine society discreetly anti-Semitic, it also was not very supportive of women. I grew up in a stifling conservative society in which, as in tango, men were supposed to be in charge, and women had to follow, looking good but saying little. Independence and intelligence in women were seen as some kind of disability. My experience in the United States was very different. I felt much freer in a culture in which gender roles appeared so removed from those of my *machista* Buenos Aires. In a much more egalitarian society, the feminist fervor of my youth with which I had challenged normativity appeared less urgent and was tapering.

In the quiet solitude of my psychoanalytic consulting room in Philadelphia, I never thought that I was going to have to revise my notions of gender and delve into the deep waters of identity politics until I heard something unusual in the complaints of my patients. I heard from my hysteric patients the question: "Am I straight, or am I bisexual?" I noted that, in fact, they were asking more and more questions like: "Am I a man or a woman?" I linked their uncertainty about their gender with the case of transsexuals since I see them as subjects from whom this question is taken for an answer. They will often claim, "I am a man trapped in a woman's body," or "Despite my male organs, I always knew I was a woman." However, when someone changes sex, the very possibility of embodying a different gender from the one he or she was born with implies that the materiality of the body is not immediately given. Therefore, both hysterics (by questioning their gender) and transgender people (by answering it) show a disjunction between the subjective sense of one's body and its material reality. Thus, for hysterics and for transgender people alike, it is indeed sexual difference that appears as a conundrum.

"I have the worst birth defect a woman can have: I was born with a penis and a pair of testicles," a patient said at our very first meeting, summing up her reason for starting psychoanalysis. According to the *Diagnostic and Statistical Manual of Mental Disorders* (American Psychiatric Association [APA], 2000), this patient should be diagnosed with gender identity disorder, an illness that requires corrective medical treatment like gender reassignment surgery and hormone therapy to achieve a sex change. However, there is a lot of disagreement over the characterization of transgenderism as a mental illness. Experts debate whether the condition should be included in a manual of psychiatric disorders at all. Some consider it to be an issue of sexual identity, sexual orientation, or even lifestyle choice.

Transgenderism is a contested umbrella term used to describe individuals whose gender expression and behavior do not match the usual expectations associated with the male–female binary system. Since the 1990s in the United States, it looks as if transgenderism has lost most of its stigma, coming into its own as an identity, but also endowed with an undeniable subversive force.

Throughout this book, I use clinical examples to show how the transgender discourse has profoundly altered and reoriented psychoanalytic practice. In doing so, I want to offer an original contribution to the theoretical and clinical understanding of transgenderism and to reframe current debates about gender and sexuality in American society. I critically investigate a wide range of discourses on hysteria, bisexuality, and transgenderism, testing their validity against clinical vignettes drawn from published sources as well as from my practice as a psychoanalyst.

Please Select Your Gender covers historical, theoretical, and clinical grounds, with the goal of exploring what can be called today's democratizing of transgenderism. Indeed, what could be more democratic, more essentially American, than giving everyone the choice of having a gender that can be changed on demand? Is this demand legitimate or only a passing fad? Since 2005, from Oprah to Barbara Walters, American television has given increasing exposure to transgenderism.[1] The views tend to be supportive. Despite the fact that gender bending appears to have gained respectability, it has also not lost its shock value. After seeing the media frenzy stirred by Thomas Beatie, the first pregnant trans man to go public, it is clear that transgenderism has acquired an extraordinary media visibility. Anyone who has turned on a television, linked to a blog, or picked up a tabloid magazine can attest to this. And yet, quite a number of people within the transgender community present a very different picture from this media glamorization of transition between the sexes. Often victims of ridicule, violence, and shrill intolerance, transgendered people still fight to protect their basic civil rights.

I will argue for a depathologization of transgenderism and thus differ from the position taken by most analysts. While avoiding the notion of sex as masquerade put forward by Judith Butler and some queer theoreticians, I take into account the rejection of certain Lacanian narratives that are often accused of phallocentrism. This allows me to engage more radically with the

---

[1] On April 25, 2005 Oprah invited transgender author Jenny Boylan to discuss whether a sex change can break a marriage. On September 16, 2005, Oprah aired a show on transgender twins followed by a September 28, 2007 show on transgender families. On April 27, 2007, Barbara Walters examined in a *20/20* special the lives of transgendered children, including a 6-year-old. On April 3, 2008, Oprah's was the first TV interview with "the pregnant man," Thomas Beatie.

political dimension of transgenderism, thus tackling the question of institutional control over the choices that regulate our bodies and our sexuality.

More fundamentally, *Please Select Your Gender* aims to revise current notions of human sexuality. Do sexual practices determine identity? When considered from the perspective of sex change operations, sexuality is both brought to the fore and questioned in its very foundation. How is a penis transformed into a vagina? While it is not so difficult from a medical point of view, it is not enough to be (or look) male or female. Sex or gender is a false disjunction.

The separation of gender and sex is a distinction that is often represented by scholars and activists as a progressive enabling move. This separation, however, was developed in relation to sex change technologies by a medical discourse that has been mostly heterosexist and normative. The contradictions in this logic emerge symptomatically in the complaints of my patients; their statements are both social and individual. I show with clinical examples that hysteria is defined by a question about the possibility of assuming a sexual positioning not fully defined by the phallus. A biological definition of sex dependent on reproductive functions is narrow and easily challenged by transsexualism. The notion of gender puts forward a masculine–feminine bipolarity that is similar to that of word classification in language. This bipolar system seems to be predicated on complementarity. Lacan formalized his theory of sexual difference by using symbolic logic and modal logic. I will not discuss these concepts at a purely theoretical level but show their concrete relevance in the analysis of cases of hysteria and transsexualism. In the following chapters, I make use of Lacan's later concept of *sinthome*, which calls up the singularity of a creation compensating for a defect in the body image and its knotting with the main elements of a subject's structure. I argue that, if for the unconscious "there is no such a thing as a sexual relation," there will always be the symptom-*sinthome* as a way of tinkering with the body.

I wish to reframe the current debate about gender and sexuality in American society by following Lacan's theory of the unconscious. I have observed in my clinical practice in Philadelphia and New York a new modality of the hysterical question: "What is my 'proper' sex?" This question around which hysteria is organized no longer appears as, "Am I a man or a woman?" or "What is a woman?" but rather as, "Am I bisexual or heterosexual?" How do recent changes in the formulation of the question affect our understanding of this phenomenon?

A little anecdote can help us contextualize the main issues. Roy and Silo were two male penguins living in New York's Central Park Zoo. A zookeeper noticed them taking turns trying to hatch a rock that looked like an egg. Seeing this, the keepers gave them the second fertilized egg of a male–female penguin couple that had been unable to hatch two eggs at once. Roy and Silo successfully hatched the egg and raised the healthy young chick, a female penguin named Tango. The story was made into an award-winning delightful children's book, *And Tango Makes Three* (Parnell & Richardson, 2005). Since the penguins were a same-sex couple, many parents in the United States objected to the book. Parents of students at Shiloh Elementary School in Illinois requested that the book be placed in a section of the library with restricted access. In a Missouri school library, after many parent's objections, the book was relocated in the nonfiction section. The American Library Association reported that *And Tango Makes Three* was the most protested book of 2006 and 2007. In 2008, one parent from Calvert County, Maryland, near Washington, D.C., arguing that the book was presenting issues of sexuality unsuitable for young children, requested that the book be removed from the children's library section and shelved with adult books on sexuality. The fact that the penguins "slept together" was claimed to be an obvious reference to sexual behavior. In other places, like in Chico, California, parents, teachers, librarians, and school administrators formed a committee and voted to retain the book in the libraries. Invoking the First Amendment, public libraries established that such censorship was unconstitutional.

This is a good example of what Lacan called the *signifier*. Its randomness (the fact that tango is both the name of a dance and the name of a penguin) is transformed into an allegory by the social context. In this allegory, I find the model for my own quandaries and those of my patients. How can we learn from these curious equivocations? Is there a logic of gender and sexuality that can teach us to make sense of new developments in sex change therapy? Are we changing the way we talk about sex and gender? But, are we thinking differently? This is what I explore by combining case studies, historical surveys, and theoretical discussions. My hope is to contribute to current controversies about the future of gender and sexual politics from the point of view of a clinician. *Please Select Your Gender* confronts psychoanalysis with questions and observations that are not directly part of its intellectual terrain but that are de facto transforming the clinic. Hence, it will advance new ideas in psychoanalysis that apply to the broader social and intellectual context; it proposes a series of critical interventions that will resonate in academic disciplines dealing with human sexuality and the broad issues of gender today.

Chapter 1

The imperative of choice

"I have made a mistake about the timing of my transition," Hera opened the session. "I should have waited to start the hormones until I had enough money to pay for the surgery. But I shouldn't waste my time or yours talking about this. I am not even sure that I can trust you. Trust is a commodity I am in short supply of." Although I was slightly puzzled, the words came out of my mouth immediately. "Is trust a commodity, then?" Hera thought for a while and finally said, "Well, I guess trust is something one has or does not have." She added, "Perhaps I have the choice of trusting you. You have earned my trust."

Hera's comment corresponds to a current assumption about the commodification of issues like love, sex, gender, and body appearance. It was important for me to state the obvious, that some feelings, emotions, and unconscious leanings may resist commodification. The ideological illusion that commodification frees one from the burden of old-fashioned hang-ups, in fact, is the key to the democratizing of transgenderism in a society based on free choice. In a free market, one should be free to choose one's preferred commodity. What could be more democratic, more essentially American, than giving everyone the choice of turning transgenderist, with a gender that can be changed on demand? In such a context, technology and market rules play a crucial role because contemporary transsexual transformations depend on a surgeon and an endocrinologist (Hausman, 1995, p. 75; Millot, 1990 p. 17). With this type of medicalized transformation, the subject is reduced to a body that is seen as a malleable natural phenomenon; its plasticity extends to sexuality. As Charles Shepherdson (2000) notes, medical science offers the possibility of a transformation predicated on the presupposition that we are dealing with an organism and not a body. This transformation assumes that what the transsexual seeks is an anatomical change and not a different embodiment. Shepherdson adds that "the surgeon works with a conception of anatomy that presupposes a natural version of sexual identity, thereby foreclosing the question of sexual difference" (p. 101).

In many cases, the idea of gender as a manipulable construct glosses over a fantasy of escaping altogether the conundrum of sexual division, both for the medical community providing the corrective treatment and for the transsexual demanding a sex change. Colette Chiland (2003) claims that the issue of transsexualism has been trivialized because "the transsexual phenomenon is surely a product of our technology-based, individualistic culture, a token of its contradictions" (p. 2). In the United States, sex change is often referred to as another consumerist lifestyle choice, comparable to becoming vegetarian or moving to a suburban community. As Jennifer Finney Boylan's (2003) accounts suggest, this is exactly what the transsexual experience is not:

> What it's emphatically *not* is a "lifestyle," anymore than being male or female is a lifestyle. When I imagine a person with a *lifestyle*, I see a millionaire playboy named Chip who likes to race yachts to Bimini, or an accountant, perhaps, who dresses up in a suit of armor on the weekend.
>
> Being transgender isn't like that. Gender is many things, but one thing it is surely not is a *hobby*. Being female is not something you do because you are clever or postmodern, or because you're a deluded, deranged narcissist. (p. 22; italics in original)

My clinical experience has exposed me to people whose whole being is consumed by this unique question. One may object that my observation sample may not be representative because it consists of my analysands, hence of people who, if they are not all pathological, at least are experiencing some level of distress. However, in his survey, Jay Prosser (1998) confirms my view that, across the transgender community, transitioning is not a minor pursuit but an endeavor that takes over subjects' lives: "As the insider joke goes, transitioning is what transsexuals *do* (our occupation, as consuming as a career)" (p. 4; italics in original).

TRANSGENDER VISIBILITY

In the 1950s, a number of cases captured the public attention. Since the 1990s, we have witnessed an enormous increase in the media visibility of transgenderism in the United States. What is new today is a discourse hinging around the availability of sexual transformation. What was categorized as either pathological or exceptional is now an everyday reality. The possibility of sex and gender changes appears as a universally accessible choice. As advances in medical technology and hormone treatment make physical changes more easily available, there is a sense that one could fashion one's sex/gender at will. Nevertheless, accessibility is limited by economical factors. Gender reassignment surgery is expensive—it can cost anywhere from

$10,000 to $100,000,[1] and few government or private insurance programs are willing to pay for it. While middle- and upper-class transsexuals may be able to afford a medicalized sex change, for poor transgender people the cost of gender reassignment is prohibitive. In 2003, Andre Geter, a 23-year-old trans woman from Alabama died in Albany, GA, after receiving injections of industrial-grade silicon (hardware store sealer) in the hips and buttocks during a so-called pumping party. This tragedy brought attention to the pervasiveness of this dangerous yet popular underground practice among preoperative transsexuals, who, unable to pay for professional care, inject poisonous hardware-quality silicon sealer into their bodies to achieve more "feminine" curves.

Is the current conspicuousness of gender modification a sign of freedom in a robust democracy, or is the trivialization of sex change a way to push it as a normalizing and prophylactic cure for gender deviance? A very puzzling situation is presented by Iran, a country in which homosexuality carries the death penalty and where women have very limited rights, but in which the government fully supports sex change operations (Fathi, 2004; Stack, 2005). In a progressive move more than 40 years ago, the Ayatollah Khomeini wrote in support of transsexuality and ruled that sex change operations were allowed, a position that has been reconfirmed by Iran's current spiritual leader.[2] Khomeini argued that "if somebody wants to undergo a sex change because he feels trapped inside someone else's body, he has the right to get rid of this body and transform into the other sex, and he is also entitled to new identification documents, in order to put an end to his plight" (Al-Arabiya TV, 2005). Since the 1990s, the number of sex change surgeries performed in Iran has surpassed the number performed in Europe (the estimation is that the number of transgender operations performed in Iran is over seven times the number of such operations in Europe.) According to Dr. Mirjalali, Iran's leading sex change surgeon, a European surgeon performs an average of 40 sex reassignment surgeries in a decade;

---

[1] Washington is one of a few states in the United States where sex change surgeries have been covered. Yet, the number there has been small. Medicaid officials declared that the state has paid for two sex change surgeries since 2000, at a total cost of about $113,000.

[2] "Changing one's sexual identity in Iran is not forbidden by religion. Hundreds of Iranians have managed to turn their dream into reality—from a man into a woman, or vice versa. Iran, which generally arouses fears in the Western world because of its conservative—some say even extreme—Islamic values, is also a country that arouses inquisitive curiosity in general. On the one hand, homosexuals are punished by death, but on the other hand, Iran is one of the few countries that not only permits transgender operations, but even shares the expense of these operations. Why not? The first to inspire that was ... the Leader of the Revolution—Imam Khomeini. Four decades ago, before he came to power in Iran, Khomeini adopted this position, and became, as some claim, the first Muslim cleric to deal with sex change this way. ... According to Khomeini, the issue of sex change does not run counter to Islamic law." Partial transcript from the TV special *Iran: Have a Sex Change on Us*. This television broadcast chronicled sex changes in Iran. It initially aired on Al-Arabiya TV on July 2, 2005.

he performed over 300 between 1993 and 2005 (Harrison, 2005). And, this is not the only surgical record held by Iran: Its surgery boom is also fueled by the high number of cosmetic plastic surgeries performed on women. As a result, Tehran has been dubbed the "nose job capital of the world" (*CBS Evening News*, 2005; Sciolino, 2000). Iranian society may still need to do some catching up. Women's rights bills have been rejected at the government level, while transsexuality, seen as an illness like any other, waits for the solution found in Islam—the idea that science can provide a cure.

Ironically, U.S. President George W. Bush had declared Iran part of the Axis of Evil in 2002, whereas an obvious common point between Iran and the United States is that the state apparatus in both countries tends to bow to religious pressures. Today's ideology of choice cannot be considered in isolation and should be viewed within such a global religious framework. Conversely, secular democracies, like those that have so far flourished in Europe, tend to stress the need to limit individual choice and put the emphasis on the rights of the citizens as a whole.

There is obviously a danger to individual freedom when gender reassignment surgery is seen as therapeutic, as a palliative measure to "fix disturbed populations." We can think here of Giorgio Agamben's (2005) book, *State of Exception* (the title refers to the German phrase for the Anglo-Saxon concept of "martial law," or the French "state of siege"), which examines periods in which the law was suspended, moments that were not exceptional but rather foundational for Western democracies. This extension of power, in which the juridical order is suspended, is supposed to protect democracies, but it has the potential to transform them into totalitarian states. Agamben successfully outlines how this "emergency" measure is a process that functions in substitution for the democratic legislation process; it is a measure by which democracy legalizes its own lawlessness. Agamben's provocative suggestion that the political model of the West is no longer the city but the concentration camp, not Athens but Auschwitz, alerts us to the fragility of democracy. Modern mechanisms of discipline used "to neutralize dangers, to fix useless or disturbed populations, to avoid inconveniences of over-large assemblies" are now being asked to play a positive role, allegedly increasing the utility of individuals (Foucault, 1979, p. 210). Similarly, I would like to call attention to the fact that the democratizing of transgenderism should not be predicated on essentialist notions of normativity. If transgenderism is not an illness, a sex change cannot be either a treatment or a cure.

The American dream rests on a fantasy of boundless mobility—you can be all you want to be. This premise erases, for instance, the overdeterminations of race or class and perhaps even gender. It also implies that identities are something one can earn rather than being something one is born into. The work of Esther Newton on female impersonation (drag) significantly influenced Judith Butler's (1990) construction of a theory of gender performativity (pp. 136–137). Newton contends that the most significant effect of drag on what she calls "the sex-role system" is that sex is no longer natural or inherited but "achieved." For Newton (1979/1972), gender "is outside. It can be manipulated at will" (p. 103).

THE WILL TO CHANGE

Is America's recent fascination with sex change also a symptom of the collapse of a certain postfeminist discourse founded on performativity? A later chapter examines Judith Butler's theories of gender seen not as substantial—it is not an attribute, as a humanist feminist position might argue, or a relation, as sustained by social constructionists—but as being purely performative. Butler's thinking has had enormous influence on a recent redefinition of gender and sexuality. If gender is purely performative, the materiality of the body can be denied. However, in the current debate around sex change, it is the materiality of the body that returns symptomatically. Under the banner of the malleability of gender, the intersexual and the transsexual movements are at opposite ends concerning body manipulations made accessible by recent technological developments. The intersexual movement opposes unwanted surgery, while the transsexual calls for elective surgery. But, both seem to support the notion that gender should be a choice rather than an external, coercive assignment. What degree of autonomy is entailed, then, in such exercise of self-determination?

From a psychoanalytic perspective, sexual identity is not determined by biology or any other innate factor; sexual identity is learned through a language one is born into and through the given dynamics of identifications. Identity is aleatory and constructed around loss, a loss that dates to the inaugural moment when we fell from a pregendered wholeness into sexual difference, the instant when someone sanctioned our being by crying out either "It's a girl!" or "It's a boy!" For psychoanalysis, unconscious choice has nothing to do with a voluntaristic free will. In this choice, the two alternatives available are not isomorphous; thus, discordances emerge between one's erogenous sex and one's declared sex. The case material I discuss in this book gives evidence that in the unconscious there is no representation or symbol of the opposition masculine-feminine. Sexual identity for both males and females is always precarious because the human infant *becomes sexed* without fully symbolizing unconsciously a normal, finished sexual positioning. Psychoanalysis attempts to throw light on the ways in which sexuality fails to conform to the social norms by which it is regulated and on the various fantasies that are constructed to veil this structural failure.

FREE TO CHOOSE

Renée Richards became a female after a sex change in 1975, at the age of 40. Discussing her life, 30 years after her transformation, in *No Way Renée: The Second Half of My Notorious Life,* Richards (2007) admits that she would have never imagined that she would become "a notable part of America's social history" because of her "unusual pursuit of the American Dream, an ideal that encourages us to make of ourselves the most we can. It is a dream my immigrant family embraced and realized. I continue to believe in it" (p. 5). The aspiration that we can be whatever we want to be, that there are infinite possibilities for self-creation and reinvention, is a dream that is not only American.

In 2004, a Portuguese transsexual woman named Nadia Almada won the reality TV show *UK Big Brother,* securing 74% of the votes. Renata Salecl noted that Nadia's words when receiving the prize were, "Now I am recognized as a woman." Wondering why a male-to-female transsexual proved so popular among the British reality TV audience, Salecl (2007) pointed to the mesmerizing allure of a transsexual as someone who embodies the ultimate project of self-transformation (p. 221). Salecl placed the fascination with self-creation within a wider social trend: the commandment to become truly ourselves, but better versions. Indeed, in postindustrial Western societies, people have the impression of being freer from the constraints of the Other, that is the entire system of laws, discourses, and languages that make up a social determinant. This relative perception of freedom versus constraint is particularly relevant in issues of sexual ambiguity. Michel Foucault (1980) has shown that from the Middle Ages, to the Renaissance, and to the 18th century, a relatively lax attitude was replaced by a sterner medicalization of choices. In the 18th century, it was the doctor who had to decide "the true sex hidden that was hidden beneath ambiguous appearances" (p. viii). This generated then a new type of medicalized discourse that left very little freedom of choice:

> From the legal point of view, this obviously implied the disappearance of free choice. It was no longer up to the individual to decide which sex he wished to belong to, juridically or socially. Rather, it was up to the expert to say which sex nature had chosen for him and to which society must consequently ask him to adhere. (p. ix)

Now that the pendulum of the zeitgeist has swung, it seems, in the opposite direction, one may wonder what role the experts will have to play. Examining sex change protocols, Charles Shepherdson (2000) concluded (based on Millot's claims) that "Gender Identity Clinics, under the guise of freedom of choice and admitting diversity (from the 'exotic' to the 'mundane' but all under the regulation of preordained 'types') are in fact in the process of becoming 'sex control centers'" (p. 103). It may be that the situation Millot was addressing belongs to the past. Now that the public at large has the impression that sex change is a pure commodity, people are troubled by a new kind of anxiety. As Renata Salecl (2004a) amply documented, this anxiety is brought about by the paradox of free choice. People are experiencing increasing pressure to choose a new self, which they have to reinvent independently of social restrictions (p. 144). Salecl (2007) wrote that

> The idea that we are supposed to be able to manage ourselves and that there is a choice in how we deal with our emotions, is linked to the very perception of the self that dominates late capitalist society. ... [T]he ideology of a limitless world is itself a product of late capitalism and the relentless drive of consumer society with its emphasis on endless choice and possibility. If, on the one hand, we live under the assumption that everything in life can be a matter of choice (on top of consumer and usual political choices, we can choose not only how we look, but our sexual orientation, whether or not to have children, what kind of medical treatment we want, etc.), on the other hand, the very choice itself seems to be anxiety provoking and deeply dissatisfying. That is why we often hear in the popular media that our society actually suffers from so-called tyranny of choice and an abundance of freedom. (pp. 221–222)

The pitfall of this consumerist ideology of self-creation is that the very availability of choice provokes anxiety and ultimately tends to be deeply disappointing. Salecl (2004a) linked the promise of endless self-invention to the difficulties subjects have to place themselves in regard to sexual difference (p. 234). The seduction of the endlessly improved self as the latest consumer object causes problems in sexual identification. Endless choice produces increase in androgyny and bisexuality, as noted by Jean-Pierre Lebrun: "Since sexuality is a matter of competitive rivalry and consummation, it does not concern anymore a choice of stable object. It is primarily a matter of seduction" (Jean-Pierre Lebrun, 1997/1999, cited by Salecl, 2004a, p. 234).

Indeed, the slogans are seductive. In 2009, one of the foremost transgender conventions in the United States had its 27th annual meeting in Chicago. Gathering under the evocative banner "BE-ALL," its main slogan is: "Everyone's welcome at Be-All! Cross-dressers, Transexuals, M2F and F2M, Wives, Partners, and Friends" (Be-All Chicago, 2009). As with any totalizing claim, there was one exception to the rule: Husbands were not invited to Be-All. Another good illustration of the ubiquity of choice is the title of the "gender workbook" by transgender writer and performer

Kate Bornstein: *My Gender Workbook: How to Become a Real Man, a Real Woman, the Real You, or Something Else Entirely* (1998).

ENJOY!

As early as 1987, French sociologist Baudrillard saw in transgenderism a new ideological horizon. He related this to one of the unforeseen consequences of the sexual revolution in the sixties: "By releasing all the potentialities of desire, the sexual revolution leads to the basic question 'Am I man or woman?'" (2002, p. 12). This would formulate anew the idea that sexual liberation first unleashed a certain feminization, later rephrased as a more generalized hesitation about sexual identities:

> Retrospectively, this triumph of the transsexual and the travestied casts a strange light on the sexual liberation of earlier generations. That liberation, far from being as in its own self-image, the irruption of a maximum erotic value of the body—with an elevation of the feminine and jouissance (the masculine having rather reserved for itself up to that point the field of power)—will perhaps merely have been a decisive stage in the journey towards transsexuality. (p. 12)

He acknowledged that this revolution triggered indeterminacy, anxiety, and consumption, but also fostered choice, pluralism, and democracy. However, the political model does not work in matters of sexuality: "But there simply is no democratic principle of sexuality. Sex is no part of human rights and there is no principle of emancipation of sexuality" (p. 13).

Baudrillard was accurate in identifying a shift not so much in the management of pleasure via liberation as in the promotion of a different modality of enjoyment. Echoing this analysis, Todd McGowan (2004) took up this issue and reflected on the premium American society now places on enjoyment (pp. 11–40). McGowan described a large-scale transformation from a society based on prohibition to one oriented toward enjoyment. He observed a movement from a society that in the past was organized around sacrifice and in which the prohibition of enjoyment carried a certain measure of dissatisfaction, to a society that commands enjoyment without any requisite of renunciation. Since sacrifice is shared and enjoyment is isolated, many current social ills appear as symptoms of this transformation: a sense of disconnection, an increase in aggression and violence, widespread cynicism, political apathy, incivility, and loss of meaning (pp. 137–196). Is the medical transformation of the body an extreme of this urge to enjoy without considering the body as a last limit? Is the surgical intervention in the body a desperate way of inscribing a prohibition to regulate enjoyment after a measure of control has been lost? Examples of this hesitation between control and lack of any form of possible control abound today in debates concerning the hormonal regulation of children's sexuality. News has broken about a new hormonal treatment that allows transgender children, defined as those who meet the controversial standards for the diagnosis of gender identity disorder (GID), to put puberty on hold; the drug, called Lupron, prevents them from developing into their biological sex. For transgender children with supportive parents, this potent and pricey new drug would usher in a new era.

Let us rapidly examine one of the Lupron cases: Marty, a 9-year-old Chinese girl who identifies as boy and lives in California. Her adoptive parents, an American lesbian couple, wish that the drug could ensure that self-determination, and not nature, is destiny. Marty has enrolled in a new school as a boy. Her breasts, which were budding to her dismay, will not grow and she will not be getting her period; thus, nobody will notice any gender variance. "You don't realize how serious this quest is until you follow the kid's lead," one mother said. "I'm convinced he feels like a boy inside." The mother's description is surprising, perhaps because we may expect a lesbian couple to be less essentialist, less constrained by prescribed gender roles, and therefore not threatened if the girl behaves in a tomboyish manner or butch style. Yet, their daughter's process of masculinization is seen as a gift, and Marty's inclinations elevated to an art form, as when the other mother interjected: "I figure if you have a Beethoven, you don't take away the piano" (Smiley, 2007). One is left wondering how far we are from the opening of Adrienne Rich's (1972) famous feminist poem: "The Ninth Symphony of Beethoven Understood at Last as Sexual Message": "A man in terror of impotence/or infertility, not knowing the difference" (pp. 171–172).

Does sexual difference make no difference? With regular Lupron injections, nature will be kept on hold, but only for the few years, during which Marty will postpone deciding whether s/he is a boy or a girl. Soon, Marty will have to make the choice that both mothers see as the next step: testosterone treatment. "Marty's body doesn't do any deciding for him, leaving the road open with Lupron until Marty can better navigate to points female, trans-male, or somewhere in between. It's a decision, essentially, not to decide. But of course that's still a decision" (Smiley, 2007). Nobody seems to notice that Marty will have been socialized as a boy for several years but will not reach puberty as a girl, and that her ability to make a free decision may not be so autonomous. If she chooses to start testosterone treatment now, will her female reproductive organs reach the maturity necessary to procreate? If in the future Marty wants to have a family, will she only have the option of being an adoptive parent? In the order of generations, the ideology of free choice turns at times into its opposite and enhances the repetition of the parent's situation.

The advancement of medical technologies poses bioethical questions with a scope that exceeds this book. Use of Lupron in children has raised quite a controversy. One vocal critic is Paul McHugh, member of the Institute of Medicine of the National Academy of Sciences. McHugh is currently cochair of the Ethics Committee at the American College of Neuropsychopharmacology. He also happens to be the Vatican's advisor on sexual matters, a member of a lay panel of practicing Catholics assembled by the Roman Catholic Church to investigate claims of sexual abuse by clergy. Most surprisingly, he is the psychiatrist who became famous when, in the 1970s, he abruptly closed John Money's sexual reassignment clinic at Johns Hopkins Hospital, thus ending sex change surgeries at the hospital. McHugh went as far as calling the Lupron treatment "a modern form of child abuse" (Smiley, 2007).

A guidebook on how to raise transgender children, marketed as the "first of its kind," pushes back the onset of transgenderism: The promotional material claims that "the authors cover gender variance from birth through college" (Brill & Pepper, 2008). If there can be gender variance at birth, is gender then simply innate? Nonetheless, some transgender adults argue that they had the awareness of being at odds with their biological sex at a very young age, and that the incongruity between their bodies and their sense of themselves caused them tremendous suffering, which could justify an early intervention. While it is obvious that children who start transitioning before puberty may have an easier time "passing," and thus will be more likely to avoid being the victims of hate crimes, on the other hand, an early change will prevent them from belonging to the transgender community. For example, Alexis Rivera of the Transgender Law Center lived as a male until age 17 and later spent several years taking hormones, finally deciding to go off hormones and settle into a middle space between male and female. Now at age 29, Rivera seems happy with the decision and finds the experience of transgenderism empowering while pointing to a potential paradox: "If medical technology keeps advancing, are we going to eradicate transgenderism?" Rivera asks. "The younger the transition starts, the younger you start socializing a biological female as a boy; they're not going to have that transgender identity. They're not going to have to walk this earth as their genetic sex" (Smiley, 2007). Behind the controversy, the questions everyone struggles with—What is a man? What is a woman?—continue to remain unanswered.

IMPOSSIBLE CHOICES

Transgenderism can be understood as a spin on hysteria, a spin that introduces a new mode of enjoyment into the social field. Any request for sex reassignment surgery should be interpreted psychoanalytically before being actualized because if the surgery is pursued as a way out of the deadlock of sexual division, it will fail as an answer. From a psychoanalytic viewpoint, one would advise taking the demand for a sex change as a subjective production, thus unique and meriting an analysis in its particularity. No predetermined norm could generalize the particulars of a subjective motivation. For instance, Catherine Millot (1990) observed:

> The feeling of being a woman trapped inside a man's body (or vice-versa) admits radically different interpretations, depending on the context. In the same way the demand for sex-change ... may also emanate from a woman hypochondriac (this has been encountered) who claims to be a transsexual in order to have her breasts removed because she is afraid she may be affected with cancer, or from a hysteric who sacrifices herself to the power drive of the doctor willing to perform the operation. (p. 26)

Millot's comments might have anticipated a controversy created by Jessica Queller's (2008) book, *Pretty Is What Changes: Impossible Choices, the Breast Cancer Gene, and How I Defied My Destiny*. Queller lost her mother to cancer. After discovering that she was genetically predisposed to develop breast cancer, she had a prophylactic double mastectomy at age 35. Queller said that now she was looking for a man who would father her children before the next step—voluntary surgery to remove her ovaries. Some commentators argued that women wanting to get prophylactic mastectomies needed to know that the risk of women dying from breast cancer is substantially lower than dying of cardiovascular disease. They contended that the fear of death from breast cancer is promulgated by a statistic that was widely quoted to promote women to have an annual mammography: that 1 in 9 women will get breast cancer in their lifetime. While this remains true, the majority of women with breast cancer can be cured, especially if the cancer is detected early (see Hartmann et al., 1999).

Millot argued that sex change discourse has promised cross-gender identifications that were motivated by something that could not be seen or imagined—a place beyond sexual difference where gender would not be simply questioned or subverted but completely transcended. She claimed that those subjects identify with an "outside sex," and that any genital change due to sex reassignment surgery was likely to fail since no anatomical transformation can grant a fantasized position beyond lack and desire. Yet, as Tim Dean (2000) noted, if reassignment surgery involves a fantasy about escaping sexual division altogether, "[t]here is a fundamental paradox, not to mention considerable pathos, in a male-to-female transsexual's undergoing orchidectomy—surgical removal of the testes—in order to elude castration" (p. 82) Millot contended that the identification "outsidesex" was in fact an imaginary identification with the phallus, an identification that can be reflected in the preoccupation of transsexuals with their genitals.

Millot's claims may need some updating. In an article published in the *New York Times* on June 22, 2008, Eve Kososfky Sedgwick commented on the media furor caused by Thomas Beatie, the first pregnant trans man to go public, noting that now "genital surgery is not what defines gender, and that will be news for lots of Americans" (Trebay, 2008). For Sedgwick, Beatie's story (born a woman, former beauty queen, changed sex to male, married, impregnated himself using frozen sperm, became the nation's first pregnant man) is "making visible the fact that a lot of people's experience of making these decisions is not about getting a penis or losing a penis" (Trebay, 2008). Sedgwick presented this story as an exemplary moral tale. "People experience gender very differently and some have really individual and imaginative uses to make of it. That's an important thing for people to wrap their minds around. He's pregnant, he seems happy. It's not in happening in any kind of a judicial, let alone criminal, context so it's not a matter of claiming a right. It's a matter of exercising one" (Trebay, 2008). But, one is left wondering why Beatie, whom neighbors described as "a quiet, regular guy," would take part in the sensational media exposure that followed his going public. What to make of his shirtless image, hairy flat chest with pregnant belly, of his television appearance on Oprah Winfrey's show followed by an exclusive interview in *People* magazine, of his surprise announcement on camera of a second pregnancy?

Thomas Beatie and his wife, Nancy, live in Oregon—in a town coincidentally named Bend. His screen-printing business is intriguingly called Define Normal. Aware that "our situation sparks legal, political, and social unknowns," Beatie refers to the universality of his desire for a child: "Wanting to have a biological child is neither a male nor female desire, but a human desire." Beatie also leans on traditional family values: "To Nancy, I am her husband carrying our child—I am so lucky to have such a loving, supportive wife. I will be my daughter's father, and Nancy will be her mother. We will be a family." His wish to remove stigma from transsexuality is laudable; to achieve it, Beatie appeals to an extended notion of normalcy. "Our situation ultimately will ask everyone to embrace the gamut of human possibility and to define for themselves what is normal" (Beatie, 2008).

REDEFINING NORMAL

I would like to reframe this discussion within the context of clinical issues, with an observation that stems from my experience with an analysand whom I will call Mitch. Mitch is a female-to-male transsexual who wants a double mastectomy but has no concern about her genitalia, which do not appear to be an erogenous zone to her. Mitch does not see her vagina as an erotic organ. Her female partner resisted the idea of surgery because she liked Mitch's breasts. All of Mitch's bodily preoccupations are focused on her external gender appearance; that is, she insists on "passing as a boy." Her breasts are a source of bafflement for those who would address her as a male, and for herself, since they serve as a painful reminder of her birth sex as a female.

Mitch, who prefers to refer to herself using the pronoun "she," is still a case in progress. Rather than escaping sexual difference, Mitch wants to inscribe in her body an unequivocal readability: She wants to be seen as a male or, to quote her more accurately, as a "boy," without any trace of doubt.

If the "virile display in human beings seem[s] feminine," (Lacan, 2006, p. 584), can we say that her masculine appearance is closer to feminine masquerade? Or, is it a virile parade? Or simply, is it imposture? Here, it is helpful to refer to a comment by Lacan that was part of a contribution to a congress on feminine sexuality, in which he opposed the female homosexual to the male transsexual: "We must still learn something from the natural ease with which such women [female homosexuals] invoke their quality as men, in order to contrast it with the delusional style of the male transsexualist" (p. 619).

Mitch is not delusional; however, she is not at ease in her quality as man; she is a careful observer of gender norms and strives to fit in the traditional male gender role. With her, I discovered that women finish their sentences by raising their voices as if they were questions, that men do not look at each other when speaking and often interrupt others, that women smile at other women, that men do not smile at strangers, that men traveling on public transportation carry their belongings away from their bodies while women keep their handbags clutched to their midriffs. The prescriptive list is seemingly endless. Even though Mitch has embarked on a gender-bending project, she subscribes to fixed gender norms. She is asking for a sanction that would confirm her being a man; she is the appearance and the masquerade, she is the proper envelope for her demand for a bodily modification.

Should we consider Mitch's concerns under the dynamics of inhibition, an inhibition that is expressed by the aversion and disgust that her breasts cause her, which make her avoid carnal contact? Sexual repulsion is so characteristic in hysteria that Freud would not hesitate to say that anyone who reacted with disgust to sexual stimulus should be considered hysteric, even when no somatic symptoms were present (Freud & Breuer, 1895): "I should without question consider a person hysterical in whom an occasion for sexual excitement elicited feelings that were preponderantly or exclusively unpleasurable; and I should do so whether or not the person were capable of producing somatic symptoms" (Freud, 1901/1905, p. 28) Mitch's paradox is that she is preoccupied with gender while expressing an aversion to sex.³ In fact, what she wants to avoid when she endlessly postpones sexual rapport is the possibility of encountering in the body of her girlfriend, and in herself, something of the Other (sex). Mitch's discontent with breasts is also her symptom: They stand out in her, as it were, like a "foreign body."

Lacan allows us to grasp how the libido in the hysteric does not necessarily follow the limits of the real body. And, to reach a more accurate understanding, we should consider Mitch's case under the psychic structure of perversion, which is characterized by a specific mechanism of negation, *disavowal*. *Perversion* does not refer to any specific behavior (sexual or otherwise) but to a specific clinical category. Freud developed the notion of a psychic mechanism he calls *Verleugnung*, or disavowal or denial, to explain the curious attitude of some boys who, when seeing a girl's genitals, claim that they see a penis. Indeed, the example of Freud's Little Hans case is very close to Mitch's experience. Very much like Little Hans, who when confronted with his baby sister during her bath, exclaimed: "Her widdler's quite small. When she grows up it'll get bigger all right" (Freud, 1909, p. 276). Mitch, as a little girl, during a bath shared with her older sister, was made aware that she was a girl, which she understood meant that she did not have a penis. In response to the shocking news, Mitch developed a twofold strategy: She disavowed the perception and secretly waited for the day her penis would grow, but she also developed symptoms that seem to indicate that the perception was registered.⁴ This reality was excised, "scotomized" (Freud, 1927, p. 153). Any pleasure that the vagina might have granted her turned into horror and disgust. From that point, Mitch did not even want to be reminded of what was "down there." Thus, a demand for a real excision in her body started to take form.

Mitch's demand for "chest surgery" highlights the libidinal importance of the breasts. Yet as an object, the erotic value of the breasts depends not so much on being part of her mother's body, but rather on the function they play in weaning, as prefiguring castration. On the basis of a loss, oneness with the mother is constructed retroactively, and the breasts, which were experienced as falling from the child's body, are invested with libido. This is illustrated in all its splendid horror by Zurbarán's painting of Saint Agatha carrying her excised breasts on a plate and by Tiepolo's portrait of the ecstatic saint after her ordeal (Lacan, 2006, p. 719).

With Mitch, I have set my refusal to be the person who would write one of the letters of endorsement required by her doctor to undergo surgery as a precondition for the treatment. This decision was based on the

---

³ "[T]he enigmatic contradiction which hysteria presents [is] the pair of opposites by which it is characterized—exaggerated sexual craving and excessive aversion to sexuality" (Freud, 1905, p. 165).
⁴ Mitch's choice of using the pronoun "she" while wanting to be seen as a "he" seems to fit with the mechanism of disavowal, which splits reality in a strategy aptly summed up by Octave Mannoni (2003) as "I know well, but all the same" (p. 68).

ethical requirement that for the analysis to work I could not be positioned as master. According to Harry Benjamin's standards of care for sex change, candidates are expected to live in their chosen gender role for 1 to 2 years (this is called real-life training, or RLT), then engage in hormone therapy for at least 1 year (which can be simultaneous with the full-time experience) before surgery can be performed (Harry Benjamin Gender Dysphoria Association, HBGDA, 1998). Candidates are required to obtain the recommendation of two mental health professionals (often, a psychologist and a psychiatrist), who can attest that surgery would not adversely affect the mental health of the patient.

Rather than being disappointed, Mitch seemed relieved by my decision because she said that she could talk more freely if she did not have to convince me of the benefits of a double mastectomy. Mitch added that she disapproved of this requirement on the basis that a patriarchal system is intolerant of gender changes, quipping that when someone requested breast augmentation, she did not need an "expert's letter as affidavit of support." I responded by stating that any demand for bodily transformation should be talked through and analyzed before the transformation is performed. Indeed, in an article on the advantages of medical skin-tightening cosmetic treatments like Botox and Restylane to combat the ravages of time, the words used by one woman to describe how her face has changed as she aged betrayed a striking resemblance to those words of many transsexuals: "My outside didn't match my inside" (Naversen Geraghty, 2007, August 2).

Similar ethical quandaries are posed by those suffering body integrity identity disorder (BIID), a new mental syndrome that may be included in the next edition of the *Diagnostic and Statistical Manual of Mental Disorders* (*DSM*).[5] BIID sufferers have the obsessive, intense, long-standing desire for the amputation of a healthy limb or digit. In one extreme case, a patient put his leg in ice to force to have it amputated, later professing still not to be satisfied because the surgeons had left the stump three inches too long. Others, in desperate efforts to force surgical amputations, injure themselves with guns or chain saws (Elliott, 2000; Marantz Henig, 2005, March 22). Since elective surgery involving mutilation or removal of a healthy tissue or organs is only accepted in cases of sex reassignment, advocates have often compared it to GID.

John Money, whom I discuss at some length in this book, happened to be the first to observe this disorder. In 1977, he called it *apotemnophilia* (literally, love of amputation) and considered it a form of paraphilia—that is, a sexual deviation (Money, Jobaris, & Furth, 1977) In 2000, Gregg Furth,

---

[5] Michael B. First, a psychiatrist at Columbia University, who was on the board of the editors of the fourth edition of the American Psychiatric Association's *DSM* is advocating for the inclusion of BIID in the forthcoming fifth edition of the *DSM*. If BIID is included, deciding whether amputations are an appropriate treatment for this mental disorder will pose some unusual dilemmas.

a New York child psychologist and one of Money's coauthors of the 1977 article, named it "amputee identity disorder." Furth also published a how-to book on "self-demand amputation" (Furth & Smith, 2002). His interest in the disorder was both professional and personal: Since childhood, he had wanted to have his right leg amputated above the knee. His coauthor in the amputation guide was Robert Smith, a surgeon in Scotland whom Furth contacted to perform his elective amputation surgery (Elliot, 2003; Kao, n.d.). Although Smith, after consulting with two psychiatrists, had agreed to operate on Furth, his hospital, the Falkirk Royal Infirmary in Glasgow, prohibited any further procedures of this type in the year 2000. Dr. Furth never received his amputation (Marantz Henig, 2005).

In 1997, Richard Bruno of Englewood Hospital in New Jersey proposed the diagnosis "factitious disability disorder." He identified three types of individuals associated with it: "devotees," that is, people sexually attracted to amputees; "pretenders," nondisabled people who act as if they are amputees, using crutches and wheelchairs; and "wannabes," those who desired to be disabled and were ready to go to extreme lengths to have a limb amputated. However, in Bruno's (1997) taxonomy, even those who managed to get an amputation continued to be called wannabes.

The new diagnosis of BIID was proposed by Michael First (2004) of Columbia University in a groundbreaking study. First's is the only article that described actual cases of BIID. The study shows the results of a survey of 52 people with the disorder: 9 of them had an arm or a leg amputated, the rest yearned for it. First claims that none of them was delusional. All subjects were asked if they ever had the "feeling of wishing to be the opposite sex, or being in the body of the wrong sex." Of the people interviewed (17 respondents), 19% answered affirmatively. David Spiegel of Stanford University, a leader in the field of psychosomatic research, treatment, and development, believes that BIID is closest to either body dysmorphic disorder or anorexia nervosa. "It reminds me a little of anorexia nervosa," Spiegel said, "where people think they're fat when it's obvious they're not" (Henig, 2005). The connection to anorexia, he added, is that people with BIID "have a clearly mistaken belief about their bodies." Indeed, the commonalities with anorexia would suggest a link also with transgender cases—for instance, both anorexic and transgender girls experience a similar horror when their breasts begin to grow, and they start to feel increasingly ill-at-ease with their femininity. Since the body is a sexual body, the rejection of the body is an attempt at having nothing to do with sexuality.

There is a problem with rejecting the body, that is, the sexual body, because it may involve a fantasy about escaping sexual difference altogether, which would suggest a psychotic structure. Spiegel disagrees with First's assertion that people with BIID are not delusional, stating that this could be a serious mental illness that looks normal on the surface: "It's often the case that people with this kind of delusion would pass a mental status screen," he said. "They can do abstract thinking, they're not disoriented, they look pretty good to the outside world as long as you don't trip over their delusion" (Henig, 2005).

First's term, BIID, distinguishes the disorder from paraphilia, psychosis, or body dysmorphic disorder (a diagnosis that is often used in cases of anorexia and bulimia), bringing the analogy closer to GID. First concludes his study by emphasizing that the diagnostic category that most resembles the phenomenology of this rare condition is GID. He built the correspondence by highlighting parallel features:

> A feeling of discomfort with an aspect of his or her anatomical identity (gender in GID, presence of all limbs in this condition), with an internal sense of the desired identity (to be the other sex in GID, to be an amputee in this condition). Other similarities include: onset in childhood or early adolescence; successful treatment by surgery for some subjects, frequently mimicking the desired identity (cross-dressing in GID; pretending to be an amputee in this condition); and for a significant subgroup of each, paraphilic sexual arousal by a fantasy of being the desired identity (in GID fantasizing about oneself as an anatomical female … in this condition fantasizing about oneself as an amputee [apotemnophilia]). (First, 2004, p. 8)

First (2004) insists that this condition might best be conceptualized in a continuum with GID. It is an extremely unusual dysfunction in the development of one's fundamental sense of physical self. "Just as GID represents a dysfunction in the development of gender identity, this disorder can be thought of as representing a particular dysfunction of the development of one's body identity" (p. 9). As a provisional conclusion of his study, First offers a provocative recommendation, "as a last resort, surgery should be considered as a potential treatment for this disorder" (p. 9). "When the first sex reassignment was done in the 1950s, it generated the same kind of horror" that voluntary amputation does now, First affirmed. "Surgeons asked themselves, 'How can I do this thing to someone that's normal?' The dilemma of the surgeon being asked to amputate a healthy limb is similar" (Henig, 2005). BIID advocates suggest in a parallel manner that, 30 years ago, being transgender was considered just as wrong as having BIID is today, and they gamble that our perceptions about elective amputations will change in the future. To accentuate the similarities with the transsexual plight, advocators have coined the word *transable*.

The press declarations of Rubén Noé Coronado, a Spanish trans man thought to be the world's first transsexual pregnant father of twins (he miscarried in June of 2009), seemed somehow to confirm the claims of BIID advocators. Rubén, who was adopted as a child, described what it was like to identify as a trans man while making use of his female reproductive organs: "It's like being born with three hands. You take advantage of them while you have them, and you get rid of one of them when they get in the way" (Telegraph.co.uk, 2009). What story has been told here? The evolution of the name of the BIID is quite evocative: It has shifted from being an "amputee" disorder to being a body integrity "identity" disorder. It is thus now positioned in a continuum with another "identity" disorder: a gender "identity" disorder. This change exposes a problem in the very logic of identity. All these cases seem to have one common feature: They start from a concept of identity that does not fit with the materiality of the body. A technological intervention via surgery or hormones will modify the body to make it fit the ideal (the opposite sex or fewer limbs). A similar situation of discordance between a preexisting ideal and the body is presented by the dilemma of intersex people, that is, of those who are born with physical gender markers that are not clearly male or female. Let us consider as an example a case from 1924, reported by Hugh Young, "the father of American urology":

> A normal looking young man with masculine instincts [athletic, heterosexual] was found to have a ... functioning ovary in the left groin. What was the character of the scrotal sac on the right side? If these were also undoubtedly female, should they be allowed to remain outside in the scrotum? If a male, should the patient be allowed to continue life with a functioning ovary and tube on the left side? If the organs of either side should be extirpated, which should they be? (p. 167, cited in Hausman, 1995, p. 180)

In this case, the doctor's dilemma was resolved because the patient was a "true hermaphrodite," and the surgical intervention could follow the sex of assignment and rearing because there was at least one testicular gonad. Currently, sex determination in intersex cases is never easily made. When a baby is born with ambiguous genitalia, it is considered a medical emergency (Fausto-Sterling, 1999, p. 45). According to the current standards of treatment, within the first 24 hours after birth the child will have to have a declared sex "and the parents must feel certain about the decision" (p. 45). Their decision is typically guided by a team of specialists: geneticists, endocrinologists, pediatric urologists, and so on (Domurat Dreger, 1998, p. 181). The imperative to rush to a decision has been influenced by one of the most prominent researchers in the field: Once more we meet John Money, whose recommendation in cases of intersexuality has been that a child needs to assume a psychosocial gender before the age of 18 months. Babies may be born "gender neutral," but to help construct their psychological identity, their anatomy must match the "standard" for their sex.

PHALLOMETRICS

Today's practitioners, "unlike the doctors of the nineteenth century ... do not search deeply into an intersexual's body in hopes of finding a material marker of ontological 'true' sex" (Domurat Dreger, 1998, p. 181). The answer is not skin deep but foreskin deep. According to the protocol, a girl cannot have a too noticeable "phallus" (as the scientific literature calls it) (Muram & Dewhurst, 1984; Newman, Randolph, & Anderson, 1992). Indeed, the medical decision concerning the assignment of sex is made on the basis of "phallic" size: "Infants with male-like structures are assigned to the male sex, while those with smaller phallic structures (micropenises or 'normal' clitorises ...) will be assigned the female sex" (Kessler, 1990, p. 13). Others may follow the protocol set up by Patricia Donohoe at Harvard Medical School. First, she tests the newborn's chromosomes to predict with some accuracy how the genitalia may develop. Once this is established, genetic females are raised as females to preserve the reproductive abilities, regardless of how much they may be virilized. In the case of the genetic male, the sex assignment is based on external anatomy, most exactly, on the size of the phallus (American Academy of Pediatrics, 2000). A phallus less than 1.5 cm long and 0.7 cm wide results in an assignment as female (Donahoe et al., 1991, cited in Fausto-Sterling, 1999, p. 57). Stressing that the uncertainties in such gender choices are determined by considerations that are more social than medical, Fausto-Sterling (1999) dubs this standard "phallo-metrics" (p. 59). What is called a "boy" or a "girl," as Suzanne Kessler (1998) has shown convincingly, is primarily a cultural convention.

Precisely, the question at issue here is how sociocultural conventions carve up and divide the body. First, let us emphasize that the semantic use of "phallus" in current medical terminology for cases of ambiguous sex is revealing;[6] it exhibits all the properties of the Lacanian phallus. Then, if we go back to the comparison with amputee disorder or BIID, we can conclude that the phallus we are talking about is clearly a Lacanian notion of the phallus and not any term in the American nomenclature. Indeed, the Lacanian phallus is an instrument: It is the mean and ratio by which sexual difference is introduced. Without regard to the anatomical differences of the sexes, both boys and girls have to renounce the fantasy of being the mother's phallus. There is the imaginary phallus, which may be detached from the body and for which the castration complex implies its renunciation, and the symbolic phallus, which is an imaginary element that circulates between mother and child to pave the way for the phallus to become a signifier. The phallus is not "an object (part-internal, good, bad, etc.) inasmuch as 'object' tends to gauge the reality involved in a relationship. Still less it is the organ—penis or clitoris—that it symbolizes. And it is no

---

[6] I am grateful to Deborah A. Luepnitz for calling my attention to this fact.

accident that Freud adopted as a reference the simulacrum if represented to the Ancients" (Lacan, 2006, p. 579). This is the trajectory of the phallus: It is just a signifier.

What did Freud and Lacan mean when they said that the unconscious knows only one sex? In the unconscious, the phallus does not have a corresponding female signifier. Due to this basic dissymmetry, both male and female assume their sexual positioning by way of one signifier, the symbolic phallus. One of the effects of the presence of the phallus as signifier is that it will designate meaning, but its presence will cause a deviation from needs. To the extent that needs are expressed in language, they are subjected to demand, they come back to the subject in alienated form. Since the sex reassignment request is formulated as what in psychoanalysis is called a *demand*, it should not be taken at face value but rather be analyzed before being actualized. "Demand in itself bears on something other than the satisfaction it calls for. It is a demand for a presence or an absence" (Lacan, 2006, p. 579).

In the simplest, schematic version of the Freudian Oedipal model, we have a binary of having or not having it, of presence or absence: Boys have it, girls do not. For Freud, castration is a loss that women think they have suffered and that men fear to suffer; hence, it organizes the sexual imaginary. For Lacan, castration is even a more fundamental loss affecting both sexes since both sexes are castrated. Nobody can have the phallus or can be it. In the mother's body, nothing is missing. Lack is purely a logical limit—the mother is deprived of something she does not have. The phallus is the object that appears to veil a symbolic lack to create it.

The phallus is a signifier without a signified (Lacan, 1998a, p. 75), and it works through absence. If we revisit the cases of amputation disorder, we may assume that the limb the sufferer wants to cut off functions like a phallus that can only be fully operative when it signifies absence. The title chosen for a very supportive documentary on the disorder was significantly entitled *Whole*, suggesting that bodies could be assumed as whole only after a part was missing (Gilbert, 2003). When a chromosomically male intersex newborn may be assigned either a female or male gender according to phallic size, we can appreciate the use of the phallus as the means to establish a relation to the order of sexual difference without regard to anatomy.

Freud made a notorious error when calling "castration" a procedure that should more adequately be called "eviration" (as any cattle raiser or veterinarian knows, castration only refers to the ablation of testicles; this is why any medical dictionary defines castration as "bilateral orchidectomy"). This mistake shows that Freud's very invention of the castration complex was affected by the castration complex; that is, that it cannot be reduced to anatomical reality and is marked by the error of taking an organ for a signifier of sexual difference. What characterizes the phallus is its ability to be embodied as a detachable and transformable object. Freud's confusion between the operation of gelding or castration with the potential amputation of the penis has been perpetuated by the doctors who determine a baby's sex in cases of "ambiguous genitalia": They look at the length of the "phallus"—which is seen as an organ both girls and boys have—and according to size, guess whether it will grow to reach an acceptable virile size and hence whether it has to be cut. Here, the phallus is displayed in its function as a "stand for" to resolve the unsolvable.

We should keep in mind that sexual difference is intractable, and castration appears as a partial, failed answer to this deadlock. In that context, it is worth examining *Transamerica* (Tucker, 2005), one of the many recent films devoted to transsexualism, perhaps the most successful in that it offers a mainstream version of "cases" relatively invisible before. Bree Osbourne is a preoperative, conservative-looking, male-to-female transsexual who is about to obtain the recommendation letter for sex reassignment surgery from her supportive therapist when she learns that, unbeknownst to her, when she was still Stanley, she had fathered a son, now a teenage runaway addict hustling on the streets of New York. The plot is full of twists and impossible to synopsize. The road movie across the United States makes the unlikely pair of travelers connect until the young man, Toby, is shocked to discover that the biological father he idealized is none other than his traveling companion, this trans woman for whom he was developing a crush, a woman claiming to be hailing from a Christian religious sect "of the potential father." Bree fails to reunite the young man with her own past and biological family since Toby runs away on discovering the truth. Bree has her surgery at the end, and thinks that she has failed with her son. The film's ending, however, reconciles them as they accept each other's differences: She is now a woman, and he is a gay-porn actor. This plot confirms that transsexualism is bound up with symbolic issues hinged around paternity. Bree can truly become a woman after she has faced the impossible task of being a father and honestly grappled with it. That she fails does not contradict this idea, for being a father is to fail, but her ordeal has been experienced and not avoided. The happy ending places both characters in a comfortable marginality, sharing a beer; it is only a matter of years before they both will be fully accepted by society.

Here, the function of the transsexual demand is crucial. Bree needs to undergo symbolic castration before being able to qualify for sex reassignment surgery. After she has gone through the symbolic hurdles, with all the uncertainties and limitations they entail, Bree's demand appears not as addressed to an absolute Other who would complete her or reducible to hysterical avoidance of her sexuality. With these qualifications, she does, indeed, make an ethical choice.

Chapter 2

The democratizing of transgenderism

On the front page of the *New York Times* style and fashion section, the headline read: "On Campus, Rethinking Biology 101: Transgender Students Gain Rights, and Respect, in College" (Bernstein, 2004, p. 1). The article reported on a new form of campus activism: In some elite universities and colleges of the eastern United States—like Brown, Wesleyan, Sarah Lawrence, and Smith—students who did not look clearly male or female and defined themselves as "transgender" demanded urgent changes to avoid harassment.

The article opened with the story of 23-year-old Luke Woodward, who arrived at Brown University looking masculine but with no plans to shift genders. "I had questioned my sexuality, but not my gender," Luke said. Luke, who then identified as lesbian, explained that during a year spent studying in Cuba, a question had arisen. People "were genuinely shocked when I said I was a woman. It was disorienting and scary. And I had to really think about it: am I a woman?" On Luke's return from Cuba, an answer started to take form. "I took more and more pains to hide my breasts and to pass as male." After meeting several female-to-male transsexuals, Luke realized that there were options. With financial help from friends and a loan, in the summer of 2004, Luke underwent a double mastectomy. If, before, Luke "had the body of a woman," noted the newspaper interviewer, Luke's transformed appearance was now more in harmony with *hir* style of sartorial choices—close-cropped hair, baggy jeans, and hooded sweatshirts. Luke described the impact of the "chest surgery" as a lifestyle improvement, asserting that now "my quality of life is better." When asked about undergoing further surgery, Luke answered: "This is often the first thing people ask me—about whether I'll get surgery 'down there,' and I think it is really weird" (p. 1).

Luke's story makes us revise our definitions of sex, gender, and even grammar. I have used an unexpected third person pronoun, *hir* (pronounced "here"), instead of his or her; I may also use *ze* and *s/he* (pronounced "shuhee") instead of he or she, hereafter, since this is the practice of some transgender people who have opted to avoid the generic division implied by usual pronouns. However, I use the pronoun each person prefers for identification; thus, I only use the transgender pronouns when either patients or authors chose it. Often, the third-person plural, they/them, overcomes the gender difficulty. I begin by talking about transsexuals in the plural, first sketching a global evolution before engaging with specific cases.

Given the current availability of sex change technologies, in the 21st century is it possible to still clearly define what is a man or what is a woman? Or, has it ever been possible? In Chapter 3, I show that under the name of hysteria, the solution to the enigma of sexual difference has been unsuccessfully pursued for over 4,000 years. Is Luke's example pushing categories of gender beyond the binary of male and female?

When people asked Luke about "surgery down there," they assumed that a specific bodily location held the key for sex determination (sex understood as genitals) to establish a congruence of sex and gender. Somehow, this confusion of sex and genitals is carried onto current designations of sex change practices because "sex reassignment surgery" would mean that the surgery is centered on the sex. Transition between genders, however, often entails several stages and body manipulations; surgery is just one of many possible interventions. Movement between genders involves body parts other than the sexual ones; for instance, the face is crucial since in everyday life interactions it tends to be one most important markers of gender determination.

In Luke's case, gender identification did not rely on one specific (sexual) body part, but rather on a combination of factors like appearance, clothing, manners, hairstyle, and so on, which together contribute to a social attribution of gender. In fact, for Luke's everyday social interactions, chest surgery may have been a much more visible indicator of gender than phalloplasty. It is noteworthy that Luke wondered whether "she" was a "he" while living abroad in Cuba, a country whose postrevolutionary culture still supports traditional gender roles under the aegis of *machismo*, or cult of the man, and *marianismo*, or cult of the one who submits. The combination of *marianismo* and *machismo* sustains fixed gender roles that foster gender inequality. Notably, Luke asked, "Am I a woman?" in a sexist context in which roles for men and women were rigidly defined. S/he became insecure about hir sexual identity because of the baffled looks of those who did not seem to be able to recognize Luke as a woman. As a first tentative answer, Luke responded to this misrecognition by hiding one physical marker of femininity, the breasts, and trying to pass as male. Today, postsurgery Luke says that s/he does not want to be identified as one gender or another, but something in between, and complained that current policy about gender reassignment "erases the space between male and female." Luke added that, in an ideal world, s/he would not have to conceal a female past to achieve a more male persona. "'I wouldn't be seen as male or female but as a female-to-male trans."

IN TRANSIT

Those who identify as transgender may call themselves male or female, man or woman, trans man, trans woman, female-to-male, male-to-female, butch or camp, or cross-dresser or they may not identify with any of these. "Transgender" today is most commonly used as an umbrella term. "Trans," "TG," or "T" are widely employed to include everyone who challenges the conventional boundaries of sex and gender. There are those who surgically change the sex they were assigned at birth (transsexuals) and those who express their gender in ways that do not correspond to their anatomical sex. Transgender can refer to those individuals who are gender variant, that is, whose gender expression does not match the expectation associated with the gender binary of male and female. In its broadest meaning, the term is also used by those who feel that their sexual identity is at odds with the social and cultural attributions of "man" or "woman." The term *transgender* is widely employed on Web sites, in support groups, in self-identity labels, and in political writings. It is sometimes understood as a very encompassing term covering all forms of gender variance. It can also apply to differentiate those people who live between the sexes without using hormones or surgery from those who change their sex.

The word itself seems to have been invented in the 1980s (Stryker & Whittle, 2006, p. 4), but in the 1990s transgenderism was enthusiastically embraced by activists as a collective category of identity with the deliberate intention of making it as inclusive as possible when negotiating legislature. By 1995, the term was widely accepted to refer to "individuals whose gender identity or expression does not conform to the social expectations for their assigned sex at birth" (Currah, Juang, & Minter, 2006, p. xiv).

Transitioning involves those in the process of dressing and living as a different gender, thus adopting an identity associated with the opposite biological sex without reassignment surgery. It also refers to those who are moving from one sex to the other by taking hormones or surgically modifying their bodies. In terms of sexual orientation, transgender people may identify as gay, straight, lesbian, bisexual, or transsexual. Transgender people who claim to be uncomfortable with their biological sex and assigned gender role are often diagnosed with gender identity disorder (GID), as defined by the American Psychiatric Association (APA).

It is important to note that the inclusion of GID in the APA's *Diagnostic and Statistical Manual of Mental Disorders* (*DSM*; APA, 2000) qualifies it as mental illness. The *DSM*, even if it is jokingly referred to as the diagnostic bible, is the gospel that stringently rules insurance companies, psychiatry and health care professionals, and policy makers alike.[1] Officially, GID is a health problem that may require corrective medical treatment. For those who suffer this disorder, gender reassignment surgery, hormone therapy, and gender role changing are recommended to help them feel "normal" or "natural," therefore healthy. There is considerable disagreement over the APA's characterization of transgenderism as a mental illness because many consider it to be an issue of sexual identity and even sexual orientation. Unlike homosexuality (which under pressure of gay activists was eliminated as a disease category by the APA), medical professionals see transgenderism as a medical and mental health condition that requires treatment. The disagreement among some transgender activists and leaders stems not only from the essentialist, almost naive way in which gender roles are portrayed in the *DSM*, but also from practical issues about discrimination—people may be less prone to discriminate against someone who suffers from "a medical condition"—and from the fact that if GID is removed from the *DSM* the few U.S. states where it is considered a medical disability will no longer grant medical coverage or disability benefits (see Hausman, 2003, p. 25).

The *DSM* (APA, 2000) characterizes GID as a "cross-gender identity accompanied by persistent discomfort with one's assigned sex" (2000, p. 535). The manual distinguishes gender identity ("the individual's self perception as male or female") from gender dysphoria ("strong and persistent feelings of discomfort with one's assigned sex, the claim to possess the body of the other sex, and the desire to be regarded by others as a member of the other sex") (p. 535). While the manual is not clear regarding whether a sexual practice is the same as an identity, it emphasizes that "gender identity and gender dysphoria should be distinguished from the term *sexual orientation* which refers to erotic attraction to males, females, or both" (p. 535; italics in the original). Confusion about sexual orientation is now listed as an identity problem. Sexual orientation confusion is lumped with other confusions regarding career choice, friendship patterns, long-term goals, moral values, and group loyalties (p. 741).

The *DSM* (APA, 2000) catalogs a variety of symptoms that determine the GID diagnosis; they are all considered manifestations of a strong identification with "the other sex." In adolescents and adults, sufferers claim that they are members of the opposite sex, often describing themselves as "imprisoned in the wrong body," for example. Other markers are obsessions with altering sexual characteristics (by way of hormones, surgery, or other means).

---

[1] For a riveting, behind-the-scenes exploration of the *DSM* apparatus and the construction of so-called mental illnesses, see Christopher Lane's (2007) *Shyness: How Normal Behavior Became a Sickness.*

The indicators specified for children are: cross-dressing (female attire in boys, stereotypical masculine clothing in girls); cross-sex roles in fantasies and play; participation in stereotypical games and pastimes of the other sex; and having a strong preference for other-sex playmates. Boys assert that their penis or testes are disgusting or will disappear, or that it would be better not to have a penis. Absence of rough play and rejection of male stereotypical games and activities are also considered indicative symptoms. In girls, the markers include wanting to urinate while standing, asserting that they will grow a penis, desiring not to grow breasts or menstruate, and developing a deep dislike of normative feminine clothing. An historical overview of the literature on cross-gender identification and behavior as mental illness concluded that, in the case of children, "the flaws in the *DSM-IV* definition of mental disorder plus the limitations of the current research" pointed to "insufficient evidence to make any conclusive statement regarding children who experience discomfort with their biological sex" (Bartlett, Vasey, & Bukowski, 2000). The authors of the study recommended that the diagnostic category of GID in children in its current form should not appear in future editions of the *DSM*.

The controversy surrounding the pathologization and treatment of cross-gender identity and behavior, particularly in children, has been evident in the literature for more than 20 years. Children who meet the diagnostic criteria for GID are more likely to become homosexual than transsexual. This leads many to conclude that the pathologizing role formerly attributed to homosexuality has been displaced onto GID. Let us note that 1980 was the year when the *DSM* no longer included homosexuality as a mental illness, but this was also the year that the diagnosis of GID was introduced. In the essay, "How to Bring Your Kids Up Gay," Eve Kosofky Sedgwick (1993) argued that while lesbian and gay became more accepted, the political separation of sexuality and gender made room for the stigmatization of gender deviance.

It takes a transsexual like Jennifer Finney Boylan to define the quandary of transsexuals while pointing out the lack of imagination of the psychiatric establishment. The memoir, *She's Not There: A Life in Two Genders* (2003), has this wonderful evocation:

> My conviction, by the way, had nothing to do with a desire to be *feminine*, but it had everything to do with being *female*. Which is an odd belief for a person born male. This last point was the one that years later, would most frequently elude people, including the overeducated smarty-pants who constituted much of my inner circle. Being gay or lesbian is about sexual orientation. Being transgender is about identity. ... In the end, what it is, more than anything else is a *fact*. It is the dilemma of the transsexual, though, that it is a fact that cannot possibly be understood without imagination. (p. 22; italics in the original)

WE ARE ALL TRANSGENDERISTS

Transsexual people take as models icons ranging from Joan of Arc to Renée Richards, the tennis champion; from 18th-century Chevalier d'Eon, a French diplomat, spy, soldier, and Freemason who lived the first half of his life as a man and the second half as a woman; to Roberta Close, also known as Miss Gay Brazil, a male-born transsexual who was voted Brazil's most beautiful woman. Thus, the references of the word *transsexual* may seem infinite. Here is the most comprehensive list according to transgender activist Leslie Feinberg (1996): transsexuals, transvestites, bi-genders, drag queens, drag kings, cross-dressers, masculine women, feminine men, intersexuals (a term that replaced hermaphrodite), androgynes, cross-genders, shape-shifters, passing women, passing men, gender-benders, gender-blenders, bearded women, and women bodybuilders who cross the line of what a female body is "supposed" to look like (p. x).

Given this plethora of uses, a brief history of the evolution of the terminology will be helpful. The term *transvestite* was invented by Magnus Hirschfeld in 1910 to describe those who occasionally wear clothes of the other sex. *Transsexualis* was first used in the journal *Sexology* in a 1949 article by David Cauldwell titled, in Latin, "Psychopathia Transexualis," a term echoing Krafft-Ebing's *Psychopathia Sexualis* (1886/1965). It is often noted that in 1923 Magnus Hirschfeld used the German term *seelischer Transsexualismus* (psychological transsexualism) (Hirschfeld, 1923). In his 1949 study, Cauldwell described the thousands of cases of "individuals who wish to be members of the sex to which they do not properly belong" (p. 275). Cauldwell also coined the term *sex transmutationist* (1947; 1951, pp. 12–16) and used both the spellings "trans-sexual" and "transsexual" interchangeably (1950). Cauldwell's (1949) initial position was at best problematic since he described transsexualism as a hereditary condition of individuals who are "mentally unhealthy" (p. 275). By 1950, Cauldwell had obviously turned a corner:

> Are transsexuals crazy? One may as well ask whether heterosexuals are crazy. Some are and some are not. Some transsexuals are brilliant. Now and then one may be a borderline genius. Transsexuals are eccentric. Some of them are not of sound mind, but this is true of heterosexuals. (p. 4)

The word *transsexualism* was popularized in the 1950s by sex change pioneer Harry Benjamin. Benjamin worked closely with Eugen Steinach, the gland specialist innovator who performed the first sex change surgeries by gland transplants and isolated the "sex hormones," and Magnus Hirschfeld, the sex reformer. By a chronological coincidence, 1952, the year in which hysteria, as a separate diagnosis, disappeared from American psychiatric texts, was also the year that a medical team led by Christian Hamburger performed the first surgical sex change on George Jorgensen, a 26-year-old American male.

On December 18, 1953, in a lecture at the New York Academy of Medicine, Benjamin used the English word *transsexual* as a medical definition for the first time. And most important, it was also in that year that the first scientific meeting dedicated to transvestism and transsexualism gathered at Benjamin's institute in New York. As early as 1954, Benjamin clearly distinguished transvestism (cross-dressing) from transsexualism (wanting to change the body) (1954/2006, pp. 45–52). In 1954, George—now Christina Jorgensen—had a third operation in the United States: the surgical construction of a vagina. The 1950s was also the decade when American popular opinion was scandalized by the results of the studies conducted by Kinsey. The Kinsey report hypothesized that, based on their activities or attractions, as many a fourth of women (15–25%) and over one third of men (33–46%) were bisexual (Kinsey, 1953; Kinsey, Pomeroy, & Martin, 1948).

As Meyerowitz (2002/2004) compellingly narrated, the 1950s marked the beginning of the popularization of transsexualism. It started when the news about Christine Jorgensen's surgery in Denmark broke out, creating a press frenzy that made sex change a household term (p. 51). "In 1952 the press discovered Christine Jorgensen and inaugurated an era of comprehensive, even obsessive, coverage. In the history of sex change in the United States, the reporting on Jorgensen was both a culminating episode and a starting point" (p. 49). In the United States, Jorgensen's tremendous public presence was emblematic of a growing cultural preoccupation with the intertwining domains of science and sexuality. It was as if, all of a sudden, Jorgensen herself embodied the crucial questions to which I return in many ways, "What is a man, and what is a woman?"

TRANSGENDER

Ever since the media explosion of Christine Jorgensen's sex change, the definitions of sex and gender have been challenged. My clinical experience has confirmed David Valentine's (2007) argument that "the 'gender' that underpins 'transgender,' and marks it as distinct from the 'sexuality' of mainstream and gay and lesbian politics, is one rooted in a sexological rather than feminist tradition" (p. 59; see also Hausman, 2001). Valentine has conducted ethnographic research among mostly poor female-to-male transsexuals of color who conceive of gender and sexuality in other terms and who did not identify with the category of transgender (Valentine, 2007). The separation of gender identity and sexual orientation is symptomatically exposed by my patients when they no longer ask, "Am I a man or a woman?" (a question of identity), but "Am I straight or bisexual?" (confusing object choice with sexual orientation). Bernice Hausman (1995) convincingly demonstrated that the gender–sex divide emerged as part of the progress of sex change medical technology.

Hausman's (1995) research has shown that, prior to the introduction of the word *gender* in 20th-century discourse as a signifier of social sex, the word *sex* was a signifier encoding both biological and social categories (p. 75). The concept of psychosocial gender identity was invented by John Money in the 1950s as part of the new technology of sex change. The protocols developed by John Money and colleagues at Johns Hopkins Hospital in the mid-1950s introduced the word *gender* to signify the social performance indicative of an internal sexual identity. The medical discourse that grounded the first practices of sex changes was heterosexist because to be recognized as homosexual would have deemed the prospective patient as unfit to undergo a sex change. The standard to identify candidates for sex change was based on anatomies that would be sexed in accordance with social categories of appropriate gender performance. "'Gender,' however, has not remained within the medical context in which it was first uttered," wrote Hausman, "nor did its inaugurators intend it to. Part of the appeal of gender identity theory is its contention that all of us have a gender identity and that it is somehow detachable from our sex" (p. 8).

Teresa de Lauretis (1987) has written a compelling exploration of the relation of technology and gender (or of gender as technology) in which she uses technology as a metaphor for scientific or industrial techniques that support her claims that representational forms are technologies. Hausman (1995) argues that gender is one consequence of the intersection of such technologies and ideological systems (p. 15). In the various feminist analyses of gender, there is an important omission—the consideration of transsexualism as a player in Western conceptions of gender. Julia Epstein and Kristina Straub (1991) contend that the recent phenomenon of medicalized sex change is nothing but an evolution of earlier historical modalities of cross-gender orientations:

> Surgical possibilities for "gender reassignment" have opened in a late modern period (and what is more *postmodern* than transsexualism?), but there is indeed nothing remotely new about transvestism or "gender dysphoria" except the official professionalizing and medicalization of the terms. (p. 11)

Hausman (1995) observed that the issue here is not that technology made sex change a reality, as Epstein and Straub suggested, but that these technologies affected the taxonomy of transsexualism. "If we consistently read back through the categories of the contemporary period, we are bound to miss the specificity of what it meant for historically dissimilar subjects to represent (in a variety of modes) the 'other sex'" (p. 13). Hausman claims that most feminist theorists attribute facticity to gender without an exploration of the semiotics of the body; that is, they use gender as a self-evident category of analysis, almost independent from sex (p. 14).

Elizabeth Grosz's (1994) examination of the development of the feminist critique of gender concludes: "Presuming that biology or sex is a fixed category, feminists have tended to focus on transformations at the level of gender. Their project has been to minimize biological differences and to provide them with different cultural meanings and values" (p. 17). The hegemony of gender can be observed in U.S. academia, in which, by the end of the 20th century, most women's studies departments had become gender studies, a category that also includes queer studies (on gay, lesbian, bisexual, and transgender issues). There is such a profusion of publications on the issue of sex versus gender that I cannot hope to list them all. In conformity with my attempt to historicize and problematize these concepts, I turn to my clinical practice.

But first, we may need to clarify the terms of our discussion. Alice Dorumat Dreger traced the first use of the word *gender* to 1915. The word appeared in the literature on human hermaphroditism and was used by William Blair Bell (1915), a Liverpool surgeon who contributed to a shift in the medical and scientific definition of what was then called hermaphroditism, and thus of "true sex." With the rise of new medical technologies—laparotomies for exploratory surgeries and biopsies to analyze living tissue—it was possible to confirm the actual presence of testes and ovaries in sex determination. Given this technological advance, Blair Bell needed a word to describe medical interventions in anomalous bodies, such as those of a patient he described as "an attractive woman, unfortunately with testes." Blair Bell's recommendations set up the precedent for the forthcoming sex change policies:

> [O]ur opinion of the gender [of a given patient] should be adapted to the peculiar circumstances and to our modern knowledge of the complexity of sex, and ... surgical procedures should in these special cases be carried out to establish more completely the obvious sex of the individual. (cited in Domurat Dreger, 1998, p. 166)

The point here is simple: Only when technology developed to the point that clinicians could intervene at the level of the body did the term *sex* begin to refer exclusively to the biological realm. John Money et al. (1955) condensed his notion of gender role as "all the things that a person says or does to disclose himself or herself as having the status of boy or man, girl or woman" (p. 254). Gender was rendered as "outlook, demeanor, and orientation" (p. 258). Money's concept of gender purposely avoided a psychoanalytic or a biological explanation—sexual identity was a psychosocial construction. In the 1960s, the psychiatrist Robert Stoller refined the notion of gender with the idea of "core gender identity," which corresponded to the internalized idea of the individual's belonging to a particular sex. "Gender identity" was distinguished from "sexual identity," which included sexual activities and fantasies. Stoller initially supported the idea of a biological force, a drive determining gender. Eventually, he developed a simplistic explanation with psychological overtones that he summed up in the formula: "dominant mother, father pushed to the side, infant cuddly and lovable, mother-son too close" (1975, p. 193).

In cases of male-to-female transsexualism, the key was an essential femininity passed from mother to son: "What his mother feels is femininity; what he feels is femininity" (p. 204). The model was one of mimetic imitation: The son copied the mother; the mother's excessive closeness to the son was considered to be a negative influence. Stoller also talked about a bisexual mother, who might have had a period of extreme tomboyishness, and of a distant father. These were factors contributing to the creation of transsexuality, especially male to female. For female-to-male transsexuals, Stoller's speculations can be rendered as "too much father and too little mother masculinizes girls" (pp. 223–244). Stoller, a believer in bisexuality, ended up moving away from a biological model to a psychological one. Money's evolution was the reverse, as he shifted from a psychological model to one in which psychology was dependent on body morphology. I will explore in depth Money's many-sided personality and his wide and long-lasting impact on issues of transsexualism.

TRANSSEXUAL REVOLUTION

As we have seen, in the 1990s transgenderism transitioned. The term that was initially coined as a noun became an adjective and with it acquired a radical edge. One can trace this specific use to 1992, when Leslie Feinberg made a call to end gender oppression under the tract *Transgender Liberation: A Movement Whose Time Has Come*. In the 1990s, transgenderism activism and scholarship launched a sexual revolution. Anne Bolin (1997) contends that "[t]he formation of a transgender community denotes a newfound kinship which supplants the dichotomy of transsexual and transvestite with a concept of continuity" (p. 26). Lately, the word *transgender* has become quite inclusive. Some welcome the term *transgender* due to its inclusiveness, and others abhor it for the same reason.

Most authors credit Virginia Prince for having proposed the designation *transgenderist* in the 1980s as a term of empowerment intended to designate an individual who adopts the role of the "opposite" gender but without undergoing a sex change. Prince, an advocate for freedom of expression, proposed a more specific term for those, like herself, who fall somewhere between "transvestite" and "transsexual." As Prince explains, "I coined the noun transgenderist in 1987 or '88. There had to be some name for people like myself who transes the gender barrier—meaning somebody who lives full-time in the gender opposite to their anatomy. I have not transed the sex barrier" (cited in Feinberg, 1996, p. x). Some critics, like Califia (1997/2003, p. 199) and Meyerowitz (2002/2004, p. 181), contend that Prince tried to distance herself from transvestites and transsexuals to reject any suspicion of sexual deviance. On occasion, *transgenderist* has been adopted by gender activists, who extend its usage to include transsexuals as a subcategory for legal purposes. This was not Prince's original intent. Although many transgenderists challenge the distinction between sex and gender, transsexual and transgender continue to be used.

Prince's neologism *transgenderist* tends to be confusing because it transforms a sexual practice (full-time cross-dressing) into an issue of identity, as if one were to refer to one's self as a "heterosexualist" or a "homosexualist" rather than a heterosexual or homosexual (or even "hetero" or "homo," for that matter). For Prince, transgenderist defines someone who traverses the divide of gender but not that of sex, therefore separating in practice gender as "performance" from sex as anatomical foundation. This seems to call up Freud's (1912) famous dictum in a "Universal Tendency to Debasement in the Sphere of Love": "anatomy is destiny." Sexual identity may be second nature, and yet many transsexuals struggle to rigidly conform to the normative demands of the opposite sex to become a "natural."

Tim Dean (2000) observed that transgenderism now situates itself in relation to transsexualism in a similar way as queer stands to homosexuality: Both refer more to political and ideological allegiances than actual sexual practices. He notes that exactly as many gays and lesbians do not consider themselves "queer" and may resent the term; many transsexuals do not think of themselves as transgender. They rather insist instead that they really belong to one sex and just happen to have been born in the "wrong biological type." They feel a discrepancy between their anatomical sex and their ascribed gender. In fact, they seem quite essentialist and normative. Their classifications are puzzling, thus betraying their arbitrariness and fragility. In the most recent scientific literature on transgenderism, male-to-female transsexuals who identify as women (whether or not they take hormones or have had surgery) are considered heterosexual if they are sexually attracted to men; if they prefer women, they are considered lesbian; and if they are not interested in sex at all, they are just asexual.

Has transgenderism been able to overcome the binary opposition of male and female? The "standard of care," the famous protocol created by Harry Benjamin, was meant to ensure professional consensus about the psychiatric, psychological, medical, and surgical management of GIDs. It asserts that having a vagina (whether natural or artificially constructed) makes someone a woman; moreover, it claimed that surgically reconstructed male-to-female transsexuals with a sexual preference for men no longer have the wrong sexual preference and are "satisfied with their ability to be a normal sex partner" (Benjamin, 1966, p. 129). Benjamin's book *The Transsexual Phenomenon* (1966) has been considered the gold standard for the treatment of transsexualism. It includes an appendix by Gobind Behari Lal suggestively titled, "Complementarity of Human Sexes." Yet, as transgender community activist Gordene Mackenzie (1994) contends, "In addition to a surplus of homophobia and sexism, Benjamin's book is also an indictment against psychotherapy" (p. 75; see also Ekins, 2005, pp. 306–328).

Judith Shapiro (1991) observed that "many transsexuals are, in fact, 'more royalist than the king' in matters of gender" (p. 253). Yet, there are many transgenderists who are not moving between sexes and prefer to describe themselves as "gender queer"—signifying that they reject the either-or male–female system. Gordene MacKenzie (1994) describes the gender movement as the civil rights movement of the 1990s. Many foresee the transgender movement as having a political impact similar to that of the gay movement 40 years ago.

THREE MILLION U.S. TRANS PEOPLE

In the United States over the last decade, transgenderism has lost most of its stigma and has become an identity. On top of that, it seems quite fashionable. "Long enshrined alongside sexual orientation as the T in LGBT [lesbian, gay, bisexual, transgender], today transgender is almost trendy" (Reischel, 2007, p. 81). The National Center for Transgender Equality calculated that between a quarter of a percent and 1% of the U.S. population is transgender—up to 3 million Americans—although other estimates are lower, and precise figures are difficult to obtain. According to Leah Schaefer, past president of the Harry Benjamin Association, in 2002 there were approximately "five thousand post operative transsexuals in the United States" (cited in Bloom, 2002, p. 37). Conservative estimates for the occurrence of transsexuality is 1 case in 23,000 individuals to 1 case in 40,000 individuals.[2] Transvestitism or cross-dressing is much more common, but even then, estimates are about 1% or 2% of the population (the Transgender Family and Friends Support Network [TFFGS]), which is similar to the number of estimated intersex cases (1.7% of all births) (Fausto-Sterling, 1999, p. 51). All these numbers should be taken as an order of magnitude estimate and not as a precise amount (for instance, intersex cases depend on a gene mutation that does not appear uniformly across the world).

---

[2] Data from smaller countries in Europe with access to total population statistics and referrals suggest that roughly 1 per 30,000 adult males and 1 per 100,000 adult females seek sex reassignment surgery (APA, 2000, p. 579).

It is impossible to have current exact frequency figures for the number of sex reassignment surgeries performed, and there is no official record of the number of transsexuals living in the United States, but there is a strong general sense that the trans movement is escalating. Even if it may be rash to claim, as some enthusiasts do, that "Transsexual people are the fastest-growing population" (Romano, 2007, p. 24), it is nevertheless evident that transgenderism has acquired an extraordinary mediatic visibility. On May 30, 2006, an article appeared on the *Village Voice* Web site about "the country's youngest transgender child" (Reischel, 2006). A 5-year-old boy claimed to be a girl and voiced his choice so convincingly that his family accepted to raise him as a girl. The child used a female name, wore dresses, grew long hair, and requested that his school treat him as a girl. In December 2006, the *New York Times* published a story on transgender children, with this opening paragraph:

> Until recently, many children who did not conform to gender norms in their clothing or behavior and identified intensely with the opposite sex were steered to psychoanalysis or behavior modification. ... But as advocates gain ground for what they call gender-identity rights, evidenced most recently by New York City's decision to let people alter the sex listed on their birth certificates, a major change is taking place among schools and families. Children as young as 5 who display predispositions to dress like the opposite sex are being supported by a growing number of young parents, educators and mental health professionals (Leigh Brown, 2006).

Indeed, in a step toward separating anatomy from what it means to be a man or a woman, New York City's Board of Health put forward in 2006 a plan to let people alter the sex on their birth certificate even if they have not had sex change surgery. The widely publicized proposal, which would have put New York at the forefront of a movement to make gender a personal choice, was withdrawn unexpectedly. Most recently, on July 29, 2007, the Metro section of the *New York Times* ran an article on how the New York Police Department trains its officers to be polite. It showed a photograph of a hefty man in drag: wearing red lipstick, a big curly blond wig, and a tight pink blazer over the police uniform. He was facing two cadets, who were in a training session that had been "designed to test their composure with Michael Cuevas ... playing a transgender victim of a robbery" (Lueck, 2007).

Transgender people may be gradually gaining well-deserved rights and overdue respect, but they continue to exert a powerful mediatic fascination. On May 21, 2007, *Newsweek* had a cover story: "The Mystery of Gender: The New Visibility of Transgender America is Shedding Light on the Ancient Riddle of Identity." Many American television shows and their hosts have focused on the topic (see note 1, Introduction; Sloen & De Landri, 2007). The views tended to be positive: Becoming transsexual was presented as the ultimate makeover. Still, a sex change seems like a complex proposition: A 2006 study published in the *Journal of Homosexuality* showed that 32% of transgendered people surveyed had attempted suicide (Abelson, 2006). Like many others, Christian Burgess (1999) suggested that most studies on transgender people are based on the self-selected transgender people in treatment, which may lead to a pathologizing stereotype. However, a great number of transgender people described in the literature have health problems, high rates of substance abuse, attempted suicides, suffered childhood abuse, been victims of sexual abuse/assault, and psychiatric disorders.[3]

TRANS IDENTITIES

Here, I want to take seriously the current debate about the freedom of gender; that is, freedom from gender oppression and the apartheid of sex promised by some transsexual and transgender activists and explore some of its clinical consequences. Many trans people like Luke are not moving between sexes; they are parked somewhere in the middle, with respect to the dichotomy of the either-or male–female system. They have arrived, as it were, neither at Ladies nor at Gentlemen. Transsexual memoirs show a recurrent sense of motion, of sexualities in transit. Terms like journey, path, crossing, passage, returning, becoming, and outing are reiterated tropes in the autobiographical accounts of sex change. This brings to mind Lacan's anecdote:

> A train arrives at a station. A little boy and a little girl, brother and sister, are seated across from each other in a compartment next to the outside window that provides with a view of the station platform buildings going by as the train comes to stop. "Look," says the brother, "we are at Ladies!" "Imbecile!" replies his sister, "don't you see we're at Gentlemen."
>
> To these children, Gentlemen and Ladies will henceforth be two homelands toward which each of their souls will be all the more impossible for them to reach an agreement since, being in fact the same homeland, neither can give ground regarding the one's unsurpassed excellence without detracting from the other's glory. (Lacan, 2006, p. 417)

The two siblings, a boy and a girl, position themselves differently in relationship to two locations in which each sex can only see one sex. One might

---

[3] See Cole et al. (1997); A. Devor (1994); H. Devor (1997); Gaines (1993); Rottneck (1999); Ryan and Futterman (1998).

take the two doors literally: the two doors, with their gender distinctions, that will allow entrance into the symbolic order. There is a binary order, and one needs to make a choice according to two mutually exclusive sexual positionings; in the public context of the train station, a sexual choice is required even to satisfy the most basic urinary needs.

The quandary of the youngsters in the train calls up Luke's account of hir trials and tribulations prior to the chest surgery. The laws of urinary segregation made Luke feel excluded and in fear. S/He said that s/he worried that if s/he entered a women's bathroom on campus, "someone might yell, 'Oh my God, there's a man here' and call security." And "in men's bathrooms I'd have to fold my arms over my chest and hope that no one would notice" (Bernstein, 2004). Luke and several other Brown students pressed the university to create more single-stall bathrooms so that students could avoid having to identify themselves as male or female to use public restrooms. At other American universities and colleges, bathrooms have already been modified and sports teams redesigned. At Sarah Lawrence, third- and fourth-year students were allowed to live with other students regardless of their sex, and certain bathrooms were designated as "all gender." The choice of words was not innocent. They could have used "unisex," but they opted for "all" precisely because this is the logic under which they operate. I will return to this point.

Wesleyan College no longer requires that students mark the male or female box in the questionnaire that they fill out when seeking help for their sexual health. In the sports arena, changes are taking place as well. Wesleyan's rugby team has eliminated the word *woman* from the name of the team, a team that previously had been defined as exclusively feminine. Transgender students felt discriminated against by fans cheering "Go girls." At Smith, a women's college, the pronoun "she" was voted out and replaced by "student" in all official documents. This gesture is somehow contradictory since Smith's ethos has been to grant an academic space exclusively to women. Students at Barnard College have also been struggling with the consequences of the fact that some students at the women's college do not consider themselves women. Although transgender people around the country have been victims of hate crimes, the students interviewed for the opening story I cited from the *New York Times* (Bernstein, 2004) said they did not feel discrimination or fear on campus; they knew they were lucky to live in privileged environments—small private colleges—with traditions of tolerance. Is it telling in some ways that these changes are primarily taking place in the educational system, more precisely in colleges and university campuses? Is there a generational issue at work?

Over 100 colleges and universities across the nation now include "gender identity and expression" in their nondiscrimination policies. On message boards, they use gender-neutral pronouns. Colleges try to ensure that restrooms and dorms are transgender friendly (open to all sexes). They adapt to the increasing number of trans college students who push boundaries and blend genders. Their presence in college and university campuses has even given rise to a reality television show, *Transgeneration*, an eight-part series that follows the lives of four college students through the 2004–2005 school year. Aired on the Sundance Channel, it featured, among others, a trans man student at Smith College, an elite institution whose graduates include not only Barbara Bush and Nancy Reagan but also Betty Friedan, Gloria Steinem, and Catherine Mackinnon.

TRANSGENDER TROUBLE

In the protected atmosphere of the elite colleges like the one Luke attended, which are considered "bisexual incubators," everyone seems "comfortable being queer" (Baumgardner, 2007, p. 209), and yet Luke's transition has not been easy. The reaction of hir immediate family "has been awesome," but for the extended family it has been more difficult to accept the change. Luke's grandparents still refer to Luke as "she." If Luke's appearance is decidedly male, hir voice still sounds female, which makes Luke hesitant to "assert myself vocally." Luke has opted not to be on the testosterone treatment that could help deepen hir voice, increase muscle and bone mass, redistribute fat, and grow facial hair for purely pragmatic reasons—s/he cannot afford the monthly expense of the hormones.

Rey was an 18-year-old freshman when he was interviewed for a *New York Times* magazine article, "When Girls Will Be Boys" (Quart, 2008). He wore baggy jeans, spiky hair, and huge tribal earrings and had a tattoo on his arm—a memento not only of a 500-mile hike through Europe the previous summer but also of the "last time he was happy" as he confesses. Several months before, when Rey entered college, he was a woman. Now, he described himself as "omnisexual." Indeed, Rey is not like most transsexuals who think that they are born in the wrong body. Like Luke, he changed his sex to have an identity that challenges the gender binary. Rey and Luke are part of a growing group of people who refuse to use gender pronouns and take a gender-neutral name. Even after they have substantially changed their appearance, they choose not to modify their bodies with surgery or hormones. Rey and Luke consider themselves as belonging to the trans community, and they identify as gender queer rather than trans man or trans male.

Rey told the interviewer that the decision to change sex started when his childhood body started to mature sexually: "My body changed in freshman year of high school, and it made me depressed" (Quart, 2008). Then, Rey began to wonder if he was really meant to become a woman. He considered the possibility of transition by midadolescence as he was inspired by a "transmale speaker guy" who gave a talk at his high school. Like many kids of his generation, Rey went home to his computer and typed "transgender" in the Google search engine, and the options exploded (a recent search for "transgendered" generated some 5,320,000 results).

The fact that there is an increasing population of trans male students in women's colleges is not a surprise for Quart (2008). She indicates that historically women's colleges have been powerful places of transformation, "where women could flourish without men." They were "incubators of American feminism" and are now open to the next generation of change. Quart contends that women's schools were the very place where young women began to question the notion of femininity. These places were a first forum for the public discussion of the contributions of Esther Newton, Gayle Rubin, Anne Fausto-Sterling, and Judith Butler who have popularized the notion that gender is socially constructed and distinct from a person's sex and sexuality. In their views, gender is fluid and variable, something to be fashioned and that can shift in character depending on the culture or the time period. The presence of trans students at single-sex colleges seems a logical extension of this tradition.

Judith Halberstam, who was interviewed for the article, agreed that the feminist theory of gender as performance did create the space for a trans self or a gender queer one and offered an option that was not available 30 years ago. This would be true for Rey, who built his own trans identity by reading queer theory. "I'm still queer even though I am a man now—it's the beauty of the term," Rey told the interviewer. "I think gender is a spectrum—gender is more complicated than sex." Rey added that everyone has "their own gender." If his identity seems fluid and evolving, his determined desire for recognition does not seem to exclude an element of defiance. "Some transmen want to be seen as men—they want to be accepted as born men," he continued. "I want to be accepted as a transman—my brain is not gendered. There's this crazy gender binary that's built into all of life, that there are just two genders that are acceptable. I don't want to have to fit into that" (Quart, 2008). Curiously, Rey wants to belong to an exclusive men's club that would not exclude anyone, above all, any women. By wishing to pass and not to pass at the same time, Rey plays the role of gender troublemaker, or he may embody a more pervasive symptom of our troubled times. What the gentle defiance of these transiting people calls up is another form of provocation that has been associated historically with hysteria. I turn to this complex history of transgression in the hope of shedding some light on these phenomena.

For these bodies in motion, arriving at a destination is not always granted or a given. This may evoke Lacan's anecdote I mentioned of the brother and sister who travel sitting across from each other in a train; when it pulls to a stop, they look at the station platform from their window, and the boy exclaims: "We have arrived at Ladies!" while the girl states: "You idiot! Can't you see we are at Gentlemen?" (Lacan, 2006, p. 417). Being in transit can be risky business, as an analysand, a formerly homeless African American transsexual woman, often tells me: "People talk about seeing the light at the end of the tunnel, but one should be careful—it might be the 6:15 train!" In all those sexualities in transit, the question is whether one can find oneself back on the platform, rather than on the tracks, when the train arrives.

Chapter 3
Genealogy of hysteria

The term *hysteria* is not only a very old name given to a mysterious disease but also a word that, since the dawn of civilization, has expressed humanity's concern for the riddle of sexuality and revealed a scientific (or not so scientific at times) preoccupation with sexual difference. Hysteria's association with the feminine dates back to the world's oldest surviving medical document. Dating from about 1900 B.C., it was named the *Kahun Papyrus* after the Egyptian city in whose ruins it was found. This ancient medical treatise deals with hysteria considered an illness of the female sex. It describes numerous morbid states, from loss of vision, to neck and teeth pain, to inability to open the mouth, to pains in the vulva and limbs, all attributed to movements of the uterus. This text is the first of many treatises to take the uterus as an independent and wandering organism. In this case, the papyrus recommends the use of sweet-smelling fumigations capable of coaxing the uterus and making it move back downward. Should this fail, the ingestion of foul-tasting potions is advised; they can repel it and send it back to its proper position (Veith, 1965, p. 34).

WANDERING WOMBS

The idea of a vagrant or errant womb floating freely in a woman's body was to remain the basis of later views, especially of all the classical Greek theories of hysteria. They saw the bodies of women in constant motion, defined by constitutional instability; moreover, sexuality was at stake: If the desire to procreate went unfulfilled, femininity turned against itself and generated a pathological condition. Frustrated, femininity attacked itself. Such a conception resonates with Plato, who famously defined hysteria as an illness caused by "the love of procreation." The uterus was "rebellious and masterful, like an animal disobedient to reason, and maddened with the sting of lust," eager to reproduce itself (Hamilton & Cairns, 1963/1973, p. 1210). The passage from the *Timaeus* in which he discusses wombs is often quoted but not always correctly. Plato wrote clearly about "the so-called womb or matrix of women":

> The animal within is so desirous of children, and when remaining unfruitful long beyond its proper time, gets discontented and angry, and wandering in every direction through the body, closes up the passages of the breath, and, by obstructing respiration, drives them to extremity, causing all varieties of disease, until at length the desire and love of the man and the woman, bringing them together and as it were plucking the fruit from the tree, sow in the womb, as in the field ... and thus the generation of animals is completed. (p. 1210)

Accordingly, Plato's prescription for hysteria was practical and relied on no-nonsense tips to young women: Marriage could solve the problem. That view entailed that womb disturbances were intrinsic to femininity: "Thus were created women and the female sex in general" (p. 1210).

If hysteria defines femininity in its classical conceptions, it will be useful to revisit its convoluted history with questions in mind: How does hysteria formulate an excess in sexuality; how does it gives shape to sexual difference? If we follow the entire debate, what stands out is that for over 4,000 years, doctors, religious authorities, and philosophers tried to solve the riddle of hysteria and failed. A modern reader curious about transgender issues should not be misled by the recent psychiatric erasure of hysteria from the official nomenclature. I treated this curious omission in my study of hysteria in urban ghettos (Gherovici, 2003). I have examined the so-called Puerto Rican syndrome, a term dating to the 1950s, and discovered that the disappearance of hysteria is simply a semantic suppression. The symptoms gathered under the derogatory label of Puerto Rican syndrome proved that hysteria is not gone but alive and well. It returns in today's *ataques,* an illness without organic cause and indifferent to traditional medical interventions, in which patients experience paroxysms of anxiety, rage, verbal or physical aggression, attacks of crying and shouting, seizure-like or fainting episodes, and unpremeditated suicidal gestures, followed by amnesia about the spectacular crises. This particular form of hysteria is at once a clinical and a political problem, bringing together mysterious clinical manifestations with issues of race, class, and language. The Puerto Rican syndrome makes of each individual case of ataque an allegory of a collective situation. This openness to the social field is not specific to this syndrome but a general feature of hysteria. Thomas Sydenham, the great 17th-century English doctor, ascribed to culture an important role in hysteria. He noted that hysterical symptoms "imitated" the culture in which they were produced. Hysteria is a cultural barometer.

Today, when I hear in my clinical practice questions about gender and sexuality it is no surprise that those questions can be traversed by a history that dates back 40 centuries. Of course, I do not believe that my patients are aware of this. But, whenever I catch these historical echoes, I cannot help thinking that what Freud called the unconscious is also traversed by history. This is why it is necessary to retrace some of the steps in the evolution of a baffling but resilient symptom. If we review the ways in which specialists have grappled with multiform manifestations of hysteria, we can hope that we will see the links between the most general issue that hysteria presupposes, namely: What is a woman? and its more pointed and recent version: How can one become a woman?

The Hippocratic corpus, which called *hysteria* certain ailments of the womb understood as a female affliction, also subscribed to the theories of errant uteruses causing different morbid states. The uterus could rise to the stomach and even jump over it; it could rush upward, push the thoracic viscera into the throat, which would cause victims to choke. Once more, fumigations and abdominal bandages were, next to marriage, Hippocratic therapies of choice for hysteria.

Despite the fact that male sufferers were occasionally identified and discussed, hysteria continued to be seen as a women's disorder. An exception was the Roman Galen of Pergamon (1976), who in the second century A.D. argued that hysteria could be found in both sexes. Galen thought that hysteria was caused by the retention of secretions like semen or menses, which would then corrupt the blood and irritate the nerves. He also thought that the main cause was sexual, mostly abstinence. As a consequence, Galen recommended genital massages for hysteric women; they would result in contractions and would release fluids until symptoms would disappear. His detailed description of genital massage, which was reproduced in medical circles until the 19th century, supports Rachel Maines's (1999) contention that for centuries female sexuality was seen as hysterical pathology. Because of that ancient myth, female orgasm was often described as a "hysterical paroxysm." Since it was a "crisis" that marked the climax of the disease, when it was produced clinically, it became a legitimate therapy (p. 11).[1] Let us note that when Galen described the treatment and its effects, his language reveals a confusion between sexes: "Following the warmth of remedies and arousing from the touch of the genital organs required by the treatment, there followed twitchings accompanied at the same time by pain and pleasure after which she emitted a

---

[1] A play by Sarah Ruhl (2009), *In the Next Room (or the Vibrator Play)*, premiered February 5, 2009, at the Berkeley Repertory Theatre, California, stages the comedic and dramatic implications of late 1800s treatment of hysteria using a strange electric-powered wooden box with a few knobs set on a platform and with a thin tube and porcelain doodad on the end, looking "like a farming implement," as one surprised female character observes. This odd mechanical box, and the central character of this play, perfected and automated a function that doctors had long performed for the patients—pelvic massage culminating in orgasm to relieve hysteric symptoms.

turbid and abundant sperm. From that time on, she was free of all the evil she felt" (p. 24). The belief that sexual massage would counteract the pervasive effects of the movements of the uterus persisted for more than 2,000 years. And, as one can expect, for the ancients and many moderns, genital manual friction could not replace frequent conjugal copulation, always the recommended cure.[2]

THE DEVIL'S HYSTERIA

For early ecclesiastical writers, sensuality, carnal pleasure, and lust were considered a sin, thus creating an important shift in the conceptualization of hysteria. Due to the growing influence of Christianity, abstinence and chastity were praised as virtues, which led to a return to supernatural explanations for hysteria. St. Augustine, who did not write specifically on hysteria, maintained that all illnesses were manifestations of original sin. Such a religious view led specialists to view the most dramatic features of hysteria as the consequence of witchcraft and demonic possession. The association of hysteria with feminine sexuality had been so ingrained that the hysteric became a heretic woman willfully engaging in sexual commerce with the devil. In the late medieval and Renaissance periods, hysterical symptoms continued to be understood as marks of the devil (*stigmati diaboli*). Supernatural explanations transformed hysterics into witches who had to be exorcised or burned at the stake in "purifying" bonfires.

One eloquent example of demonization of hysteric symptoms is the 1494 *Malleus Maleficarum* (republished in 1951). In this immensely popular religious treatise on medieval misogyny, known in England as the "Witches' Hammer," not only partial anesthesia, mutism, blindness, deafness, and convulsions but also women's ability to experience sexual pleasure were considered satanic stigmata, confirmatory of evil possession; vicious punishments were prescribed for the "bewitched" women. The cause of demonic hysteria was femininity—women were witches *in potentia*. "What else is woman," exclaim the authors, "but a foe to friendship, an inescapable punishment, a necessary evil, a natural temptation, a desirable calamity, a domestic danger, a delectable detriment, an evil of nature, painted with fair colours! ... It is indeed a necessary torture" (Veith, p. 63). It was considered entirely natural that women would form alliances with the devil. Indeed, the trials at the courts of inquisition, in which a woman was presented to a mostly male audience to witness her demonic possession, were the distant and nightmarish precursors of Charcot's more scientific clinical presentation of hysterics to a bourgeois public at La Salpêtrière.

---

[2] For an engrossing excursion through the disease paradigm of hysteria from ancient times to the 19th century, see Veith (1965) and Maines (1999).

After centuries of witch mania leading to wholesale persecution of hysteric women, Edward Jorden wrote in 1603 *A Briefe Discourse of a Disease Called the Suffocation of the Mother. Written Upon Occasion Which Hath Beene of Late Taken Thereby, to Suspect Possession of an Evil Spirit, or Some Such Supernaturall Power. Wherein Is Declared That Divers Strange Actions and Passions of the Body of Man, Which in the Common Opinion, Are Imputed to the Divell, Have Their True Natural Causes and Do Accompany This Disease.* This book's main argument is disclosed in its title, and such a key text indicates a secularization and medicalization of hysteria (Jorden, 1603; reissued in MacDonald, 1991). Although Jorden was the first to identify a mental component in hysteria—he proposed a cure involving the elimination of "some melancholike or capricious conceit" (Jorden, p. 26); nevertheless, his tract describes the womb or "Mother" as the primary site of the disease (p. 5).

In early 17th century France, Charles Lepois was the first to offer a truly revolutionary conception that would lay the foundations for a systematized idea of hysteria (Bercherie, 1983, p. 22). Lepois (also known as Caroli Pisoni) saw hysteria as a primitive illness of the brain, close to epilepsy and affecting also men. He was not the first to consider that hysteria occurred in both sexes—as we saw, this view was anticipated by Galen but had been forgotten for two millennia. It took half a century for his ideas to be accepted, thanks to the contributions of the English doctors Thomas Willis and Thomas Sydenham. In Willis's (1684) theorizations, hysterical fits were produced by "Spirits inhabiting the Brain, being now prepared for Explosions" (p. 71). Finally, the "spirits" found a precise anatomical location from which it was be hard to move higher upward, that is, within the head. Finally, the identification of the cause and the locus of hysteria paved the way for early psychiatry.

HYSTERIA BECOMES AN ILLNESS

Sydenham considered that "hysteria is the commonest of all chronic diseases" except fevers, "responsible for one sixth of all human maladies" and even though he clearly recognized the occurrence of hysteria in men (called *hypochondria*), he claimed that "women ... are rarely free from it" (Payne, 1900, p. 143). Sydenham's groundbreaking contributions confirmed that the etiology of hysteria was not supernatural but natural: Hysteria, a medical pathology, only required medical care, not religious condemnation or legal punishment. Sydenham offered, by the same token, an explanation for the pathogenesis of hysteria; it came from an imbalance in the distribution of "animal spirits" between mind and body and was caused by "commotions of the mind, arising from sudden outbursts of anger, pain, fear of other similar emotions" (Veith, 1965, p. 143). Shortly after Sydenham's death, his follower Georgio Baglivi (1723) advanced the understanding of hysteria as a disease caused by "the Passions or Commotions of the mind" (p. 161) and indicating a shared emotional basis for all "Disorders of the Mind" (p. 163). He also emphasized the profound influence of the physician on the patient, noticing the curative power of suggestion:

> The Physician ought to employ his greatest Sagacity and Industry in raising the depress'd Spirit of his Patient, by any means whatsoever; either by smoothing him with fair Words, or humouring him with agreeable Medicines, and pretending that such Med'cines are the only effectual and sovereign Means to cure him. ... I can scarce express what Influence the Physician's Words have upon the Patient's Life, and how much they sway the Fancy; for a Physician that has his Tongue well hung, and is a Master of the Art of persuading, fastens, by the mere Force of Words, such a virtue upon his Remedies." (p. 171)

Here, one comes closer to the conception shared by contemporary psychoanalysts since, for Baglivi, hysteria involved the mind *and* body at once. More momentously, Baglivi held that both could be cured by the effect of speech. Whereas for Sydenham emotions accompanied hysteria, for Baglivi they became its central cause. Baglivi's ideas started to be disseminated, but almost two centuries passed before the understanding of hysteria was truly revolutionized.

The return of the medical conception of hysteria during the 17th century introduced major innovations in theorization but did not translate into any change in clinical practices or the association with the feminine. The professional contemporaries of Willis and Sydenham, and even Sydenham himself, remained faithful to the traditional Hippocratic and Galenic treatments for hysteria: They prescribed "antihystericals" that included putting bandages or plasters on the navel to compel the uterus back into its correct anatomical position or applying sweet-smelling pessaries[3] to secure the womb in place.

During the 17th and the 18th centuries, another important development was the emergence of a neurological model of the disease. The new explanatory principle combined the old humoral conception with the contemporary knowledge of neurology, chemistry, and mechanics. In the 18th century, Robert Whytt (1767) attempted to trace the origin of hysteria by following the connections between body and soul in an effort to determine the role of the mind in hysterical body ailments. Yet, as causes for hysteria he included wind, worms, "aliments improper in quantity or quality," obstructions in the viscera of the lower belly, and "tough phlegm"

---

[3] The pessary was a contraption introduced in the vagina to correct the "defective" position of the uterus.

together with "violent affections of the mind" (p. 183). Whytt claimed that the violent affections of the mind were responsible for the most sudden and surprising changes in the body. Sudden nervous symptoms were caused by "doleful or moving stories, horrible or unexpected sights, great grief, anger, terror, and other passions" (pp. 206–207). This last series of causes gets closer to the Freudian conception of trauma as the basis of hysteria and lays the foundation for the inclusion of the role of emotions. In spite of that, Whytt's treatment followed Sydenham's tradition: vegetable bitters, mineral waters, quinine, cool and dry air, light and sparing food, small amounts of wine, exercise, amusement (to deal with grief and anxiety), and opium.

William Cullen (1781) was a contemporary of Whytt who described hysteria as "neurosis" on his neuropathological essays. This innovation, however, had little to do with our present-day understanding of the term for he still militantly promoted vomiting, bleeding, and purging as treatment (see Riese, 1958). For him, hysteria was produced by gastric and genital disturbances that affected the brain and caused hysterical conversions. And, he also found hysteria to occur more frequently in women. Here was a crucial twist in hysteria's winding path: The late 18th and early 19th centuries marked an exacerbation in the association of hysteria with female sexuality. In Cullen, the uterine theory was revived to explain the pathogenesis of hysteria, the past returning with a vengeance.

In America, Cullen, internationally famous and one of the most distinguished physicians of his time, found a fervent follower in Benjamin Rush. One of the signatories to the Declaration of Independence, Rush became the father of American psychiatry when he introduced a "moral treatment" at the Pennsylvania Hospital in Philadelphia. Rather than fumigations, smelling salts, or vapors, his treatment for hysteria, understood as a moral rather than a physical disease, consisted of regular and lengthy conversations with the patient. For Rush, hysteria was a disease of the privileged, idle, and self-indulgent class, a sign of distinguished social status.

On the other side of the Atlantic, Philippe Pinel, already famous for having freed the mentally ill from the asylum's shackles and chains, also freed the uterus and the brain from any etiological connection with hysteria. His observations on nymphomania underlined sexuality as an important causal factor in the development of hysteria and marked a reerotization of the disease. Despite differences, his ideas anticipated Freud's elaborations, especially concerning a distinguishing feature of hysteria: that it concerns the body as sexed. However, Freud's originality in his view of that enigmatic area of human life—sexuality—was to discover a common foundation in "normal" and "abnormal" sexuality. Freud's work on hysteria called attention to the "skewed" relation of subjects to their sexuality that takes an oblique course that separates them from sex.

HYSTERIA, THE FEMALE MALADY

Hysteria etymologically refers to the uterus; thus, for many hysteria was tantamount to "women" or "femininity." "As a general rule," wrote Auguste Fabré in 1883, "all women are hysterical" (Showalter, 1993, p. 287). Like most of his contemporaries, Fabré saw hysteria and woman as a tautology: "Hysteria, before being an illness is a temperament, and what constitutes the temperament of a woman is rudimentary hysteria" (Showalter, 1993, p. 287). This led Elaine Showalter (1997) to generalize that "Hysteria is inevitably a feminist issue because for centuries doctors regarded it as a female reproductive disease" (p. 9). She observed that feminist theorists tended to take 19th-century hysteria as the epitome of feminine oppression; hysteria was presented as a proto-feminist rebellion against patriarchal oppression.

With feminist scholarship, a reconceptualization of the medical history of hysteria took place to address the role of science and medicine in female oppression. Showalter (1993) notes that throughout its history "hysteria has been always constructed as a 'woman's disease,' a feminine disorder, or a disturbance of femininity," adding that "this construction has usually been hostile" (p. 286). Showalter adds the important observation that the feminist appropriation of hysteria has overlooked the crucial fact that although constructed as primarily feminine, it has also been a disorder of men. As Mark Micale (1989) observes, "No line of evolution within the historiography of hysteria is more complicated than the feminist one" (p. 331).

In the production of a feminized hysteria, the gender divide is always clear, as Peter Brooks (1993) noted: Male observers have constructed the female hysterical body as the embodiment of female nature (pp. 54–87). For Danielle Gourevitch (1984), "Hysteria is the disease ... of women in their relationship to men" (p. 27). Similarly, Micale (1995) describes the history of hysteria as "a body of writing by men about women" (p. 67) that "expresses the immense incomprehension between the sexes through the ages" (p. 70). Furthermore, Eliot Slater (1982) calls the quintessential femininity of hysteria "a product of machismo, of male chauvinism" (p. 39). Paul Verhaeghe (1997/1999) generalizes when he observes: "Hysteria is the name of the age-old relationship between man and woman" (p. 245). There is no doubt that hysteria appears as a combat zone for the battle of the sexes. Moreover, for Micale (1995) the construction of the hysteric as incomprehensible, irrational, convulsive, sexual, female, Other, exposes that the stigmatizing power of past medical writing about hysteria is ultimately a defeat, "a symbol of the limit of male knowledge about the opposite sex" (p. 70). In the same vein, Maines (1999) sees the "sexist" understanding of hysteria in Western medical tradition that she dates back to the Hippocratic corpus, as indicative of androgenic definitions of sexuality and [of] the construction of ideal female sexuality to fit them; [of] the reduction of female sexual behavior outside the androcentric standard to disease paradigms requiring treatment; and [of] the means by which physicians legitimated and justified the clinical production of orgasm in women as a treatment for these disorders. (p. 2)

Maines points out that in current English common usage, the word *hysterical* is applied to a person to mean "upset to the point of irrationality." This use "combines in its connotations the pejorative elements of femininity as and of the irrational." She notes that there is not an analogous word like "testerical" to describe, for example, out-of-control male sports fans' behavior (p. 21). Moreover, Maines interpreted hysteria as a disease produced by "discontinuities between male and female experiences of sexuality" (p. 7). Both observations call on Lacan's (2001) dictum "there is no such a thing as a sexual relationship" (p. 455), an expression repeated over the years, which pertains to the fact that between man and woman there is no relation of complementarity. Hysteria therefore appears a symptom of the discontinuity between the sexes, it emerges as the pathologization of the nonrapport, and it manifests the heterogeneity of feminine sexuality.

It is no coincidence that psychoanalysis, which was invented to treat hysterics, should be dealing with the momentous psychic consequences of a lack of symmetry or proportion that would guarantee a perfect union between man and woman. Rather than a convergence, Lacan (2006) even declares that between man and woman there is a wall—a wall that stands for a void or an absence (p. 239).[4] The omission of male hysteria reveals the void, the inexistence of complementarity between male and female; it is as if one was saying in the sexual distribution of hysteria that there is no such thing as a rapport between the sexes. It is true that psychoanalysis was invented by Freud while listening to hysterical women. But, even though psychoanalysis emanated from work done mostly with women, its inaugural claim completely altered the disease paradigm—men could also be hysterical.

I have surveyed the female sexual character of hysteria as defined by ancient, medieval, Renaissance, and modern medical authorities before Sigmund Freud. At the time of the invention of psychoanalysis, the association of women with hysteria was stronger than ever: Hysteria and femininity were seen as a natural fate of character. Once more, women were

---

[4] Lacan quoted a poem by Antoine Tudal, "Between man and love, there is woman/Between man and woman, there is a world/Between man and the world, there is a wall." He revisited this poem in his unpublished *Seminar XIX: Le Savoir du Psychanalyste, 1971–1972*, class of January 6, 1972. This time, Lacan likened this wall with castration and made up the word (*a*)*mur* as a condensation of wall (*mur*) and love (*amour*), mediated by the object cause of desire (*a*).

hysterical because they were women. Hysteria was "rooted in the very nature of being female" (Mitchinson, 1986, p. 90). Hysteria became a caricature of femininity (Chodoff, 1982), "the embodiment of a perverse or hyper-femininity" (Smith-Rosenberg, 1985, p. 198). The whole 19th century was caught in a contradiction between the suggestion that women required sexual gratification for reasons of health and the assumption that women were not interested in the pleasures of the flesh. Often, the conflict was resolved by echoing the Platonic idea that women only yearn for maternity and not for sexual enjoyment.

It was in the 19th century that the appeal of hysteria increased dramatically to the point that it became "the great neurosis," as Charcot called it (Charcot, 1877). Not only did it trigger vast medical interest, but also it emerged to cultural prominence. At the same time, though, the ancient link between hysteria and the female reproductive apparatus was preserved. This century of great medical advances brought about invasive treatments for hysteria—large doses of opium, removal of ovaries, hysterectomies, clitoridectomies—together with a strange array of machines to apply pressure to the ovaries or keep the womb fixed in place. In this evolution, Jean-Martin Charcot appeared both as a major synthesizer and as a true discoverer.[5] He gave dignity to hysteria, thus allowing Freud to progress significantly. In the late 19th century, at last, the uterus was left alone in the imagination of the interpreters of hysteria when the emerging field of psychiatry moved the cause of hysteria upward from the uterus and attributed hysteric fits to lesions of the brain. Charcot (1877) emptied hysteria from its uterine content and from its feminine determination by instructing his students to assume "that the word 'hysteria' means nothing" (p. 37).

Hysteria may have, by then, lost its primary sexual localization, yet in Charcot's own words hysteria "*c'est toujours la chose génitale, toujours—toujours—toujours* [it is always a genital cause, always—always—always]." Freud (1914/1959) was shocked by Charcot's revelation: "I know, that for a moment I was almost paralyzed with amazement and said to myself: 'Well, but if he knows that, why does he never say so?'" (p. 295). Freud's reason for surprise was not so much the "genital" source but the emphasized "always" of Charcot's remark, which suggests an inevitable determinism. Freud wondered why, if Charcot knew about the role sexuality played, he was so absorbed by brain anatomy and the experimental production of hysterical paralysis, unsuccessfully trying to find a correlate of the psychiatric nosography in neurology. After years of performing autopsies twice a week that did not provide any organic basis for his claims, he was unable to sustain his theory of an anatomical lesion. Later in his career, Charcot abandoned the idea of an organic lesion and leaned toward a functional or

---

[5] Jean-Martin Charcot was one of the greatest neurologists of France (1825–1893). For more on Charcot, see Trillat (2006).

dynamic explanation of hysteria. One of his biggest contributions was to reproduce the hysterical attack, inducing and stopping under hypnosis the dramatic seizures of *grande hystérie*. The "artificial" production of hysteric symptoms proved to be crucial in the later Freudian discovery of their origin. Freud would not neglect the essential role of sexuality.

HYSTERIA IN THE TEMPLE OF SCIENCE

At the height of Charcot's fame, during hysteria's heyday, Freud spent 4 months in Paris (between October 1885 and February 1886) to study with the "master of hysteria." The form of hysteria that Freud discovered at La Salpêtrière was both medicalized and theatrical. At the time, the hospital of La Salpêtrière was the biggest in the world. Charcot's spellbinding Tuesday night lessons were attended not only by doctors but also by the intellectual and artistic Parisian elite.

Freud admired Charcot, but he also took into account the criticism of the rival School of Nancy, where Hippolyte Bernheim questioned the role of suggestion in the spectacular hysterias that Charcot was treating. Most hysterias Charcot treated at La Salpêtrière were extremely "Charcotian," which raised the question of whether hysteria was "natural" or produced by suggestion. Bernheim violently opposed Charcot's methods and denounced the great hysterical crisis of La Salpêtrière's clinical demonstrations as an artifice, a symptomatology constructed by suggestion. For Bernheim, a subject could become "hysterizable" after the repetition of a number of crises. He thought that the susceptibility to suggestion was not restricted to the mentally ill, and that the majority of persons can be readily inclined towards it (Bernheim, 1913). This nonpathological hysterical basis common to most human beings is an interesting precursor to Lacan's notion of hysteria as the norm of human condition (Lacan, 1998a, pp. 466–467).

THE CONSEQUENCES OF BAD HYPNOSIS

Bernheim (1917) argued that suggestion "is an act by which one idea is introduced into the brain and accepted by it" (p. 113). If hysteria is induced by the persuasive words of the hypnotist, then hysteria, caused by suggestion, becomes an effect of discourse. Ironically, it was by way of hypnosis that Freud invented psychoanalysis: Less skilled than Bernheim at inducing hypnotic trances, he stopped his attempts and began listening to what his hysteric patients had to say when awake. Freud's first treatments of hysteria combined talk therapy and hypnosis. Still, it was his inability to successfully hypnotize some patients that allowed him to discover psychoanalysis through the cathartic cure after giving up hypnosis entirely. He created a method that bypassed hypnosis and was conducted in a state that differs little from the normal one. In this way, Freud developed an original way of understanding hysteria, one that includes an investigation of the unconscious. Freud deliberately broke away from hypnosis, but not without learning a key lesson from Charcot's hypnotic powers since Charcot had been the first to remove hysterical symptoms with hypnosis, thus revealing the "psychic" origin of hysteria (Freud, 1893).

Pierre Janet followed Charcot's steps like a disciple and paved the way for a new clinical perspective that he would not exploit to the fullest although it was to be of great use for his contemporary and rival, Freud. Charcot had spent years unsuccessfully trying to find physical lesions that explained idiosyncratic hysterical bodily symptoms. Janet's genius was to argue that hysteria followed a peculiar anatomy, one that derived from popular knowledge rather than from science. Janet noted that, for a patient, her hysterical paralysis of the hand ended at the wrist, like a glove and did not follow the path of the muscles and nerves that extend well into the forearm. Janet (1965) concluded that hysterical paralyses and anesthesias had "something mental, intellectual, in them" (p. 158). Hysteric symptoms split the body "mentally" and "intellectually" in a manner that follows popular ideas and not the structural divisions of real anatomy. Hence, Janet broke the Cartesian mind–body dichotomy and, without being fully aware of it, proposed a novel correlation between mind and body through language. If hysteria is an illness of the mind and the body, how can one differentiate which affects the other? Janet's observations implied that an idea is incarnated in the body, that knowledge—even in its popular conception—traverses the body, defying the rules of anatomy. In the same way, Freud (1888/1893) wrote that the hysterical symptom "takes the organs in the ordinary, popular sense of the names they bear: the leg is the leg as far as its insertion into the hip, the arm is the upper limb as it is visible under the clothing" (p. 169). Nothing corresponds to the pathways and topography of nerve branches. For the hysteric, popular knowledge writes symptoms on the body, symptoms that are more faithful to language than to anatomy.

What Charcot had discovered and Janet confirmed was that the hysteric's body is imaginary. With hysterical symptoms, the psychical becomes physiological, following an anatomy that depends on language and the imagination. Therefore, it reveals the human body as something that belongs to another logic, a logic that, for Lacan, is marked by the material side of language, hence the signifier. As we have seen, hysterical anesthesias follow a given culture's popular notions of the function of organs. This very fact gives us interesting insights into the primacy of the signifier for humans taken as speaking beings. This throws new light on the way in which culture is articulated in the body. A body is not just a collection of organs, but a place onto which culture inscribes itself. The result of such inscription we may call *subjectivity*. The particular words that the symptoms represent are very idiosyncratic, each patient's "writing" being a matter of subjective style that identifies him or her like a signature. The anatomical defiance of hysteria can reveal a lot about the structure of the speaking subject. The hysterical body shows that the human body is not simply the body of flesh and blood but a network of signifiers. This is the body with which I engage in this book—for psychoanalysis, the body is a speaking body linked with culture and a specific imaginary realm. Transgender issues all revolve around this particular body.

HYSTERIA GAVE BIRTH TO PSYCHOANALYSIS

Hysteria must be given pride of place above all because it was with hysterics that Freud reached a new understanding of the human psyche. This insight is shared by Ilza Veith, whose magisterial history of hysteria was published in 1965 and has been universally used by scholars.[6] Her study, the first full-scale intellectual history written in English, became the "definitive" history of hysteria (Lowenfeld, 1968, p. 101). As Micale (1989) writes, "No single text in the historiography of hysteria has had a wider readership" (p. 38). Veith grounded her study in a Freudian historical teleology. Today, it continues to be considered the most authoritative source of information.[7] A review of the current literature on hysteria confirms that all authors rely, explicitly or not, on Veith's narrative covering 4,000 years of hysteria.[8] However, work by British classicist Helen King has called into question much of the canonical interpretation that treats hysteria as a historical constant and attempts to discredit Veith's idea that hysteria pre-dates the Hippocratic corpus.

King (1993) powerfully challenges Veith's contention that the name *hysteria* has been in use since the time of Hippocrates. She argues that medieval and Renaissance scholars looked back to the Hippocratic text, selected the symptoms that fit their concept of hysteria, and made up glorified ancient roots for hysteria. King confirms that the ancients had a version of the female body in which symptoms were dependent on movements of the wandering womb.[9] Yet, King's criticism radically separates the adjectival form *hysteric* from the noun *hysteria*. As it turns out, King states that the word

---

[6] Veith's book has been widely praised for its excellence; see Meskey (1985).
[7] See Micale's (1989) discussion of Veith's importance (pp. 38–46).
[8] I will just mention a few representative names: Joan Acocella (1999); Jacques André, Jacqueline Lanouzière, and Francois Richard (1999); Julia Barossa (2001); Charles Bernheimer and Claire Kanahe (1985/1990); Janet Bleizer (1994); Elisabeth Bronfen (1998); Diane Chauvelot (1995); Charles Melman (1984); Mark Micale (1989); Juliet Mitchell (2000); Gisèle Harrus Revédi (1997); Alec Roy (1982); J. M. Stevens (1975).
[9] For an overview of Hippocratic gynecology and the female body in Ancient Greece, see King (1998).

used in the Hippocratic texts is the adjective *hystericus,* meaning "from the womb," to show the part of the body from which symptoms emanate, and not the noun. As such, *hystericus* is purely a physical description of cause—it just means that the symptom is caused by the womb moving, putting pressure on an organ. King observes that for Hippocrates there was no concept of hysteria as a disease entity but rather the belief in an all-powerful womb capable of causing all sorts of disturbances. As a Hippocratic text put it, "the womb is the origin of all diseases." Even when one could say in all fairness that for the Hippocratic corpus all diseases in women are hysterical, the implications of this word were entirely different for the ancients.

Clearly, Veith uses secondary sources and 19th-century translations of the Hippocratic corpus, yet King (1993) underscores that the main problem is the distortion of the ancient approach to illness when imposing a diagnosis of hysteria—for the Hippocratic texts just describe symptoms and do not give a single disease name to a group of symptoms. For King, the alleged classical pedigree of hysteria is an early modern invention to validate through dignified ancient Greek origins the newly founded humanism that remedicalized hysteria in the late Renaissance. Yet, to be fair, what remained as a constant through the millennia was the association between hystericus and the female body.

King (1993) contends that before the 1600s the "hysteric affection" was a gynecological problem, attributed to the womb. Only after the 17th century did hysteria acquire its contemporary features. Still, in the early 17th century, hysteria was linked to conditions found in both sexes, like hypochondria and melancholy. The shift took place in the late 17th century when, as J. M. Boss (1979) notes, hysteria "is united with hypochondria and annexed parts of melancholy's crumbling empire" (p. 237). With this transformation, the cause of hysteria is no longer restricted to just the womb but seen as being located in the brain and affecting the whole person.

One may wonder in which century the inaugural moment of hysteria actually took place and suspect the claims about hysteria's universalism and essentialism. Although King rightfully disowns Hippocrates as the adoptive father of this hybrid child, even such an illuminating piece as hers does not, however, fall outside the "discourse of hysteria" as defined by Lacan, a discourse whose very structure she unwittingly repeats and reenacts. This misleading nosological entity makes wombs move freely in the body, marks bodies with demonic stigmas, unleashes massive witch hunts, produces convulsions or panic attacks, but above all has made "experts" question not only its roots and origins but also their own capacity to produce a reliable explanation. Most of hysteria's medical interpreters agree to define it as undefinable. The most cautious "commentators repeatedly warn that hysteria defies definition" (Bleizer, 1994, p. 3).

HYSTERIA DEFIES DEFINITION

Is hysteria one illness or many? Has a definite causal mechanism for hysteria been established beyond any doubt? Can a single pathogen be identified for hysteria? Can hysteria be even called a disease? Gérard Wajeman (1982) sums this up well: "There doesn't seem to be anything medicine has not said about hysteria: it is multiple, it is one, it is nothing; it is an entity, a malfunction, an illusion; it is true and deceptive; organic or perhaps mental; it exists, it does not exist" (p. 11). Charcot had affirmed that hysteria existed in all places and at all times, believing that hysteria was a constant entity over time and place; qualifying this thesis, Veith (1965) adds that if "hysteria … has adapted its symptoms to the ideas and the mores current in each society, yet its predispositions and basic features have remained more or less unchanged" (p. viii). The problem with hysteria is that it is not a clearly identifiable disease entity. Already in 1685, Sydenham described hysteria as "a farrago of disorderly and irregular phenomena. … Hence it is extremely difficult to describe a history of the disease" (Micale, 1995, p. 109). Bernard de Mandeville accurately describes the protean nature of hysteria in his 1711 *Treatise on Hypochondriack and Hysterick Diseases*, "the word HYSTERICK must be of a prodigious latitude, to signify so many Different Evils, unless you mean by a Disease, that, like the Sin of Ingratitude, includes all the rest. … The very name has become a joke" (Micale, 1995, p. 267).

Following this admonition, King's criticism has historicized hysteria and warned us against a transhistorical use of the word. My research on the Puerto Rican syndrome proved her contention right, but even within a purely historicist approach one cannot deny that hysteria refers us to a pattern that has crossed centuries (Gherovici, 2003). Even though hysteria is not the only enigmatic disease that has left specialists clueless, hysteria has always triggered an interest that surpasses all other mysterious nonfatal ailments. Hysterical symptoms raise question after question. Is hysteria cyclic and repetitive? Or, do its symptoms involve a particularity of form unique to each patient, thus accounting for the difficulty observers have had in identifying a finite number of symptoms for hysteria? Sydenham remarked on the polymorphic manifestations of hysteria, "[t]he frequency of hysteria is no less remarkable than the multiformity of shapes which it puts on" (Veith, 1965, p. 141). When Whytt (1767) tried to restrict his listing to only the most common symptoms, the epigrammatic selection occupied four full pages of his *Nervous, Hypochondriac or Hysteric Disorders*. Nineteenth-century psychiatric clinical practice was based on very precise observations and meticulous description of symptoms and phases, which allowed for the construction of a diagnosis. Thus, Charles Lasègue (1878), a contemporary of Charcot, facing the innumerable personal manifestations of hysteric symptoms, simply gave up: "The definition of hysteria has never been given and will never be" (Micale, 1995, p. 109n.3). This sense of inescapable failure is echoed in the 20th century by Edward Shorter (1994): "Writing a history of something so amorphous, whose meaning and content keep changing, is like trying to write a history of dirt" (p. 26).[10]

DO YOU SPEAK HYSTERIA?

The general nosological frustration that the multiple mutations of hysteria have elicited reveals why hysteria has left an indelible imprint on the evolution of the health sciences and illuminates one of its most interesting aspects, an aspect that helps explain why psychoanalysis is so indebted to hysteria. The chameleon-like quality of hysteria exposes the confines of the anatomo-clinical method, which, as Michel Foucault (1975) notes, is used by the medical sciences to articulate space (body), language, and death (p. 197). Hysterical symptoms are unconditionally faithful to the cultural mandates in place at any given time. This is why certain symptoms appear only during a particular time period and in accordance with its prevailing medical knowledge. This openness to medical discourse shapes hysterical symptoms: The hysteric shows what the physician "wants" to see even while revealing the limits of this gaze. Hysterical manifestations often seem to confirm medical knowledge, only to challenge it in the end, reducing the practitioner to a position of impotence. Hysteria is undoubtedly culture specific; its manifestations are based on the dominant theories of disease for each culture and are syntonic with the rest of the cultural beliefs. Hysterical symptoms come and go with the fashions. Like other aspects of human culture, hysteria is constantly changing. The fact that hysteria is so susceptible to the collective explains why certain modalities of hysteria will be produced only in particular cultures and in specific time periods.

If from the very beginning of modern medicine we have a hysteric, her symptoms, and a doctor,[11] what is important is how these elements are articulated. Inevitably—and this has become more evident with contemporary medical practice—medical knowledge erases subjectivity by reducing subjects to a set of organs, symptoms, and clearly ascertainable complaints. Hysteria, however, appeals to the subject's most entrenched resistance to all these coercive systems. This resistance takes effect by actively baffling or provoking the dominant medical knowledge. The manifestations are so

---

[10]To challenge Shorter's pessimism, see Curtis (2007).
[11]This suggests, as Bronfen (1998) observed, an interesting relationship, a "romance" between medicine and hysteria in which hysteria and the medical discourse about hysteria are mutually constitutive (p. 102). For an exploration of the elusive yet powerful ties between doctors and their hysterics, see Israël (1979), Melman (1984), and Wajeman (1982).

numerous and even contradictory that they manage to expose the fault lines and blind spots of the medical perception. In this struggle, what manages to prevail is subjectivity. Indeed, hysteria presents us with the idiosyncrasies of intractable subjectivity. The clinical revolution introduced by Freud began by restoring subjectivity to the hysteric.

Before we set aside King's powerful critique as one twist in hysteria's sinuous path and sweep it away as another version of the ever-present hysteric riddle, let us note that King's objection to the diachronic account of Veith converges with the insights provided by Thomas Laqueur. Laqueur (1990) argued persuasively that in the course of medical and philosophical history prior to the 17th century there was no opposition or sharp boundary between the sexes. "Sexuality as a singular and all-important attribute with a specific object—the *opposite* sex—is the product of the late eighteenth century" (p. 13; italics in the original). Laqueur does not think that earlier scientists were mistaken. They carefully recorded what they observed. However, because their view did not include two sexes, the anatomical parts were identified accordingly. Later political developments created a distinction between men and women; thus, the materiality of the body was interpreted in a different way.

Laqueur's analysis goes back to Aristotle, who although he apparently supported the idea of two different sexes did not regard these as in total opposition. The boundaries of male and female were of degree and not of kind. Unlike 19th-century commentators, who used facts like menstruation or metabolism to locate women in the world order, for Aristotle the distinct qualities of each sex were better and lesser versions of each other. In sex, which existed for the purpose of generation, the male represented the efficient cause and the female the material cause. Aristotle, like Galen five centuries later, aligned reproductive organs with the alimentary system, common to all flesh. For Aristotle, all of the male organs were similar to the female. The similarities extended even to the uterus, which presumably the male does not have, and Aristotle assimilated it to the male scrotum since the vagina was a tube (*kaulos*) "like the penis of the male, but inside the body" (*HA* 10.5.637a, pp. 23–25, quoted in Laqueur, 1990, p. 33) Indeed, the notion of a reversibility between the sexes (the idea that the vagina is an inverted penis) is actualized in the most recent techniques of male-to-female sex reassignment surgery, in which the skin of the scrotum is used to build the labia of the neovagina. This is illustrated by a line from the movie *Transamerica* (Tucker, 2005) in which the protagonist, Bree, explains: "They don't cut it off! It just becomes an innie instead of an outtie." The reversibility of the sexes, however, does not extend to female-to-male sex change—phalloplasty in the female-to-male transsexual remains a challenge (Hoebecke, 2001).

Laqueur (1990) observes as well that, "For two millennia the ovary ... had not even a name of its own. Galen refers to it by the same word he uses for the male testes, *orcheis*. ... Herophilus had called the ovaries *didymoi* (twins), another standard Greek word for testicles" (pp. 4–5). Also within what Laqueur called the "one-sex body" paradigm, for Galen women were inverted and lesser versions of the male, with man's external genitalia turned inward.[12] Although Latin and ancient Greek, like most languages, had a plethora of words to refer to sex and sexual organs, the experts in the field did not produce a precise vocabulary of dimorphic genital anatomy: The female body was then a lesser version of the canonical body. If the vagina was thought of as an internal penis or the womb as a female scrotum, this would imply that there existed several genders but only one adaptable sex (pp. 34–35).

Laqueur contends that well into the age of print, people believed that there were male and female subjects indeed, but only one kind of human body. Men and women were seen as slightly diverging modifications of one sex. Of course, everything changed when sexual difference was established, as Laqueur (1990) explains:

> Sometime in the eighteenth century, sex as we know it was invented. The reproductive organs went from being paradigmatic sites for displaying hierarchy, resonant throughout the cosmos, to being the foundation of incommensurable difference: "women owe their manner of being to their organs of generation, and especially to the uterus," as one eighteenth century physician put it. Here there is not only a repudiation of the old isomorphisms but also, and more important, a rejection of the idea that nuanced differences between organs, fluids, and physiological processes mirrored a transcendental order of perfection. (p. 149)

The new model of sexual difference created an opposite sex. Laqueur's claim that sex was invented destabilizes our modern ideas about the sexed body as an unchanging, transhistorical entity—sex becomes situational, any boundary between male and female is cultural. Here, a detour through psychoanalytic perspectives about sexual difference is necessary since for the unconscious, curiously perhaps, there is only one sex.

FOR THE UNCONSCIOUS, THERE IS ONLY ONE SEX

The human infant is initially not aware of the existence of two sexes and will eventually discover sexual differences and assume a sexual positioning.

---

[12] "Turn outward the woman's, turn inward, so to speak, and fold double the man's [genitalia], and you will find the same in both in every aspect" (Galen of Pergamum, quoted in Laqueur, 1990, p. 25).

This is a complex process in which one particular organ will be privileged, the penis for Freud, which will be for Lacan a signifier only, the phallus. Freud (1925) argues that both boys and girls attribute a special value to the penis, and that the discovery that certain humans have it while others do not will have psychical consequences. Lacan differs from Freud on this point when he argues that both sexes must assume castration, that is, renounce the fantasy of being the mother's phallus. For Lacan, the phallus, far from being an organ, is a theoretical speculative assumption applied to both women and men. Lacan's distinction of phallus and penis emphasizes that sexual difference is irreducible to biology (see Mitchell & Rose, 1985). It is not identification with a parent of the same or opposite sex (Freud's Oedipus complex) that determines the subject's sexual positioning, but the subject's relationship to the phallus. As there is no signifier in the symbolic order for sexual difference, sexual difference will be assumed by one signifier, the phallus. It does not have a feminine equivalent and operates for both sexes, thus establishing a fundamental asymmetry.

Since there is only the phallus to define two sexual positions, this implies a failure to inscribe the opposition between masculine and feminine. And, the unconscious does not seem to be able to recognize this elaborate system of difference we call gender. This seems to run parallel to Laqueur's claim that the idea of two sexes is not the necessary, natural consequence of corporeal difference. Even if psychoanalysis has a different set of concepts and different priorities, it corresponds to an age-old problem in the distinction between the male and the female. The issue for psychoanalysis, as we will see, is not purely culturalist or exclusively somatic. Both the post-Foucaultian investigation into a genealogy of the sexed body and the post-Freudian explorations of bisexuality agree that culture could not make the body fit into the categories necessary for biological and cultural reproduction.

According to Laqueur (1990), before the modern period only one sex existed, differences between men and women were of degree not of kind, and the female body was seen as a lower version of the male. However, for centuries, hysteria articulated a sharp corporeal sexual distinction. The disease had been associated since ancient times with an unstable female body whose "wandering uterus" proposed a radically different version from the unproblematic, stable male body, hence allowing hysteria's intractable idiosyncrasies to embody an otherness that contested the male body as a model and a canonical form.

King's (1993) careful philological exploration of the word hysteria shows that since the Greeks its meaning changed many times; what in Newton's time was considered classical hysteria was a European interpretation of the newly translated texts of Hippocrates and Galen (p. 7). The origins of "hysteria" remain elusive, but it is important to note that the beginnings of the modern conceptualization of hysteria coincides with what Laqueur

(1990) identifies as the moment when the view that women were a reversed, if less-perfect, version of the male was abandoned. Two sexes in fact meant that women became increasingly seen as radically "other" and, according to Roy Porter (1993), not just other but bizarre (p. 250). The breakdown of the one-sex model and the establishment of two sexes, together with the creation of a "tradition" of hysteria, engaged the science of sex with the demands of culture, both deeply complicating the emerging politics of gender.

Let me underline this fact: King (1993) contended that a model of hysteria with alleged ancient roots was constructed as Cartesian science swept through Europe (see Porter & Rousseau, 1993, pp. 91–221). This occurred just at the time of a momentous transformation that Laqueur (1990) identified as the moment when the categories of "male" and "female" became opposites (p. 154). Porter and Rousseau (1993) remarked that Western culture was transformed under the regime of a newly founded science dominated by secularism and political reform. In that context, hysteria emerged at the center of the debate about nerves, gender, sexual differences, and the fabric of human culture, far exceeding the strictly medical domain. It is in this sense that they can claim that hysteria was construed as "almost a philosophical category rather than as a medical diagnosis or a set of therapies" (p. xii). They argued that as certain tenets of Enlightenment culture gained strength, "especially the reliance on reason, observation, logic, predictability, secularism, and the waning of a faith in superstition and magic, hysteria continued to find itself reinvigorated and regenerated" (p. xii). In this self-renewing discourse, hysteria became both a medical category and a critique of male–female relations.

The history of hysteria (*pace* Veith, 1965) has haunted modern theories of subjectivity and representation since Freud and is as much the history of Western modern civilization, a history that certainly starts with the Cartesian revolution and finds in psychoanalysis a very productive symptom bringing together language, body, and sexuality. For Foucault, the 17th and 18th centuries marked a period of great change in concepts of sex and sexuality. Foucault (1979) thought that the change from feudalism to capitalism modified the concept of the body (p. 1979). This line of argument supports Laqueur's claim and seems to fits with an important contention made by Lacan (1981), the idea that the Freudian field was made possible by the emergence of the Cartesian subject (p. 47).

This historical context introduces something analysts often hear in the office, "the most profound alienation of the subject in our scientific civilization, and it is this alienation that we encounter first when the subject begins to talk to us about himself" (Lacan, 2006, p. 233). Lacan repeatedly asserted that the psychoanalytic subject was superposable with the Cartesian *cogito*. "It is unthinkable that psychoanalysis as a practice and the *Freudian* unconscious as a discovery, could have taken on their roles before the birth—in the century which has been called the century of genius, i.e. the seventeenth century—of science" (Lacan, 1989, p. 6; italics in the original).

The inaugural step of modern science generated the divided subject of the unconscious. "Divided into what?" asks Verhaeghe (1997/1999), and responds, "two *differentially sexed* creatures" (p. 141; italics in the original). I return to the clinical effects of subjective division. One of them is the fantasy of original fusion, which is illustrated by Aristophanes' myth since the longing for the unity of a lost paradise plays a crucial role in hysteria, as noted by Verhaeghe (pp. 140–144). He observes that the nostalgia for an original mythical wholeness avoids assuming a sexual identity. This fantasmatic return to a state preceding sexual differentiation sends us back to a time, as Laqueur would say, before sex was invented.

It is commonly accepted in the literature that "subject" and "gender" are historically constructed, while "sex" is a natural category around which "gender" is socially constructed. Even if the ideas of Lacan and Laqueur partially overlap, it is important to keep in mind that Laqueur sketches a history of sexual difference, proposing viewing "sex" as constructed as well, which is what in Lacanian terms is the "Symbolic." Yet, this is not a psychoanalytic position since for psychoanalysis sexual difference is neither a social construction nor a fact of nature and rather an impossible imperative leftover of symbolization. If one can historicize sex and even psychoanalysis, it remains that sexual difference is essentially ahistorical. The imperative of sexual difference is not a human law; thus, sexual difference cannot be reduced to gender. As Charles Shepherdson (2000) observed:

> Psychoanalysis does not advocate a "biological" account of sexual difference, or even a version of "psychic essentialism" (grounded in a fixed ideal of "masculinity" and "femininity"), but neither does it amount to a form of historicism, focused on the symbolic construction of "gender." ... Sexual difference is neither "sex" nor "gender." (p. 2)

The theoretical specificity of psychoanalysis lies precisely in this position, which offers a third option for the old debate over nature versus nurture. In psychoanalysis, the body is not a natural entity governed purely by biological laws, and the body cannot be reduced to projections or representations as if it was a "contingent historical formation" (Sheperdson, 2000, p. 3). Psychoanalysis has the advantage of being able to operate in this problematic intersection between the signifier and the flesh, between body and language.

GENDER IDENTITY CONFUSION

Bernice Hausman (1995) stressed the importance of Laqueur's claim that "sex" was "not always the conceptual ground (the biological 'original') of gender (the cultural 'copy')" (p. 183). Hausman remarked on a conceptual confusion Laqueur falls into when he explores several cases of individuals who "change sex" or are defined juridically as being a sex other than the one they have been living, for example, Marie de Marcis in the 17th century. Marie was almost burned at the stake for falling in love and wanting to marry a female servant with whom she shared a bed (Laqueur, 1990, p. 136). Marie, who had been baptized a girl and lived as a woman (medical testimony corroborated that she had been born female, and her master and mistress confirmed that she had menstrual periods), had revealed that she had a penis and therefore she was a man who wanted to exercise his right to marry a woman. Instead, Marie de Marcis was accused of sodomy and convicted. De Marcis was saved from dying at the stake by Dr. Jacques Duval, who, after the trial, examined Marie's vulva and found the member and proved that it was not a clitoris by massaging it until it ejaculated.

Despite the evidence, the court did not grant a gender change. Hausman noted that in his discussion, Laqueur is cognizant of his use of the words *sex* and *gender* as interchangeable terms, but that when he referred to how in the 17th century there was little regard for the sex "the protagonists felt themselves to be, what they were inside" (Laqueur, 1990, p. 138), he was employing the concept of *gender identity*, which he explicitly defined as "the sense infants acquire very early on of whether they are girls or boys" (p. 138).

Hausman (1995) rightfully noted that this specific use of gender is quite new. As we have seen, the idea of a psychosocial identity in sex was codified in the 1950s as gender, and it then entered the medical lexicon of the new technology of sex change (p. 7). Laqueur used gender as a contemporary psychosocial category describing social roles and identities, which would have been unthinkable for pre-20th-century subjects. Besides, he applied it to analyze a period when there was no linguistic or semantic construction denoting the inner certainty of one's gender identity. This mistake is part of a general trend in which gender replaces sex, even to signify biological events or signs specific to sex. Hausman's criticism points out the limitations of a systematic historicization of sex and gender.

From a Lacanian perspective, sexuality in human beings is not the realization of a relation between opposite poles, a quasi-mathematical equation. Neither sex nor gender, there are no easily available opposites. Instead, we have the mystifying function of the phallus as a symbol. This is why hysteria is so loaded with meaning. The history of hysteria reviewed via Veith (1965), revised by King (1993) and Laqueur (1990), entirely hinges on a womb taken for a phallus, which is why it is hidden, mobile, starved, inverted, and so on.

From the vantage of today's scientific knowledge, the concept of a wandering womb appears at best as a quaint mistake. However, the image of an errant womb can be read more symptomatically—or etymologically: the "errancy" was underpinned by a mistake, a category mistake when one talks of an "error of nature" to explain monstrosities and aberrations. In this case, there may have been a logical necessity for such an error. The error consisted at root in taking an organ for a signifier of sexual difference, and it may be such an error that is being made repeatedly by some transsexuals. In themselves, wombs or penises are failed answers for the riddle of sexual difference. Freud tried to solve the riddle like Oedipus before him, and he made use of a first notion of "bisexuality." This was part of his own "erring" progression, an "errancy" that describes a trajectory. I try to reconstruct such a trajectory, a theoretical wandering that goes from bisexuality to the phallus and libido and leads to the Lacanian idea of mobile sexuation patterns.

Chapter 4

Freud's sex change

Freud's career began inauspiciously with a huge setback. In the fall of 1886, after returning from Paris where he had gone to study with Charcot, Freud gave a lecture on male hysteria at the prestigious Vienna Society of Physicians. Wishing to share with his colleagues what he had discovered in Paris, he presented a case that he had followed at the Salpêtrière Hospital; it was the traumatic hysteria of a man who had fallen from a scaffold. Freud expounded on Charcot's observations that there was no link between hysteria and genital organs or any difference between male and female hysteria (Jones, 1953, pp. 229–230). As a matter of fact, Freud's lecture was poorly received. One old surgeon objected: How could Freud talk of "hysteria" in males when the very word came from the Greek word for "womb"? The rejection exasperated Freud, intensifying his sense of alienation from his Austrian colleagues. Irritated and impatient, he abandoned hope of being recognized by the local medical society and concentrated on establishing his private practice. Freud wrote or published relatively little between 1886 and 1891, but he continued refining his treatment of hysteric patients. His exposure to Charcot's work on male hysteria and other neuroses in men, however, played a significant role in his later formulation of a general theory of psychosexuality and on the non-gender-specific idea of universal bisexuality (Micale, 1995, p. 166).

Meanwhile, Freud focused on his bread-and-butter job, dealing with the intractable complaints of neurotic patients for whom medicine provided no answer. Their mysterious ailments betrayed something that was sexual in nature. To explain these baffling symptoms, Freud developed a theory of sexuality in collaboration with his close friend William Fliess. Finally, their friendship came to an end amidst bitter accusations of plagiarism regarding the theory of bisexuality (Strachey, 1962, p. xi).

For years, Freud and Fliess had talked and exchanged correspondence about the new concept of bisexuality (1887–1904). In 1897, Fliess published what he thought was going to be a revolutionary contribution to the current debate on sexuality, *Die Beziehung zwischen Nase und weiblichen Geschlechtsorganen in ihrer biologischen Bedeutung dargestellt*

[*The Relation Between the Nose and Female Genital Organs Presented According to Their Biological Significance*] (Fliess, 1897/1977). Fliess, who was an ear-throat-and-nose specialist in Berlin, believed that he had found the proof of universal bisexuality by observing links between genital organs and noses. Basing his observations on the morphological similarity of erectile tissue found in the nasal cavity as well as in the clitoris, penis, and nipples, he identified two cycles in the body. These cycles would underpin the most dramatic changes in the patients he observed, like falling ill, being cured, or dying. One cycle was feminine and lasted 28 days, the other was masculine and lasted 23 days. Men and women would experience regular nose bleeding corresponding to women's menstruation. He even calculated that Goethe's life was a ratio of cycles of feminine cycles of 28 days. "Goethe thus died when his 1,077th feminine menstruation had deconstructed the last particle of his admirable organism" (p. 252). Fliess's apparently absurd thesis was well received in his time as it shared many assumptions shared by his scientific contemporaries (Sulloway, 1979, pp. 147–169).

Subsequent to the publication of Otto Weininger's *Geschlecht und Charakter* [*Sex and Character*] (1903, 2005), a treatise on sexuality in which Weininger made great use of the notion of bisexuality, Fliess accused Freud of intellectual burglary since he assumed that Weininger had heard of his own theories via Freud. This incident shattered their friendship. Freud had a patient, Hermann Swoboda, who was an intimate friend of Weininger. During the analysis, Freud discussed with Swoboda some of Fliess's new ideas on bisexuality. Those ideas were then relayed to Weininger, who included them in his 1902 doctoral dissertation, which became the basis for *Sex and Character*. Fliess had reasons to worry. Soon after the publication of *Sex and Character*, Weininger committed suicide. He shot himself in the house where Beethoven had died, and the book became an instant best-seller. Its impact on a whole generation cannot be overestimated.[1]

Without developing the complex links between Freud and Fliess, I just mention that Fliess played a major role in Freud's self-analysis, the invention of psychoanalysis, the discovery of the unconscious, and the experience of transference love. The Fliess–Freud relation offers an excellent example of acting out, understood here as transference without analysis. From a purely psychoanalytic perspective, a protracted dialogue, like the one Freud and Fliess maintained for more than a decade, excludes the possibility of ownership of concepts.

---

[1] Published in 1903, it reached its 25th edition by 1925. The book was admired by Ludwig Wittgenstein and received glowing reviews by August Strindberg. Weininger was hailed for having solved the hardest of all problems, the "woman problem." For more on Weininger and the "woman question," see Sengoopta (2000b, pp. 135–136).

BISEXUALITY STOLEN

Freud announced in a letter dated August 7, 1901, that he was planning to write a book, *Human Bisexuality*, and asked Fliess to coauthor it. "The idea is yours. You remember my telling you years ago, when you were still a nose specialist and surgeon, that the solution lay in sexuality." Freud added, "[s]everal years ago you corrected me, saying that it lay in bisexuality—and I see you were right" (Moussaieff-Masson, 1985, p. 448). However, their friendship was fading, and as Kris (1954/1977) notes, "Freud tried to revive it by once more suggesting that the problem of bisexuality was one that lent itself to a harmonious co-operation between them" (p. 39). The rift was already too deep and their relationship ended soon after. "I do not comprehend your answer concerning bisexuality," Freud wrote just 1 month later in an apologetic style that could be also read as ironic:

> It is obviously very difficult to understand each other. I certainly had no intention of doing anything but working on my contribution to the theory of bisexuality, elaborating the thesis that repression and the neuroses, and thus the independence of the unconscious, presuppose bisexuality. ... Since almost everything I know about it comes from you, all I can do is cite you or get this introduction entirely from you. (Moussaieff-Masson, 1985, p. 450)

The joint writing project never took place. Nonetheless, Frank Sulloway (1979) notes that the book that Freud wanted Fliess to coauthor was eventually published: "That seminal work eventually came out—minus Fliess's cooperation—under the better-known title *Three Essays on the Theory of Sexuality*" (p. 187). In the last letter of their correspondence, Freud asked Fliess to review the proofs of the *Three Essays* to verify his remarks on bisexuality, giving him freedom to change them to his satisfaction. Freud even offered to postpone publication until Fliess had published his own text. These were all, as Peter Gay (1989) writes, "decent gestures" (p. 155) but Fliess chose not to accept them. This was the end of their correspondence but not of the quarrel.

In 1906, Fliess published *Der Ablauf des Lebens: Grundlegung zur exakten Biologie* [*The Course of Life: Foundation of Exact Biology*], which expounded his theories of periodicity and bisexuality (Fliess, 1906/1923). That same year, three books publicized the controversy: A friend of Fliess, Richard Pfennig (1906), published a pamphlet accusing Weininger, Swoboda, and (indirectly) Freud of plagiarism. Not only was the title explicit enough: *W. Fliess and seine Nachentdecker O. Weininger und H. Swoboda* [*W. Fliess and His Epigones O. Weininger and H. Swoboda*], but also the text exposed fragments of the personal Freud–Fliess correspondence.[2] Swoboda replied with a defamation lawsuit, which he lost, and in 1906 published *Die gemeinnützige Forschung und der eigennützige Forscher: Antworten auf die von Wilhelm Fließ erhobenen Beschuldigungen* [*Research of Interest to the Public and the Researcher's Own Self-Interest: Response to the Accusations Launched by Wilhelm Fliess*].[3] And, Fliess (1906) circulated *In eigener Sache* [*For My Own Cause*]—whose subtitle is revealing, *Gegen Otto Weininger und Hermann Swoboda* [*Against Otto Weininger and Hermann Swoboda*].[4]

Freud also responded quickly by writing to two key figures: Karl Kraus, editor of the newspaper *Die Fackel* [*The Torch*] and the most important polemist in Austria at the time, and to Magnus Hirschfeld, editor of the Berlin *Yearbook for Sexually Intermediate Stages* and the principal advocate of a scientific treatment of transsexualism (Sulloway, 1979, p. 227). By calling Hirschfeld's attention to Fliess, Weininger, and Swoboda, Freud was panning the arc of the emergent science of sexology and establishment of transsexuality.

Freud's last letter to Fliess, which was not included in *The Origins of Psychoanalysis* (Freud, 1954), summed up the conflict that ended the relationship:[5] "For me personally you have always (since 1901) been the author of the idea of bisexuality; I fear that in looking through the literature you will find that many came at least close to you. The names I mentioned to you are in my manuscript" (Moussaieff-Masson, 1985, pp. 466–467). Freud appears ambivalent in his apology and incurs yet another parapraxis—he forgets that he had learned about the theory of bisexuality from a "friend" (Fliess) whose name is not mentioned at all in the published text (Freud 1901/2003). Wrongly dating the incident as it would have occurred in the summer of 1901 (it was actually in 1900), he admits, however, that he and his friend had exchanges about the theory of bisexuality two and a half years earlier (Freud, 1901/2003, p. 138). But, Freud makes another mistake in the date of Fliess's discovery of bisexuality: Fliess sent Freud the manuscript in the spring of 1896 and not in 1901. Surely enraged, Fliess made this personal letter public along with the rest of their 1904 correspondence.

---

[2] A translation into French of abstracts of the text can be found in Porge (1994).
[3] Translated abstracts are available in Porge (1994).
[4] See Scheidhauer (1994, pp. 17–53).
[5] The Freud–Fliess correspondence ended officially in 1902. The 1904 letters were not part of the lot saved by Marie Bonaparte. Not all of Freud's letters to Fliess were published—of 284 letters, postcards, and drafts, only 168 were selected for *The Origins of Psychoanalysis* (1954). But, the terse correspondence between Freud and Fliess in 1904 was included in Fliess's *In eigener Sache* [*For my own cause*]. The 1904 letters first appeared in an English translation in an article by Patrick Mahoney (1979). See also Moussaieff-Masson (1985) and Vincent Brome (1984).

The relationship ended on an inauspicious note, and the animosity over the priority dispute persisted over the years. Yet, in this last letter Freud did not deny Fliess's accusations: "I see that I have to concede that you were more right than I originally was prepared to" (Moussaieff-Masson, 1985, p. 466). In a previous letter he had described Weininger as "a thief with a key he picked up" (p. 464), but now Freud admits having glossed over the fact that he had seen Weininger himself and had read the manuscript before its publication, recognizing the underlying theme of bisexuality. "I must have regretted at the time that via Swoboda, as I already knew, I had handed your idea to him" (p. 466). In the same letter, Freud was openly skeptical about claiming ownership of ideas and protested that he had always acknowledged the work of others and never appropriated anything that belonged to anyone else. As René Lew (1994b) notes, the belief in intellectual property is not only imaginary, but "it belongs to the order of a constant *acting out*" (p. 6; italics in the original). Lacan (2006) remarked that an accusation of plagiarism was "a fine opportunity to perceive that if there is at least one bias a psychoanalyst should have jettisoned thanks to psychoanalysis, it is that of 'intellectual property'" (p. 329).

"Do not forget that it was through him [Fliess]," Freud told Karl Abraham in a letter of March 3, 1911, "that both of us came to understand the secret of paranoia" (Abraham & Freud, 1965, p. 103). Le Gaufey (1987) observes that this is why Freud could maintain that his theory of paranoia preceded his reading of Schreber's memoirs—he had already learned about homosexuality and paranoia firsthand through his conflict with Fliess (p. 59). For Paul Roazen (1968), "the theme of plagiarism can be found almost everywhere one turns in Freud's career" (p. 88). Kurt Eissler (1971) contends that

> the correct biographical approach would be to cite Fliess as the prototype of the scientist whose efforts are hampered by his paranoid tendencies, and who wastes time and effort in a useless and destructive fight about priorities—a fight that, if anything, makes him appear like a fool in the eyes of posterity. (p. 171)

Eissler underscores that Fliess's accusations were unfounded; indeed, Fliess had mentioned his idea of universal bisexuality in his 1897 book, so that by 1904, it was impossible to consider it a secret.

The estrangement left major wounds for Freud. In October 1910, after sharing a holiday with Sándor Ferenczi in Sicily, Freud felt that the Budapest student expected not just a working collaboration but also a closer relationship, and he wrote to Ferenczi explaining why he did not wish to have an intimate friendship:

> Not only have you noticed that I no *longer* have any need for that full opening of my personality, but you have understood that and correctly returned to its traumatic cause. ... This need has been extinguished in me since Fliess' case, with the overcoming of which you recently saw me occupied. A piece of homosexual investment has been withdrawn and utilized for the enlargement of my own ego. I have succeeded where the paranoiac fails. (Brabant et al., 1992, p. 22; italics in the original)

In a much more candid tone, Freud explained to Jung his prudence with Ferenczi (McGuire, 1974/1994):

> My traveling companion is a dear fellow, but dreamy in a disturbing kind of way, and his attitude towards me is infantile. He never stops admiring me, which I don't like, and is probably sharply critical of me in his unconscious when I am taking it easy. He has been too passive and receptive letting everything be done for him like a woman, and I really haven't got enough homosexuality in me to accept him as one. These trips arouse a great longing for a real woman. (p. 159)

Freud's assertions of not having "enough homosexuality" in him while greatly "longing for a real woman" deserve some attention because in his analysis of Schreber's paranoia he pointed to the absence of Schreber's wife due to a trip as a trigger factor for the disease. The presence of a real woman would serve as a limit for the homosexual urge. In the absence of a real woman, the homosexual drive can become unrestrained—whether it is Schreber's or Freud's. Freud's longing for a woman also points to the importance of the presence of a real woman for a man's masculinity. We further explore this issue in Chapter 8 when analyzing the pressure to become a woman experienced by some transgender people.

When Christopher Lehmann-Haupt (1985) discusses "the pitfall and dragons" at the end of Freud and Fliess's friendship, he claims that the split offers "material for a thousand monographs, not a few of them focusing on what Freud refers to in an unpublished 1910 letter to Sándor Ferenczi 'the greater independence that results from having overcome my homosexuality.'" Louis Breger (2000) looks into the intellectual motivations of the dispute over the idea of bisexuality, noting that Freud was of two minds about it—first he was skeptical but later embraced it. Breger observes that the final conflict was not about facts or the validity of the concepts but over priority—who had used the concept first, who owned it. "How ironic that their friendship should end in an argument over bisexuality when Freud's love for Fliess—bisexual or 'homosexual' in his own words—was so central to it all along" (p. 152). One can attribute the split to bisexuality—that is, to the repressed homosexual feelings between Freud and Fliess.

With his notion of bisexuality, Fliess had hoped to explain homosexuality, the mechanism of repression, the etiology of neurosis, and the nature of the unconscious (Sulloway, 1979, p. 183). It is clear that Freud followed Fliess's idea that all human beings are bisexual (Jones, 1953, p. 317; Kris, 1954/1977, p. 42; Strachey, 1962, p. 127), but it is harder to assess how extensively Fliess's biological theory of bisexuality influenced Freud's psychoanalytic theories. It is also difficult to have a linear sense of Freud's theory of bisexuality—Freud is equivocal on this issue.

HUMAN BISEXUALITY, ALL TOO HUMAN

No matter what the exact chronology is, Freud's realization of the importance of bisexuality and of the undercurrent of homosexuality in every neurotic owes a lot to Fliess. Freud (1905) publically acknowledged Fliess in a footnote for the idea of bisexuality, dispelling the claim that it could be Weininger's, but this reference was deleted from the second and later editions of *The Three Essays*, possibly in response to the Pfennig–Fliess publications. In the same footnote, Freud also listed eight authors who used the idea of bisexuality, five of them before Fliess (p.134).[6] The idea of bisexuality was neither new nor original by 1860, as noted by Pierre Fédida (1973/2000/2004, p. 242). On one occasion, Freud even forgot that he had learned about bisexuality from Fliess. Ernest Jones (1953) called Freud's lapse of memory "a severe case of amnesia" (p. 350), which appears in Freud's *Psychopathology of Everyday Life* (1901/2003) as an example of "forgetting impressions and knowledge." In the text, Freud quotes the wrong year (a mistake that, as we have seen, he also made in a letter addressed to Fliess). And, Fliess's name is not even mentioned. Freud writes:

> In the summer of 1901 [actually 1900], I once told a friend with whom I used to have lively exchanges of scientific ideas at the time that neurotic problems can be solved only if we take it as read that individuals are originally bisexual. He replied: "But I told you that myself two and a half years ago in Br., when we were out for an evening walk, and you wouldn't hear of it at the time." It is painful to be required to surrender one's claim to originality in this way. I could remember no such conversation in question, nor what my friend had said. One of us was obviously mistaken, and on the principle of who benefits—*cui prodest?*—it must be me. Over the next week I did in fact remember everything just as my friend had tried to remind me of it. I even remember what I had

---

[6] These were Gley (1884), Kiernan (1888), Lydston (1889), Chevalier (1893), and Krafft-Ebbing (1895).

replied at the time. "No, I can't agree with you, and I don't want to be brought into that line of argument." (p. 138)

The incident changed Freud's perspective on claims to originality: "[S]ince then I have become more tolerant if I come upon one of the few ideas with which my name can be linked elsewhere in the medical literature, and I find that I have been given no credit for it" (p. 138).

In the same way that there was a public controversy and bitter fight between Freud and Fliess around issues of bisexuality and plagiarism, it may be said that the concept of bisexuality itself leads to "gender trouble" (to quote Judith Butler, 1990), a "trouble" that leads to the notion that there are only copies without an original or travesties without an authentic model as soon as one tried to define gender identity. When analysands ask: "Am I straight or bisexual?" could it be that they are asking in fact: "Am I a copy or an original?" Since the traditional question of sexual identity at the core of hysteria has shifted from a question of gender identity ("Am I a man or a woman?") to one of sexual orientation ("Am I straight or bisexual?"), an exploration of the post-Fliessian concept of bisexuality in Freud is necessary. Bisexuality is a key concept because it can guide us into two divergent paths: One sends us toward hormone treatments and the medical reassignment of sexual identity, the other comes closer to the thesis defended by Steven Angelides (2001) that bisexuality has functioned historically as the structural other to sexual identity itself, undermining assumptions about heterosexuality and homosexuality.

FREUD'S BISEXUALITY

In *The Interpretation of Dreams*, Freud (1900) describes bisexuality in relation to the polymorphous and infantile characteristics of human sexuality—the "unexplained problems of perversion and bisexuality" (p. 607). He was, however, quite invested in its progress, as revealed by the analysis of a dream that realized his desire of "laying before my friend [Fliess] a difficult and long-sought theory of bisexuality; and the wish-fulfilling power of the dream was responsible for our regarding this theory (which, incidentally, was not given in the dream) as clear and flawless" (p. 331). Freud compared this dream to one of a female patient that dealt with "the somewhat commonplace story of a servant-girl who was obliged to confess that she was expecting a baby but was in doubts as to 'who the (baby's) father really was'" (p. 332). Not only was the theory of bisexuality problematic and incomplete, but also it was not clear who had fathered it. Fliess's accusations of plagiarism and his estrangement from Freud can appear as a paternity dispute that has little to do with originality over the theory but rather with paternity, or the place from which someone lays down the law, be it of sexual difference, of language laws, or of prohibition of incest.

Christian David (1992/1997) sees bisexuality as "a major concept" in the Freudian theoretical edifice (p. 47), but Robert Stoller (1975) notes that Freud often "handles the subject with little more than a phrase: 'bisexual constitution,' 'bisexual disposition,' 'bisexual organization,' 'innate bisexual constitution,' 'cross inheritance' indicating the subject is a given almost to be taken for granted" (p. 8). Thus, Serge André (1999) proposed to treat bisexuality not as a concept but rather "as an original signifier" (p. 13). This signifier formed and unformed the relationship of Freud and Fliess; bisexuality also became "the foundation on which the edifice of psychoanalysis was built" (p. 13).

Against the backdrop of transference in the Freud–Fliess exchange,[7] bisexuality acquired peculiar value, leading Freud to declare in 1904 that he preferred to "avoid the topic of bisexuality as far as possible" (Moussaieff-Masson, 1985, p. 464). Sulloway describes Freud's attitude on bisexuality as wavering between extremes, from "hot to cold and back again" (p. 222). I understand this oscillation as a back and forth between loyalty to the biological Fliessian position, what Fédida (2004) calls an illusion of symmetry reinforced by the idea of periodicity based on the coupling of mirroring opposites (masculine-feminine, left-right), and Freud's growing awareness of the limitations that such perspective has for psychoanalysis.[8] At the end of the complex case that I develop in the next chapter, *A Case of Homosexuality in a Woman*, Freud briefly mentions the sex change experiments of Eugen Steinach. Immediately after, Freud (1920) wrote three sentences that eloquently sum up the conundrum of bisexuality:

> Psychoanalysis has a common basis with biology, in that presupposes an original bisexuality in human beings (as in animals). But psychoanalysis cannot elucidate the intrinsic nature of what in conventional or in biological phraseology is termed "masculine" or "feminine": it simply takes over the two concepts and makes them the foundation of its work. When we attempt to reduce them further, we find masculinity vanishing into activity and femininity into passivity, and that does not tell us enough. (p. 171)

It is important to reiterate that Fliess's notion of bisexuality is based on feminine and masculine characteristics that would constitute the complementary halves of a whole. For Freud, bisexuality opened the problem of

---

[7] For bisexuality in Freud's self-analysis, see Anzieu (2004).
[8] Marx Schur (1972) referred to an unpublished letter in which Freud discussed Fliess's theory with the ironical designation "bi-bi" (p. 140).

how to formulate a theory of sexuality in which there is only one (male) libido but two sexes.

In his "Three Essays on the Theory of Sexuality," Freud (1905) had ascribed to bisexuality equal importance for both sexes. It was "a decisive factor" in the "understanding of the sexual manifestations that are actually to be observed in men and women" (p. 220). Much later, at the time of "Civilization and Its Discontents," Freud (1929/1930) still sustained the idea of a universal bisexual disposition but admitted that it became an "impediment" because it was psychologically unsound (since it presupposes two symmetrical halves) and also incompatible with his monolibidinal theory:

> We are accustomed to say that every human being displays both male and female instinctual impulses, needs and attributes; but though anatomy, it is true, can point out the characteristic of maleness and femaleness, psychology cannot. For psychology the contrast between the sexes fades away into one between activity and passivity, in which we far too readily identify activity with maleness and passivity with femaleness, a view which is by no means universally confirmed in the animal kingdom. The theory of bisexuality is still surrounded by many obscurities and we cannot but feel it as a serious impediment in psychoanalysis that it has not yet found any link with the theory of the instincts. (p. 105)

Freud's understanding of bisexuality did not advance much when he tried to give a more psychoanalytic definition of *masculine* and *feminine* because in the binarism implied by bisexuality, the key question that runs through all of Freud's speculations is what bisexuality consists of—what the two parts of the "bi" actually are.

In a 1915 addendum to the "The Differentiation Between Men and Women" section in Three Essays on the Theory of Sexuality (Freud, 1905), three meanings are given for the concepts of masculine and feminine: in biological terms, in their sociological connotation, and as the opposition of activity and passivity. The last definition led Freud to conclude that libido is always active, in that sense "invariably and necessarily of masculine nature" in both men and women, irrespective of the object. Already the dualism contained in the term "bisexuality" pointed to the aporia of sexual difference because

> the concepts of "masculine" and "feminine," whose meaning seems so unambiguous to ordinary people, are among the most confused that occur in science. ... Pure masculinity or femininity is not to be found either in a psychological or biological sense. Every individual on the contrary displays a mixture of the character traits belonging to his own and the opposite sex. (p. 219, n. 1)

Freud (1919) underlines the limitations Fliess's idea of bisexuality as bilaterality, which "can only have an intelligible meaning if we assume that a person's sex is to be determined by his genitals" (p. 201).

Bisexuality's riddle seems inextricably related to the "enigma of woman."[9] In a later lecture devoted to resolving "the riddle of the nature of femininity," Freud (1932/1933) avoided falling into the trap of an impossible task, describing "what a woman is," but rather enquired "how she comes into being, how a woman develops out of a child with a bisexual disposition" (p. 116). The paradox is that "when you meet a human being, the first distinction you make is 'male' or 'female'? and you are accustomed to make the distinction with unhesitating certainty" (p. 141). And yet, one "cannot give the concepts of 'masculine' and 'feminine' *any* new connotation. This distinction is not a psychological one" (p. 142; italics in the original). Freud deepened the paradox by pointing out the fact that when there are admittedly two sexes, there is no conceptual unity to be had in bisexuality. From one sex to the other, there is a logical jump. Rather than bridging the gap, bisexuality exacerbates this discontinuity. It opens the way to Lacan's dictum that "there is no sexual relation" in the sense that one can grasp how, if for the unconscious there is no representation of the female sex, then the unconscious is monosexual or homosexual; there is only one signifier for both sexes, the phallus.

For Freud, bisexuality is, as Fliess (1906/1923) proposed, universal, although bisexuality is not bilaterality or complementarity. Fliess described psychosexual attraction in terms of "bisexual complementarity"—a feminine man tends to attract a masculine woman and vice versa (p. 508). In the Freudian view, men are not from Mars and women from Venus, but rather, as Lacan (2006) observed, sexual difference opens up an insurmountable chasm:

> Gentlemen and Ladies will henceforth be two homelands toward which each of their souls will be all the more impossible for them to reach an agreement since, being in fact the same homeland, neither can give ground regarding the one's unsurpassed excellence without detracting from the other's glory. (p. 417)

Neither gender nor sex can explain what psychoanalysis detects as operating as unconscious sexual difference.

NO LADIES OR GIRLS

Lew (1994a) summed up the issue concisely: "From bisexuality to the absence of direct rapport of one sex to the other—a rapport that would not

---
[9] For more on bisexuality and "woman's enigma," see Kofman (1985).

pass through the third term of the phallus—Freud's trajectory is absolutely straightforward" (p. 91). At least, Freud's trajectory entailed a divergence with Fliess that became clearer in 1919:

> The dominant sex of the person, that which is the more strongly developed, has repressed the mental representation of the subordinated sex into the unconscious. Therefore the nucleus of the unconscious (that is to say, the repressed) is in each human being that side of him which belongs to the opposite sex. (pp. 200–201)

Here, one needs to understand that the repressed "opposite sex" is the Other sex, "this sex which is not one," as Luce Irigaray (1985a) would say, the woman's side.

In "Analysis Terminable and Interminable" (1937), Freud refers to "the repudiation of femininity" as a "biological fact, a part of the great riddle of sex" (p. 252). The great riddle of sex is what all psychoanalysts struggle with and cannot reach through the usual processes of analysis. Although Freud's description of the "wish for a penis" and the "masculine protest" as a biological bedrock relies on a language still close enough to that of Fliess (Pontalis, 1973, p. 26), the idea of a sexual dissymmetry persists, but as mediated by the Oedipal structure. In both sexes, castration is violently opposed, but the difference is that men experience castration as an impending danger, whereas women discover it as something that has already happened. Thus, Freud's (1937) own concept of bisexuality can be understood as a precursor to Lacan's formulae of sexuation: Even when men and women all experience castration anxiety (pp. 252–253), there is no equivalence between men's sexuality and women's sexuality.

To better understand this point, let us return to an often-quoted passage in Freud's letter to Fliess of August 1, 1899:

> The farther the work of the past year recedes [writing *The Interpretation of Dreams*] the more satisfied I become. But bisexuality! You are certainly right about it. I'm accustoming myself to regarding every sexual act as a process in which four individuals are involved. We have a lot to discuss on this topic. (Moussaieff-Masson, 1985, p. 364)

One can note a discrepancy between Freud's certainty that his work is on the right track and his hesitations here barely concealed—"certainly right," "accustoming myself," "a lot to discuss." Freud's vivid summary of Fliess's theory suggests that he is trying to push it to a limit, and that he is probably already thinking in terms of the Oedipus complex: Indeed, if "every sexual act [is] a process in which four individuals are involved," then every sexual act entails the presence of the parents and thus redoubles each partner because each partner arrives to a sexual act with the introjected superego of the parents (Freud, 1924, p. 177). Freud's contention in the dissolution of the Oedipus complex is that one inherits the parents' superego, that is, the symbolic internalization of each of the parent's parental figures; following this formula, one even could say that the sexual act of any 2 partners should involve 14 people at least.

MOVING BEYOND OEDIPUS

Freud considered the Oedipus complex, the triangular relation between mother, father, and child, as producing universal psychological distinctions between the sexes. Nevertheless, Freud's limitations in making compatible his libidinal theory and the theory of bisexuality are hindered by the constraints brought by the Oedipus complex, understood as a matrix of sexual identity. Conversely, Jung's proposition of an Electra complex as the feminine version of the Oedipus complex provides a good counterexample as this theory appears tainted by the hope of finding the other half capable of complementing sexual difference. Freud's evolving understanding of the Oedipus complex moved from mirroring halves to the impasses made evident by feminine sexuality. Freud's bisexuality dead ends result not only from Fliess's theoretical flaws but also from prompting by certain essentialism of the Oedipus complex. As I discuss, Lacan's (1998b) formulae of sexuation pick up where Freud left off and follow a trajectory that moves beyond the dyad. Thus, one needs to move the Oedipus complex and see sexuality not in terms of gender but in terms of modes of enjoyment (*jouissance*) (pp. 5–7) (see also Lacan, 1973).

Fundamentally, bisexuality is not a "third kind" of sexual identity that would stand between or beyond homosexuality and heterosexuality. On the contrary, it is something that puts in question the very concept of a symmetrical notion of sexual identity. This is why Freud concluded his analysis of a case of homosexuality in a woman with a critique of the notion of "third sex." In this discussion, he referred to Eugen Steinach, who along with Magnus Hirschfeld had speculated that the so-called third sex of homosexuals might be explained by bisexuality, which would be understood as the presence of both male and female sex hormones. "[I]t would be premature, or a harmful exaggeration, if at this stage we were to indulge in hope of a 'therapy' of inversion that could be generally applied" despite "the remarkable transformations that Steinach has effected in some cases by operations" (Freud, 1920, p. 171). As he sums up, Steinach had been "carrying out experimental castration and subsequently grafting the sex-glands of the opposite sex" and had successfully managed "to transform a male into a female and vice versa. The transformation affected more or less completely both the somatic sexual characters and the psychosexual attitude" (Freud, 1905, p. 144). The claim was that Steinach had "cured" male "inversions" by transplanting an undescended testicle from the body of a "healthy" heterosexual into that of a homosexual man. Freud (1905) describes such a sex transformation

> actually effected in a man who had lost his testes owing to tuberculosis. In his sexual life he behaved in a feminine manner, as a passive homosexual, and exhibited very clearly-marked feminine sexual characters of a secondary kind (e.g., in regard to growth of hair and beard and deposits of fat on the breasts and hips). After an undescended testis from another male patient had been grafted into him, he began to behave in a masculine manner and to direct his libido towards women in a normal way. Simultaneously his somatic feminine characters disappeared. (p. 144)

Some of the groundbreaking transformations performed by Steinach and discussed by Freud were of cases of "physical hermaphroditism" (Freud, 1920, p. 171), which raises the question of whether those patients were actually homosexual or, rather, intersex. Freud is extremely cautious about expecting Steinach's sex changes to become "cures" for homosexuality, but he remarks that eventually Steinach's experimental sex modifications "will produce a direct confirmation of the presumption of bisexuality" (Freud, 1905, p. 144). The ideology of sex change ended up concealing a belief in sexual complementarity that both Freud and Lacan would challenge.

Steinach's sex change experiments took place during "a crisis of gender," that is, at "a moment when the boundaries and norms of male and female shifted, disintegrated, and seemed to intertwine" (Sengoopta, 1996, p. 466). As we have seen, Fliess's theories of bisexuality had been popularized by Weininger's notorious book *Sex and Character* (1903), and they provided the tenets that justified Steinach's experimentation in the 1910s on animals and humans in Vienna. Hirschfeld's first reported incomplete sex reassignment surgeries in female-to-male patients took place in Berlin in 1912. The female-to-male sex change involved a double mastectomy and a hysterectomy (Hirschfeld, 1918; see also Pfaefflin, 1997, and Meyerowitz (2002/2004, pp. 18–21). "The European scientists grounded their medical interventions in a new definition of sex that cast all humans as bisexual, or partly male and partly female. Stated simply, the new definition challenged the more widely known nineteenth century vision of separate and opposite sexes" (Meyerowitz, 2002/2004, p. 15). In the absence of a point in the body to anchor sexual difference, the counterintuitive model of opposite sexes, which, as we have seen, Laqueur argued was invented just a few centuries ago, dissolves into bisexuality.

FREUD GOT "STEINACHED"

Although Steinach was well known for his sex change operations in rats and guinea pigs by means of castration and transplantation of endocrine glands, it was for the vasoligations that he administered that he became a medical celebrity in Europe and beyond. The "Steinach operation," promised rejuvenation, made him famous, and even became a verb—people were "Steinached" (Sengoopta, 2003, p. 123). This is why in November 17, 1923, at the age of 67, Freud underwent this procedure, hoping that it would prevent a return of his oral cancer and might improve his "sexuality, his general condition and his capacity for work" (Gay, 1989, p. 426).[10] Freud had shown a certain trust in the curative powers of the "Steinach" by undergoing it, although afterward he seemed more than ambivalent about the effects of his vasoligation, even if "at least some of the time he seems to have felt that it had actually made him feel younger and stronger" (p. 426).

When Harry Benjamin, the father of sex change operations and fervent supporter of Steinach, visited Vienna, Steinach himself, who was on friendly terms with Freud, arranged a meeting with Freud.[11] Freud, who was very serious, laughed briefly when Benjamin jokingly declared that a disharmony of souls might perhaps be explained by a disharmony of endocrine glands. Freud spoke of Steinach, fully recognizing the great value of his biological experiments. He told Benjamin that he himself had undergone a Steinach operation. The vasoligation had been performed by a close collaborator of Steinach, Professor Kun. Benjamin claimed that Freud seemed satisfied with the result.[12] Benjamin said that Freud confided that his general health and vitality had improved, and that the malignant growth of his jaw had been favorably influenced. In Benjamin's view,

> Freud was very much biologically oriented, and, in this sense, he was not a Freudian. ... Freud asked me not to tell anyone about his operation until after his death, and I have kept that promise. He also asked

---

[10] Freud underwent a Steinach operation, a ligature of the vas deferens on both sides. The surgery was mentioned by Freud in a letter to Sándor Ferenczi, January 22, 1924. Freud wrote: "I have felt nothing reassuring from the effects of the Steinach operation" (Falzeder, Brabant, Giampieri-Deutsch, & Hoffer, 2000, p. 119).

[11] According to Pfaefflin (1997), Benjamin wanted to meet Freud to consult him because of problems with sexual potency. Freud suggested Benjamin's erectile dysfunction was due to his latent homosexuality. Pfaefflin claimed that this short interaction between the two men resulted in Benjamin's permanent skepticism against psychoanalysis, if not a thorough dislike, which since then has been claimed to be a marker of many encounters of transsexuals and their psychoanalysts.

[12] "The Steinach operation of eight and a half months ago has achieved nothing," Freud wrote to Sándor Ferenczi on August 6, 1924 (Falzeder et al., 2000, pp. 160–162). Harry Benjamin contradicted the statements in Freud's correspondence when he claimed that Freud confided to him the positive effect that the Steinach operation had.

me if I had been analyzed. I mentioned my relative short analysis by Arthur Kronfeld in Berlin.[13] Freud warned me that Kronfeld had "a very bad character." (Haeberle, 1985)

Thus, the sex change doctor and the psychoanalyst met and had a friendly exchange that started with a lighthearted admission of psychic and endocrinal disharmony. It might be a good time to continue a debate that was cut short by the widening distance between the two discourses, psychoanalysis and the clinic of transsexualism. On the whole, Freud did not reject Steinach's attempts, and he paid tribute to Steinach's discoveries by quoting him on several occasions. Freud's involvement with the colleague of Hirschfeld, however, was not limited to a purely theoretical dialogue. It is noteworthy that Freud, who had a rigorous medical training, underwent the rejuvenation operation (literally, a "castration") promoted by the sex hormone researcher. This is a testimony to Freud's confidence in the operation and to the prestige that the physiologist Eugen Steinach enjoyed in the Vienna of Freud, Krafft-Ebing, and Otto Weininger. Steinach had been nominated for the Nobel Prize in physiology six times between 1921 and 1938, although he was never to receive it (Sengoopta, 2000c). Interestingly, Freud, who was "impressed" by the experimental work of Steinach, stated that his disagreement with the idea of a third sex was partly based on the axiom of the natural bisexuality of all living beings acquired from Fliess "and about which he could never be shaken" (Jones, 1955, p. 281).

The Freud–Steinach connection is important as well because Steinach played a pivotal role in the history of transsexualism. Originally, sex change technology evolved from the developments of endocrinology and plastic surgery. By 1912, Steinach had succeeded in hormonally changing the sexuality of guinea pigs—the transplantation of sex glands into females and vice versa modified their sexual behavior. The male guinea pigs developed female sexual behavior: They presented their posteriors to other males, inviting copulation. The females began to act like males, mounting other females. The transplantation of ovaries into infantile castrated male guinea pigs caused physical and psychic feminization that included the development of the mammary glands and nipples, milk production, willingness to give suck, feminine direction of the sex instinct and skeletal form, hirsute character and type, and deposition of adipose tissue of the female type. Simultaneously, male characteristics were extensively inhibited. Testicular transplants in infantile spayed female guinea pigs brought about development of masculine *Anlagen* (masculinization): clitoris grown

---

[13] Benjamin met Kronfeld in 1921 at Hirschfeld's First International Conference for Sexual Reform on a Sexological Basis in Berlin. Benjamin knew Hirschfeld from before the war; in the meantime, he had opened his institute in Berlin, which he visited regularly in later years; see Haeberle (1985).

to penis size, masculine sex instinct, skeleton, and pilosity. Simultaneous transplantation of testicle and ovary into infantile guinea pig castrates produced development of masculine and feminine sex characteristics (experimental hermaphroditism) (Steinach, 1912, 1913, 1916).

This breakthrough that denotes the shift from neural to chemical theories of sexuality was encouraged by the prominent sexologist Hirschfield, who discovered the "chemistry of sex"—endocrinology—and suggested Steinach do experiments with animal's gonads (Hirschfeld, 1956, pp. xiii–xiv; Money & Musaph, 1977, p. 56). As Anne Bolin (1993) observes,

> It is important to note that transsexualism, as a historical phenomenon, was defined by the development of two important medical technologies that made possible the innovative alterations of the male body: hormonal reassignment therapies and sex reassignment surgery. These treatments circumscribed the medical creation of male-to-female transsexualism. However, Vern Bullough notes that the significance of this field has been neglected in the history of transsexualism. (pp. 454–456)

We have referred to Catherine Millot's (1990) observation: "There is no transsexuality without the surgeon and the endocrinologist" (p. 17). Steinach turned out to be one pioneer endocrinologist who made contemporary sex changes possible.

For Freud and Steinach, the notion of castration had connotations that run against common assumptions—both used the terms "castration complex," Steinach (1940) only in a purely biological sense: "The elimination of the germinal part of the gland did nothing to impair its hormonic effectiveness; its integrity was proved by the fact that the castration complex did not appear after reimplantation" (p. 98).[14] Both saw in castration an enabling and positive "operation" that could either rejuvenate people for Steinach or open the way for desire in the Freudian view.

Steinach's research followed the model of embryologist Wilhelm Roux, who studied normal biological development by artificially inducing abnormalities and monstrosities to infer from them the course of normal development. Steinach castrated prepubertal animals' sex glands and replaced them with the glands of the opposite sex. He also castrated prepubertal animals and implanted the sex gonads of both sexes. The reimplantation of gonads and the experimental feminization and masculinization of rats and guinea pigs helped Steinach investigate the

---

[14] Steinach proved experimentally that the sexually active internal secretions of the testes were produced by the interstitial cells, which had nothing to do with the production of spermatozoa, a hypothesis that generated great controversy at the time, although it was eventually accepted as correct. See Benjamin (1945); Sengoopta (1998); Meyerowitz (2002/2004), pp. 15–29).

effects of hormones on body characteristics and on behavior. His experiments took as point of departure a 1,000-year-old practice—castration. "How could I overlook anything so obvious? It was almost certainly not unknown that to those experimenters who carried out castrations several thousands years ago that these glands have not only a specific sexual significance, but other influences much more widespread," wrote Steinach (1940, p. 36).

Steinach's work was based not only on human castration (eunuchs for harems, the European 18th-century production of high-pitched soprano male voices, castrated followers of religious sects like the Russian Skoptsy and the Romanian Lipovans) but also on the quite common agricultural use of castration.

> Farmers and cattle-breeders did not remove the sex glands in order to produce impotence. Their purpose was to influence the appearance and temperament of their domestic animals. Repeated experiments have taught them that a castrated bull becomes not only a more patient beast of burden as an ox, but is a more favorable subject for beef production. (p. 36)

Castration produced more useful animals; it also proved that it affected the entire body configuration and influenced the psychic characteristics of an animal (p. 37). Sengoopta (2000c) underscores the important contribution of Steinach to contemporary endocrinology:

> By castrating rats and guinea-pigs and reimplanting testicular or ovarian tissue in the castrated animals, Steinach showed that male or female development in rats and guinea-pigs were not, as some leading scientists were arguing at the time, programmed ab ovo, with the sex glands merely exerting a protective or stimulatory function over them. ... The sex characters, then, were generated and maintained by the internal secretions of the sex glands and constantly modifiable to some degree. (p. 5)

Current standard hormone therapy for menopause and sex change transition treatments derive from Steinach's innovative research.

Steinach's work is directly connected to that of Harry Benjamin, a medical endocrinologist and sexologist, who pioneered the surgical treatment for transsexualism. Benjamin was Steinach's most enthusiastic supporter in the United States. Benjamin had met Steinach in Vienna in 1921 and was greatly impressed with Steinach's sex change operations in rats and guinea pigs. From that point, Benjamin became his disciple and visited him almost every summer well into the 1930s.

Sengoopta (2000c) studied the Benjamin–Steinach correspondence and made revealing discoveries. A true acolyte, Benjamin kept every letter, postcard, and note Steinach sent him from 1921 until Steinach's death in 1944 and because of Steinach's almost illegible handwriting had most of it transcribed and typed. Benjamin personally revised, edited, and saw through press the English translation of Steinach autobiography. Benjamin took to heart the promotion of the work of Steinach in the United States and made many efforts to popularize his master's works. Benjamin tried to bring Steinach to the United States in a visit that he expected would be as high profile as the coming of Einstein. That tour never materialized, and Steinach did not achieve the recognition Benjamin had hoped. Then, the field of endocrinology became a biochemical rather than a physiological discipline as American institutions and pharmaceutical companies showed little interest in Steinach's studies.

The correspondence records some of Benjamin's successes in propagating Steinach's name and message. He would keep the press interested in Steinach's discoveries. He actively encouraged the publication of the first book in English describing Steinach's work, *Rejuvenation: How Steinach Makes People Young* (Corners, 1923). The book had been written under the pseudonym of George F. Corners by German American journalist George Sylvester Viereck, who interviewed Steinach in Vienna. Benjamin also revised the English translation of Steinach's autobiography *Sex and Life* (1940) and saw it through to publication (Sengoopta, 2000c).

SEX CHANGES

In early 20th-century Vienna, Steinach's experiments provided verifiable answers to the questions raised by Fliess–Weininger's metaphysics of gender. Weininger had presented the human "permanent bisexual condition" in his influential *Sex and Character* (2005/1903) not as a metaphor but as a biological fact (Sengoopta, 2000b, p. 86). Weininger relied heavily on embryology, and he claimed that even with distinctive anatomies, males and females each contained both male and female sex-determining substances (plasmas) in every cell.[15] The proportions of plasma varied for each individual and were to explain the variations in range of masculinity and femininity in humans. Making Fliess's influence obvious, Weininger (2005/1903) follows Fliess's assumption that a sexual positioning implies a

---

[15] Le Rider (1982) summed up Weininger's book as "a dreadful pandemonium teeming with the worst forms of fanaticism: anti-feminism, anti-Semitism, a passion for irrationalist metaphysics" (cited in Delavenay, 1987, p. 137). For more on Weininger and Fliess, see Fausto-Sterling (1999, pp. 151–154), Sengoopta (2000b, pp. 47–85), and Sulloway (1979, pp. 223–232).

repression of its opposite, assuming that unisexuality is never complete; the characters of the underdeveloped sex never disappear entirely.

Steinach's experiments confirmed the Fliessian–Weiningerian theory of universal bisexual constitution. Steinach thought that all mammals had rudimentary dispositions or tendencies (Anlagen) for both sexes. The hormonal products of ovaries and testes (which Steinach called *puberty glands*) determined the boundaries between male and female, thus influencing either feminine or masculine growth. Anne Fausto-Sterling (1999) notes that Steinach described hormonal processes in militaristic terminology (p. 159). This was another trait that he shared with Freud, who also favored martial expressions such as defenses, attacks, formations, and so on. For Steinach (1913a), "inhibitions" soon led the way to "battles of the antagonistic actions of sex hormones." Steinach described the evolution of gonad transplants as if "a battle raged between the two tissues" (p. 320). Fausto-Sterling (1999) argues that Steinach's language of conflict "reflected preexisting ideas about the natural relationship between male and female" (p. 161). The conundrum of sexual difference was still couched in the language of strife and of the battles of sexes.

Although the notion that sex had a genetic determination was starting to be accepted at the time, Steinach laid the emphasis on the idea that sex glands stimulated those characters associated with one sex and actively "inhibited" those associated with the other. The sex glands, in short, were "antagonistic" in their functions. His physiological descriptions became political allegories of the way sexual difference was socially constructed in prewar Vienna.

A controversial aspect of Steinach's work that had been discussed by Freud (1905, p. 144) was his treatment of human homosexuality by transplantation of testicles. Steinach (1916, 1920) believed that his experimental findings in animals were applicable to humans, and he claimed that hermaphroditism and homosexuality were due to lack of sexual differentiation in the gonads, which caused the production of both male and female secretions. This hypothesis emerged from exchanges with Hirschfeld, who had already placed a biological responsibility for homosexuality in the action of hormones that he named "andrin" and "gynacin." As we have seen, it was Hirschfeld who had suggested that Steinach experiment with the gonads of animals (Money & Musaph, 1977, p. 56).

Steinach's highly debatable—and quickly abandoned—"cure" for masculine homosexuality, in which one testicle was surgically removed and replaced with a testicle from a heterosexual donor (Herrn, 1995, p. 45), was not revolutionary but fit the general drift of current science. Sengoopta (2000a) emphasizes that even

> in the purely intellectual sense, Steinach's homosexuality-cure represented a logical outcome of his "analytic" experiments on the sex

glands—it proved ineffective, to be sure, and was significantly influenced by contemporary cultural politics, but it was not the bizarre piece of quackery it might seem at first glance. Steinach's involvement with homosexuality was but one result of his experimental research on the development of sex. (p. 457)

Steinach's research illustrated the complex and, at times, even contradictory relationship among glandular medicine, biological experimentation, and the social notions of gender and sexuality. Steinach treated masculinity and femininity not as immutable qualities but rather as morphological and psychological attributes capable of being modified by the effects of glandular secretions. Males could be feminized and females virilized, which was a revolutionary gender-bending notion. For Steinach, humans are bisexual when they are embryos and thus remain bisexual: "Even men whose instinct is normally heterosexual," wrote Steinach (1940), "may contain in their organisms minute vestigia of a female character even though under normal conditions they never come to functional expression" (p. 91). Yet, both his experiments of "rejuvenation" by vasoligation and his "cure" for homosexuality by glandular transplantation implied an essentialist notion of gender roles (the operations helped males again become strong, muscular, energetic, hairy, creative, libidinous, and heterosexual). Steinach's research was used by Hirschfeld to validate scientifically his construction of a new homosexual identity as a biomedical condition.[16]

THE BRAIN IS THE MOST IMPORTANT AND RELIABLE ORGAN OF SEXUAL IDENTITY

In 1862, under the pseudonym of Numa Numantius, Karl Heinrich Ulrichs gave the name of "Urnings" or "Uranians"[17] to men who were sexually attracted to men. He wished to eradicate the association of homosexuality with pathology by arguing that these men had "a woman's mind trapped in a man's body" (*anima muliebris corpore virili inclusa*). Ulrichs transposed new knowledge about embryology to sexual orientation to decriminalize

---

[16] For a brilliant analysis of the Steinach–Hirschfeld collaboration and of Hirschfeld's use of Steinach's research to support homosexual emancipation, see Sengoopta (1998).

[17] Uranian alluded to Pausanias's distinction between two types of love in Plato's *Symposium*. Aphrodite was born of a male, Uranus (the heavens). This Uranian Aphrodite is associated with a noble love for male youths. Another account had Aphrodite as the daughter of Zeus and Dione and is associated with a common love of women as well as of youths and is of the body rather than of the soul. After Dione, Ulrichs gave the name "dioning" to men sexually attracted to women. For Ulrichs, unlike Plato, male Urnings were essentially feminine and male dionings, masculine.

homosexuality and challenge sodomy laws. "Urning" became *conträre sexual,* in German, and later, *Empfindung* (contrary sexual feeling) (Westphal, 1869). Empfindung was eventually translated as "sexual inversion" in English (Ellis, 1942). But, the semantic efforts at eradicating prejudice still encountered linguistic bigotry—between 1886 and 1923, in the English versions of Krafft-Ebing's classic, the now-obsolete term "antipathic sexual instinct" was used in the title, *Psychopathia Sexualis: With a Special Reference to the Antipathic Sexual Instinct. A Medico-Forensic Study* (1886/1962). Westphal, Krafft-Ebing, and other sexologists supported Ulrichs's advocacy for the biomedicalization of sexuality to decriminalize male homosexuality, also known as eonism, after the Chevalier d'Eon (Ellis, 1942). The term *Urning* was eventually replaced by "sexual inversion" and later by "homosexual," a term coined together with "heterosexual" by Karl Maria Kertbeny in 1869 (see Katz, 1995/2007, p. 10).

Magnus Hirschfeld, like Ulrichs, explained sexual orientation in terms of the bisexuality of the developing human embryo. Where Ulrichs used the "mind," Hirschfeld, taking a biological turn, spoke of the "brain." Hirschfeld's investigations about the neural centers for sexual attraction in fetuses destined to become homosexual remain ideologically close to current neuroanatomical research on homosexual, heterosexual, or in between sexual orientation. Simon LeVay (1991b) stirred a big controversy with his monograph, *The Sexual Brain.* He argued that there were differences in the brains of straight and gay men. LeVay more recently wrote *Queer Science: The Use and Abuse of Research Into Homosexuality* (1997), in which he explored the biology of homosexuality in the social context. To justify his claim that sexual behavior is biologically motivated, he went back to the work of Ulrichs, Hirschfield, and Kinsey. Recent biomedical explanations of sexual difference can be aptly summed in the words of Milton Diamond: "The brain is the most important and reliable sexual organ" (Angier, 1997).[18] This idea is not new; it was already defended in Victorian times by Ulrichs.

It is well known that the human embryo until approximately the 12th week has a double generative principle, male and female. Until that time, the embryo is potentially capable of developing male and female sexual parts. This bisexual potential of the human embryo was linked to evolutionary Darwinism by Freud (1905) when he followed Ernst Haeckel's postulate that ontogeny recapitulates phylogeny, that is, that the developmental sequence of an individual parallels the historical sequence of evolution: "Ontogenesis may be regarded as a recapitulation of phylogenesis" (p. 131). For Haeckel, development provided a way to establish homologies; those structures that were derived from the same embryological

---

[18] "And it is the head, Dr. Diamond added, that holds the primary sexual organ, the source of one's identity, and the organ that does not lie" (Angier, 1997).

precursors (Steinach's *Anlage*) could be considered to be homologies and used for the reconstruction of phylogenies. Haeckel's views also influenced Fliess's early theories of bisexuality, whose importance for Freud's theory of sexuality we have already established (Sulloway, 1979, p. 150).

Freud (1920) contends that mental sexual character and object choice do not necessarily coincide and disapprovingly refers to the naiveté of Ulrich's contentions. He mentions ironically the simplistic "popular expositions— 'a feminine mind, bound therefore to love a man, but unhappily attached to a masculine body; a masculine mind, irresistibly attracted by women, but alas! imprisoned in a feminine body'" (p. 170). Ulrich's idea of sexuality is simplistically heteronormative; it implies the assumption that all women are naturally attracted to men, including women trapped in male bodies. Freud knew all too well that there is no biological programming to fully determine either sexual orientation or object choice.

PHYSICAL OVERDETERMINATIONS, PSYCHIC DESTINY

One could claim that the concept of bisexuality might explain how with the help of hormones a male could become female and a female could become male. This is exactly what Steinach's experiments with the sex changes of guinea pigs had proved. On the other hand, Steinach, the biologically inclined scientist, had a concept of sexuality whose similarity to Freud's is striking. Steinach (1940) wrote: "For even in nature the line of demarcation between the sexes is not as sharp as is generally taken for granted. Absolute masculinity or absolute femininity in any individual presents an imaginary ideal. A one hundred percent man is as non-existent as one hundred percent woman." All humans have the "primordial disposition (*Anlage*) or potentiality for either sex" (p. 67; italics in the original).

In 1948, Steinach's most important follower in the United States, Benjamin, was referred by Alfred Kinsey an "effeminate boy" who wanted to become a girl and whose "mother supported him in this." Benjamin narrates:

> Kinsey had never seen a case like this, and it was new even for me. It went well beyond the by then recognized transvestism. The concept of transsexualism did not yet exist, it only gradually took shape in my thinking, not least because of this first case. I introduced the term only in 1954, and my book on the subject did not appear until 1966 (*The Transsexual Phenomenon*). Anyway, I asked for the boy's psychiatric examination under the aspect of possible surgery that would make his body more female in appearance. (Haeberle, 1985)

Benjamin treated the child with estrogen (commercially introduced in the United States in 1941 as Premarin). The treatment had a "calming effect." The child was later sent to Germany for partial surgery. The next year, 1949, Kinsey referred another patient to Benjamin, someone who according to the medical report expressed a "desire to be changed surgically" and "refused any other alternative" (Meyerowitz, 2002/2004, p. 47). It was not until 1952, when the U.S. public opinion was extremely moved by the very publicized sex reassignment surgery of Christine Jorgensen in Denmark, that a new era of sex change in the United States started. Collaborating with endocrinologists, surgeons, psychiatrists, and colleagues of various disciplines, Benjamin became Jorgensen's doctor and the U.S. pioneer of sex change treatment. In the aftermath of Jorgensen's story, the American press published a great deal of material on the theory of bisexuality, a theory to which both Christian Hamburger (Jorgensen's Danish endocrinologist) and Benjamin subscribed. The theory of bisexuality was nicely summed up by Jorgensen during an interview. Answering the question, "Are you a woman?" Christine gave what became her standard explanation: "You seem to assume that every person is either a man or a woman. ... Each person is actually both in varying degrees. ... I am more of a woman than I am a man." She added what rings like a paraphrase of Steinach: "Society has decreed that there are men and there are women. ... People, both men and women, are both sexes. The most any man or woman can be is 80 percent masculine or feminine" (Meyerowitz, 2002/2004, p. 98). The theory of bisexuality normalized her condition by giving it a physical cause—Jorgensen was an extreme case of the universal bisexual predisposition.

Until the invention of the notion of "gender identity" in the second half of the 20th century, an identity that was experienced as an immutable psychic "sex" felt internally, the loaded term *bisexuality* had defined the foundations of sex. What is more, in the end, the discourse of bisexuality led paradoxically to the newer practice of sex reassignment surgery. How did this happen? As we saw, Fliess, Steinach, and Benjamin tried to locate bisexuality in the body; their notion of physical or biological bisexuality entailed that human beings were not purely of one sex or the other since the balance was shown to vary; it was above all a matter of proportions. They attempted to demonstrate that one is not 100% "man" or "woman," and that it was the predominance of feminine or masculine quantities that would determine gender. In the second part of the 20th century, however, the notion of bisexuality tended to be seen more as a "psychic bisexuality," which made it depend on the old binary, man or woman. Thus, with the emergence of the notion of "gender" seen as gender identity, sexual identity became a holistic notion for the psyche—one would feel either entirely male or entirely female at a psychic level, independently from what one could exhibit as organs present or not in one's body. As Benjamin (1966) put it, a "gender feeling" was an irrevocable destiny "so deeply engrained that the morphological sex" had "to yield" (p. 113) Gender became a drive.

Hence, we are now witnessing a development to a third moment in which one has somehow returned to a sexuality located in the body itself, but it has remained coupled with a holistic sense of being one or the other sex. The technologies of gender modification have of course evolved in one century, even when many of them were launched by pioneers like Steinach, but they are now grafted onto a discourse of essentialist identity. For many transsexuals, starting as they do from a perceived problem presented as a birth defect, the issue is simply how to change their bodies to reach the ideal of being just the other sex. The apparently infinite progress of surgery and hormonal treatments has lent credence to an ideal of bodily reassignment collapsed with a new psychic holism. It is now possible to change one's gender on demand by specific interventions on the biology of sexuality. However, developing sex change technologies that allow people to move more easily from one sex to another have highlighted a question that often remains unanswered: What makes a man a man and a woman a woman?

What makes a man a man and a woman a woman is a question that has come to psychoanalysis from hysteric patients. The position on bisexuality held by Fliess, Steinach, and Benjamin seems closer to a queer notion of sexuality in which genders are placed in a continuum beyond a strict binary. Paradoxically, the liberal discourses of gender identity support a sort of essentialism about gender identification. It will be useful to be cognizant of the hysteric discourse about bisexuality because it may open the way for an alternative. This is what I do in the next chapters.

Chapter 5

Falling into sex like falling in love

In spite of Dora's reluctance, after years of irritability and depression, capped by a suicide note and a brief episode of delirious convulsions, she was brought to Freud by her father to be treated for a mysterious chronic cough and loss of voice. Freud revealed that this 18-year-old woman, who was on quite bad terms with her mother, was so devoted to her father that she helped him sustain an extramarital affair. Dora not only took care of the children of her father's mistress during their illicit encounters but also ended up as an object of barter since she was offered as a token to the husband of her father's lover. Freud was suspicious of Dora's apparently "innocent" complicity and speculated that Dora's collaboration was not without motivation. Dora's adoring attitude toward her father's mistress caught Freud's attention. He noticed her interest in the "other woman" who embodied a compelling mystery for the young woman and figured that this mystery held the key to a femininity that Dora was discovering. It is true that Dora praised the mistress, Frau K.'s "'adorable white body' in accents more appropriate to a lover than to a defeated rival" (Freud, 1901/1905, p. 60). Was it only that Dora's homosexual love was a love of knowledge and her infatuation with Frau K. a wish to acquire the latter's knowledge of sexual matters (p. 120)? It took almost two decades to start resolving the mystery.

Dora's case was initially written to demonstrate what a psychoanalyst could gain from dream interpretation. It was completed in 1900 but published in 1905, and it became Freud's first "novel" about a patient. It was the first detailed account of a treatment of a young hysteric using the then-new psychoanalytic method. Twenty years after the treatment of Dora, Freud found the key to her problems and to his own failure (just as he was about to solve the riddle, she abruptly left the treatment). When another "beautiful and clever girl of 18" (1920, p. 147), who had attempted suicide and was in love with a woman, was taken to him by a distraught father, Freud could not help seeing similarities. Dora was treated as a hysteric, and the new patient's difficulties were centered on her homosexuality. Freud, however, was all along aware that "a hysteric symptom is the expression of both a feminine and a masculine fantasy" (1908, p. 165).

HYSTERICS ARE BISEXUAL

It seems to be common knowledge that hysterics are bisexual; indeed, Freud (1908) himself saw at the heart of hysteria the irreducible presence of a bisexual fantasy. Juan-David Nasio (1998), who took Lacan's insights as a point of departure, decided to go further when he asserted that hysterics were not just bisexual but not sexual at all; for him, indeed, "they are asexual, outside sex" (p. 56). This radical exteriority would derive from a structure of indecision, in which, fundamentally, a hysteric is someone who cannot know whether he or she is a man or woman—for Nasio, the hysteric has not managed to "appropriate the sex of his body" (p. 57). This view makes Nasio diverge from the standard view proposed by Charcot and his followers, a view also shared by Freud, since they all attempted to distinguish a masculine hysteria—which was the novelty at the end of the 19th century—from a traditionally feminine hysteria. To make his position clearer, Nasio adds: "The expression *masculine hysteria* is a contradiction in terms, since the noun *hysteria* means sexual uncertainty (neither man nor woman) while the adjective masculine, by way of contrast, makes a choice precisely where choice turns out to be impossible" (p. 57; italics in the original). Provocative and counterintuitive as it sounds, nevertheless, I would be tempted to follow this theory, if only because my practice as a psychoanalyst in the United States has led me to deal mostly with hysteric analysands, that is, with patients who pose the question of their own sexual identity not in terms of "Am I a man or a woman?" or as "What is a woman?" but mostly as "Am I bisexual or heterosexual?" All the hysterics whom I have treated found it exceedingly challenging to assume a sexual positioning. And, whenever they did, it tended to take on the appearance of a sudden choice, a jump into the unknown, in other words, a "fall."

Even when I find a useful insight in Nasio's remarks, this idea is at variance with the thesis defended by Lacan in his later seminars. In the last decade of his life, Lacan (2006) was in the habit of speaking of hysterics only in the feminine. Was this because, as he repeated, one begins learning about desire from female sexuality, more precisely by standing in "the doorway that leads from female sexuality to desire itself" (p. 619)? I try to disentangle these notions by following the same path from sexuality to desire but in reverse, that is, by going back to the discussion of a famous case of female homosexuality. Lacan had written that "in all forms of female homosexuality, even unconscious, the supreme interest is in femininity" (p. 619), and like Freud, he ascribed an exemplary value to female homosexuality; female homosexuality was for him invaluable in discerning the various stages traversed in the process of becoming a woman (1994, pp. 95–96).

To test these claims as well as the theses deployed by recent queer theory, I revisit the controversy that has surrounded Freud's (1920) treatment of the woman described in "The Psychogenesis of a Case of Homosexuality in a Woman." Despite its clumsy title, whose syntax and style suggest a dry medical report, it was considered by Lacan (1994) as "one of the most brilliant texts of Freud," although he immediately added that it was "also one of the most disquieting cases," that it even seemed "archaic" or "out of fashion" (p. 102). The Freudian case study, which was his latest, became one of Lacan's favorite examples. The case has attracted attention lately via gender studies, with the publication of an interdisciplinary collection (Lesser & Schoenberg, 1999). More information has been made available through the publication in German, and translations into French and Spanish, of a biography of the protagonist of this 1920 case. Giving her the pseudonym Sidonie Scillag, Ines Rieder and Diana Voigt (2003) chronicled the life of Freud's former patient. Sidonie died in 1999, at the age of 99. After her death, her real name was disclosed: Margarethe Trautenegg, née Csonka. *Csillag* in Hungarian means "star," and *Csonka*, "mutilated." In October 2004, the material used by Rieder and Voigt to construct the narrative biography of Sidonie Scillag (a large photo collection, personal documents, and numerous interviews with Margarethe Trautenegg) was donated to the Sigmund Freud Museum in Vienna by the authors of the biography.

DORA, SIDONIE, ANNA, AND THE LADY

Why would Freud (1920) take into treatment a patient who, as he admitted, "was not in any way ill—she did not suffer from anything in herself nor did she complain of her condition" (p. 150)? First, it is possible that Freud's interest in Sidonie's case was motivated by his wish to elucidate lesbianism, given his own daughter Anna's inclinations. This is what Jean Allouch (2002, 2004) has suggested; indeed, at the time Anna had been in analysis with her father for a year. Such claims are persuasive but perhaps reductive since Freud would locate homosexual tendencies at the heart of feminine sexuality anyway, independently of any sexual orientation, and saw in them a general female manifestation of interest in the female Other. This is also why in the 1923 postscript to Dora's case, Freud (1901/1905) does not mention lesbianism, just as he acknowledges that he neglected Dora's strong unconscious gynecophilic attraction to her father's mistress (p. 120, n. 2). By then, Freud had started considering homosexual feelings quite normal among neurotics.

Despite their differences, Dora and Sidonie shared a similar pattern—they were fascinated by a woman who was thought to have deep knowledge about sexuality. This knowledge was based on experience: While Frau K. was unfaithful and wily (she knew how to pleasure an impotent man, Dora's own father), Sidonie's lady was a cocotte who led a pleasantly dissolute life. The lady (or baroness, which she was) was also openly bisexual as she was rumored to live with a married couple in a ménage à trois, all the while having affairs with several men.

Here is the main plotline for the young homosexual woman treated sometime between 1918 and 1919, whom I will continue calling Sidonie. A vivacious 18-year-old woman from a Viennese family of "good standing," she was brought to treatment after a love affair with a woman that first unleashed a social scandal, then followed by a dire suicide attempt. Given all this, Freud was aware of the unfavorable circumstances for a psychoanalytic treatment and never promised Sidonie's parents that their daughter would immediately seek a heterosexual life, as they had wished. For him, psychoanalysis could not and was not meant to "cure" homosexuality, which Freud did not consider pathological. It was a sexual orientation as contingent as heterosexuality. The situation Freud had to deal with was not the most propitious for psychoanalysis. Thus, in October 1920, echoing his discomfort with the case, Freud wrote a letter to Edoardo Weiss in which he discussed situations when a psychoanalytic treatment was not recommended: He named those in which there was no "painful conflict" or when a patient was "in fact very happy with himself and his only suffering is caused by the resistance of exterior circumstances" (Freud & Weiss, 1975, p. 49). Indeed, this was a case in which there was no "conflict of suffering," as Weiss (1970) called it. Freud (1920) was fully aware that Sidonie "had never been neurotic and came to the analysis without even one hysterical symptom" (p. 155). His task to be was more delicate; it "did not consist in resolving a neurotic conflict but in converting one variety of the genital organization of sexuality into the other" (pp. 150–151). This "variety" of "genital organization" meant that for Freud homosexuality was as much an outcome of the Oedipus complex as heterosexuality. "In general, to undertake to convert a fully developed homosexual into a heterosexual does not offer much more prospect of success than the reverse," he added, at the same time seeing bisexuality as the key to success. "I have found success possible only in especially favorable circumstances, and even the success essentially consisted in making access to the opposite sex (which had hitherto been barred) possible to a person restricted to homosexuality, thus restoring his full bi-sexual functions" (p. 151).

MANLY TYPES

Like Dora, and for similar reasons, Sidonie never completed her analysis. Agnès Aflalo-Lebovits (1984) pointed out that the two cases were linked:

After treating Sidonie, Freud revisited Dora's case and attempted to resolve the issue in a new light (p. 23). What was the real problem? It came from the fact that Sidonie insisted on maintaining an intimate relationship with an older lady who, as Freud (1920) wrote, "in spite of her distinguished name" was "nothing but a *cocotte*" (p. 147; italics in the original). The young woman's parents had tried everything to prevent her from maintaining a relationship with the ill-reputed lady. Defying the prohibitions, their daughter continued the relationship until one day, when the father saw them walking together on the street, he threw a furious glance at the pair before proceeding on his way. When the lady asked about the man who had cast such an irate look at them, the young woman confessed that it was her father, who had forbidden their friendship. Incensed, the lady stated that under those circumstances she did not wish to see Sidonie ever again. On hearing those words, Sidonie rushed to the overpass of a railway line nearby and jumped. She was badly injured in this serious attempt at suicide even though in the end she survived with little permanent damage—she nevertheless had to spend months on her back recovering.

Freud noticed that the verb she used to describe her fall had been *niederkommen,* meaning both "to fall" and "to deliver a child." Freud linked this to a moment in her adolescence when her Oedipus complex had been revived, that is, that she had wished to have her father's child when her mother gave birth to a younger brother. Even though she unconsciously hated her mother for this, she then turned to her, renouncing her womanhood, and having "changed into a man," for a while took her mother in place of her father as a love object, thus overcompensating for the hostility she had felt for her mother. This is a phenomenon that Lacan (2004) called "reactive" (p. 108).

Freud noted a curious discrepancy in the parents' attitude regarding Sidonie's homosexuality: The father was furious and unforgiving, while the mother, who had remained her daughter's confidante all along, appeared completely at ease with the new development. The mother's tolerance was an implicit appreciation of the secret meaning of her daughter's choice— Sidonie's obvious lack of interest in men was a way of avoiding rivalry between daughter and mother since the latter was still a youngish woman who cherished male attention. On his side, the father was quite embittered because of his daughter's defiance: Her turning away from men altogether meant that she was turning away from him as well.

All in all, Lacan tended to follow Freud's (1920) analysis of the attempted suicide as having represented both a punishment fulfillment and a wish fulfillment—"the wish to have a child by her father, for now she 'fell' through her father's fault" (p. 162). Her desperate gesture contained the ultimate and original meaning of the situation (Lacan, 2004, pp. 106–110). Her fall on the railways was a symbolic act according to Freud, it was the Niederkommen of a baby during childbirth. Lacan's discussion of Freud focused neither on hysteria nor on homosexuality but on female sexuality, specifically on the disadvantages in which women find themselves when they access their own sexual identity. In a subsequent seminar, Lacan (1993) argued that this disadvantage was "turned to her advantage in hysteria owing to her imaginary identification with the father, who is perfectly accessible to her, particularly by virtue of his position in the composition of the Oedipus complex" (p. 172). Lacan then located an analogous structure in Dora and Sidonie: Both women loved a woman like a man, following what Freud described as "manly type" (*männliches Typus*) to address a question to a woman. In both cases, there was a father, a daughter, and an older woman. As with Dora, the object that Sidonie desired was located beyond the woman she worshipped. For Sidonie, her fervent love was close to the devoted adoration of courtly love. It was an impossible love that took as object what the loved woman was lacking. Lacan concluded that in the extremity of her passionate love, what she looked for in the loved woman was the phallus.

It is clear that Dora's and Sidonie's cases were determined by a whole economy, and that they followed a circuit of gifts (Lacan, 2004, p. 140). For both, the fathers' inability to give the phallus yielded a new twist to the idea of giving. Dora remained attached to a father whose virile gift she could not receive. Yet, she loved her deficient father all the more, her love growing stronger in proportion to his diminished status. Similarly, Sidonie loved the lady with total devotion and expected nothing in return. She wanted above all to demonstrate to her father that true love is disinterested (p. 144), which corresponds rather neatly to Lacan's notion that the true sign of love is to give what one does not have. Sidonie had wanted to show to her father that one could love someone not for what this person *has* but rather for what the person literally *does not have*.

Lacan's reading of the cases is underpinned by a system of exchanges influenced by Lévi-Strauss's structural anthropology, in which the basic rule of kinship and exogamic exchanges is summed up in the formula "I received a wife and I owe a daughter" (p. 143). This principle transforms any woman into an object of exchange. In the social exchange, the male is reduced to being the holder of the phallus (p. 106). It is the dissymmetry in the phallic function that creates the opposition summed up by Freud as "having" and "not having," a couple that becomes for Lacan a starker opposition between "having" and "being." Man "has" the phallus, while woman does not have it. Because of that, she can embody it, and thus "be" the phallus.

In all this, the function of the father in the mother's discourse has a decisive role to play since hysterics are sustained by their love for the father, even when they deny it. Indeed, the love for the father played a decisive role in Sidonie's attempted suicides. The biography mentions two subsequent attempts, one with poison, the other with a gun, both having the father as main addressee. In 1922, Sidonie, rejected, hopeless, and disappointed in the lady, feeling trapped after consenting to be courted by a male suitor just to please her father, drank poison (Rieder & Voigt, 2003, p. 129). The third attempt against her life was in 1924. Sidonie was engaged and about to get married. The white bridal dress was already ordered, the reception was scheduled, and the honeymoon plans with visits to Venice and Florence were advancing, but she panicked at the idea of life with a man. Desperate, through the father of a friend, an arms collector, she bought a revolver under the excuse that it was a wedding gift for her fiancé. Sidonie's reason to commit suicide was that "she was afraid of telling her father the truth" about her misgivings about the wedding (p. 155). Not long after a lush engagement party, at night, while all the family was home sleeping, she took the gun and, aiming at her chest, pulled the trigger. Everyone heard the shot and ran to her help. Sidonie survived because her father promptly took her to the hospital: "Daddy's big Steyer convertible car madly sped through the streets carrying Sido, groaning in pain, on the back seat" (p. 156). Incredibly, the bullet missed her heart by half an inch.

A few months earlier, in August 1924, Sidonie had made a firm decision to end her relation with the lady. The way she chose to break up reveals the crucial role played by her father in her love affair with the baroness. Sidonie sent the baroness a telegram. The text was hers, but she signed it with her father's name. The telegram forbade the lady from establishing any contact with "his daughter," Sidonie. Thus, we can see that Sidonie's love for her father found its expression in revenge against the lady. Sidonie defied the father's desire while trying unsuccessfully to sustain it. Sidonie gives a twist to the formula "hysteric's desire is desire of/for desire," because, as Lacan (1981) observes, "the formula that originated in the experience in the hysteric—*[hu]man's desire is the desire of the Other*—it is in the desire of the father that the female homosexual finds another solution, that is to defy the desire of the father" (p. 38; italics in the original). The father is also is at the center in the interruptions of both Sidonie's and Dora's analyses.

TWO SEXES, ONE SIGNIFIER

For Dora, in Lacan's (1993) commentary, what Freud missed was the fundamental "question on the subject of her sex" (p. 171). This derived from a more general principle:

> For the girl as much as for the boy the castration complex assumes a pivotal value in bringing about the Oedipus complex; it does so precisely as a function of the father, because the phallus is a symbol to which

there is no correspondent, no equivalent. It is a matter of dissymmetry in the signifier. (p. 176)

Thus, we have seen that the Symbolic, which defines the main structure of the link of the unconscious with kinship, lacks a corresponding female equivalent to the phallus. Following Lacan's analysis of how the phallus operates for Dora and Sidonie, we verify that the phallus cannot be reduced to an anatomical organ. Lacan (1994) talked about the phallus as symbolic object (p. 152) and as a signifier (p. 191). The idea that the phallus should function as a signifier was taken up again in *Seminar V* (1957–1958) (Lacan, 1998a) and became a central element in the formulation that "the phallus is the signifier of the Other's desire" (2006, p. 290).

What was Lacan trying to illustrate with this idea? In his theoretical itinerary, the phallus played an essential role as signifier of sexual difference. Initially, Lacan had distinguished the phallus from the penis, when this phallus was first and foremost an image. The imaginary phallus, as conceived of in the 1950s, was imagined as a detachable object that materialized the object of the mother's desire. It circulated between mother and child in a dialectic that paved the way for the notion of the phallus as a signifier. The imaginary phallus is an object of a desire located beyond the child and with which the child tries to identify. The Oedipus complex entails renouncing the fantasy of becoming the imaginary phallus.

Finally, Lacan took the idea of the imaginary phallus further by developing the theoretical and technical implications of the idea of the phallus as a signifier, while revisiting the Freudian castration complex. For Freud, castration was not only the real "castration," but also the symbolic lack of an imaginary object. In short, castration could be understood as the relationship of desire with a primal "mark" comparable to a tattoo, to circumcision, or to signs branded on animals (Lacan, 1998a, p. 308). This mark, the sign that sustains castration, later called S1 by Lacan, can also be illustrated by examples of tattooing given in Freud's *Totem and Taboo* (1912–1913). In Lacan's (1998b) later formulation, the phallus is no longer either a fantasy or an object, it becomes a signifier without signified (p. 81) or the pure signifier of jouissance (2006, p. 696).

Having explained terms and their logical operations, we need to return to the main question: How can a hysteric, above all a hysterical woman, signify binary sexual difference with only *one* signifier, the phallus? This was the problem that complicated Dora's itinerary, her quest motivated by a desire to know about love and sex. In that sense, Dora was always asking a question about being: "What is it to *be* a woman?" Unable to answer or comprehend this, it was at a metaphoric level that her neurosis was to acquire its full meaning. Thus Freud's failure with Dora was tied to his attempt to bring in a real "object," a man whom she might love, that is

Herr K., and not to work with her metaphors. As Lacan (1994) puts it: "Freud did not see that the introduction of Herr K. as a normalizing object of heterosexual love could only remain metaphorical, as a last attempt to comply with the law of symbolic exchanges" (p. 146). Indeed, quite often the introduction of a real object, like the baby brother in the case of Sidonie, only impedes the possibility of displacement and substitution.

In the text "The Agency of the Letter in the Unconscious or Reason Since Freud," Lacan (2006) connects metaphor with "the question of being" and metonymy with the lack of being (p. 439), developing insights provided by Roman Jakobson's structural poetics.[1] Like Jakobson, Lacan identifies metonymy with the principle of prose narratives, with a drift to narrate that he called "fabulation."[2] As Jakobson had it, it was in metonymy that one found the recipe for a good novel: A novel brings together bits and pieces, traces of the real that have no value in themselves but acquire a harmonious meaning by resonating with one another. In concordance with this principle, Sidonie's first failed suicide has unmistakable echoes of Anna Karenina's death when Tolstoy's heroine hurled herself under a train in a paroxysm of shame and revenge.

FREUD'S ERROR

To better understand the logic of what can be called Freud's "mistake" (his "category mistake" to be more precise) with Sidonie, let us return once more to analogies with Dora's case. In both cases, the young women were brought to Freud by their fathers, a disposition in the treatment that was far from ideal. Rather than consulting the psychoanalyst on their own initiative, they were sent to Freud to be "cured." Freud's solution proved fatal for the progress of Dora's treatment. She abruptly ended the treatment after he had forced on her the name of the object of her desire: "You love Herr K." Freud's "error" betrays his blind spot not only about feminine homosexuality but also about hysteria. Similarly, when Freud (1920) noticed Sidonie's violent "bitterness

---

[1] For an excellent analysis of metaphor and metonymy, see Russell Grigg (1989). Grigg pointed out that only in 1957 did Lacan attach true importance to the concepts of metaphor and metonymy (p. 67). Grigg distinguished metonymy from three different structures of metaphor (substitution, extension, and apposition). Whereas metonymy and substitution metaphor are produced via substitution (one term for another term that remains retrievable), Grigg argued that extension and apposition metaphors are not. He also showed that although Lacan suggested that all metaphors are substitution metaphors, some of the examples used by Lacan are best described as apposition metaphors. Grigg demonstrated that "[o]nly in the case of substitution metaphor we can talk of metaphoric meaning" (p. 76).

[2] "*La métonymie est le principe de ce que l'on peut appeler, dans l'ordre de la fabulation et de l'art, le réalisme*" [Metonymy is the principle of what we may call, of the order of fabulation and art, realism] (Lacan, 1994, p. 145).

against men," he decided to break off the treatment and referred her to a female colleague for reasons he considered "obvious" (p. 164).

Was it the case that Freud (1920) could not tolerate the young woman's repudiation of men? Perhaps it was his identification with her father, "an earnest, worthy man, at bottom very tender-hearted" (p. 149), that posed a problem, and yet he saw the reawakened love for her father as positive transference. Was he suspicious because she brought him heterosexual "lying dreams" that tried both to please and to betray him (p. 166)? Freud concludes his description of Sidonie's pronounced "masculinity complex" with the declaration: "She was in fact a feminist" (p. 166). It is quite striking that Freud qualifies Sidonie's repudiation of men and challenge of masculine authority as ideology. Some women, like the famous Anna O. (Bertha Pappenheim), have reinvented themselves by feminism. Anna O's transformation from famous case study into women's rights activist is quite admirable. Yet, if Sidonie was trying to change the social condition of women, she was at a disadvantage, as Harris (1999) notes, "If 'she was in fact a feminist' she was a feminist quite without the support of feminism" (p. 157). The information one gathers in the biography confirms that if she was touched by feminism, she was not transformed. We see her always as a willing captive of her father's approval, with no indication of a desire to fight and challenge her own dependence, social status, or fears.

Was Freud reacting to his own prejudices dealing with Sidonie's same-sex love for an "older" woman? (The "older" lady was twenty-eight years old.) Needless to say, it is obvious that Freud was full of contradictions; he both went along and broke with the prejudices of patriarchal thinking on femininity and homosexuality. A few paragraphs further, Freud offered this insight, still relevant today in current discussions of confusions between object choice and sexual identity: "The literature of homosexuality usually fails to distinguish clearly enough between questions of choice of object on the one hand, and of sexual characteristics and sexual attitude on the other, as though the answer to the former necessarily involved the answers to the latter" (p. 170). How to understand his abrupt interruption of the treatment? Its root may be Freud's initial skepticism about "treating" homosexuality, a skepticism that is reiterated at the end, when he stated that "it is not for psychoanalysis to solve the problem of homosexuality" (p. 171). Or, was it that Freud could not continue this treatment of female homosexuality before he had solved the problem of femininity, this "dark continent" that still eluded him?

Fundamentally, the mystery of the "other sex" is a question that concerns both men and women. During his first open seminar, Lacan had spoken of Dora as someone whose object was homosexual. Five years later, he stated that the hysteric's same-sex interest was to figure out how one can be either male or female (Lacan, 1993, p. 284). Dora's hysterical homosexuality was thus not so much concerned with her choice of a love object as it was the consequence of a process of identification that allowed her to access desire. Dora's "homosexuality" stemmed from an identification mediated by desire: Dora found her desire in the other. This is mostly true of hysteria in general, for which identification operates at the level of desire. In short, one may say that hysterical desire takes desire for its object.

Desire remains always as an enigma for the hysteric. When Lacan (2004) reopened the case of the "Young Homosexual Woman" in 1963, it was in the context of the discussion of the function of the object that caused desire, which he designated with the letter *a* (p. 129). This object emerged with brutal force in Sidonie's first suicide attempt, especially in view of the diverging version that has emerged in the recent biography (Rieder & Voigt, 2003, pp. 27–28).[3] Lacan interpreted Sidonie's defiance, strolling down the street in the arms of the lady, as an "acting out," which is when things are "offered to be seen" (*donné à voir*). According to Freud, the suicidal attempt took place immediately after she saw her father's anger, which led to the lady's rejection. In the biography, the two women see Sidonie's father, who is accompanied by a colleague, at a certain distance, about a block away, after which Sidonie, taken by surprise and panicked, runs down the street, fleeing from the lady. When she returns a few minutes later, the father has gone, having boarded a trolley. In this version, Sidonie's father had not even seen his daughter, while it was the lady who saw the scene. The biography introduces a huge difference: The precipitating factor for the suicide would have been the lady's reproach that the young woman was not seriously in love if she could run like that to hide from her father. In this version, the father's "blindness" was the key.

In fact, the father had most likely seen the daughter because, as Thomas Gindele (2003b) observes, it was the father who had brought his daughter to the treatment, and thus it is likely that he gave Freud a true version of this event (p. 397). Sidonie's diverging account, however, gives more poignancy to her suicide attempt. Whereas Freud describes a disapproving paternal gaze that triggers the suicidal gesture, Sidonie places her father at the end of the street talking to a colleague and then immediately taking the tramway. Afraid of being seen by him, Sidonie ran away from the lady before noticing that her father had left on the tramway. She was not sure whether he saw her walking with the baroness and pretended not to see her or if he even noticed her at all. Freud (1920) notes a remarkable element in the lady's rejection:

> The fact that at that moment the "lady" had spoken in just the same terms as her father, and had uttered the same prohibition, forms the connecting link between this deep interpretation and the superficial one

---

[3] See Thomas Gindele's (2003a) illustrative annex, including a map and photographs of the scene of the suicide (pp. 40–43).

of which the girl herself was conscious. ... For analysis has explained the enigma of suicide in the following way: probably no one finds the mental energy required to kill himself unless, in the first place, in doing so he is at the same time killing an object with whom he has identified himself, and, in the second place, is turning against himself a death-wish which had been directed against someone else. (p. 162)

The father's furious glance could not have been seen by Sidonie if, according to the biography, he was too far away to discern who these two women were. By throwing herself onto the tracks, Sidonie did three things at once: She killed the imaginary gaze of the father that she had interiorized, she reinscribed a symbolic father via her possible death (since the dead father is the symbolic father, and this was the father with whom she identified), and she acted out in the Real, the absolute seriousness of her affection for the lady. Thus, Sidonie's uncertainty regarding whether her father had seen her or not ends up disclosing an object, the gaze, in all its importance. Symptomatically, the privileged position of the gaze as object *a* reappeared in Freud's farewell to Sidonie at the end of treatment. He told her: "You have very cunning eyes. I would not like to find myself later in life as your enemy" (Rieder & Voigt, 2003, p. 77).

SOME POSTFEMINIST READINGS OF SIDONIE'S CASE

Sidonie's case history has been discussed at some length by Diana Fuss in an essay that has been often quoted and anthologized.[4] Given Fuss's reputation as a renowned deconstructive feminist, I examine closely an essay that I find exemplary. It stems from a moment "when feminist indignation pairs with rigorous, critical scholarship," as Virginia Goldner has it (1999). Fuss (1995) herself is in a postfeminist tradition attentive to language and materiality, a tradition concerned with discerning the true meanings of "gender" and "sexual difference." Her point of departure is an examination of "the cognitive paradigm of 'falling' which Freud provides in this case study to 'explain' female homosexuality" (p. 57). Fuss contends that the young woman's fall is not so much a "fall" as a regression, a "gravitational fall back into a preoedipality" through a concomitant desire for the mother and identification with the father. Fuss uses this as a springboard to investigate critically psychoanalytic theories that depict female homosexuality

---
[4] Diana Fuss's essay appears as "Fallen Women: Identification, Desire, and 'A Case of Homosexuality in a Woman'" in Warner (1993); "Fallen Women: 'The Psychogenesis of a Case of Homosexuality in a Woman'" in Fuss (1995); "Fallen Women: 'The Psychogenesis of a Case of Homosexuality in a Woman'" in Lesser and Schoenberg (1999).

in terms of "pre-" something: preoedipal, presymbolic, prelaw, premature, presexual, and even pretheoretical. All these tend to "position their subjects *as* foundational, primeval, primitive, and indeed as pre-subjects, before the normative, heterosexualizing operations of the Oedipus complex" (p. 58; italics in the original). The problem that Fuss sees in Freud's approach is bound with the Oedipus complex in all its forms, not just with feminine sexuality.

Like Lacan, Fuss is skeptical of the way in which Freud explains the shift in Sidonie from a maternal attitude (wanting to *be* a mother) to a homosexual one (wanting to *have* a mother) as the result of her mother's late pregnancy and birth of a younger brother. Fuss questions the key role of the promise of a substitute object, challenging Freud's theory of femininity, a theory that is just sketched in this 1920 case and was expanded in the next decade with three crucial contributions. These crucial texts in which Freud expounds his theory of femininity are "Some Psychical Consequences of the Anatomical Distinction Between the Sexes" (1925), "Female Sexuality" (1931), and "Femininity" (1932/1933).

On this account, Fuss's project is quite worthwhile. Freud himself was aware of his theoretical shortcomings when elucidating the formation of sexual identity and, particularly, of feminine sexuality. Whereas an earlier stage of Freud's theoretical elaboration asserted that the Oedipus complex was similar for both sexes, his later texts on libidinal organization stress differences in object choice, in the effects of the castration complex, and in the narcissistic investment of the genital organs. Freud's last works underline the fact that the first object for the girl is the mother, and that later variations will determine whether she can reach a feminine positioning via identifications that will guide object choice.

Thus, Fuss is unconvinced by Freud's explanation of the daughter's movement toward the mother, following what in 1920 was described by Freud as an "enigmatic disappointment" and in 1932 was theorized as an "inevitable disappointment." This generalization was made in the 1932 lecture "Femininity," in which Freud put forward the idea of a "masculinity complex" in women as a regression from the attachment to the father. Here is Freud's (1932/1933) hypothesis:

> Female homosexuality is seldom or never a direct continuation of infantile masculinity. Even for a girl of this kind it seems necessary that she should take her father as an object for some time and enter the Oedipus situation. But afterwards, as a result of her inevitable disappointments from her father, she is driven to regress into her early masculinity complex. (p. 130)

Fuss (1995) questioned the use of the word *regress*, which she understood as a backward motion, as "a retrenchment rather than an advance, a retreat *from* the father rather than a move *toward* the mother" (p. 64; italics in the original). Fuss thought that Freud's speculation about a displacement of the heterosexual daughter–father incest onto the mother contains a disavowal of the homosexual daughter–mother incest (p. 64). She dismissed Freud's idea that for girls the "early masculinity complex" *is* the daughter–mother incest.

Against these strictures, one can adduce Lacan's idea that incest is always an incest with the mother, who stands for the first Other, the first *heteros*. The mother occupies the place of the only incestuous object thanks to her primal role due to the state of helplessness in which the baby finds itself when born, a fact that makes it depend on an other (the mother) for its survival. But, she is also from the Other sex, thus opening the way to the heteros of sex. The psychic importance of the mother can be shown by the devastating effects of maternal deficits for the child, as proven by the studies of Renée Spitz (1945, 1966) on hospitalism, in which she studied institutionalized infants who failed to thrive physically and psychically due to lack of consistent care despite adequate nutrition and health care. Similarly, Jenny Aubry (1983) demonstrated that children who lacked adequate maternal care (often children who were separated from the mother or mother substitute and from their environment at birth) presented autistic characteristics and behaviors of self-aggression and self-mutilation. This chimes in with Lacan's (2001) analysis of the devastation caused by maternal deficits: "If the child is not the object of a particularized life desire, even if presented through the lack in the mother, it can neither develop nor get structured" (p. 371). The consequences of early maternal deficits can be catastrophic, but on the other hand the separation from such important first love is not easy, especially for a girl. This sends us back to the question posed by Freud (1932) in his "Femininity" lecture: "How does a girl pass from her mother to an attachment to her father?" (p. 147).

The answer may address Fuss's criticism. The initial symmetry between boys and girls in their love for the mother ends when castration introduces a logic that distinguishes boys and girls in reference to a tertiary term, the phallus. The paternal prohibition works in a twofold manner: "do not reintegrate your product" (to the mother) and "you will not have sex with your mother" (to the child). Under the dominance of phallic criteria, "boy" now means "having a penis" or "not without not having it," "virile," "being a man," and so on. Similarly, the signifier "girl" acquires a phallic signification and loses its anatomical connotations to adopt other meanings, such as "feminine," "mysterious," "lacking," "demure," "beautiful."[5] For the boy, the phallus and castration resolve the Oedipal problems. For the girl, things are more

---

[5] See Chapter 9 for a discussion of Geneviève Morel's (2000c) elaboration on the three temporal registers of sexuation (pp. 30–32).

complex. The resolution of the Oedipus complex orients both boys and girls toward a masculine position (both love the mother and have to renounce to her).

Serge André (1999) assessed this early period of Freud theorization on femininity and contended that the girl, to avoid homosexuality and move to a male object, had to undergo "a change of sex" in fantasy (p. 173). To test the claim that homosexuality is inscribed in the structure of the feminine Oedipus complex and that a heterosexual object choice implied a change of sex in fantasy, André discussed the case of the young homosexual woman (pp. 173–184). Freud could never fully account for why not all girls go on to become homosexual. The so-called normal outcome of the Oedipus complex, the relation to the father, could be in fact reeditions of the earlier attachment to the mother.

BROKEN PROMISES

We have seen that Fuss rejects Freud's argument that the desire for the mother is a return to a "hated rival," a regression that would be caused by the frustration in her Oedipal inclinations for the father. She asks: "Why, in short, is the daughter's 'rivalry' assumed to be with the mother and not with the father?" (Fuss, 1995, p. 62). According to Freud, in the resolution of the Oedipus complex, the girl resents her mother for having deprived her of a penis, and she will turn to her father in the hope that he will provide a child as a symbolic substitute for the penis. Fuss is absolutely right; Freud's theory of femininity ends in an impasse: The outcome of the feminine Oedipus is nothing other than a regression to the preoedipal connection to the mother.

Lacan's way out of this conundrum is first to question the efficacy of the Oedipus complex to understand femininity. It seems to explain so well boy's sexuality but does not seem to be fully operative in the case of girls. Lacan will put less emphasis on castration, and to the claims it leads to, and more on the division that the primacy of the phallus creates for the girl.

For Lacan (1994), the privation of the phallus in the girl is the real lack of a symbolic object (the symbolic phallus); the missing penis is already a symbolic notion imposed onto the Real, in which nothing is missing (p. 218).[6] Thus, the mother is deprived of an object that she actually never had. If there is anything perceived as lacking, what is absent is already the symbolic phallus, and the agent of privation is the imaginary father. As

---

[6] To talk about the lack of the penis already implies a process of symbolization that created such lack. To illustrate this point, let us say that, for instance, Freud's standard edition is a set that consists of 24 volumes; if we have only 20 in our library, we would be missing 4 volumes. But, in the shelves nothing is missing; if we consider some volumes missing, it is only because of the symbolic idea of a "complete" set.

exemplified by Sidonie, the girl displaces the resentment she felt for her mother for not giving her a penis onto her father when he fails to provide the desired child.

According to Freud (1932/1933, 1937), this resentment will be the moving force: It makes women desire a penis in sexual intercourse and want a child from a man. Lacan, however, claimed that no object can be sufficient because privation is imaginary: No matter how many children a woman may have, the dissatisfaction may persist because desire has no exact corresponding object. Then, the mother will desire other things beyond the children (like a lover, her job, watching television, and so on). The mother's dissatisfaction is propitious because it introduces the dialectics of desire that allow the child to see beyond the mother's desire. This helps the child look outside the dyad.

Let me emphasize this point: Fuss's antiessentialist avoidance of the concept of the phallus gives the impression that she is not aware of the fact that children notice anatomical differences only after the symbolic event brought about by the threat of castration. Anatomy, with its chromosomes, gametes, and genitalia, becomes then part of a mythical Real that acquires signification on this second stage, when the values of the sex assigned at birth are structured and a sexual positioning is assumed. Finally, an object choice is made.

In Dora's case, the promise was that she could access the paternal phallus by way of Herr K., who stood out as an object of desire structured around Herr K.'s connection to Frau K. This is the promise that was broken by Herr K. in a scene by the lake. In this labyrinth of connections, when Herr K. made a more clear sexual advance, taking Dora in his arms while disavowing any interest in his wife, she slapped him in the face. He had said: "You know I get nothing out of my wife" (Freud, 1901/1905, p. 98). Lacan, following closely the syntax of the phrase in German ("*Ich habe nichts an meiner Frau*"), noted that Herr K. was severing the previous circuit, as if he had been telling Dora: "There is nothing in me of my wife." To add insult to injury, Dora may have heard the same complaint from her father's lips since we know that Dora's father used the exact phrase when he talked to Freud about Dora's mother (p. 26, n. 106).

If Herr K. was interested only in Dora, then her father was interested only in Frau K.; such an alleged "normal" set of attractions had the effect of breaking the circulation of gifts, of collapsing the regime of exchanges. Excluded from the quadrangle of desiring connections, Dora was no longer essential to the continuation of the saga. The fateful confession of Herr K. suddenly short-circuited the circuit of desire sustained by the mediating function of the other woman. This why when Freud first met Dora, she complained that her father had wronged her, and thus she required reparation; frustrated, torn by jealousy and resentment, she had moved to the level of demand.

Similarly, Freud (1920) claims that Sidonie's homosexuality was the result of a broken promise based on an exchange or economy of the gift. The lingering question is whether the "symbolic gift of a child" is equivalent to a woman's desire to have a child, and if that wish can be the same as her desire to become a mother. This is why Fuss (1995) is quite right to stress that Freud's case begins with the word *homosexuality* and concludes with the word *motherhood* (p. 66). Indeed, the missing word here would be *femininity*, a word that seems to remain out of reach not only for Freud but also for the unconscious. The case of Sidonie can be understood in terms of frustration considered as a failure in the paternal discourse.

For Freud, the love for the father was shaped by a "defaulting on a promise for which one has given up everything" (Lacan, 1991b, p. 353). In this case, the broken promise shattered Sidonie's trust in a symbolic chain of gift exchanges. Sidonie's tender, loving exaltation (*Schwärmerei*)[7] of the fallen lady combined with her humble devotion reveal a dynamic of exchanges in which the young woman expected little and asked for nothing. Her lack of pretensions (*"che poco spera e nulla chiede"* ["hoping for little wanting nothing"]) was rather a phobic *"noli me tangere"* ["do not touch me"] (Diamantis, 2004, p. 60). The counterpoint to the strategy of demanding nothing from the lady is that Sidonie was actually demanding something from the father (Feltzine, 1995, p. 18). As with Dora, frustration made Sidonie move to the level of demand: She had been, wronged, and the father goes from being a symbolic father to become the imaginary father. In her frustrated love, she identifies with the imaginary father, who becomes the addressee of her demand for love, staged in the scene that he is forced to witness. As Freud (1920) puts it, Sidonie had been frustrated in "the wish to have a child by her father, for now she 'fell' through her father's fault" (p. 162). One may conclude that Sidonie did not simply "regress," as Fuss claims, but rather that she "fell" into the barrenness of the Real.

If, as she believed, the phallus was received by her mother (in German, "to receive" is *bekommen*), the same phallus had been denied to her, so that it fell (it falls, *es kommt nieder*). Nonetheless, her attempted suicide was at the same time—as the word itself reveals—a giving birth, that is, a symbolic parturition. Freud noted that she was identified with the missing object: She became the baby she was denied. In her *Niederkommen,* she was at once having the child and destroying herself, in a symbolic stillbirth. Whereas Dora remained in metaphoric substitution, Sidonie's desperate act was the last element in a long chain of displaced objects.

Fuss, critical of Freud's study, denounces the limitations of the theory of female sexual inversion, a theory that she claims is based on a single case history. Yet, she falls into the same trap since she criticizes Freud's theory

---

[7] For an enlightening discussion of Freud's clinical understanding of Schwärmerei in this case, see Monique David-Ménard (2004).

of female sexuality from a single case history. She never proposes an alternative theory of female sexuality or of homosexuality. There is an element of truth in Jack Drescher's (2001) observation about the "pivotal role" that this 1920 Freud essay played in the psychoanalytic theory of female homosexuality and his reproach that "its biased views toward lesbians ... became codified into the psychoanalytic canon" (p. 1447). However, such "biases" have issued from highly selective, if not tendentious, readings of Freud's theories of sexuality.

Fuss (1995) attacked Freud for reducing homosexuality to identification. As stated, her analysis of Freud's theory of female homosexuality is based on the paradigm of falling that she translates into the Latin *cadere* ("to fall"); this etymological connection then conjures up cadavers, an "insatiable oral drive," and a view of homosexuality as "identification in overdrive" (p. 77). Is this criticism in "overdrive"? Fuss's assessment of Freud's theory of homosexuality focuses on the verb niederkommen (to fall or to be delivered of a child), a verb that had been given to Freud by Sidonie. Freud did not employ it to "explain" female homosexuality, as Fuss argues, but to analyze the logic of her suicidal attempt. Here, Fuss's reading strays from the close textual attention that her critique would require. As a result, she gives the impression of not knowing Freud very well or of willfully distorting the letter of his texts. How else can one make sense of her claim that "for Freud every fall into homosexuality is *inherently suicidal* since the 'retreat' from preoedipality entails not only the loss of desire but the loss of a fundamental relation to the world into which desire permits entry—the world of sociality, sexuality, and subjectivity" (p. 77; italics in the original)?

Fuss (1999) criticizes Freud for not having elaborated a theory of homosexual desire. She dismisses the fact that Freud did not use "desire" as a theoretical concept (as Lacan did), and that properly speaking Freud did not have a theory of desire, whether homo- or hetero-. In a series of curious interpretive inversions, Fuss aligns object choice with heterosexuality and identification with homosexuality, believing that for Freud "desire is the province and privilege of heterosexuals, homosexuals are portrayed as hysterical identifiers and expert mimics" (p. 71). Rather than follow Freud's development of his theory of identification from the Oedipus complex to "Totem and Taboo" (Freud, 1912–1913) and *Moses and Monotheism*,[8] Fuss treats it as a consistent whole and then attacks its coherence: "Freud in spectacular circular fashion, resubmits homosexuality to its own alleged entropic 'tendencies,' so that 'homo' subsumes 'sexuality' and identification incorporates desire" (p. 71–72). On the other hand, Fuss is right to refuse the idea that homosexuality would appear as a regression when the choice of maternity is frustrated. Indeed, she poses the question of whether this

---

[8] For a discussion of Freud's theory of identification, see Grigg (1987).

might be a case of identity formation, of "homosexuality" versus "motherhood," or of same-sex desire and same-sex identification. Fuss's essay convincingly exposes the limitations of Freud's Oedipus model, showing how identity and desire may not always overlap.

If Freud can be blamed for not having elaborated a theory of homosexual desire beyond his contention of regression to a primeval identification, Fuss (1993, 1995, 1999) does not escape similar charges. Since she did not propose an alternative theory of homosexuality, her claims become increasingly contradictory. In a sweeping gesture, she asserted that female homosexuality is psychoanalysis' very foundation, contending that out of Freud's six completed case studies, two are studies of object choice inversion in women (Fuss, 1995, p. 59). Fuss neglected the fact that Freud treated more than six patients during his whole analytic career. Besides the four prepsychoanalytic cases published in the *Studies on Hysteria*, none of them on homosexuality, there is evidence (reports or autobiographies, letters and interviews of analysands, letters by Freud, published works by Freud, and clinical records of subsequent treatment) that Freud treated *at least* 43 patients between 1907 and 1939 (Lynn & Vaillant, 1998). Similarly, Fuss (1999) claimed that Lacan's early focus on paranoia was because "Lacan was interested only in *homosexual* women" (p. 56; italics in the original). Lacan's interest was not in homosexual women but in paranoia. While one may indeed argue whether the Papin sisters' incest that led to a notorious massacre should be considered as "homosexual" (Christine Papin believed that in a former life she was her sister's husband), at least Aimée, the paranoiac patient studied by Lacan in his dissertation, was clearly not homosexual (Roudinesco, 1997).

Like Judith Butler, Fuss (1999) thinks that in Freud's model the child's homosexual desire for the parent of the same sex is a fundamental, yet disposable, component of desire, and that it is a component that has to be repudiated and repressed. According to her, the "inessentiality" of homosexuality reflects a secondary reaction formation against the attraction of psychoanalysis to an economy of the same (homo) and a fascination with its own origins. Yet, if one pushes the thesis to its rigorous conclusion, it becomes absurd as it implies that from the start girls only love their mothers and boys only their fathers, and that they repress that homosexual first choice to become heterosexual. This repressed homosexual primer would reduce all sexual forms to heterosexual choices; that is, if two people of the same sex desire one another, one has to have identified with the opposite sex, thus reproducing a heterosexual matrix within homosexual desire.

While one cannot seriously say that Freud ever dehumanized homosexuals, one can grant that Freud lacks a full theory of feminine homosexuality, a theoretical failing that led to a well-known controversy on femininity. For a long time, Freud answered the question, *"Was will das Weib?"* ["What does a woman want?"] (Jones, 1995, p. 421) by saying that he knew well what women wanted. He called that desire "penis envy": Since they did not *have* it, they chose the man who *had* it. But in 1923, Freud took a dramatic turn and admitted that he had been wrong (Freud, 1923b). It is not a penis but love for the mother that the girl wants, and for that, like the boy, she has to renounce something in the Oedipal struggle. Is for Freud the female homosexual a girl with an arrested psychosexual development, as Fuss claims (1999)? The details of Freud's reversal and the understanding of regression from object choice to identification have stirred a long debate in feminist criticism. The debate has not been closed and keeps eliciting more conflicting views.

ONLY TIRESIAS COULD TELL

In an influential essay dating from 1980, Adrienne Rich (1986) turned the argument of heterosexual object choice on its head: If the first erotic bond is to the mother, she asked, could not the "natural" sexual orientation of both men and women be toward women (pp. 23–75)? In fact, there is nothing "natural" about either heterosexuality or homosexuality. More recently, commenting on the "heterosexual matrix" that prevails in our society, Judith Butler (1997) discussed the predicaments of a culture that struggles to mourn the loss of the homosexual attachment (pp. 132–150). Butler then stated that any sexual position is acquired, at least partially, not through mourning but rather as a repudiation of homosexual attachments. Concerning femininity, she asserted that "the girl becomes a girl through being subject to a prohibition which bars the mother as an object of desire and installs that barred object as a part of the ego, indeed, as a melancholic identification" (p. 136). Fundamentally, Butler has challenged the idea that sexual identity is built around object choice. She wrote: "If one is a girl to the extent that one does not want a girl, then wanting a girl will bring being a girl into question," adding that within this matrix, homosexual desire challenges gender (p. 136). Lacan (2006) acknowledged the inability of psychoanalysts, male and female alike, to elucidate feminine sexuality with a challenge: "A convention on female sexuality is not about to cause to weight upon us the threat of Tiresias' fate" (p. 613). In 1972–1973, Lacan (1998b) argued that woman's sexuality was structured differently from man's. Castration could not fully account for the feminine positioning because femininity was a position in regard to sex not fully determined by the phallus. There was nothing mysterious about feminine sexuality; mystery was a fantasy to cloud over the lack of a rapport between the sexes. The problem of femininity was centered around how the phallic function (which worked in an asymmetric manner for each gendered sexual positioning) was unconsciously signified and depended on how each subject acknowledged her subjection to the law of sexual difference. Following up on this, in the next chapter I engage with Butler's influential theories of performative gender that have powerfully impacted recent discussions of transgenderism.

Chapter 6
Gender and sex as performance

In her enormously influential book, *Gender Trouble*, Judith Butler (1990) observed that contemporary feminism had "gotten in trouble" by becoming a "woman's" movement, that is, by assuming that women were a uniform group with shared identity, interests, and goals. The critique of patriarchal culture made on behalf of the presumed universality of "women," she argued, produced an "unwitting regulation and reification of gender relations" (pp. 5–6). It would reinforce the binary view of gender relations (in which culture builds masculine and feminine genders on male and female bodies), the very template from which feminism was trying to break away. She argued that making political claims in the name of women, thus treated as a seamless category, was a self-defeating gesture. This argument partly overlapped with Lacan's formula: "Woman does not exist," which means that, unlike masculinity, which is a universal function founded on the phallic exception of castration, woman is a nonuniversal (Lacan, 1998b, p. 7; p. 72).

Without making any explicit reference to Freud, however, Butler (1990) seemed to reformulate the distinction between "being" and "having" the phallus when she observed that people refer to gender not only as something they "have" but also as a state of "being," as in the question "What gender are you?" (p. 7). This was immediately followed by an exploration of the feminist claim that gender is a cultural interpretation of sex. If gender was socially constructed, Butler continued, could it be constructed differently, or did social conditions impose some sort of determinism? Did construction offer the possibility of agency and transformation? Since for Butler the notion of a gendered self, which Robert Stoller (1985) called "gender core" (pp. 11–14), is produced along "culturally established lines of coherence" (Butler, 1990, p. 24), gender, in this sense, is not simply an attribute that persons are supposed to have (as a humanist feminist position may claim) or a relation (as sustained by social constructivists) (p. 10). Butler's proposition was that "being" a sex or gender is fundamentally impossible (p. 19). Her thesis resonates with Luce Irigaray's (1985b) critique that grammar can never be a true index of gender relations because it presumes a model of gender as a binary relation between two positive and representable terms. Irigaray has claimed that this binary masks the univocal, hegemonic male discourse that silences the feminine as site of subversive multiplicity. This refers to the impossibility of a grammatically denoted substance that would correspond with a word like "feminine" as defined by grammar: The feminine sex becomes a point of linguistic absence (Butler, 1990, p. 19).

Then, gender is neither a noun nor a set of attributes—gender is always a doing, constituting the identity it is purported to be (Butler, 1990, p. 25). This is one of Butler's most important arguments in her effort to move beyond the binary frame: Gender is always performative. This appears most clearly in practices like drag, cross-dressing, and butch or femme identities. The performance of drag emphasizes the discontinuity between the anatomy of the performer and the gender that is performed, highlighting three contingent dimensions of gender embodiment: anatomical sex, gender identity, and gender performance. "In imitating gender, drag implicitly reveals the imitative structure of gender itself—as well as its contingency" (p. 137). Parody is praised not as a copy of an original but as a fantasy of a fantasy. Sexual identification is akin to gender parody, both revealing that they are an imitation without an original—a production that postures as an imitation. Furthermore, gender parody overrides the very notion of a natural origin: "Gay is to straight not as copy is to original, but, rather, as copy is to copy" (p. 31). Butler borrows Fredric Jameson's idea of pastiche as the postmodern form of parody without laughter, a parody that has lost its satirical impulse. When "normal" loses its meaning, there is still subversive laughter "in the realization that all along the original was derived" (p. 139). Butler celebrates the subversive potential of gender parody, in which notions of core or fixed gender identities can be exposed as fictions. In her view, the notion of gender loses consistency and is liberated by being pluralized. "Genders can be neither true nor false, neither real nor apparent, neither original nor derived. As credible bearers of those attributes, however, genders can be rendered thoroughly and radically *incredible*" (p. 141; italics in the original).

Whether one complies with the ascribed traditional gender roles or traverses gender boundaries, according to Butler (1990), one *always* puts on a gender performance:

> Gender is always a doing, though not a doing by a subject who might be said to preexist the deed. ... There is no gender identity behind the expressions of gender; that identity is performatively constituted by the very "expressions" that are said to be its results. (p. 25)

When Butler stated that gender is performative, she was challenging the feminist critique of sex as produced by discourse, the sex–gender divide, and the idea of compulsory heterosexuality as ineffective strategies. Gender, sex, sexuality all became performances.

The idea of gender, sex, and sexuality as free floating is one of the main tenets of queer theory. This is how David Halperin (1995) defines it: "Queer is by definition whatever is at odds with the normal, the legitimate, the dominant. There is nothing in particular to which it necessarily refers. It is an identity without an essence" (p. 65). According to queer theory, identities are not fixed and immovable, and thus one can transcend them. Yet, the promise of infinite plasticity may produce what Ken Corbett (2001) called "queer theory's utopianism" (p. 329). Thus, if there is no sex but only gender, and if gender is performative, it must be radically free—the materiality of the body seems vacated, or ignored, or negated—disavowed, even. In *Bodies That Matter,* however, Butler (1993) picks up the lost body and reworks the category of sex and the problem of materiality to explore why sex itself is construed as a norm. There, Butler follows Lacan's idea that sex is a regulatory norm by which bodies become materialized. "'Sex' is, thus, not simply what one has, or a static description of what one is: it will be one of the norms by which the 'one' becomes viable at all, that which qualifies a body for life within the domain of cultural intelligibility" (p. 2). The blurring of sex into gender becomes obvious:

> If gender is the social construction of sex, and there is no access to this "sex" except by the means of its construction, then it appears not only that sex is absorbed by gender, but that "sex" becomes something like a fiction, perhaps a fantasy, retroactively installed at a prelinguistic site to which there is no direct access. (p. 5)

Butler appropriated the criticism that her earlier account of gender as performative may elicit, and she spelled it out for the reader: If everything is discourse, are bodies purely discursive? If gender construction is reduced to a speech act, who is the subject speaking, and who constructs this subject (p. 6)? Butler suggests that some constructivism presumes a construction that operates deterministically, "making a mockery of human agency" or presupposes a voluntaristic subject that rehabilitates the voluntaristic subject of humanism that constructivism has sought to put into question (p. 7). Her claim is that gender materializes sex, and subjects are subjected to a gender that neither precedes nor follows the process of gendering, subjects can only emerge "within and as the matrix of gender relations themselves" (p. 7). Gender does not require any willful appropriation, "it is the matrix through which all willing first becomes possible"; furthermore, "the matrix of gender relations is prior to the emergence of the 'human'" (p. 7). When a baby is born, the interpellation "It's a boy" or "It's a girl" shifts that infant from being an "it" into a "she" or a "he." In that naming, the child "is brought into the domain of language and kinship through the interpellation of gender" (p. 7). Such attributions or interpellations that in *Gender Trouble* (Butler, 1990) were placed under the notion of "heterosexual matrix" became "heterosexual hegemony" in *Bodies That Matter* (Butler, 1993). This shift opens the possibility of a matrix that will be malleable. The materiality of the body becomes a process of materialization working over time through repetition (p. 9). Butler's contention that both sex and gender are the result of historically contingent processes of materialization could be easily assimilated to Laqueur's (1990) argument that the existence of two sexes is a modern invention.

ACTING OUT SEXUALITY

Butler's notion that sex is discursively constructed derives, at least partially, from psychoanalysis—sex and gender are effects of language on the body. The subject psychoanalysis works with is a split subject, a speaking body, a desiring subject who is brought into being and split by language. Butler's (1993) intention in *Bodies That Matter* was "to challenge the structural stasis of the heterosexualizing norm within the psychoanalytic account" (p. 22). Yet, as Tim Dean (2000) persuasively argues, theorizing gender and sexuality in terms of the performative, Butler was dealing just with imaginary and symbolic effects, which leaves aside "the limit to language that Lacan calls the real" (p. 77) and thus leaves subjectivity and the ego "calmly untroubled" (p. 192). Dean contends that Butler's omission is regrettable because the Lacanian Real, which is "asubstantial, unsexed, and ungendered" (p. 210), provides potential for queer theory to exploit (p. 217). For psychoanalysis, sexual difference is not a norm but a real impossibility, which is to say, it is a limit to the speakable and thinkable. "By distinguishing sexual desire and jouissance from the irresistible pull of genitalia, Lacan denaturalizes and deheterosexualizes desire," notes Dean (p. 195). Lacan theorizes sexuality not in terms of gender, but of modalities of jouissance that refer to what cannot be accounted for within a binary pairing of complementary opposites (Lacan, 1973, 1999b). Dean (2000) adds that the assumption that psychoanalysis is heterosexist (it argues that desire is desire for the other sex) can be challenged by Lacan's contention that desire has no object other than its satisfaction. The object that causes desire "takes forms that are gender neutral—the gaze, the voice, the phoneme, the lips, 'the rim of the anus,' 'the slit formed by the eyelids'" (p. 194). Lacan detached desire from gender (p. 216). Desire is partial, and not necessarily gendered, which suggests the potential to conceive of sexuality outside the confines of normative heterosexuality.

To further discuss Butler's theses on gender, we can return to the scene that precipitated the suicide attempt of Sidonie. The young woman was, as Butler would say, "performing her gender," parading her "knight dyke" persona in a scene carefully staged for her father's gaze. When the lady discovers in the street that the whole scene was a spectacle of passionate devotion with the purpose of infuriating the father, she brutally rejects Sidonie. The lady refuses to continue the relationship with the young woman not just because she sees a public display of romantic courtship addressed to the father through a rebellious transgression, but also because, echoing the young woman's father, she sanctions her behavior as tarnishing her reputation, bringing her a bad name, but "being of good birth as she was," she still plays by the rules and honors her "distinguished name" (Freud, 1920, p. 153). Above all, it was because she suddenly became aware of her secondary role in a scene performed mostly for Sidonie's father, and that the baroness found her part unacceptable and like a spurned prima donna, left the scene. Here, there was no more room for laughter as the parody has rung too true.

The performance enacted by Sidonie had posited the baroness as a capricious master not bound by moral laws. For her, the baroness was the mythical She, the Woman, whose legendary primordial repression constitutes the symbolic order. Sidonie was promoting the Woman to the level of the Name-of-the-Father to make up for her father's deficiency. She performed a scene in which she could find in her lady an absolute phallus with which he could signify her sexuality. This is why in Chapter 8 I explore Woman as Name-of-the-Father, in a logic of supplementarity that organizes jouissance according to the tangled knots of a *sinthome*. For the moment, I would like to stay with Lacan's double notion of acting out—a subject's performance of a scene for the gaze of the Other—and *passage à l'acte* (passage to the act). These two terms also address the premises that provide the foundation for Butler's ideas of gender as performative. Since both Dora and Sidonie present cases of women's "virile" inclinations (*männliches Typus*) whose sexual object is someone of the same sex, they offer a good ground to test Butler's ideas on sex and gender. This allows us to reframe the critiques of the work of Lacan and Freud by queer theory and feminist theory.

WHAT IS THE GENDER OF LOVE?

We have seen that Fuss's (1993, 1995, 1999) model of gravitational pushes and pulls made the mistake of collapsing object choice and sexual identity. To avoid this slippage, one needs to reopen the case of Sidonie by taking into account her "significant other." As Lacan (1998b) noted in a seminar in which homosexuality was a key issue, as far as love is concerned, gender seems irrelevant. He said: "*Quand on aime il ne s'agit pas de sexe*" ["When one loves, it has nothing to do with gender"] (p. 25). With this in mind, I follow the grid proposed by Lacan in a passage of the seminar *On*

Anxiety in which he calls the suicidal attempt a "passage to the act" and also describes Sidonie's adventure with the Lady as an acting out.

The pair *acting out* and *passage to the act* can serve to analyze Dora's case. Lacan (2004) argues that Dora's paradoxical complicity in the continuation of the extramarital saga was an acting out, that is, an attempt to make the object causing desire—which was outside—appear in a scene: Dora helped her father sustain an adulterous affair in the hope of making him appear potent and thus able to offer the promise of a virile gift. As we saw, the confession of Herr K., who blurted out that he got nothing from his wife, precipitated a passage to the act under the form of a withdrawal from the stage—the subject, identified with the object, dropped from the scene. Dora's answer to his confession was a slap that changed the story forever. Of course, the consequences of Dora's passage to the act were less severe than in the case of Sidonie, but they were regulated by a similar pattern.

Let us revisit both the scene of Sidonie's suicide attempt and that of Dora at the lake and explore them as performances staging an encounter with the object cause of desire (object *a*). Both were anxious encounters not filtered by desire and deprived of the veil of the fantasy. As we have seen, Herr K.'s declaration disrupted the desiring chain and produced a collapse of identifications in Dora, which resulted in a charge of anxiety. Herr K. interrupted the circuit of exchange by which Dora could have had symbolic access to the paternal phallus. One can say that without her connection to Frau K., Dora was confronted with the enigma of sex with nothing to safeguard her. Dora's father was rich (*vermögend*) but impotent (*unvermögend*) and therefore unable to give the phallus. Before the lake scene, all went relatively well for Dora: She knew that her father was impotent and helped him by sustaining his desire for Frau K. If up to that point Dora was complicit in enabling the continuation of an extramarital affair, now she saw the crude reality. She could no longer tolerate it and then denounced it. She had been wronged: The Other had broken its promise. She understood that she had been a convenient pawn, that her father had used her to maintain the affair. Having gained such knowledge, Dora wanted the adulterous relation to stop.

By slapping Herr K., she produced a passage to the act and fell from the scene. Dora now demanded absolute love. The slap Dora gave Herr K. and Sidonie's suicide attempt were ploys that attempted, at least temporarily, to ward off anxiety. Although anxiety was at work in both the acting out and the passage to the act, Lacan (2004) establishes a clear distinction between them. While both are strategies deployed against anxiety, in the acting out the subject remains in the scene, whereas in the passage to the act the subject leaves the scene altogether. Dora's and Sidonie's acting out were addressed to the Other, first taken as the father. The passage to the act, however, implies a flight from the Other into the dimension of the Real; it is an exit from the symbolic network, bringing along a dissolution of the social bond. Thus, the jump on the railways and the slap of Herr K.'s face were messages that had been addressed to anyone and no one in particular. They entailed a disintegration of the subject, who for a moment turned into a pure object *a*, a leftover of signification.

The acting out of Sidonie and Dora occurred before they began their treatments, and it functioned as the event that precipitated bringing them to analysis with Freud. This evokes Lacan's (2004) claim that the acting out was "transference without analysis," that is, a "wild transference" (p. 148), as illustrated in the Freud–Fliess controversy over plagiarism discussed in Chapter 4. Unlike certain symptoms that may not beg for an interpretation because they are not a call to the Other but pure jouissance addressed to no one, an acting out always calls for an interpretation (p. 147). Roberto Harari (2001) alleges that acting out is untamed transference insofar as it questions and overwhelms the subject to a much greater extent than the symptom: "In acting out, we must take into account that the subject is experiencing phallic jouissance" (p. 85). In that sense, an acting out has a stronger power of demand than the symptom: "It is a peremptory demand for interpretation, given the shattering it bears" (p. 85). Whether gender is a performance, an acting out, or a passage à l'acte, what matters for a psychoanalyst is the negotiation between the subject and the object *a* with which the performance plays. Following Butler's (1988, 1990, 1993, 1997, 2004) theoretical progression, we will find in mourning a good example of the complex circuit of the object as it determines subjective positions.

GENDER AND MELANCHOLY

Butler (1997) builds gender on a certain conception of melancholy that derives from Freud's (1917) "Mourning and Melancholia." As is well known, Freud differentiates melancholy from mourning: *Mourning* refers to an experience of grieving or of working through an external identifiable loss (a loved person, an ideal), while *melancholy* corresponds to a state of endless grief that develops into a morbid condition (the ego identifies with the lost object itself). Freud contends that the mourner gives up the lost object by "offering the ego the inducement of continuing to live" (p. 257). Grief work (*Trauerarbeit*) is a task that allows a certain economy to be restored; one attachment is severed to make others possible. Butler's model describes a subject unable to forget or repress, incapable of grieving the loss of the homosexual object, ill-equipped to cut ties and move on.

Let us distinguish more clearly Butler's (1997) position from that of Fuss (1993, 1995, 1999). Fuss attacked the Freud of "Mourning and Melancholia" (1917), who claimed that the loss of an object produces a regression to identification and therefore neglected the revised theory of mourning offered in "The Ego and the Id" (Freud, 1923a). Butler is much closer to the Freud (1923a) of "The Ego and the Id," who often contradicted the claims in "Mourning and Melancholia." While Fuss criticizes Freud's use of regression, for Butler it is regression that allows women to come closer to the nexus of attachment lost in the compulsory production of heterosexuality. For Butler, the inability to accept the loss of the homosexual attachment comes in the way of the possibility of a regression and stalls a progression to the next object; as a consequence, subjects remain trapped in a primeval melancholy.

Six years after "Mourning and Melancholia" (Freud, 1917), Freud (1923a) revised his explanation of the dynamics of mourning in "The Ego and the Id," in which he suggested that mourning is not always possible: With very significant objects, the process of mourning may never be completed (p. 31). Freud's theoretical turn can be traced back to his daughter Sophie's death. In a 1929 letter to Binswanger, Freud mentioned the persistence of mourning and generalized the experience of having lost his daughter 9 years earlier:

> Although we know that after such a loss the acute state of mourning will subside, we also know we shall remain inconsolable and will never find a substitute. No matter what may fill the gap, even if it be filled completely, it nevertheless remains something else. And actually, this is how it should be. It is the only way of perpetuating that love which we do not want to relinquish. (E. Freud, 1960, p. 386)

If the people we love deeply are eminently irreplaceable, the possibility of true mourning seems challenged. In 1923, Freud (1923a) redefines the ego's character as "a precipitate of abandoned object-cathexes," that is, an embodied history of lost erotic attachments (p. 29). This is the claim that Butler (1997) follows when she contends that no final severance of attachments "could take place without dissolving the ego" (p. 196).

SEXED IDENTIFICATIONS

In Section III of "The Ego and the Id," Freud (1923a) may surprise the reader by stating that it is not bisexuality but identification with the rival object that governs the formation of "normal" sexual identity (thus contradicting Fuss's assumptions once more). In his discussion of the "simple positive Oedipus complex in a boy," which is characterized by an "ambivalent attitude to his father and an object-relation of a solely affectionate kind to his mother" (Freud, 1923a, p. 32), Freud argues that to cope with the loss of the mother, the boy substitutes this maternal object cathexis regressing to two forms of identification: "either an identification with his mother or an intensification of his identification with his father" (p. 32). In his own theorizing, Freud turned a corner: "These identifications," Freud suggests in reference to the "more normal" identifications emerging in the Oedipus complex, "are not what we should have expected, since they do not introduce the abandoned object into the ego" (p. 32). In the case of "the more complete Oedipus complex, which is twofold, positive and negative" and due to "the bisexuality originally present in children" (p. 33), the boy may not simply be ambivalent about his father and affectionate with his mother; he may behave like a girl facing his father and be jealous and hostile with his mother. Freud, however, continues to imply that identification with the rival constitutes the norm. Identification preserves the loved and hated rival within the ego, but an ego subject to the violently critical, obscene, and ferocious superego.

MOMMY DEAREST

If we return to Sidonie, we can see that she appeared to have substituted her love choice for her Oedipal rival. Indeed, Freud (1920) claimed that "analysis revealed beyond all shadow of doubt that the lady-love was a substitute for her mother" (p. 156). It is true that the lady was not herself a mother, yet Freud asserts that for Sidonie, "Motherhood [w]as a *sine qua non* in her love object" (p. 156), even when her own mother favored her sons and was not very kind to her. Freud suggests that when the girl was experiencing a revival of the Oedipus complex, she suffered a great disappointment. She had already developed a strong affection for a little boy whom she would often see in a playground. She was conscious of her wish to have a baby boy, as when her mother gave birth to her youngest brother. Her true disappointment came from the fact that, being unable to become the mother of her father's child, she repudiated her wish for a child and threw the baby out with the bath water, as it were—and rejected femininity altogether. The flaw in her logic was the following: Being a mother was the only answer to the question, "What is to be a woman?" Since she was unable to be a mother, she could not be a woman. Then, a major transformation occurred—Sidonie became a man. She "changed into a man and took her mother in place of her father as the object of her love" (p. 158). As her relation to her mother was hostile, she was able to overcompensate via a substitute mother to whom she could be passionately attached. As we saw, Sidonie discovered that by letting her mother know about her homosexual inclinations, she would leave men to her mother; thus, she would overcome the mother–daughter rivalry by avoiding any antagonism, or as Freud said, she decided to "retire in favor of her mother"(p. 158), a point to which I will return.

Her father's dislike of her homosexuality reinforced the success of the strategy—Sidonie could both regain her mother's love and take revenge on her father. She wanted the father to know because her behavior followed a retaliatory principle. In effect, according to Freud (1920), she thought: "Since you have betrayed me, you must put up with my betraying you" (p. 159). The broken promise, however, got reenacted in the transference. Unhappily, Freud missed the opportunity of an analytic intervention that would have allowed the young woman to abandon a purely egoic discourse and engage with her unconscious desire. This moment is described as one of "positive transference" (p. 164) and relates to a period in the treatment at which Sidonie had a series of dreams of getting cured, longing for husband and children. Freud did not believe these dreams, declaring them "false or hypocritical." He concluded that Sidonie "intended to deceive me as she habitually deceived her father" (p. 165).

This fits with Freud's (1920) general description of Sidonie. Freud had painted her as someone who was "full of deceitfulness," who "disdained no means of deception, no excuses, and no lies" to get what she wanted (p. 148). While he was quite suspicious of her, the deceiving dreams first had positive elements; he evokes these with a dose of skepticism: "Beside the intention to mislead me, the dreams partly expressed the wish to gain my favor; they were also an attempt to gain my interest and my good opinion—perhaps in order to disappoint me all the more thoroughly later on" (p. 165). Sidonie's lying dreams had a purpose, not only to deceive him just as she deceived her father, but also to make a promise to Freud that she knew she was going to break. This is how she would reenact her own drama of frustration in the transference. No doubt Freud felt wronged and imaginarily wounded. He reacted strongly to the lies, which he saw as a provocation that precipitated the termination of the treatment. What Freud missed in this situation is that the unconscious usually lies to tell a truth. Sidonie's unconscious had lied to expose the truth of the promise that the father could not fulfill. The main issue in this case was not the object (whether a baby, a husband, or a cure) as much as the promise. Freud's decoding of this message would have allowed for the constitution of a demand of analysis in what up to then was just a preliminary stage. Indeed, Freud exposed the deception, but he missed its symbolic value as a message; therefore, he fell as well into the trap, he "fell through the father's fault" (p. 162). If Sidonie was staging an acting out for Freud, she was providing her analyst with a unique belvedere onto her object cause of desire because, as we have seen, the acting out as such is a scene that makes the object *a* appear. Freud was not aware that in his position as analyst he was actually playing the role of object cause of desire. He simply fulfilled the destiny of the object *a*, which is to fall: "The *a*, the object, falls. That fall is primal. The diversity of forms taken by that object of the fall ought to be related to the manner in which the desire of the Other is apprehended by the subject" (Lacan, 1990, p. 85).

"DADDY, I HAVE HAD TO KILL YOU"

For Lacan (2006), there is no doubt: Here, Freud makes a mistake, he "errs when he regards himself as the object aimed at in reality by the negative transference" (p. 534). The broken promise was related to an object supposed to guarantee the movement from the mother to the father. Her intention was not to betray her father but to denounce the deception that Sidonie had experienced. Freud had missed a chance to truly start the analysis when he ended it. "What a pity it had to be broken off!" was the conclusion of Lou Andreas-Salomé after reading the case (Pfeiffer, 1972, p. 102). She told Freud: "Behind the negative transference to you there lay hidden no doubt the original positive transference to the father. Would not this original basis come to light eventually in the acting out of the negative transference?" (p. 102). Her critique went to the heart of the matter: Freud blamed everything on negative transference, making the superficial assumption that it was all a "virile protest." This gesture was in fact more Adlerian than Freudian. Andreas-Salomé was openly skeptical about the hypothesis that the young woman became homosexual and was ready to commit suicide to take revenge on the father. This is, however, how Jones (1955) read the case, arguing that her homosexuality was to take revenge on her father, and that the suicide attempt was motivated by an identification with the father as the lost object (p. 279).

Sidonie's negative transference was constituted by her hate for masculinity, which was necessary to assume her sexual identity. If Freud (1920) had been able to tolerate the moment of negative transference and, instead of breaking off the treatment, had taken the broken promise as a signifier of the Other, he could have turned the tables in the transference. Then, by working around the unkept promise implied by the "lying" dreams, he could have engaged the young woman in her desire, thus transforming an imaginary wound into a necessary lack. If, as Lacan (2004, p. 152) argues, Sidonie was telling the truth from the veiled position of a lie, she was already then negotiating castration by talking from a position of semblance, of make-believe.

Let us take a last look at Freud's theory that at the end of the latency phase the promise of a penis substitute is expected from a man who will always disappoint the girl, never fulfilling the promise. This is because he is no other than the father, whose exclusion is always demanded by the laws of exogamy. Taking a Freudo-Lacanian look at the logic of female homosexuality, Gérard Pommier (2000) offers a genealogy that slightly differs from Freud's but that applies handsomely to Sidonie's case. Pommier links female homosexuality with castration anxiety and its denial. His reconstructed logic goes as follows: The father refuses to give the penis to his daughter and has to physically reject her; otherwise, he would commit incest and cease being a father. This rejection may be greeted by violence and rebellion, which is often seen in the period preceding female homosexuality. Only love will be able to appease the castration anxiety thus unleashed and replace penis envy. Hence, the daughter will love a woman like a man, and she will acquire a penis vicariously. Female homosexual love, according to Pommier, would stem from a fantasy of masculinization. Sexuality would then turn phallic by focusing on the clitoris.

For all its clarity, Pommier's (2000) systematization does not fully explain Sidonie's sexuality. Sidonie comes across as someone who has rejected sexuality altogether—she rejects her own femininity and repudiates masculinity while playing the part of the devoted knight toward her baroness. In her biography, a photograph shows her in male period costume that makes her look like an 18th-century roué, which seems to indicate that, for her, femininity was a transgressive virile disguise. Indeed, Sidonie had a hard time becoming a woman. Freud (1920) confirmed that she had rejected the sexual advances of a lesbian of her age and generally "had a physical revulsion to the idea of sexual intercourse" (p. 153). According to the biography, during her life, Sidonie experienced profound aversion to intimate sexual contact with male and female lovers alike (Rieder & Voigt, 2003). Sidonie's disgust toward sex reminds us of classical hysteria. The young woman assumed in her behavior toward her love object "the masculine part" (Freud, 1920, p. 154) and "could not conceive of another way to be in love" (p. 153) with a mother. Was the young woman wondering, "What is a woman?" or more pointedly, "What am I for my mother?"

It is in this context that Marcianne Blévis (2004) paid attention to the excessive love that Sidonie's mother had for her sons and the detestation that she flaunted toward her daughter, an attitude that she kept even on her deathbed. "I find my mother so beautiful that I will do anything for her, but she only loves my brothers," Sidonie recalled telling Freud (Rieder & Voigt, 2003, p. 62). Blévis describes the delirious jealousy of Sidonie's mother. This jealousy determined and constituted the homosexuality linking mother and daughter.

The narrative biography documents many painful instances of rejection. On one particularly humiliating occasion, which happened the year before the treatment with Freud, Sidonie and her mother were staying at a health spa, a place that Emma Scillag visited frequently to cure her nervous problems, such as anxieties and fears. Away from her husband, Emma seemed much happier, enjoying the male attention she commanded and behaving, to Sidonie's embarrassment, as if she were not a married woman. When one of her admirers, struck by Sidonie's beauty, congratulated Emma Scillag for having such a pretty daughter, the mother responded to the compliment by pretending that Sidonie was not her daughter (Rieder & Voigt, 2003, p. 63). Denying that she had a 17-year old daughter, the mother tried to appear younger. The real motivation was her wish to disavow that her daughter could be beautiful and thus be a potential rival. The daughter understood the message:

> Sidonie's pain was so intense that she ran away in tears to her room, and spent the next days alone in the forest to avoid the sight of such a horrible woman that had a real hatred of everything that was feminine. Every woman was a contender, an adversary, even her daughter. (p. 63)

It was the mother's wish to appear as the only desirable beauty that led to a deterioration of Sidonie's sexuality. Sidonie's symptoms can be interpreted as an attempt to repress maternal jouissance in the hope of salvaging her subjective and sexual identity from the mother's jealousy.

Sidonie's serene avoidance of the pleasures of the flesh calls up the figure of the angel. The angel's identity is not based on sex. The angel is an asexual creature, outside time, and hence immortal. As a messenger, the angel invokes the annunciation of something. Lacan (1998b) suggested that this figure helps us visualize the gap between the Symbolic and the Real, between the boundary of the sexual symbolic body and the real of the flesh (pp. 8–9). If we were to assign gender to angels, the gender of choice would be feminine, with a maternal touch. Angels are supposed to be in a state of perpetual bliss, a bliss that leaves nothing to be desired. Like a devoted mother, angels do not desire; they render a service—they love.

When Freud (1920) tried to justify his having interrupted the treatment, he adduced the fact that he had become aware that Sidonie "transferred to [him] the sweeping repudiation of men which had dominated her ever since the disappointment she has suffered from her father" (p. 164). This is the repudiation of masculinity that has triggered the interest of feminists and queer theorists. Lacan (2006) maintains that observation shows that female homosexuality "is oriented by a disappointment that strengthens the axis of the demand for love" (p. 583). Over and over again, Freud insisted that for the girl the threat of castration is experienced as a fear of loss of love.

Why is love so important for the female homosexual? It is that, according to Lacan's (1998b) sexuation formulas, women are positioned as "not-all," which gives them a different relation to the phallus. To make full sense of the case, one needs to think in terms of Lacan's formulas of sexuation, a grid that he invented to account for how a subject may live as a man or as a woman given that there is a disconnection between men and women: "the impossibility of inscribing the sexual relation between two bodies of different sexes" (p. 120). This is a grid I bring to bear on my clinical cases in the following chapters. The formulas of sexuation are Lacan's attempt

| $\exists x$ | $\overline{\Phi x}$ | $\overline{\exists x}$ | $\overline{\Phi x}$ |
| $\forall x$ | Φx | $\overline{\forall x}$ | Φx |

Figure 6.1 Lacan's masculine and feminine modalities.

at formalizing sexual realizations for men and women by using a model derived from formal logic. Lacan presented his formulas of sexuation in their most accomplished form in Seminar XX. I reproduce the general scheme but return to it in the next chapters. It is important to remember that what Lacan calls the "male side" and "female side" are not determined by biology but by the logic of unconscious investments, to the point that, for instance, a man, biologically speaking, can nevertheless inscribe himself on the female side (see Figure 6.1).

Using the symbols of formal logic, Lacan (1998b) inscribes a masculine modality (phallic jouissance) on one side and a feminine modality on the other (Other jouissance). The formulas contain the symbols $\forall$ (the universal quantifier), $\exists$ (existential quantifier), Φ (phallus). On the upper left side of the table, we have $\exists X \, \overline{\Phi X}$. "There exists at least one that is not submitted to the phallic function." On the lower left, there appears the formula $\forall X \, \Phi X$, that reads, "All are subject to the law of castration." On the female side, the upper right line reads: "No X exists which is not determined by the phallic function." In other words, castration is an absolute that functions for all. On the lower line, there is a negation marked by the barring of the universal quantifier, which is quite inconceivable from the perspective of formal logic $\overline{\forall X} \, \Phi X$. Lacan proposed that it be read as "not-whole," woman is not wholly subjected to the phallus. On this side, there is no exception that could serve as the basis for a set of women (therefore there is no universal of women).

We can then reopen the question of femininity as neither sex nor gender but from the pole of jouissance. Whereas for Freud there is only one libido (masculine), Lacan took a very important step forward in the debate around sexual difference when in 1972 he proposed a division based on two forms of being, masculine and feminine, corresponding to two forms of jouissance: phallic and Other. Lacan located phallic jouissance on the male side and gave it the force of necessity (All men), which relies on the exclusion of one man, the unlawful or impossible jouissance of the primal father. In this model of sexual division, we encounter two positions: one, that of the phallic one ("man") who is limited by the father exempted from castration (the exception to the phallic rule that provides its support), and on the other side the unlimited jouissance of a woman who is "not all" subjected to the phallic constraints.

To go further, we will see that the female side of his sexuation graph is elaborated on the basis of contingency: It is possible and conditional. The feminine side is not all determined by this phallic logic. Femininity is where the Other jouissance comes into being. "Man" and "woman" are therefore signifiers of imprecise meaning, and they stand for sexed positions relative to a phallic premise. Initially, the child ignores sexual difference. Only by undergoing the castration complex will the child note the existence of sexual difference.

However, to avoid confusion, we need first to explore the notion of jouissance to better understand the psychoanalytic concept of the phallus, a phallus seen not as an obstacle to femininity but as the very condition of sexual differentiation. According to Freud (1905) and Lacan (1993, 1998b), there is no signifier that defines the female sex since only one libido animates both men and women and splits them according to different modes of satisfaction. Thus, we have to reexamine the issue in terms of Lacan's (1992) concept of jouissance.

Jouissance is a word that does not translate easily into English. Lacan himself suggested a combination of "enjoyment" and "lust." Jouissance is also equivocal in French. Indeed, jouissance is a form of enjoyment not necessarily accompanied by pleasure or joy. Often, in the experience of jouissance, pain and pleasure are indistinguishable. Jouissance conveys the enjoyment of an object, but an enjoyment not simply yielding advantageous returns or results; rather, it produces not a gratifying surplus benefit but a violent, climactic bliss closer to loss, death, fragmentation, and the disruptive rapture experienced when transgressing limits. This is made explicit in a definition given by Lacan (1966/1967):

> What I call jouissance—in the sense which the body experiences itself—is always in the nature of tension, in the nature of a forcing, of a spending, even of an exploit. Unquestionably, there is jouissance at the level at which pain begins to appear, and we know that it is only at this level of pain that a whole dimension of the organism, which would otherwise remain veiled, can be experienced. (p. 60; see also Braunstein, 1992/2005)

It is in connection with jouissance that Lacan's sexuation formulas show the universal character of castration. To pose the existence of the universality of castration, Lacan took a mythical character from the Freudian literature—the father of the primal horde as presented in "Totem and Taboo" (Freud, 1912–1913). This mythical father of the primal horde represents a father not subjected to castration, a despotic leader who enjoys all the women and offers them an absolute jouissance. There is thus a universal of men, the group of all men subjected to castration and one exception, the fantasy of one man who has access to a jouissance that is absolute and inaccessible, one man who is not subjected to castration. This universal allows for the general expression "man."

On the other hand, "Woman" (*la femme*) cannot have a universal value. It is in this sense that Lacan would say that "the" woman does not exist. Lacan's sexuation formulas assign two places for sexuation, eliminating a multiplicity of choices of positions: The phallus organizes a distribution on either side of the formulas in a way that does not depend on the possession of an organ. Since the phallus is not an organ but a symbol, it has astonishing plasticity. This plasticity allows for the diverse identificatory assignation of sexes according to various cultures. The theory of the phallic jouissance and the Other jouissance reiterates that the sexuation formulas can grant only two modalities of jouissance.

Here, we see that women, because of their positioning as not all, have a different rapport to the phallus. On their side, there is no exception founding the universal (the law is absolute because there is no one who is not submitted to the law of castration). Since the female side knows no universal, there is no universal signifier of femininity (the Woman does not exist), thus there is no primal mother who can indicate a feminine trait valid for all women.

Let us apply to Sidonie's case the teachings of Lacan's formulas. Sidonie wanted to find in her father's gaze the love that would compensate for the privation of the phallus. As we have witnessed, her access to femininity was not easy: Not only did her father betray her, but also her mother prevented her from being the object of male attention since she had to "retire" and let her mother enjoy men exclusively. Here, we see that it is the mother who is in the position of exception. Sidonie's mother was in the place of an x that did not fall under the law of castration. Sidonie rejected her femininity as a way of refusing her mother as an exception (or $\exists X \overline{\Phi X}$). This formula implies that there exists at least one x that is not submitted to the phallic function; it is the exception that sustains the universal of $\forall X \, \Phi X$ that is the male norm that entails for all men to be submitted to the phallic function by way of castration. Sidonie sacrificed her "normal" femininity and chose an angelic femininity. Thus, we can say that Sidonie made a semblance of homosexuality, thereby negotiating her castration and reducing love to being just its declaration.

We have seen how the frustration caused by broken promises made Dora and Sidonie move to the level of demand and how demand turned into an obstacle on their path toward assuming a sexual positioning. The psychodynamics of demand that we have explored in this chapter will appear as crucial in the clinic of transsexualism. All sex changes are formulated as requests that need to be analyzed first at the level of demand. If demand is ultimately a demand for love, extreme caution should be exercised because no object can fulfill it. Lacan's (1998b) grid of sexuation and his conception of love as *sinthomatic* formation, that is, as supplement for the lack of rapport between the sexes, will have to be explored in its dialectical tension with Judith Butler's (1990) concept of performativity. Both will prove relevant with analysis of concrete cases in the next chapters.

In the next chapter, I continue discussing Judith Butler's thesis about gender as performance but with the objective of testing her claims in a case of gender change that became a cause célèbre.

Chapter 7

Boy girl boy

Joan/John, Bruce/Brenda, or David Reimer was born a twin baby boy (XY chromosomes). At 7 months, he had his penis severely burned during a relatively risk-free circumcision to treat a phimosis, a condition in which the foreskin narrows at the tip, eventually preventing urination. Apparently, the surgeon used a new machine (an electrocautery knife) with which he was not familiar and burned away most of the penis. The damage was so severe that it could not be repaired surgically. The prognosis given by the doctors was grim. They predicted that baby Bruce "will be unable to live a normal sexual life from the time of adolescence: that he will be unable to consummate marriage or have normal heterosexual relations, in that he will have to recognize that he is incomplete, physically defective, and that he must live apart" (Colapinto, 2000, p. 16).

Just months later, the anguished parents happened by chance to see a television program in which Dr. John Money was discussing sex reassignment surgery. Almost at the end of the show, someone asked a question about treatment options for intersex babies, whom Money had called earlier in the program "newborns with unfinished genitals." Money explained with great optimism that through surgery and hormone treatments one can veer a baby toward whichever sex seemed best, so that the child would be raised happily in that sex. The twin's parents wrote to him immediately. Money answered promptly and invited them to come to Johns Hopkins University.

Money was the chief of the John Money Gender Identity Institute and believed that children were gender neutral at birth—gender identity depended exclusively on socialization and "correct"-looking genitalia. Money was also the person who had coined the term *gender identity* and had a reputation as a leading specialist on the psychological repercussions of ambiguous genitalia while making headlines for his pioneering work at his John Hopkins clinic for transsexual sex reassignment. He recommended that baby Bruce be raised as a girl that they would call "Brenda." The parents agreed. In July 1967, at age 22 months, Bruce had both testicles removed at Johns Hopkins by surgeon Dr. Howard Jones, the cofounder of

Money's clinic. This new surgery started the process for feminization of Brenda that would eventually lead to the creation of an artificial vagina.

ABLATIO PENIS: NORMAL MALE INFANT SEX REASSIGNED AS A GIRL

In 1975, Money published an article documenting the amazing progress of a normal male child who was reassigned as female and brought up as a girl, who was known in the literature as John/Joan. The case provided proof that children were psychosexually neutral at birth, and that the development of stable gender identity depended on socialization reinforced by the appearance of anatomy, even when the "normal-looking" appearance was achieved by hormones and surgery. Money wrote that at 9 years old, this child had "differentiated a female gender identity in marked contrast to the male gender identity of her [identical twin] brother." Money gave a very good prognosis for this reassignment: "The twin can expect to be feminine in erotic expression and sexual life. Maintained on estrogen therapy, she will have normal feminine physique and a sexually attractive appearance. She will be able to establish motherhood by adoption" (p. 65). Bruce/Brenda (John/Joan) was the ideal subject to test Money's ideas because he had an identical twin. His brother provided an ideal control case—a perfect genetic double with an intact penis who was raised as a male. Money had found the ultimate subject to prove that conditioning combined with hormones and surgically reconstructed genitals, and not biology, determined sexual identity. Despite Money's optimism, between the ages of 9 and 11, the child started to feel that there was something inexplicably odd with her:

> There were little things from early on. I began to see how different I felt and was, from what I was supposed to be. But I didn't know what it meant. I thought I was a freak or something. ... I looked at myself and said I don't like this type of clothing, I don't like the types of toys I was always being given, I like hanging around with the guys and climbing trees and stuff like that and girls don't like any of that stuff. I looked in the mirror and see my shoulders are so wide, I mean there is nothing feminine about me. I'm skinny, but other than that, nothing. But that is how I figured it out but I didn't want to admit it, I figured I didn't want to wind up opening a can of worms. (Diamond & Sigmundson, 1997, pp. 299–300)

This type of realization, however persistent, lacked the certainty often heard in transgender people. There was no internal truth in contradiction with the body. Although the young Reimer was aware that he felt different, he remained uncertain about what made him feel that way. He did not have either a conviction or any alternative explanation about himself. The truth was repressed, and he just kept on entertaining doubts: "I didn't want to admit it, I figured I didn't want to wind up opening a can of worms" (Diamond & Sigmundson, 1997, p. 300).

Although Money described the girl in the study as having many "tomboyish" behavioral traits, he contended that a female gender identity had been differentiated. Thus, he maintained his thesis that gender identity is not sufficiently differentiated at birth, and that a genetic male could be successfully raised as a girl (see Bradley et al., 1998). For Money (Money & Tucker, 1975), the favorable evolution of the reassigned girl was a milestone:

> Although this girl is not yet a woman, her record to date offers convincing evidence that the gender identity gate is open at birth for a normal child no less than for one born with unfinished sex organs or one who was prenatally over or underexposed to androgen, and that it stays open at least for something over a year after birth. (p. 98)

The prognosis for the sex reassignment was auguring a well-adjusted future: "The girl's subsequent history proves how well all three of them [parents and child] succeeded in adjusting to that decision" (p. 95).

OPENING AND CLOSING THE GENDER GATE

Despite Money's optimistic claims, the experiment did not go smoothly. Brenda was not just "tomboyish," she adamantly refused to do "feminine" things: She did not like her dresses, sat with legs opened, played with her brother's toys, got into physical fights with boys, wanted to shave like dad, hated makeup, and preferred to urinate standing, a habit that horrified the girls at school, who barred Brenda from the girls' bathrooms. (Brenda sneaked out from school to a back alley to urinate; she later reported this was one of the many humiliating experiences she went through during her childhood.) Very occasionally, Brenda would behave in a manner that her mother described as "feminine," keeping herself "so neat and tidy as she can be when she wants to be" (Money & Ehrhardt, 1972/1996b, p. 119).

Brenda was taken periodically to Money's Gender Identity Institute to monitor her adaptation to being a girl. When Money mentioned that she was getting old enough to have a vagina constructed, she ran out of the room screaming. Money showed Brenda pictures of vaginas and women during childbirth in the hope that it would inspire her to become a "normal girl." Money went as far as forcing the twins to perform mock coital exercises with one another, on command (Colapinto, 2000, p. 87). The children were so scared and confused that they did not dare tell their parents about it.

When Brenda reached the age to have a vagina surgically constructed, she rebelled. On her last visit to Money in Baltimore at age 13, a male-to-female transsexual talked to her to persuade her of the advantages of having a vagina surgically constructed. She became very upset and ran away from the hospital. After this episode, Brenda threatened to commit suicide if forced to make another trip to Baltimore to see Money. And, in spite of the fact that the parents had been instructed never to tell her about what that had actually happened, Brenda's father broke down and eventually told the truth. "I was relieved." Brenda/David recalled. "Suddenly it all made sense why I felt the way I did. I wasn't some sort of weirdo. I wasn't crazy." After hearing the unbelievable events, the boy who was raised as a girl asked only one question to his father: "What was my name?"(Colapinto, 2000, p. 180).

Almost immediately, Reimer decided to revert to her/his birth sex. The first gesture was an act of nomination: She did not want to go back to the name Bruce, which she considered "a name for 'geeks and nerds.'" She liked Joe "because it had no pretensions; it was a name for Everyman" but finally chose David after the biblical king and giant slayer because "it reminded me of the guy with the odds stacked against him" and commented that David was "the guy who was facing up to a giant eight feet tall. It reminded me of courage" (Colapinto, 2000, p. 182). The final choice between "Joe, the Everyman" (the universal, all men) and David was left to the parents. They decided on David and thus, under that name, he began his life again as a male.[1]

In his transition back to male, David Reimer changed the hormonal treatment from estrogen to testosterone. The breasts grown with female hormone pills were surgically removed, and something that medical records called a "phallus" was constructed. David's "normalizing" wish was to get married to a woman who already had children because, above all, he wanted to be a father: "I could be a good husband if I was given a chance; I think I could be a good father if I was given a chance" (Colapinto, 2000, p. 191).

FEMALE BY DEFAULT

In a saga with protagonists who have surnames that sound like works of fiction, Money's work was closely monitored by another research team, led by another psychologist, Milton Diamond, who believed in an innate basis for gender. Diamond got in touch with Dr. Keith Sigmundson, who was in charge of Brenda's psychiatric care in her Canadian hometown, and

---

[1] David's decision to revert back to male changed the way the case was known: Now, it is often referred to as the John/Joan/John case to better describe the movement between genders.

was aware that the experiment was not working. Diamond believed that prebirth factors prevail over culture, that learning and environment have little effect on gender in humans. For Diamond, gender identity is present virtually from conception. To prove his point, in 1997 Diamond published a denunciation of the case in a scientific journal (Diamond & Sigmundson, 1997). At that time, the identity of the patient was not revealed. David only decided to reveal his identity when Colapinto's best-selling book was published 3 years later.

Until the case was denounced as a failure, it set a precedent for sex reassignment as the standard treatment for thousands of newborns with similarly injured, or irregular, genitals. Money's theories of gender identity are still at the center of current debates on how to respond best to intersex. Money's emphasis on a combination of rearing and appropriate genital appearance has meant that most intersex babies would undergo "normalizing" surgeries and hormone treatments when the newborn's penis was deemed small or the clitoris was considered too long.[2] This quotation illustrates the prevailing direction in treatment of intersex babies during what Alice Domurat Dreger (1999) called "the age of surgery" (p. 11):

> The choice of gender should be based on the infant's anatomy. ... Often it is wiser to rear a genetic male as a female. It is relatively easy to create a vagina if one is absent, but it is not possible to create a really satisfactory penis if the phallus is absent or rudimentary. Only those males with a phallus of adequate size which will respond to testosterone at adolescence should be considered for male rearing. Otherwise, the baby should be reared as a female. (Donahoe & Hendren, 1976, p. 369)

Money's recommendation that the Reimers's son would be surgically sex reassigned and raised as a girl was in accordance with the standard pediatric procedures for intersex babies since the 1950s, when the availability of hormones and better surgery made the body malleable. With the Joan/John case, Money (1975) was reassigning as female an "entirely normal male" who was apparently giving indications of being "feminine in erotic expression and sexual life" and was even able to "have normal feminine physique and a sexually attractive appearance" (p. 65). This case was seen as a triumph for the power of sex change technologies and of the advancement of science; it also questioned notions of sexual difference. In 1973, the magazine *Time* (January 8, 1973) ran an article on the Joan/John story,

---

[2] For a discussion on the controversial practices of sex reassignment for people with ambiguous genitalia, see the videotapes *Redefining Sex* and *The Child With an Intersex Condition: Total Patient Care* (sometimes screened under the name *First Do No Harm*), both published by the Intersex Society of North America (http://www.isna.org/). Also see Fausto-Sterling (1999, pp. 45–77). For an illuminating account of intersex cases and their impact on medical knowledge and technology, see Alice Domurat Dreger (1998).

and the report is a good example of how the case was being portrayed in the media.

> This dramatic case ... provides strong support ... that conventional patterns of masculine and feminine behavior can be altered. It also casts doubt on the theory that major sex differences, psychological as well as anatomical, are immutably set by the genes at conception. (Colapinto, 2000, p. 69)

The case was promising proof of gender as a social construct and therefore potentially malleable—plastic at both a behavioral and glandular level. The feminists picked up on it, and this case became a touchstone for the feminist movement in the 1970s, when it was cited as living proof that the gender gap is purely a result of the cultural environment. "Even Kate Millet cited the case in making the argument that biology is not destiny," observed Butler (2004, p. 61). Indeed, Kate Millett (1970) quoted Money's articles as scientific proof that the differences between men and women reflect not biological imperatives but societal expectations and prejudices. Butler remarked that Suzanne Kessler coauthored several essays with Money in favor of the social constructivist thesis only to later disavow her alliance and attack Money harshly after the news about the John/Joan case was made public (see Kessler, 1998).

THE GENE PULL

Such was the failure of this fantastic case that it has become the ultimate example used as evidence against Money's (1961b) notion that "erotic outlook and orientation is an autonomous psychological phenomenon independent of genes and hormones, and moreover, a permanent and ineradicable one as well" (p. 1397). The old debate of nature versus nurture was once more revived. Money's failed experiment fueled the controversy about intersexual surgery. Diamond & Sigmundson (1997) claimed that the John/Joan case failed partly because sexual orientation is prenatally organized or at least predisposed. David's case seemed to prove that any baby born with the Y chromosome—the most overt mark of a male—is likely to have been affected by male hormones in the womb. Prenatal exposure to hormones, Diamond & Sigmundson (1997) contended, determined the brain's "psychosexual bias" in either a masculine or feminine direction. Cheryl Chase, the founder of the Intersex Society of North America (ISNA), declared that "Diamond's recommendations [were] not going to help." "Instead, clinicians who treat intersex children will start assigning more of them as males, and doing a different sort of horrible intervention," she argued, for example, by trying to construct a phallus from a small amount of tissue. "They can't conceive of leaving someone alone," Chase complained (Angier, 1997).

The intersex movement advocates a delay of surgery in the case of babies born with ambiguous genitalia, that is, babies whose genitals challenge what is considered normal. This condition results from chromosomal and hormonal abnormalities and occurs once in every 1,000 births. The majority of such infants are designated female, largely because, as discussed, it is considered surgically easier to turn ambiguous genitals into a vagina than into a penis. The intersex movement claims that babies should not receive an operation before they can talk, as if only access to speech would ratify sexuality.

PRENATAL OR POSTNATAL GENDER

In 1997, Milton Diamond denounced the failure of John Money's famous sex reassignment case, the John/Joan/John case. This case study has become the most powerful example supporting the hypothesis of an innate gender identity. The outcome of the controversy is profoundly paradoxical since the very case used by John Money to prove his theories of gender fluidity ended up supplying the strongest evidence against them. The case, however, is not a perfect experimental test of innateness since the baby was raised as a boy for his first 17 months of life; besides, the parents chose not to move to another town, and neighbors were aware of the child's male past.

To better approach Money's general ideology, and with it that of sex change therapy, we need to turn our attention to an article published just a few years before the scandal in which Money reported the results of a careful study of bisexuality. He claimed that bisexuality had great importance and underpinned the gender debate in the guise of androgyny, especially in light of the then-recent neurobiological discoveries of the brain's prenatal or neonatal bipotentiality. Money (1990) contended that even though the male–female dimorphism of the hypothalamus had been recognized, its determinants and stages of differentiation, both prenatal and postnatal, remained to be fully ascertained.

Today, we have learned that the effects of sex hormones on brain organization occur so early in life that the uterine environment acts differently on the brains of boys and girls. Throughout life, testosterone and estrogen remain essential for maintaining aspects of sex-specific differences in the adult human brain. For example, an article (Hulshoff Pol, Cohen-Kettenis et al., 2006) with the suggestive title, "Changing Your Sex Changes Your Brain: Influences of Testosterone and Estrogen on Adult Human Brain Structure," seemed to show that sex hormones not only are involved in the formation of reproductive organs but also induce sexually dimorphic brain development and organization. It suggested that cross-sex hormone administration to transsexuals affects brain morphology in young adulthood, and that gonadal hormones change the brain volume of young adult transsexuals. The findings indicated that, throughout life, gonadal hormones remain essential for maintaining aspects of sex-specific differences in the human brain.[3]

There is evidence suggesting that some brain regions are structurally different in women and men and may vary in morphology between homosexual men and heterosexual men. This allegedly produces sex differences in brain structure and organization (LeVay, 1991a), but the process of sexual differentiation of the human brain has not been fully elucidated (Arnold et al., 2004; Dalery & de Villard, 1981). Despite many studies conducted to determine how hormones act on human brains to produce the sex differences reported in behavior or cognitive patterns, both genetic and hormonal mechanisms remain not fully accounted for (Skuse, 2006). In this regard, Money's questions are still relevant.

SEX STEMS FROM THE ABSENCE OF TRUE HARMONY BETWEEN MEN AND WOMEN

In his 1990 piece, "Androgyne Becomes Bisexual in Sexological Theory: Plato to Freud and Neuroscience," Money started a discussion on bisexuality by returning to the work on hermaphroditism with which he had started his career. In that context, he mentioned Plato's myth of "the conjunction of male and female in the primordial androgyne" (p. 392). Money contended that the myth of the primordial androgyne had existed since time immemorial in oral tradition and had even found its way into the book of Genesis, "where it is written that man and woman were made in God's own image—two people united as one, in other words" (p. 392). Money alluded to Parmenides' idea that there was a male and a female generative principle, and that differences in their proportions accounted for variations in degree of masculinity, femininity, or androgyny.

For a doctor who used surgery and hormone treatments so readily, it is surprising to see that in that piece Money's attention was focused on the writings of Plato, in particular the answer given by Aristophanes to the question "What is love?" in the *Symposium*. According to Aristophanes' myth, the original human race was made up of people who had a double back, four hands, and an equal number of legs. These creatures had one head but two faces, thus four ears and two organs for reproduction.

---

[3] For a review of most recent studies providing evidence of how androgens produced in fetal or neonatal life act on the brain to induce sex differences in neural structure and cognitive functions, see Knickmeyer and Baron-Cohen (2006).

One would find three types of pairs, male-male, female-female, and male-female. Their strength made them so formidable that the gods became jealous. To put an end to their insolence, Zeus decided to cut them in half. So, to this day, we are left wandering, in search of our missing half to return to our original nature as double beings. The story gives a mythical dimension, albeit ironically (Aristophanes' whimsy is praised in the *Symposium*), to the old notion that love means the wish to return to an archaic state of unity that would heal all the wounds previously suffered. When we look for the perfect "other half" whom we can never find, love arrives always too early or too late—it is either too much or not enough. Alas, it seems that there is always something that does not work, as if the other half is never able to re-create the original whole. According to Aristophanes' myth, sexual generation is an accidental by-product of the absence of a harmonious relation between men and women, who in their longing for a lost unity seek each other to recapture the previous state of androgyne completeness rather than reduplicate their divided selves in their children.

Money notes that Aristophanes' characterization of love entails an experience of fusion (the dream of finding the part that would complete us). In the experience of falling in love, one feels the pull of mutual attraction as if, indeed, two halves wanted to be joined. To illustrate this idea, Money refers to Aristophanes' description of the moment when one half meets the other:

> [One] is overwhelmed, to an amazing extent, with affection, concern and love. The two do not want to spend any time apart from each other. These are people who live out whole lifetimes together, but still couldn't say what it is they want from each other. I mean, no one can think that it's just sexual intercourse they want, and that this is the reason why they find such joy in each other's company and attach such importance to this. It's clear that each of them has some wish in his mind that he can't articulate; instead, like an oracle, he half-grasps what he wants and obscurely hints at it. (Plato, Gill (Ed.) 1999, p. 25)

Money's view of an androgynous sexual order ruled by complementarities faces an impasse: the impossibility of creating the One for which love longs. Money's endorsement of the myth of finding a perfect other half betrays his sentimentalism and suggests a romantic longing for fusion that seems to be at the root of his scientific investigations and aligns him with Eugen Steinach. Money's logic betrays the essentialist ideology that guided his manipulations of sex and gender: From the manipulations on the anatomies of docile guinea pigs to the militant quest for another sexual body, a single vector seems to characterize the utopia of sexual transformation.

Money used medical technology to modify sex and affect gender, but his experiments revealed a belief in gender roles that are not far from those guiding Steinach's "cures" of homosexuality by transplantation of testicles as they are all based on rigid gender roles and a dream of complementarity. Money enthusiastically praised what he described as the moral, erotic, biological, and ethnological bipotential principle of androgyny, a principle that he claimed had been long known in sexological science as bisexuality. Fliess could then logically appear as Money's predecessor. Their concept of bisexuality presupposes two symmetrical halves, like those in Aristophanes' description. This supposition of complementarity permitted them to claim that a better understanding of bisexuality would explain homosexuality and heterosexuality, as if they were reciprocally related. From a Lacanian point of view, homosexuality and heterosexuality are not the two sides of the same coin. Bisexuality can never be the Rosetta stone for sexuality, as Money and Fliess hoped, because bisexuality is not a developmental stage. Human sexuality is based on a lack of a sexual rapport, which means a lack of relation, a lack of proportion. Sexual division is asymmetric. Masculine and feminine positions are predicated on contradictory systems; they follow dissymmetrical logics that are two ways of exemplifying how language fails to signify sex. Money's (1990) and Fliess's (1918, 1923) accounts are only satisfactory insofar as they describe the phallic side of sexuation. We shall see that one has to take into account both sides to gain a more comprehensive perspective. To understand sexual choice, we need to take into account the drive, identification, and object choice.

Money's intersex reassignments were based on two basic postulates: The first was that individuals are psychosexually neutral at birth and the second that healthy psychosexual development is intimately related to the appearance of the genitals—both ideas can be traced to early theories of bisexuality. The malleability of gender could be built on a physical neutral substratum (bisexuality), but the social construction required an anatomically correct body to succeed. Since David was born "normal," that is, not intersex, Diamond noted the irony that the John/Joan case failed to demonstrate what it was designed to prove: a universal theory of psychosexual development (Diamond & Sigmundson, 1997, pp. 299–300; see also Fausto-Sterling, 1999, pp. 66–77). Money claimed that nurture defined sexual identity, nevertheless, here nature reasserted itself. How else to explain Brenda's habit of urinating in a standing position despite its costly social consequences? This behavior displays the contradiction between what she identified with and what she was supposed to be. Money's method reshaped the body to make it correspond to a gendered sexual identity; it artificially naturalized the body to make it fit into prescribed gender norms.

A MAN BORN MAN, CASTRATED, FEMINIZED, MASCULINIZED

When Natalie Angier wrote in the *New York Times* (1997) about how psychologist Diamond help topple Money's theory, she said that David's story had the "force of allegory." "But which force was that? And is this an allegory with closure?" inquired Judith Butler (2004) in *Undoing Gender* (p. 62). In a piece titled "Doing Justice to Someone" (pp. 57–74), Butler summarized David's story, while she tried awkwardly to make sense of the moral of a case that disproved her contentions about gender as performative. She noted that David saw himself as "a man born a man, castrated by the medical establishment, feminized by the psychiatric world, and then enabled to return to who he is" (p. 65). Butler pointed out an interesting paradox: "But in order to return to who he is he requires—and wants, and gets—a subjection to hormones and surgery. He allegorizes transsexuality in order to achieve a sense of naturalness" (p. 65). However, Butler omitted the fact that David's wish to "trans" back to male was not simply a wish to change sex but to undo the violent transformations that medical technologies had done to him. The domino effect first was triggered by a faulty medical intervention that attacked the materiality of his body, a materiality at odds with Butler's insistence on the malleability of performance.

Butler observed that the Money Gender Identity Institute enlisted a male-to-female transsexual whose task was to explain to Brenda the virtues of having a vagina "in the name of normalization." At the same time, Diamond's team applauded David's transformation back to male, a sex change achieved through hormones and phalloplasties, which was already the usual transsexual protocol "in the name of nature." Butler (2004) noted that David's experience from boy to girl and back to boy shows that Money's alleged malleability of gender requires a forceful application, and that the "nature" that the endocrinologists defend also calls for hormonal and surgical means. "Malleability is, as it were, violently imposed. And naturalness is artificially induced" (p. 66). The quandary here is that naturalness had to be artificially reintroduced because his sex had been made malleable by multiple medical interventions.

Given that this story has the potential to demolish her gender claims, Butler's contention that "the story as we have it does not actually supply evidence" is a weak argument. It is true, as Butler remarked, that David's relationship to his sexuality implied an always present, biased medical audience observing, measuring, and probing his reactions. Still, David seemed to have had a suspicion about the truth of his gender all along, as a repressed knowledge, while never pushing to find things out. This differs from what is heard in candidates for sex change; they experience a sudden revelation about their gender as an epiphany. Despite the fact that David had always had the experience that something was odd about his assigned female gender, he was deeply unhappy but still uncertain about what was happening. He always remained afraid of exploring things further, unwilling "to wind up opening a can of worms."

Most sex change histories include a moment of when the Rubicon is crossed, when the awareness of being in the body of the wrong sex is achieved. This was never the case with David. He was dissatisfied being Brenda and felt all along that something was wrong, but it was not until he heard the truth as told by his father that he, in an après coup movement, was able to reinterpret the past. For David, it was someone else's speech (his father's) that confirmed and made sense of his feelings. In most transsexual accounts, the realization of the "true" sexual identity felt to be at odds with body type appears as a self-imposed thought, a conviction brought by an inner voice that does not require any external confirmation.

David's situation calls up the infinite image created by two opposing mirrors: One technological intervention is used to repair a failed technological intervention caused by a failed technological intervention. Butler's difficulty lies not in the lack of evidence of the case, as she argued. Butler found herself in a very delicate position. Not only were Money's limitless ambition and questionable scientific honesty revealed by the case (well into the mid-1990s, Money's published works extolled the success of his sex reassignment; the 1996 edition of his best-selling *Man and Woman, Boy and Girl* report the twins' case as a success), but Money's claims about gender's extraordinary malleability are embarrassingly similar to her own. Perhaps Butler was uncomfortably aware that the theories that she developed in the 1990s about gender performativity could look like a revamped version of John Money's 1955 invention of the notion of gender roles:

> All those things that a person says or does to disclose himself or herself as having the status of boy or man, girl or woman, respectively. [Gender] includes, but is not restricted to sexuality in the sense of eroticism. Gender role is appraised in relation to the following: general mannerisms, deportment and demeanor; spontaneous topics of talk in unprompted conversation and casual comment; content of dreams, daydreams and fantasies; replies to oblique inquiries and projective tests; evidence of erotic practices and, finally, the person's own replies to direct inquiry. (cited in Money, 1973, p. 397)

LESSONS FROM THE INTERSEXED

Money started his career in 1949 by studying Freud's concept of "hermaphroditism" in the first of the "Three Essays on the Theory of Sexuality" (Freud, 1905). This project paved the way for his 1952 Harvard doctoral dissertation on the psychology of hermaphroditism (Money, 1952). The study of intersex children made Money arrive at his conclusions about psychosexual development.[4] With the twins' case, Money extended his theories to a biologically unambiguous male child. Although David's body was surgically altered to fit his new female status, Money's treatment put great emphasis on what we may call the performative aspects of gender. These are aspects that Butler defined as the culturally constructed, stylized bodily acts that, in their repetition, establish the appearance of an essential "core" gender. Money (1961a) claimed that human beings are sexually neutral at birth by revising Freud's drive theory: "The direction or content of erotic inclination in the human species is not controlled by the sex hormones. Hormonally speaking, the sex drive is neither male nor female but undifferentiated—an urge for the warmth and sensation of close body contact and genital proximity" (pp. 239–240). Characteristically, he waxed lyrical when describing the plasticity of sexuality: "To use the Pygmalion allegory, one may begin with the same clay and fashion a god or a goddess" (1996b, p. 152).

Diamond (1965) had long claimed that Pygmalion's clay is not malleable but adaptable: "Although humans *can adjust* to an erroneously imposed gender role, (a) it does not mean that prenatal factors are not normally influential, and (b) that they do so with difficulty if not prenatally and biologically disposed" (p. 50; italics in original). Without relying uniquely on a purely biological determination like Diamond, who argued that hormones and not the environment are decisive in gender, sex, and sexuality, the twins' tragic lives (David's twin, Brian, the experiment embedded "control" subject, was diagnosed with schizophrenia and died of a drug overdose not long before David's suicide) dismantle Butler's notion that gender is purely performative. If there is no identity behind the acts that supposedly "express" gender, and if these acts constitute—rather than express—the illusion of the stable gender identity, how can we explain David's pathos? Furthermore, David's "inner truth" about his being a man contradicts Butler's (1990) argument that "being" a gender is only an effect of culturally influenced acts without any solid, universal basis, that gender acts are constituted through the practice of performance. In the case of David, his gender did not remain contingent and open to interpretation and "resignification," despite the multiple attempts at erasure and reinscription.

When Butler (2004) criticized practices of sex reassignment of intersex babies to surgically remake the body as if "gender had to be borne out in singular and normative ways at the level of anatomy," her arguments come across as weak. "Gender is a different sort of identity, and its relation to anatomy is complex" (p. 63). This is precisely because Money's logic of attribution of gender brings back the materiality of the body, which was absent in her claim of gender as purely performative. She noted

---

[4] For a Lacanian reading of Money's notion of gender, see Klein (2003, pp. 51–60).

that the mutilation of the bodies was rationalized in the name of making the child look normal, even at the expense of sexual function and pleasure (p. 63).

I appreciate Butler's (2004) description of the ease with which Money describes how a female body can be reconstructed as if femininity was "always little more or less than a surgical construction, an elimination, a cutting away" (p. 64). But, when Butler compares Money's contention that how anatomy looks and is seen is the basis for sexual identity with Diamond's claim that the genetic presence of a Y chromosome is the most compelling evidence for an "invisible and necessary persistence of maleness" (p. 64), she does not seem to consider that for both gender is purely a behavior. In the case of Money, this can be either a set of behaviors triggered by the body's appearance and its responses to it, or in Diamond's by a chromosome that will model the behaviors. Perhaps this omission is the result of the proximity of their notion of gender as a set of behaviors, with Butler's (1990) earlier claim that "gender is a always a doing" (p. 25). She diverges from Money and Diamond in her nonessentialist approach to gender identity: "There is no gender identity behind the expressions of gender; that identity is performatively constituted by the very 'expressions' of gender that are said to be its results" (p. 25). What remains is an uncomfortable similarity: Milton and Diamond could compare the failure or success of their respective approaches only on the basis of results, of "expressions of gender" in David's gender performances.

One does not know what to admire most: Butler's honesty and courage in tackling a difficult case or the series of embarrassed qualifications with which she accompanied each statement. Butler (2004) was "undoing" and came out "undone." David seems to fall somewhere between her gender contentions and the norm:

> David's discourse puts into play the operation of critique itself, critique which, defined by Foucault, is precisely the desubjugation of the subject within the politics of truth. This does not mean that David becomes intelligible and, therefore, without value to politics; rather he emerges at the limits of intelligibility, offering a perspective that on the variable ways in which norms circumscribe the human. It is precisely because we understand, without quite grasping, that he has another reason, that he *is*, as it were, another reason, that we see the limits to the discourse of intelligibility that would decide his fate. David does not precisely occupy a new world since he is still ... positioned somewhere between the norm and its failure. And he is finally neither one ... as he speaks to the limits of what we think we know. (p. 74)

Butler noted with poignancy that David's case is paradoxical because it has been at the center of many debates on intersexuality, even though he was not intersex, and about transsexuality, even though David was not transsexual. It is clear that David Reimer's highly touted case was produced by the incredible accumulation of medical mistakes, a scientist's perverse ambition, and the confusion of organ and signifier. This is a confusion that was incurred both by Money and Diamond. Money because he thought that the phallus was an anatomical organ, and therefore a man without a penis not only could no longer be considered male but was better off as a girl. Diamond mocked Money, saying that in this confusion he was "echoing Freud" (Domurat Dreger, 1999, p. 176). But, Diamond incurred the same confusion of organ with phallus when he calls the penis that David had surgically constructed between the ages of 15 and 16, "phallus."

Yet, David's sexual identity was subjected to the phallic premise that functioned independently of the actual presence of the organ. David seems to prove the psychoanalytic definition of sexuality as sexuation. As we have seen, according to Lacan's formulas of sexuation, one the male side, regardless of the biological sex, everyone is subjected to the phallic premise: "All are subject to the law of castration" (this is the universal law of symbolic existence). And, on the female side, "No x exists which is not determined by the phallic function." This side of the formulas indicates an inevitable inscription within the law—even without a penis, there is no subject that is not determined by the phallic function.

THE PHALLUS, UNIT OF EXCHANGE

The phallus is just a signifier. David employed this signifier in its function as masquerade when at age 18 he used part of the settlement money he obtained in compensation for the penis ablation to buy what one may call "a phallus on wheels." This was a vehicle that he called "the shaggin' wagon," a windowless, wall-to-wall carpeted van equipped with a bed and bar that he acquired in hopes of "lassoing some ladies" (Colapinto, 2000, p. 187). This strategy eventually failed. His surgically constructed penis did not resemble the usual organ and did not perform well (for instance, it could not become erect). The shaggin' wagon granted him many dates, but he would stop sexual encounters when they would become intimate. On one occasion, he got drunk, passed out, and probably revealed too much. David's "accident" became immediately the object of gossip and ridicule. As a result, David made a suicide attempt by taking a bottle of his mother's antidepressants.

David could attract women with his phallic van; he could handle masculinity as masquerade but could not perform as a man when what was expected from him was based exclusively on the proper functioning of the virile organ. From the male side of the sexuation formulas, one can say that it is from the phallic signifier and the paternal exception that the sexual position is formulated. David also tried to become a man by becoming a father. But, sexual positioning is always a failed accomplishment; there are two sexes but no relation. Given the two positions that the paternal metaphor inscribes, the father cannot be assimilated to the man, and the woman is always contaminated by the mother.

After the van fiasco, David had a second phalloplasty that allowed him to have sex genitally, and he focused all his energies on becoming a husband and father. After a blind date set up by his sister-in-law, he fell in love with Jane, a single mother with three children. Jane attributed a phallic value to other things. Above all, she was looking for love: "I was looking for love in the wrong places. I wanted a relationship. I wanted someone to love me" (Colapinto, 2000, p. 193). Jane knew about David's situation and that he had received a substantial amount of money as a settlement. She almost sounds ironic in her emphasis on the word "convertible," for during the matchmaking process, Jane recalled: "She [the wife of David's brother] had said he's got this *van* and a *convertible*. I said, 'Does it really, matter how much money he has or what he has between his legs?' If he's not good to me or the kids, he can go his own way" (p. 194; italics in the original).

After dating her for 1 year, he exchanged one phallic symbol for another—he sold the shaggin' wagon and bought a diamond engagement ring. On September 22, 1990, David and Jane got married. This relation seemed to be based on a different dialectic of love and desire. Early in their relationship, David was very concerned about how to tell Jane about his dramatic life. When he gathered the courage to tell her, she surprised him. "She said that she had known all the time and that she didn't want to tell me because she figured it would bother me," David recalled. "That's when I knew it was the real thing; I knew she cared for *me*" (Colapinto, 2000, p. 194; italics in the original). According to the sexuation formulas, one can say that love makes a phallic necessity of the contingent, the traumatic encounter with the Real. Jane and David's love, a love determined by the nonrelation, was not fully regulated by the phallus and in that sense was similar to the feminine position; the feminine position is not all governed by the phallus. With love, for a few years, David seemed better able to tolerate the impossible real truth of his history, the impossible horror that did not cease to not write itself.

On the feminine side of the formulas, the law is absolute: There is no one who does not fall under the phallic function. Thus, David could be a man even without having a penis. Money's plan of having a vagina surgically constructed for Brenda was not going to grant him access to femininity. In taking a fetishistic approach to sexual difference and operating according to the left or male side of the sexuation formulas, Money and his team seemed to rely excessively on the presence of an organ, albeit artificially constructed, as part of a general behavioral conditioning. David himself gave a very illuminating insight about his situation that can be read as a critique of the confusion between penis as organ and phallus as a signifier that prevails among the specialists who conducted his experiment. David recalled how his whole being was summed up by the presence or absence of a penis:

> Doctor [Money] said, it's gonna be tough, you're going to be picked on, you're gonna be very alone, you're not gonna find anybody unless you have vaginal surgery and live as a female. And I thought to myself, you know I wasn't very old at the time but it dawned on me that these people gotta be pretty shallow if that's the only thing they think I've got going for me; that the only reason why people get married and have children and have a productive life is because of what they have between their legs. ... If that's all they think of me, that they justify my worth by what I have between my legs, then I gotta be a complete loser. (Diamond & Sigmundson, 1997, p. 301)

There are in fact quite a number of losers in this story: David, who ended up committing suicide; Money, whose reputation was damaged; and even Judith Butler, who was alarmed by the proximity between Money's initial position and her own thesis.

SEX FOLLOWS GENDER

John Money started his career working with people who bring gender trouble—intersex people cannot fit in the binary classification of sexual difference; often they embody either or both sexes. Money's work with intersex people confronted him with people whose legal and social status was in discordance with their chromosomal, gonadal, or body status. He introduced the gender paradigm to free sex from biological determinism or sexual function. *Gender* referred to a realm of sexual difference not determined by the body: a person's social, personal, and legal status. Gender was both *gender identity*, the private "inner" experience of gender, and *gender role*, the public presentation as male or female. These concepts were developed further by other intersexual researchers like Anke Ehhardt as well as psychoanalyst Robert Stoller.

One of the lessons of the John/Joan case is to reveal the contradictions in Money's contention that gender is constructed in social conformity with cultural norms was a liberation of gender from the biological limits of sex. The liberation of gender from sex implied the conditioning of sex to gender. According to this logic, if anatomy was not destiny, then gender was purely social. In this case, one wonders why it was so important, even necessary, to dress the body in the gender of choice by intervening with hormones and multiple mutilating surgeries. The key is that Money argued that the sex of assignment and rearing was the best indicator for gender role and orientation. But, his idea was not that since gender role was postnatal it therefore could be "easily modifiable. Quite the contrary! The evidence from examples of change or reassignment of sex in hermaphroditism ... indicate that gender role becomes not only established but also indelibly imprinted" (Money, Hampson, & Hampson, 1955, p. 308). Money aligned himself with the behavioral tradition: An anatomically correct body needed to be constructed to imprint and condition the appropriate gender behaviors and ensure the expected gender role and orientation. Sexual orientation "is not defined on the basis of chromosomal sex, nor of any of the internal and concealed variables of sex. Instead it is defined on the basis of the external sexual anatomy and the sexual characteristics of the body in general" (Money, 1990, p. 34). Gender was "performative," yet the binary of gender was enforced through the material production of sex.

There is another ideological element underlying the debate: The term *intersex*, which replaced *hermaphrodite*, was introduced in the 1920s by German researcher Richard Goldschmidt, who contended that all mammalian hermaphrodites were in fact "intersexes." They all begin life as one sex or the other, but undergo a sex reversal as embryos. The sex reversal during the fetal development would thus determine the intersexuality. While Goldschmidt's theory of reversibility as the etiology of intersexuality has been proven wrong, his influence continues to be important (Hausman, 1995, p. 78). In fact, the theory of physical bisexuality still looms large.

One element that could help us enormously in this discussion is an unpublished study produced in the early 1950s—around the same time that George Jorgensen became Christine. The extensive study followed the lives of 250 young adults born with unusual genitalia but who had not undergone any surgery or received hormone treatments. In spite of experiencing some "sexual ambiguity of no mean proportions," all the people studied expressed great satisfaction with their lives. They seemed normal. There was "no suspicion of psychopathology." They were "almost a model of what the average citizen believes a healthy, well-adjusted American youth should be," the author observed: "confident, self-reliant, and optimistic" with a "'conspicuously low' rate of neuroses and psychoses" (Colapinto, 2000, p. 235). No experts on the debate of intersex treatment ever made reference to this important study. It is not surprising since the thesis was never published or distributed and can only be accessed through special permission at the Widener library at Harvard University, where it was submitted in fulfillment of the requirements for the degree of doctor in philosophy. The author of the thesis was a 30-year-old doctoral candidate named John Money.

What happened to Money? Money began his career by studying Freud's theories of sexuality. He later abandoned Freud in the name of U.S. behaviorism, more precisely of psychoendocrinology, that is, imbued by an ideology of science that was positivistic and smacked of coercive reductionism. Against this tendency, Lacan's path toward a deeper understanding of sexuality proves that one can be Freudian and keep progressing while remaining close to the clinic, keeping an openness to ethics and aesthetics.

Chapter 8

Lacan's transsexuals

Currently, the image of a pregnant trans man—upper body naked, flat hairy chest, ripe round belly, square jaw framed by a beard—is no longer news. But, it responds eloquently to the conclusion of Freud's essay on Sidonie Scillag, our "Young Homosexual Woman." In 1920, Freud expressed his skepticism about the "remarkable transformations that Steinach had effected in some cases by his [sex change] operations" (p. 171). He felt that it would have been "premature" or "harmful exaggerations" to consider this type of bodily intervention a "therapy" that could "be generally applied" (p. 172). In the case of women, the tone of Freud's speculation was cautious: "A woman who has felt herself to be a man, and has loved in masculine fashion, will hardly let herself be forced into playing the part of a woman, when she must pay for this transformation, which is not in every way advantageous, by renouncing all hope of motherhood" (p. 172). In Freud's time, the kind of sex transformations brought about with hormones and plastic surgery by Benjamin and Money would have seemed improbably far-fetched. Nowadays, it is a matter of fertility treatments, and these trans men are able to conceive, be pregnant, and give birth. With several trans men having shown the mass public that they were able to retain their identities as men while keeping their female reproductive organs, becoming pioneer pregnant fathers, usual notions of what is male or female are challenged even further. Still, we do not know enough about the limits of our bodies. Technological developments push our comprehension and reiterate that for gender, anatomy is not destiny. Now, the questions are mostly issues of ethics and deontology. Are these the new symptoms of our times?

Freud was not afraid of sharing publicly his difficulties and even his shortcomings, courageously exposing his failures in the hope of learning from his mistakes. Here is how he described the problematic conditions with Sidonie Scillag that made him decide to stop the treatment:

> The analysis went forward almost without any signs of resistance, the patient participating actively with her intellect, though absolutely tranquil emotionally. Once when I expounded to her a specially important

part of the theory, one touching her nearly, she replied in an inimitable tone "How very interesting," as though she were a *grande dame* being taken to a museum and glancing through her *lorgnon* at objects at which she was completely indifferent. (1920, p. 163; italics in the original)

Why was Sidonie so dismissive? Why were Freud's interpretations discarded as uninteresting, dusty, old, museum pieces? Besides Freud's own resistances, the analysis failed because, fundamentally, Sidonie was a patient without symptoms. Her only reason to be in analysis was the "passage to the act" that took place before she came to see Freud and thus was outside the bounds of transference. Remember that the controversy around the suicidal attempt of Sidonie had revolved around the interpretation of *niederkommen*: Did the verb "to fall" yield the meaning of "giving birth," as Freud and Lacan maintained, or could one see more in it? Lacan offered the additional interpretation that Sidonie was searching for the father's gaze because she wanted to be seen as *lovable* for the Other that he embodied for her. But, as discussed in Chapter 5, the encounter on the street went awfully wrong. Sidonie fell outside the scene she had staged, and she herself became this "fallen" thing that she was aiming at making appear.

Niederkommen can be glossed as "falling together," which calls up the etymology of "symptom" (in Greek, *symptom* literally means "falling together"—*syn*, "with," and *piptein*, "to fall"). If Sidonie's fall was a symptom, if all her unconscious issues fell together in a quasi-fatal precipitation determined by her unconscious positioning, it was a symptom without an addressee. This fall will also bring us closer to Lacan's later work on another form of symptom, one that he rewrote as *sinthome*.

The coining was made apropos of James Joyce in 1975. In the year-long seminar that he devoted to Joyce, Lacan defined the sinthome as a creative knotting together of the registers of Real, Symbolic, and Imaginary. The sinthome served to analyze the function of art in Joyce's life and to give a more comprehensive interpretation of the function of the father in the Borromean knot.[1] Structurally, this knot has one main characteristic: If one ring is unknotted, the other three come loose. The sinthome is a fourth ring that knots tripartite registers not arranged harmoniously, thus providing a palliative solution. In Joyce's case, the name of the father could the take place of a fourth ring, keeping the other three knotted.

When Lacan turned his attention to Joyce's writings, he discovered a new paradigm and a new relation to the body. He observed that Joyce had a peculiar body, one that could fall, slip away, like an open envelope letting

---

[1] One can trace a nonclinical use of the symptom to Lacan's *Seminar XIX Ou Pire* (1971–1972), unpublished, session of January 19, 1972. Lacan implicitly referred to the Althusser notion of symptomatic reading by discussing the symptom and necessity in the context of a new reading of Marx.

go of its contents. Lacan focused on a passage of *A Portrait of the Artist as a Young Man* (Joyce, 1992), when Stephen remembers a moment of rage at his schoolmates that suddenly faded away: He had felt his anger falling from him "as easily as a fruit is divested of its soft ripe peel" (p. 87). For Lacan (2005), such a transformation of anger was curious and revealing. It could be generalized as encompassing a Joycean body, a body that could fall from one's self, like a wrapping that does not fully hold (p. 149). In Joyce's case, it was writing that would "hold" the body.

Taking into account the complex relationship that transsexuals have to their body—they often say that their souls are trapped in a body of the wrong (opposite) sex—I claim that an art similar to that of actual artists, if not necessarily with the genius of Joyce, can be found in transsexual artificiality. In some cases, it gives birth to an art that, I argue, is tantamount to a creative sinthome. As I discuss, the later Lacanian contribution proved illuminating when dealing with transgender clinical issues.

Three years after having launched the notion of the sinthome, Lacan (1979) further developed the link with a fall:

> A *sinthome* is not a fall, even if it looks like one. It goes as far as making me consider that all of you out there, you have as sinthome each his or her partner. There is a she-sinthome and a he-sinthome. That is all that is left of the so-called sexual rapport. The sexual relation is an inter-sinthomatic relation. (pp. 219–220)[2]

One main contention in this book is that Lacan's theory of the sinthome permits a new approach to the paradoxes of gender, an insight shared by Bracha Lichtenberg Etinger (2002), who wrote that Lacan's 1975–1976 seminar allowed grasping the impossible relation between the sexes. Developing Lacan's idea that a man can be a woman's symptom, she wrote: "The sinthome is therefore the other sex, it is what 'woman' is to 'man' and is a product of art" (p. 91). Used in this sense, the sinthome puts in operation the difference between "man" and "woman," and at the same time it never reduces the difference between "woman" and "woman," that is, an originary feminine difference.

I discussed Sidonie's "fall" within the parameters of Lacan's theory of acting out. In light of what precedes, it is clear that her fall was not a sinthome. As she was fully in the hysterical structure, she performed repeated passages-to-the-act for want of finding a sinthome instead. We have seen that the new biographical information mentions two other suicide attempts

---

[2] "*Un* sinthome *n'est pas une chute, quoique ça en ait l'air. C'est au point que je considère que vous là tous tant que vous êtes, vous avez comme* sinthome *chacun sa chacune. Il y a un* sinthome *il et un* sinthome *elle. C'est tout ce qui reste de ce qu'on appelle le rapport sexuel. Le rapport sexuel est un rapport intersinthomatique*" (Lacan, 1979, pp. 219–220).

addressed to her father, which indicates that Sidonie did not renounce the dialectical vortex forcing her to move from acting out to passage to the act. Hence, Sidonie fell because she could not let her father fall; at the same time, she thought that she had fallen from the protection of her love for him. Sidonie's virile display of love for the baroness and the fateful encounter preceding her first suicide attempt put the father at the center of the scene. We have also seen that Freud interrupted the treatment when he noticed that he had replaced her father in the transference. Is the father an obstacle in the progress of the treatment?

Lacan gives a new twist to Freud's Oedipus complex when he reformulated it as evincing the domination of the Name-of-the-Father. Later, Lacan (2005) went beyond the Oedipus complex and finally proposed the sinthome as a way of reknotting what had been left unknotted because of the father's failure. This applied above all to Joyce's case but could be generalized somewhat. If we may suppose that Sidonie had been able to remain in analysis with Freud, she might have had an opportunity to go from her negative feelings about her father to her positive ones. In other words, she would have let her father fall in the end. She would have been able to "make do without the father, having made use of him" (p. 136).[3] Since the sinthome is not a complement but a supplement, it is a vehicle for creative unbalance, capable of disrupting the symmetry. The sinthome is what helps one tolerate the absence of the sexual relation (Lacan, 1973, p. 47). Instead of grief and reproaches for broken promises addressed to the Other as demands, the sinthome employs the Name-of-the-Father as a way of naming, as a path in the invention of new signifiers (Lacan, 1977). Lacan's notion of the sinthome thus connected fantasy, demand, the system of the Symbolic, and the place of the Real with the infinite possibilities that it allows for jouissance.

To give concrete examples of these abstract concepts, I study an early case of transsexualism that was treated by Lacan not only with remarkable prudence but also with great zeal. I try to show that Lacan's caution hints at an ethics of sexual difference. The case of a transsexual patient called Henri constitutes a rare exception to the paucity of Lacan's case studies. Although Lacan did not publish this case, it had a strong impact on his rereading of Freud's discussion of Schreber.

"IT REALLY MUST BE RATHER PLEASANT TO BE A WOMAN ... "

Schreber's case is an exception in Freud's case studies because he never met the person he analyzed. Freud first read a book and then wrote a long analysis

---

[3] "One can very easily do without [the Name-of-the-Father] on condition that one makes use of it."

of the author's delusions, which suggested to him a case of paranoia. Judge Daniel Paul Schreber, a highly intelligent and learned jurist, became presiding judge of the Saxon High Court of Appeals in Germany at the age of 40. This promotion became overwhelming and triggered a breakdown. After spending 6 years in a private psychiatric clinic, he felt sufficiently recovered. Determined to secure his release from the asylum, Schreber wrote a detailed account of his illness to argue in court for his discharge. The court determined that even though Schreber still suffered hallucinations and delusions, he was competent to live outside the asylum. *Memoirs of My Nervous Illness* was published in 1903. His memoirs have attracted so much scholarly attention that they may be the book most written about in all psychiatric literature.

Daniel Paul Schreber was born in 1842 to an upper-class family in Leipzig. His father was a prominent orthopedic physician, writer, educator, and reformer of missionary zeal, a reputed authority on hygiene and child rearing. The complex delusional world of Schreber (1903/2000) had a center—his body, which was the place of an astounding transformation:

> The month of November, 1895, marks an important time in the history of my life and in particular in my own ideas of the possible shaping of my future. ... During that time the signs of a transformation into a woman became so marked on my body, that I could no longer ignore the imminent goal at which the whole development was aiming. In the immediately preceding nights my male sexual organ might actually have been retracted had I not resolutely set my will against it, still following the stirring of my sense of manly honor; so near completion was the miracle. Soul voluptuousness had become so strong that I myself received the impression of a female body, first on my arms and hands, later on my legs, bosom, buttocks and other parts of my body. (p. 163)

Beset by persecutory delusions about his doctor, Schreber had been dominated by the conviction that he was going to change into a woman; then, he would become God's bride, a consenting prey to God's voluptuous pleasures. One can say that Lacan's highly original interpretation of Schreber's memoir was buttressed by his contemporary treatment of a transsexual patient called Henri.

UNRIVALED UNDERSTANDING

Jean Delay, a pioneer in the psychiatric treatment of transsexuals in France and the author of a famous psychobiography of André Gide (Delay, 1956, 1957), provided the most adequate summary of Lacan's innovative work with Henri, a male patient who requested a sex change:

During his hospitalization in this ward, he was in psychotherapy with Dr. Lacan between 1952 and 1954, meeting on an average of one session a week. Henri said that he had found in him [Lacan] an "unrivaled understanding." Notwithstanding, they both agreed on the uselessness of pursuing an attempt at changing his condition, a change to which the patient apparently never subscribed. (Delay et al., 1956, p 53)[4]

Not only was Lacan the first psychoanalyst in France to conduct psychotherapy with a transsexual, but also he undertook the treatment of a patient who was already a famous case since he was "not just anybody but Delay's 'Henri'" (Pierre-Henri Castel, 2003, p. 351).[5] At the same time, he was rereading Freud's text on Schreber. Lacan treated Henri between 1952 and 1954 and then started his seminar on psychosis in 1955, a year later. Moreover, Lacan wrote both "On a Question Prior to Any Possible Treatment of Psychosis" (1957–1958) and "Guiding Remarks for a Convention on Female Sexuality"(1958) at the same time, which suggests a thematic connection. It looks as if the questions posed by psychotic transsexuality and female sexuality were related. Observing Schreber's delusional transformation into a woman, Lacan gave new meaning to a phenomenon often observed in psychotic patients: feminization. This was a key element in Lacan's unorthodox reading of the case—he replaced Freud's interpretation of Schreber's case as being determined by the patient's "rejection of homosexuality" (for Freud, Schreber had to imagine that he was turning into a woman in order to accept the idea that he was going to have sex with a man or with a male father figure). Lacan discovered an emblematic feature in Schreber's transsexualist delusions. In Schreber's delusion of being transformed into a woman, Lacan found the lineaments for a new theory of sexual identity.

PSYCHOGENESIS OF A CASE OF MALE TRANSSEXUALITY

During the 2 years that he was hospitalized, Henri was in weekly psychotherapy with Lacan.[6] He was placed in Jean Delay's ward, Clinique des Maladies Mentales et de l'Encéphale (Mental and Encephalon Disease

---

[4] Note that one of co-authors, Jean-Marc Alby, had completed a groundbreaking thesis on transsexualism in 1956. This article was both a case study of a male patient (Henri), who solicited a surgical sex change to obtain the physical appearance of a woman, and a review of the existing literature on transsexualism at the time.

[5] The description of the case was not Lacan's since after all it was not "his" case but Delay's "Henri."

[6] For an interesting description of the collaboration of Lacan and Delay at Saint Anne, see Major (1995/1996).

Clinic) at the Sainte Anne Hospital in Paris,[7] where he underwent a long and meticulous examination after he had requested an experimental sex change surgery. To be fair, Henri's childhood had been "deeply troubling" (Delay et al., 1956, p. 42). He had been born with undescended testicles (cryptorchidism) and presented a case of hypotrophy, a condition in which a full-term baby is born with the characteristics of a premature newborn. He was declared a girl at birth and named Anne-Henriette. His aunt had foretold: "The baby will not last; it is not worth the trouble taking care of it" (p. 43). However, the baby survived and was raised as a girl. When he was 1 year old, his mother died before weaning him. After his mother's "brutal death of unknown cause," his great-aunt, whom Henri called "Grandmother," raised him. Henri was extremely attached to her: "He would practically never leave her alone" (p. 43).

Henri wore dresses, had long hair, and played with dolls. He recalled with longing the praise he had earned as "the pretty little girl I was." At age 16, his father, who up to that moment had remained detached and utterly indifferent, suddenly intervened. The father noticed Henri's romantic interest in a male friend who was 2 years older and abruptly forced Henri to wear male clothes with the injunction: "You can't help but make a choice" (p. 45). Henri "welcomed that transformation with obvious indifference and a lack of surprise that still astonishes him today. He was already aware that he was not like other people" (p. 45). This was the beginning of a period of "moral suffering" (p. 45). Between the ages of 15 and 16, his testicles descended, and "he found 'that' disgusting" and kept praying for feminization, wishing "that it could all be arranged and that the thing would retract and disappear completely" (p. 46). Henri never wore female clothes again, and until his hospitalization at age 40, he was "leading the apparently normal life of a man" (p. 43). His sexual life was limited to rare erections accompanied by severe anxiety and occasional nocturnal emissions.

However, on his hospitalization in 1952, he asked to be admitted to the women's section because he could not tolerate getting undressed in front of men. He was at the time unemployed and depressed and complained of multiple bodily pains—in the abdomen, thorax, and especially in his genitalia. He suffered rectal bleeding (caused by hemorrhoids), which he interpreted as menstruation. The testicular biopsy proved normal, and an exploratory laparoscopy did not find any female organ. The findings "disappointed the patient very much" (p. 49). Henri was an avid reader. Reading Magnus Hirschfield's *Le sexe inconnu* (1936), he discovered the possibility of a sex change. Henri had learned about new hormonal treatments and the experimental surgeries performed by Felix Abraham in Germany in the 1930s. Since he was a very pious person who strongly

---

[7] For more on Delay's work at Saint Anne's Mental and Encephalon Disease Clinic, see Thullier (1999).

opposed homosexuality because of religious convictions, he had found further justification for his request in a 1952 papal encyclical on medicine concerning mutilating interventions "to mend severe wrongs" (Delay et al., 1956, p. 52). Henri explained:

> I have a feminine soul, I'm morally like a woman, I do the cleaning, above all I love cooking. ... This question often has come to me: "Why not stay like this?" because for that there was no need of doctors, I would have found that myself, it could have happened that I evolved in another way, this not being the case, it is natural that I abhor everything that is masculine in me, from the physical appearance to the clothes. (p. 50)

Henri dreamed of a relationship with a heterosexual man because he could not tolerate a homosexual relationship. To be able to "unite with a person of the opposite sex" and thus "repair the mistakes of nature removing the undesirable glands and improving the physical aspect," Henri requested "a castration with amputation of the penis, plastic surgery of the scrotum to make it into a vulva, creation of an artificial vagina, and treatment with feminizing hormones" (p. 52).

Delay and others (1956) concluded the case review by saying that, despite the lengthy process of observation, his request should not be granted. Delay and his team were hesitant, considering that he was raised as a girl, but found that his absolute conviction was pathological. Notably, they observed that Henri, on hearing their decision, did not seem too anxious to convince the doctors otherwise, as if the pursuit of his request were more important than its realization. There is no record of Henri's life after his hospital discharge.

METAMORPHOSIS SEXUALIS PARANOICA

A year after Lacan completed Henri's therapy, he started the study of the Schreber case in the first two terms of the 1955–1956 seminar *The Psychoses* (Lacan, 1993).[8] After returning more rigorously to his 1932 thesis on paranoia, the seminar moved to explore hysteria by addressing the question "What is a woman?" The thematic progression of the seminar confirmed that psychosis opens the way to a new formulation about hysteria and feminine sexuality. Lacan rewrote Freud's theory of psychosis and summed up Freud's Oedipus complex in his formula of the paternal metaphor. Lacan offered an almost line-by-line reading of Freud's text alongside Schreber's *Memoirs of My Nervous Illness* (2000). As we have

---

[8] Jean Delay hosted Lacan's seminar at Sainte Anne and invited Lacan to give a talk on "Freud in the Century" that was later published as part of the seminar.

seen, Lacan differed from Freud's speculation that Schreber's psychosis was the result of the repression of his passive homosexual position vis-à-vis the father. According to Freud, Schreber's foreclosed homosexual relationship to his father was reawakened by his relationship to his doctor, Professor Flechsig. Schreber developed a massive transference that led to his persecutory delusion, which centered on his eventual transformation into God's wife (Freud, 1911, pp. 1–82). Lacan insisted that what was foreclosed was not homosexuality but the Name-of-the-Father, a signifier that intervened in the mother–child dyad and offered a substitute for the child in the desire of the mother. The Name-of-the-Father was thus defined as a key signifier granting access to phallic signification; it was the factor that allowed the subject to bestow meaning to signifiers and adopt a position as male or female in the basic sexual division.

Summing up Lacan's 1958 discussion of Schreber's transsexualism, Hervé Hubert (2001) stated that since the Name-of-the-Father was foreclosed, it was the Real that was summoned in place of the Symbolic (p. 206). We can attribute Henri's severe anxiety when he had erections to his confusion between the organ and the signifier: Henri could not symbolize the turgescent organ; the erected penis was experienced as a foreign body—it was a meaningless real piece of flesh. Henri, deprived of the symbolic function by which the penis plays the part of the phallus, saw his whole body become a foreign body. His demand for a sex change may illustrate that sexual difference needs to be embodied both imaginarily and symbolically. Henri was passively trapped in interactions in which he experienced the figures of authority, like his father or the doctors, as embodiments of a capricious all-powerful Other. One could hypothesize that his request for a physical transformation could be a demand for a cut in the real of the body that would subtract a privileged piece of flesh from the Other's jouissance.

Delay and his colleagues (1956) wrote that both Henri and Lacan had quickly "agreed on the uselessness of pursuing an attempt at changing his condition, a change to which the patient apparently never subscribed" (p. 53). If Henri was described as not having subscribed to a sex change, it was because a surgical bodily transformation into a woman was a project to which he had not subscribed fully. It was a change that he had not endorsed contractually, that is, by mutually binding symbolic responsibility as he seemed divested from the symbolic aspects of sexual difference. One can speculate that this was the main reason why Lacan decided that Henri should not undergo sex change surgery: A surgically reconstructed feminized body would have been a change to which the patient never subscribed because he was unable to imaginarize, least to say, symbolize, the other sex he wished to embody. Henry lacked the libidinal investment of specular identifications that support the body as a whole. Lacan (2006) called this "a lethal gap in the mirror stage" (p. 476). In Schreber's illness, he also saw a regression to the mirror stage when Schreber experienced his body as an aggregate of colonies of foreign "nerves," a depository of detached fragments of his persecutors. For Henri, a sex change that implied cutting off pieces of his body would replay the mortal impact of the mirror stage's disintegration. Apparently, Henri had never subscribed to the formative, unifying function of the mirror stage.

This divestment of the body as image brings to mind another example from a female-to-male transsexual I treated. She told me, after having had a double mastectomy, that she could only then feel that her body had a limit. Before, she felt her body to be boundless. The surgically found limit revealed a relationship to the body in which the imaginary was accessed through the Real. Whereas in the case of this female-to-male transsexual the intervention in the real of the body (a double mastectomy was later followed by a hysterectomy) was successful and allowed for a libidinal investment in the image by way of a real lack, in the case of Henri, everything appeared to indicate that his sinthome was not the actual sex change, but its pursuit only. The sinthome had to be deferred. Here resided all his art.

THE TROUBLE WITH HENRI

We can explore Henri's demand with the hypothesis that his sex change request was an attempt at reaching his sinthome, granting him a form of suppletion, making up, as a stand-in, for the deficiencies at the level of the Symbolic.[9] Henri was trying to invent something that limited jouissance while functioning as an indicator of the fault it remedied. His wish to change sex held him together and allowed him to make an attempt at an insertion in the Symbolic. Henri claimed that his desire for transformation permitted him to identify with "the suffering segment of humanity" (Delay et al., 1956, p. 52). It was what would humanize him, albeit magically. Delay et al. (1956) noted that "the desire for transformation" had a "clear-cut magic signification." They observed that Henri lacked any awareness of the "actual and normally scary characteristic of the realization" of his request (p. 52). His longing for a sex change left, however, an important piece outside—the Real.

Henri had stipulated that once his testicles had been amputated, they should be given to a man deprived of his sexual glands as the result of an accident or an illness. Henri imagined his sex change as a sex exchange, that is, as an inscription in a lineage, but on a purely imaginary level. By donating his organs to someone who would be more deprived than he was, he

---

[9] Lacan did not employ the word *suppléance* until 1975. See Lacan (1976/1977, p. 6; session of November 18, 1975).

engaged in a circulation of gifts, all the while treating his undesirable body parts as detachable organs that could only be reclaimed or offered as gifts. A similar logic was illustrated by "N.," one of Stoller's (1975) patients, who could only reclaim his penis after he had lost it in his sex change surgery: "I mean, after all, I have still got the same penis. It's just differently arranged, that's all. [Penile and scrotal skin were used by the surgeons as the vaginal lining]" (p. 89). Stoller's N. might have echoed Laqueur's contention that in ancient times the vagina was considered an inverted penis. N. tried to confirm the implausible infantile sexual theory based on the assumption of the same (male) genitals in everyone: The premise that "everyone possesses a penis" was proved by his own body as "everyone possesses a penis, even those who do not."

One feature of Henri's sex change request is worth mentioning: He assumed that his surgically feminized body was going to grant him the ability to "unite with a person of the opposite sex," that is, to have a rapport with the opposite sex. One can say that his penis prevented him from having access to sexuality. And yet, sexual difference was there from the start—his very body belonged to the sex that was the opposite of his soul. His fantasy was that the sexual rapport could be attained if he were to have a penile ablation. This calls up a logic in which one affirms as evident what is paradoxical, a logic described by Patricia Mercader (1994) as "tautological strategy" (p. 247). Mercader argued cogently that most transsexuals affirm that they truly belong to a sex from which they are excluded. Thus, Henri's idea of sexual difference seemed independent from the phallic organization and distribution of difference.

Henri's persistent request for a sex change, neatly described as "the pursuit of his chimera" (Delay et al., 1956, p. 53), was nevertheless a pursuit that evinced no haste to be realized. It seemed closer to a strategy of deferral—postponing access to a devastating jouissance. This points to the structural function of the pursuit as a regulator of jouissance. Henri wished to sacrifice his male sexual organs not only to inscribe sexual difference but also to mediate jouissance by his embodiment of a female ideal: He abhorred feminized male homosexuals but found great pleasure in daydreaming fantasies in which he was a woman in the company of a man. Likewise, Schreber's feminization granted him "bliss" (*Seligkeit*), a bliss that constituted a very specific form of jouissance. Schreber became both the signifier of the phallus and the object of the Other's jouissance (Quinet, 1988, p. 38). Caught in the radical dependence that a newborn experiences with the coming and going of the mother, thriving in her presence and succumbing to severe anxiety in her absence, Schreber would cultivate a voluptuous connection with God. Even Schreber's physical transformation depended on the direct influx of God's rays—when God was near, his bosom swelled, and it receded when God withdrew. Alone in front of the mirror, his upper body naked, with the exception of a few feminine adornments,

Schreber (1903/2000) had the impression of being "a woman in the height of sexual delight" (p. 249). Schreber experienced his transformation into a woman as God's commandment. His transsexual transformation was to turn him into the woman whom God lacked. This God was, however, a capricious, unbarred Other. As Lacan highlights, Schreber stated that the divine Other, who was constantly seeking satisfaction through him, was in fact nothing but a whore (*Hure*) (Schreber, 1903/2000, p. 331). In this way, Schreber's process of feminization provided a partner for God, Woman, the one who only exists in psychosis.

One can say that for both Schreber and Henri it was the subjectivation of sex that was extremely problematic. Whereas Schreber's was clearly a case of paranoia, in Henri's case Delay et al. (1956) can talk about "monomania"—a delusion limited to his conviction of being a woman despite contrary anatomical evidence (p. 54). Henri had no other visible sign of psychosis. One should take into consideration that Henri was born with genital anomalies, and that he had been mistakenly assigned to the female sex. He was raised as a girl; his birth certificate and identity as a citizen confirmed his sex as female. This error was corrected all at once by his father, but only when he was 16 years old. If gender was socially constructed, he was definitely a woman. Let us take a closer look at the circumstances surrounding his second sex change. Being a widower for 10 years, after the passing of Henri's great-aunt, his father married the great-aunt's cleaning lady and had two more children—a girl and a boy who died at age 4 of typhoid fever. The father forced Henri to abandon abruptly his feminine persona and obliged him to wear only male clothing precisely at the exact same time of the birth of Henri's sister. Like Henri's, his sister's sex was not easily determined at birth. She was eventually declared to be a girl. It was at the moment of the birth of a sibling with ambiguous genitalia that the father intervened and forced Henri to "decide," that is, he ordered him to assume a male persona. Henri's response was extremely passive, as if the commandment had the effect of an absolute law on which Henri was reduced to total impotence. A similar lack of protestation could be observed when his sex change request was denied after 2 years spent in the hospital.

Henri responded as if the events had taken place somewhere outside discourse and did not implicate him as a subject. It seemed that Henri was divested of his body, to which he referred as an alien thing; his pursuit of a sex change was a way of recapturing his body by the artifice of a transformation into a woman. Henri's ability to extricate himself from his body suggests that his body had fallen away as an imaginary projection of a whole and was then reduced to the real of a body turned into a collection of fragmented, painful organs. The dramatic events that Henri suffered seemed relatively meaningless to him, calling to mind Claude Rabant's (1992) contention that "[T]he orientation of the real forecloses meaning" (p. 165). Without the Symbolic, reality is all too Real, that is, meaningless.

Let me insist on this point: Henri had placed Delay and his colleagues in the role of weighty authority figures. Not unlike Schreber's Professor Flechsig, they were endowed with a power that could only elicit total subjection. For Schreber and Henri, neither fathers nor doctors appeared as representatives of the law—they were the law itself. Their injunctions functioned like categorical imperatives that imposed rules without any dialectical suppleness, but these imperatives would at the same time enact a destruction of the law itself because they deprived the law of any normative meaning. It corresponded to the arbitrary dictates of Henri's father, who had let him be raised as a girl and only intervened when Henri was 16 years old. In this case, the father's lack was no longer symbolic, but real. Such a lack was similar to the lack that Henri wanted to carve out in his body and organs. Since Henri's father did not work as a substitute for the mother's desire, the pursuit of a sex change was an attempt to make up for this real absence. Henri's pursuit of a sex change did not substitute for the father or engage with the paternal metaphor. His pursuit of a sex change was an attempt at reverting not an "error of nature" but an error that had been rectified in the legal inscription of his civil status.

As one can deduce, Henri's father played a very important role in his son's transformation from girl to boy, from young man into a woman. This is how Lacan (2006) theorized this movement:

> Furthermore, I must point how the structure I am isolating here [Schreber's and Henri's] may shed light on the unusual insistence played by the subjects of these [transsexual] case studies histories on obtaining their father's authorization for, one might even say his hand-on assistance with, their demands for the most radical rectifications. (p. 474)

Here, the "rectification" that the father may authorize is not similar to the rectification that operates in the case of the young homosexual woman, who wanted to show to her father that she could give the lady what she herself did not have: Lacan (1971–1972) said that the female homosexual sustains sexual discourse in all its security (December 8, 1971). In Henri's and Schreber's cases, there was no secure sexual discourse. The universality of the phallus as differentiating men and women and signifying jouissance was foreclosed. Neurotics accept the inscription of jouissance under the phallic coordinates, first by finding it in the mother's jouissance and desire and then by giving it a phallic signification when they make a sinthome of the Name-of-the-Father.

Is transsexualism thus "the impossible relation between a subject and the phallus" (Frignet, 2000, p. 41)? These are the terms used by Henry Frignet when he discusses Christine Jorgensen's autobiography, a book to which I return in another chapter. To be more accurate, we should reverse the terms. The terms of Frignet's quote should be rephrased as Henri's case shows the impossible relation between a subject and the penis. This is because, in his case, the phallus did not operate as a universal signifier of particularity. On the other hand, Castel (2003) referred to Henri's hypochondria as a "phallic hypochondria" (p. 391), a term that may be too loaded or even inappropriate since for Henri the penis was not a support for the symbolic phallus taken as a signifier of sexual difference. With both Henri and Schreber, the fantasy of transformation into a woman produced signs that were at first hypochondriac in nature; both had a delusion of pregnancy, another indication of a feminine identification outside the phallic register.[10] Henri's hypochondria confirmed his fragmented relationship to his body, but it did not concern the phallus, only the penis, in this case, an organ taken as pure flesh. It was moreover an organ that could acquire value only insofar as it was be rejected, denied, or excised.

It may have been that in Henri's case the "phallus" did not refer to the symbolic phallus but to an imaginary phallus not yet symbolized; it would still be attached to a maternal body that needed to be mutilated. It was in excess, and its disappearance would allow Henri to come to terms with the ideal image he had of himself. As Moustapha Safouan (1974) observed, while the neurotic is not content being just a man but also wants to become a *real* man or a *real* woman, the transsexual asks not to be the phallus. Henri's sex change demand implied that something had to be missing in the real of the body. That would introduce an imaginary lack, literalizing in the flesh what psychoanalysis calls *castration*.

We can note similarities with respect to the function of the father. Schreber's case shows a father who was an exceptional, excessive father, an apostle of child education who operated as an unbarred Other not subjected to symbolic castration—not just as a representative of the law but rather as the law itself. Henri's father appeared entirely bent on obtaining his own jouissance, not subject to castration; he gambled, was a man of the night, had many lovers, and finally ruined himself financially. On the whole, he seemed unable to show any interest in his son, which is why he first complacently consented to Henri's feminization. Again, he was not so much the bearer of the symbolic law as the bearer of the commandments of an absurd law, which legitimated nothing.

How could Henri abide by the law of phallic signification when that law was foreclosed? As Geneviève Morel (2000a) contends, the freedom of the psychotic resides precisely in this rejection that forgoes the phallus and the Name-of-the-Father together and that ends up requiring an invention to anchor jouissance (p. 184). According to Morel, the male-to-female transsexual implicitly reasons in this way: "You see that I have a penis, and you say I have a phallus. But I do not experience that phallic jouissance. Then,

---

[10] For Freud's misreading of Schreber's hypochondria, see Cottet (2000).

cut off my penis and you will not make the same mistake" (p. 186). In the case of the female-to-male transsexual, the reasoning would be:

> With the excuse that I have a feminine sexual organ, you make me into someone who is subjected to phallic logic. But I do not assume that phallic lack. Then give me an organ, and that mistake will not be made again. I am at the margin of your norms. (p. 186)

Morel identifies these two positions, which explain the "error" of nature, as ways of rephrasing the sexuation formulas according to the phallic premise. When Henri wanted to have his male sexual organs removed, he wanted to get rid of the "mistake of nature" by addressing the real organ and not the signifier. He thus exposed the aporia of sexual signification founded on the need to take the phallus as a signifier of sexual difference (Lacan, 1971–1972, December 8).

The recurrent expression "error of nature," so dominant in transsexualist discourse, was not coined by Lacan (1971–1972, December 8), but borrowed from Jean Marc Alby's 1956 unpublished thesis (p. 28). The phrase "error of nature" is not a neologism, but it recurs in classical discourses about transsexualism; it is often heard in patients. It was employed in 1840 by Charles Marc in one the first documented medical observations of a desire for a sex change dating from 1678. This was the case of M.V., who was presented as a man from Barège in his 40s who went by the name of Mademoiselle Rosette. Until his father's death, he dressed like a man. When his father died, he changed domicile and started to wear women's clothing, amidst self-accusations of transvestism and of having offended women by cross-dressing as a man. When the examining doctor pointed to the fact that he grew a beard and did not look at all like a woman, Mademoiselle Rosette argued that considering that he was convinced that he was a woman, those contradicting anatomical facts were "nature's error" (Marc, 1840). He complained of getting menstrual periods and at times would think that he was pregnant. Eventually, he concluded that even when he was not born a girl, he was in the process of becoming one. He had a vision in which a beautiful woman assured him that if he remained chaste and ate only fruits and milk, he would have the power to fully become a woman (Alby, 1956, p. 28).

Henri and Schreber were "Freudian cases" for whom sexual positioning was predicated on an "error" that consisted of taking the real organ for a signifier of sexual difference. Their transformation into women was the consequence of not being able to make a common "error," which is that of taking a natural organ for an *organon*, a system of principles, an organizer. This common error can be what the rectification proposed by some transsexuals is all about: "If you think that because I have a penis I am a man, that is an error; I can be a woman who has a penis." Or conversely, "If you think that not having a penis makes me a woman, this is an error because I am a man without a penis." And, they are absolutely right because for the unconscious somebody with a penis can be a woman or someone without a penis can be a man. Sexual positioning is not based on organ attribution.

A LACANIAN TRANSSEXUAL

I now move to a later case of transsexualism examined by Lacan to probe more accurately the meaning of the transformation into a woman, which is something often observed in psychotic patients but also found in other psychic structures. I focus on the case of a patient called Primeau to test Lacan's hypothesis that these men are destined to become women, not because they are foreclosed from the penis but rather because they have to be the phallus. This is the strategy, according to Lacan (2006): "[U]nable to be the phallus the mother is missing, there remained the solution of being the woman men are missing" (p. 472).

Gérard Primeau (as he was called to protect his identity) was a patient suffering from imposed speech (that is, he would hear voices speaking in his head). This was his second hospitalization. At that time, he no longer believed that he was the reincarnation of the philosopher Nietzsche or the poet Artaud, or that he needed to save France from "the fascists." He had been hospitalized this time after a suicide attempt triggered by the certainty that he was a "transmitting telepath," and that his thoughts could be heard through his radio by people who were "receiving telepaths" (Schneiderman, 1980, p. 35). Primeau, who was 26 years old at the time, had already received 25 electroshocks. He was interviewed by Lacan while hospitalized at the Henri-Rousselle Hospital. The interview was done as a live clinical presentation before a group of psychiatrists and psychoanalysts. Primeau was clearly anxious, aware that Lacan was a rather well-known figure and had difficulties explaining himself. He felt "a little disjointed in regards to language" (p. 19), which meant that he had a hard time distinguishing dream from reality. It was by telepathic transmission that he received full "[s]entences"; they had "no rational meaning in banal language" but were "imposed" on his brain, on his intellect (p. 20). The imposed sentences were "like intellectual drives that come to me, which are born brutally, and which impose themselves on my intellect" (p. 33). Primeau told Lacan that the imposed speech would create "a kind of mini-theater" in which he was "at the same time the creator and the director" (p. 23). "It's a dream, a kind of waking dream, a permanent dream" (p. 21). Primeau, disturbed by the imposed sentences, conceded nonetheless that they played a restorative function, as "bridges between the imaginative world [his own] and the world that is called real" (p. 22).

When Lacan started his interview by asking Primeau about his name, he discovered that this was not such a simple issue. As Primeau explained, "I had decomposed my name. ... In a somewhat ludic way, I had fragmented my name to create" (Schneiderman, 1980, p. 20). We could see in this, as Harari (2002) did, a Joycean pun calling up the sinthome. Harari established a link between Primeau's creative gesture of self-nomination with the strategies he used to ward off the invasion of imposed sentences (p. 182). As soon as a sentence imposed itself, Primeau would have to "counterbalance" its effect: "I have a sentence that counterbalances, which is my reflection; there is a disjunction between the imposed sentence and my sentence, a reflexive thought. I say, *But...*" (Schneiderman, 1980, p. 20). Primeau only acknowledged the second "counterbalance" sentence as his own. This "but" was a form of refusal, a way of not adapting to the external world, hence of not being captured too easily. Such a but alludes to the place of the subject as emitter, which is usually the case in the production of a sinthome, yet in this case, Primeau's imposed speech placed him in the role of a receiver. It was when he thought that his thoughts were heard on the radio, that is, when he was switching from the position of receiver, of "receiving telepath," to the position of emitter, "transmitting telepath," that he was unable to symbolize this transition and then attempted suicide.

During the interview, a few stern details of his family background came across. Gérard Primeau was born in 1948, he was an only child, his father traveled a lot and was home only on weekends, and his mother was mostly silent (Schneiderman, 1980, p. 28). Even if he was thought to be intelligent, he dropped out of a very competitive course of preparatory study for the entrance examination to a very good university because, as he said, he had "a problem with a girl" whom he described as beautiful, "radiating." Then, he added: "Sexually, I am as much in love with a woman as I am with a man" (p. 27). Indeed, Primeau had engaged in sex with both men and women. While relating the story of another woman he loved, Primeau turned his attention to one of the women in attendance to illustrate what he called female "radiance." He commented that this woman was quite beautiful, radiant despite the fact that she wore makeup. Lacan immediately asked him if he ever wore makeup, and Primeau explained that he would occasionally put on makeup: "It has happened to me, yes." Smiling, he explained that he would do this because he "had a lot of sexual complexes ... because nature endowed me with a very small phallus" (p. 30). Asked to elaborate further, Primeau continued: "I had the impression that my sex was shrinking, and I had the impression that I was going to become a woman. ... I had the impression that I was going to become a transsexual" (p. 31).

"A transsexual?" inquired Lacan. "That is to say, a sexual mutant," responded Primeau. Lacan retorted: "That is what you mean. You had the feeling that you were going to become a woman." "Yes," confirmed Primeau: "I had certain habits. I used to put on makeup, I had this impression of the shrinking of the sex and at the same time the will to know what a woman was, to try to enter into the world of a woman, into the psychology of a woman, and into the psychological and intellectual formulation of a woman" (Schneiderman, 1980, p. 31). Primeau, well aware that he still had a masculine organ and that he never felt what it was to be a woman, nevertheless had seen himself as a woman in a dream and thus hoped to become one. He experienced himself as a woman, "feeling it psychologically" (p. 31). He did not explicitly express a demand for a sex change. Lacan had Primeau spell out what he meant by being a transsexual; this referred to a transformation without any medical intervention—he was not changing sex, but rather undergoing a spontaneous change into a woman. Primeau had the impression that this transformation resulted from the feeling of shrinkage of what was in place of the phallus. As illustrated in ancient Greek comedies, the phallus carries a weight and size that no human organ can emulate. By comparison, Primeau had experienced a shrinkage of the phallic support; it was this that made him want to enter the domain of women by just becoming a woman.

Primeau seemed as disjointed in language use as he was in his sexuality. He had written a poem in which he created a neologism, "Venure," as the conflation of Venus and Mercure, feminine and masculine condensed in what he called "an elegy" (Schneiderman, 1980, p. 30). In that elegiac poem, he had spliced the French verb meaning "to fall" (*choir*) with the noun for choice (*choix*) to create the neologism *choixre*. He explained this coining as his wish "to express the notion of falling conflated with the notion of choice (*choix*)" (p. 30). This inevitably calls up the case of Sidonie, and here Primeau offered yet another meaning to the notion that sexual choice is akin to a fall. However, Primeau could not "fall" together into sexuality as with a sinthome but in his usual "disjointed" manner.

Talking about the pattern of imposed speech (it was getting worse, as indicated by the recurrent persecutory feelings of telepathy), he said that language had no boundaries. When he used the word *creation* for his imposed speech, Lacan asked him what he meant, and Primeau responded:

> At the moment it emerges from me, it is a creation. It is a little like that. One must not become intimate. The fact of speaking of these solitary circles and of living without boundaries, there is no contradiction. In my mind I do not see a contradiction. How can I explain that? I am in a solitary circle because I have broken off from reality. It is for that that I speak of a solitary circle. But that does not prevent living at an imaginative level, without boundaries. It is precisely because I have no

boundaries to put a stop to this, you can no longer struggle. There is no more struggle. (Schneiderman, 1980, pp. 33–34)

Primeau's contention that there were no boundaries refers to a language with no interdictions, deprived of any law. Why was Primeau so detached from the external "real" world, "broken off from reality"? He saw the imposed speech as a language with no contradiction, an imaginary language without boundaries. One suspects that this is due to the foreclosure of the function of the father as Name-of-the-Father. Not unlike Schreber, Primeau's lack of the Name-of-the-Father may be related to his fantasy of becoming a woman, of occupying the position of a woman. The missing signifier of the Name-of-the-Father is what the imposed speech made up for, creating "a bridge," an invention to anchor jouissance. The imposed speech was also the expression for the unbridled excess of a noncastrated Other who could read this thoughts and force irrational sentences onto his mind. Primeau's remark that "there (was) no more struggle," suggests his eclipse as a subject, finally confirming the pessimistic prognosis given by Lacan: "There are suicide attempts which end up succeeding" (p. 41).

Lacan concluded his interview with a brief comment that he shared only with the audience. Noting that several months before he had examined someone who could have been labeled as having a Freudian psychosis, he announced: "Today we have seen a 'Lacanian' psychosis ... very clearly marked" (Schneiderman, 1980, p. 41). Lacan closed the interview with the following statement: "This is a clinical picture which you will not find described even by good clinicians. ... It is to be studied" (p. 41). Lacan met with Primeau sometime between 1975 and 1976; this was the time when Lacan was teaching a seminar on Joyce, *Le Sinthome,* which proposed a new theory of madness and of sexual difference. Primeau's dominant problem lay in his transformation into a woman. Is this the crux of the clinical picture that had not yet been described and remains to be studied?

LACAN AND MICHEL H.

I call upon another of Lacan's interventions regarding the transsexual wish. This occurred in an interview that he conducted on February 21, 1976, with a male cross-dresser then under psychiatric observation after a nervous breakdown. The patient was contemplating the option of a sex change.

Michel H. was brought for consultation with Lacan by Marcel Czermak at the Henri-Rouselle Hospital. Michel H. explained that since he had been a very young boy he had enjoyed wearing his sisters' underwear: "I do not know how far it goes back because I was very little. I recall some facts, being very young, I would fondle feminine clothing, particularly full-slips, nylon." (Lacan, 1996, p. 312). Every morning and evening, at the time his sisters were changing clothes, Michel would hide in the bathroom for periods of 15 minutes and slip on some of his sisters' undergarments. Occasionally, he would fall asleep wearing one of his sisters' undergarments and was caught once by his parents in this state. They concluded that their son was a somnambulist. "I continued to cross-dress in hiding," Michel recalled, which elicited Lacan's intervention: "Then, you acknowledge that this is cross-dressing [*travestissement*]" (p. 312). Michel confirmed this. Lacan insisted: "Therefore you acknowledge that this has ruined everything in your life, and you call that, yourself, cross-dressing. Therefore this implies that you know very well that you are a man." Michel replied: "Yes, that's something I'm very much aware of" (p. 313).

Michel explained that when he had women's clothing on his body, he felt happiness. Michel described that the satisfaction granted by female clothing was not sexual: "It is not on the plane of sex. It's on the plane … well, I call this the plane of the heart [*coeur*]." To further clarify, he added, "I have already the entire character of a woman, on the sentimental plane as well" (Lacan, 1996, p. 313). Michel claimed to have had a happy childhood, but with a recurrent nightmare of a terrifying woman with a blonde wig who came to the house to cut off people's limbs. He had been a drug user and as a cross-dresser would wear a blonde wig. Once while high on drugs, he made an attempt at self-castration with a blunt razor blade—the pain stopped him, and he was hospitalized.

He had sexual experiences with men and women alike and reported not having any deep pleasure with either. It seemed to have been a mechanical act that had to be accomplished because it was expected of him but whose necessity he did not feel spontaneously. He said: "I was in the arms of a woman; I had a lot of trouble penetrating her; I was out of my depth. I never felt like a man." Lacan interjected: "Nevertheless, you must have felt like a man, you are endowed with a male organ." To which he answered: "Only at the moment when I felt pleasure during a sexual encounter. For me it was a pleasure one cannot refuse. One is obliged to take it" (Lacan, 1996, p. 317). With this, Michel H. seemed to say that he felt that the only moment that he possessed a virile member was when he experienced pleasure, with the qualification that this pleasure was so perfunctory that, in consequence, his organ was perfunctory as well. The way that he talked about being obliged to take pleasure betrayed a relationship to the Other as marked by a jouissance that made him its object without allowing him to identify with his own enjoyment. This separation from his enjoyment during sex seems to account for the unhopeful prognosis given by Lacan at the conclusion of his assessment. Michel clearly identified as a transvestite and not as a transsexual. Cross-dressing gave him the assurance that he knew what his sex was and granted him access to a jouissance that he could own and that produced what he called "happiness."

Indeed, Michel H. was not ambivalent about his sexual identity. During the interview, he acknowledged several times that he was a man and that he was struggling with his effeminate tendencies. Lacan (1996) remarked: "And you say that when you were drugged with morphine and cocaine you felt more at ease." Michel responded: "More energy, yes, I forgot everything except that I was a woman because I was dressed as a woman." Lacan added: "You forgot everything except ..." Michel: "Except myself dressed as a woman." Lacan: "While you were under the influence of drugs you felt what?" Michel: "I forgot that I was a man" (p. 325).

The drugs regulated the painful enjoyment of being a man who experienced happiness in feminine garments: "When I am dressed like a girl, I realize that I am a man, I realize that I am a transvestite. This is very hard" (Lacan, 1996, p. 326). He talked about feeling embarrassed and humiliated. And yet, this was the way Michel experienced jouissance.

Before he was hospitalized, he would lock himself up in his apartment and spend days dressed as a woman. He would be "drugged to better feel his character [*personnage*]" (Lacan, 1996, p. 326). Michel H. was addicted to drugs, felt suicidal, and thought that the only solution was to have a sex change operation. He had read about it and planned to travel to Morocco to undergo the surgery. He was mostly interested in changing his face, to make it become truly beautiful.[11] To achieve this end, he was even ready to become a prostitute. "I learnt many things: that one can get a castration; that one can have breasts with hormones; that one can really manage to metamorphose a man into a woman" (p. 332).

All through the interview, Lacan (1996) paid heightened attention to the young man's mannerisms, to his errors, to his peculiar syntax, and above all, to a poem in which Michel had described his desire to be transformed into "the eternal, the blonde woman" (p. 336). The first three stanzas of the poem read as follows:

The eternal: The blonde woman

Pinet hospital
I tell a project of wanting to forget myself
in the perseverance
to find my most beautiful personality
adorable Corinne

Transvestite I hate
I am very embarrassed to know I am effeminate

---

[11] Michel's interest in beauty is similar to the sign that appeared in Schreber's hypnopompic idea that it would "be *beautiful* to be woman submitting to the act of copulation" (Freud, 1911, p. 36; emphasis added). Beauty, as a denial of castration, plays an important imaginary function for the ego.

and the suffering
of ridicule
wounds my sensibility
Corinne is emptied

Michel is born again
I am secure because I think
that I have a chance
to kill myself one day if I am desperate
Corinne executed. (p. 336)

The poem was signed three times: "Michel, Michelle, and Corinne." Corinne, he explained, was his new name, a name he had chosen since his childhood; it was the name of a little girl who was then 6 years old, which was coincidentally the age at which he started cross-dressing (p. 338). In the facsimile reproduction of the poem, one can notice that the frilly C of Corinne is identical to the M of Michel, as the leftover letter of his male self. Also, it is hard not to hear *corps* (body) in Corinne. Lacan commented on the poem:

LACAN: "You are the one speaking, therefore you adore yourself?"
MICHEL: "That's it, yes."
LACAN: "In short, do you speak to yourself?"
MICHEL: "Yes, that's it, I ask myself questions."
LACAN: "Corinne, who is she?"
MICHEL: "It's me. I changed my name; it's better to receive my feminine state." (p. 338)

It looked as if Corinne manifested the fact that the body can be changed by language; this was the body that Michel acquired via the Corinne/corps persona of his cross-dressing reveries. What remained was the indelible mark of his masculinity on his face, a face he felt was imperative to transform because it could not be hidden in feminine clothes. His face betrayed his maleness.

Michel's desire to modify his face reveals that he did not experience his body as fully his. Had his body fallen? Because a body can fall, a body can fall away like a fruit's soft, ripe peel, as we have seen was the case for Stephen in Joyce's *A Portrait* (1992). Lacan notes that this falling away of the body is imposed on Stephen, like imposed speech, resembling the voices heard by Primeau. Once the peel has slipped away, some sort of reparation takes place, and Stephen relates to his body as alien and disgusting (Harari, 2002, p. 338). Primeau also achieved some reparation and experienced the voices as a bridge and as a theatre where he was both creator and director. For Michel, his body was reclaimed by an act of nomination when he renamed himself Corinne, in an effort to reunite his male body (corps) and his feminine heart (coeur). Michel's sinthome was not clearly related to the need for a complete transformation of the real of the body and may not have guaranteed the success of a sex change surgery. Michel's demand for a surgical change appears to be a demand for a facial feminization rather than a genital change. And, the key to his jouissance was predicated on possessing a female "quality"—being tender or sweet. But, he hesitated between the masculine (*je suis doux*) and the feminine (*je suis douce et gentile*). When he was a man in women's clothes, he was a complete woman, that is, one with a penis.

On the whole, Lacan sounded quite pessimistic about this case. He did not recommend a sex change for Michel because Michel did not evince the usual transsexual discourse; for instance, he never declared that he was a woman trapped in a male body. Although Lacan (2006) noted a clinical proximity between psychotic transsexualist practices and perversion, the difference is that in perversion the father is addressed defiantly, while in psychosis the issue is to obtain the father's authorization (p. 474). This corresponds to the way in which the father (or the-name-of) is called on to regulate a jouissance perceived as invasive and all too real. This was not the case with Michel, who was nevertheless a tormented fetishist.

Michel used drugs to diminish the awareness that he was a man and to better identify with the feminine role he was playing. Drugs helped him confirm the disavowal of castration. In this case, a sex change would have meant the actual realization of the push-towards-woman (already present in the terrifying blonde woman of his childhood nightmares) and thus would have been a dangerous solution. The sex change would have jeopardized Michel's possibility of experiencing jouissance. Lacan (1996) was clear about the psychic cost of the surgery: "As he has said it himself clearly, he will not experience any jouissance, neither with a man, nor with a woman. He will not have greater satisfaction, even less than he had had so far" (p. 348). The poem contained a warning: "I have a chance/to kill myself one day if I am desperate/Corinne executed." The risk of suicide loomed large: A sex change could be the *execution* of Corinne, in both meanings of the word, both as an implementation and as a death sentence for corps/coeur/Corinne, who was himself—a man with a feminine heart, a woman with a penis.

CHERCHEZ LA FEMME

We have observed a correlation between the foreclosure of the Name-of-the-Father and the "unstoppable yearning to be a woman"[12] often witnessed in

---
[12] I heard this once from a patient.

transsexualist practices. This would be true of Schreber, as Russell Grigg (1999) stated:

> Schreber's symptoms are not really homosexual at all and it would be more accurate to call them *transsexual*. These transsexual and other phenomena, for which Lacan coined the phrase "push towards woman" (*pousse-à-la-femme*) are the result of the initial foreclosure of the Name-of-the-Father and the corresponding lack in the imaginary of phallic meaning. (p. 55)

Here, Grigg used Lacan's (1973) tag of *pousse-à-la-femme* ("push-towards-Woman") (p. 22). The tricky phrase could be rendered in English as "driving one to become a woman," if "drive" was not already a technical concept translating Freud's *Trieb*. The concept could be exemplified by Renée Richards, the famous transsexual tennis player, who created a media frenzy in 1976 when she went to court and won the right to play as a woman in the U.S. Open. She was asked at age 72 about the motivations for her sex change more than 30 years before. She described her decision to change sex as resulting from an unyielding "pressure to change into a woman." This could be an adequate translation of Lacan's expression pousse-à-la-femme. Richards also said that she wished she could have something that could have stopped that "pressure" and prevented the surgery: "What I said was if there were a drug, some voodoo, any kind of mind-altering magic remedy to keep the man intact, that would have been preferable, but there wasn't" (Walder, 2007, February 1). By then, she seemed to have regrets about something that she had felt earlier as inevitable: "Better to be an intact man functioning with 100 percent capacity for everything than to be a transsexual woman who is an imperfect woman." However, the imperative to turn into a woman had been a way of warding off suicide: "The pressure to change into a woman was so strong that if I had not been able to do it, I might have been a suicide" (Walder, 2007, February 1). Was that a psychotic moment or an acting out? How does the push-towards-Woman generate such a performative femininity?

Let us try to circumscribe the context of the discussion more rigorously. Is the femininity at play in the complex case of Schreber a natural, innate femininity copied from the mother, as Stoller proposes in male-to-female transsexualism? Stoller considers "protofemininity" as an innate predisposition in both females and males:

> Though it is true that the boy's first love is heterosexual, and though fathers are too-powerful rivals, there is an earlier stage in gender identity development wherein the boy is merged with mother. Only after months does she gradually become a clearly separate object. Sensing oneself a part of mother—a primeval and thus profound part of

character structure (core gender identity)—lays the groundwork for an infant's sense of femininity. This sets the girl firmly on the path to femininity in adulthood but puts the boy in danger of building into his core gender identity a sense of oneness with mother (a sense of femaleness). Depending on how and at what pace a mother allows her son to separate, this phase of merging with her will leave residual effects that may be expressed as disturbances of masculinity. (Stoller, 1985, p. 16)

On the other hand, one might want to see in Schreber and Richards manifestations of a phallic femininity, a femininity flaunted as masquerade, as one may find in hysteria. Can this phallic femininity be found in cross-dressing practices, considering the position vis-à-vis castration that grants the transvestite the jouissance of his organ veiled in feminine clothes? Or, is this femininity related to a "jouissance beyond the phallus," like the one Lacan attributed to the mystics (Mahieu, 2004, p. 28)?

"PUSH-TOWARDS-WOMAN"

In his study of the famous president's memoir, Freud (1911) had stated that Schreber's "idea of being transformed into a woman was the salient feature and the earliest germ of the delusional system. It also proved to be the one part of it that persisted after his cure, and the one part that was able to retain a place in his behavior in real life after he had recovered" (p. 20).

Following Freud's path, Lacan (1993) stressed the core function of Schreber's transformation into a woman and wondered whether this was a "properly psychotic mechanism, one that would be imaginary and that would extend from the first hint of identification with and capture by the feminine image, to the blossoming of a world system in which the subject is completely absorbed in his imagination by a feminine identification" (p. 63). What should interest us at this point is that it was in his commentary of the Schreber case that Lacan presented imaginary mechanisms that he later systematized under the name of the push-towards-Woman.

Freud's thesis has the merit of simplicity. For him, Schreber's transformation into a woman implied a feminine position toward the father, that is, a castration. In this view, Schreber's evolution showed first a rejection, then an acceptance of his transformation into a woman. Finally, in his cure, the cultivation of a female persona itself was to acquire a stabilizing effect. The transformation originally experienced by Schreber as an invasion by God was understood by Lacan (1993) also as connected with some basic bisexuality: "In President Schreber's case this rejected meaning is closely related to the primitive bisexuality" (p. 85). But for him, homosexuality played a secondary role in the interpretation of the case: "In no way has President Schreber ever introjected any type of feminine form" (p. 85). The missing meaning for Schreber was related to bisexuality insofar as bisexuality "involves the feminine function in its essential symbolic meaning ... at the level of procreation" (p. 86). What precipitated Schreber's psychosis would have been "an irruption in the real of something he has never known, the sudden emergence of a total strangeness that will progressively bring on a radical submersion of all his categories to the point of forcing him into a veritable reshaping of his world" (p. 86). In the end, this drive had to transform Schreber into a woman, not just any woman, but God's wife, the anointed person who would be the bearer of a new human race.

For Marie-Hélène Brousse (2003), Lacan's reading of Freud's analysis in the Schreber case reveals the push-towards-Woman not to be a contingent feature but a logically and necessary element that one should look for in psychoses, even when it does not manifest itself clinically. Lacan used the phrase in 1972 when he referred to Schreber's transformation into a woman, a transformation that he explained as the result of the sudden, violent entrance of a father.[13] Interestingly, Brousse dates Lacan's invention of the concept to 1957, just 1 year after the publication of Henri's case.

Indeed, the coining of the phrase *push-towards-Woman* in 1972 looked back to Lacan's "On a Question Prior to Any Possible Treatment of Psychosis." In 1972, the push-towards-Woman appears as the result of the "irruption of *One-Father*, (italics in the original)" the same One-Father alluded to in the 1957–1958 text "On a Question..." In the earlier text, the One-Father was present at the dramatic conjuncture that marked the beginning of each case of psychosis. This One-Father is not the subject's own father, but the signifier of paternity as a legal fiction. This unique father is the agent for a metaphor, an agent represented by a signifier summoned by a contingency of life. This missing or foreclosed signifier "presents itself to a woman who has just given birth, in her husband's face, to a penitent confessing her sins in the person of her confessor, or to a girl in love in her encounter 'with the young man's father'" (Lacan, 2006, p. 481). This One-Father, foreclosed in the symbolic, comes back as real jouissance, and it can also be embodied in a female form.

As we have seen, the concept of push-towards-Woman refutes completely the Freudian hypothesis of an unconscious homosexuality as determinant for the sexual causality of psychosis. If, as Brousse (2003) claims, "(t)he push-towards-woman is a theory of the sexual partner in psychosis, a way of thinking about the sexual partner" (p. 81), it is more specifically the sexual partner's jouissance that is at stake. This jouissance

---

[13] "I could here, by developing the inscription that I made through a hyperbolic function of Schreber's psychosis, demonstrate in what it contains of the sardonic the effect of the push-to-the-woman which is specified in the first quantifier; having made very clear that it is from the irruption of *One-Father* as without reason that is precipitated here the effect felt as of forcing, in the field of an Other to be thought as the most foreign in every sense" (Lacan, 1973, p. 22).

cannot be symbolized because the phallic signifier has been foreclosed. Brousse identifies in the push-towards-Woman a specific way by which the subject related to the Other, not just any Other, but an Other of sensual pleasure, in other words, of jouissance. The push-towards-Woman is thus a construction that expresses an interpretation of jouissance in terms of its very feminization.

A good example of this could be given once more by Schreber's case since the first indication of a transsexual delusion in progress came in a thought linked to women's sexual enjoyment. Schreber indeed speculated "that after all it really must be rather beautiful to be a woman submitting to the act of copulation" (Freud, 1911, p. 36). In Schreber's mind, this notion evolved and finally led to the voluptuous debauchery that he would not hesitate to attribute to God. Similarly, for Henri, the push-towards-Woman was a way of approaching jouissance in the idealized bliss, thanks to which he imagined a female version of himself when he saw himself engaged in a total rapport with the opposite sex.

BEYOND OEDIPUS, WOMAN

What stands out, as Brousse (2003) has reminded us, is that the push-towards-Woman is a not an Oedipal phenomenon (it is not a push-towards-mother), and, moreover, that the Freudian thesis of unconscious homosexuality fails as a cause of psychosis: It tries too hard to assimilate psychosis to the Oedipal structure, and the thesis "does not work" (p. 83). Brousse claims that the framework of Oedipal laws does not apply in psychosis in the same way as it applies to neurosis. Correcting the usual interpretation that psychosis occurs when "something is wrong in the maternal desire" because of a paternal weakness, she reiterated Lacan's argument that a so-called weak father may be a father who is all too strong; often, he finds himself in the position of a legislator making the law rather than representing it, or he is an all-too-pure, too good, too perfect father (and Schreber's father is an egregious example of this), which prevents the Name-of-the-Father from functioning as a signifier.

Thus, if we follow the terms that Lacan uses to define clearly the push-towards-Woman, it appears that they are not correlated with the Oedipal model but with the modes of jouissance proposed in the sexuation formulas. Schreber's imposed feminization was a way to write the jouissance of the Other.[14] Jouissance was equated with a signifier, "the" woman, who was placed in the position of Other. Schreber was to become "the" woman that was needed to grant the jouissance of the Other. One may introduce variations in this logic, such as "being the phallus that the

---

[14]Lacan (1986) contended that paranoia places jouissance in the place of the Other (p. 7).

mother lacks," "being 'the' woman men lack," "being the woman God lacks." These inscribe several forms of the sinthome, stabilizing a psychosis, supporting jouissance while securing a sexual rapport that does not exist.

Schreber's feminization, described in 1957–1958 by Lacan (2006) as only imaginary, must be understood more generally as having effects at the level of the three registers of the Symbolic, Real, and Imaginary (p. 476). His feminization grants him a "transsexualist jouissance" in which we can see the real manifestation of jouissance in his body. It is also imaginary, as witnessed by Schreber's bliss in looking at his feminized image in the mirror. It has also a symbolic reference: The woman as an exception, "the" woman, who will copulate with God and create a new world order by providing a new generation is a Name-of-the-Father in disguise, as we shall see. The push-towards-woman functions for Schreber like a sinthome; later in his illness, he knew that he will not fully become a woman, but the certainty of the prospect of a future, potential transformation still sustains him because it makes up for the deficiencies in the Name-of-the-Father and is a correlate of his transsexual jouissance.[15]

PUSH-TOWARDS-WOMAN AND FANTASY OF FEMINIZATION

Millot (1990) also used to refer to the feminization often observed in psychosis when she would note that primary transsexuality does not involve psychiatric symptoms (p. 42). This may make us question whether the push-towards-Woman is specific to psychosis or whether it can be considered as a more generalized phenomenon. Going further, Franz Kaltenbeck (1992) proposed the application of the *pousse-à-la-femme* to all clinical structures, while always keeping in mind a differential diagnosis. Kaltenbeck considers the "push-towards-Woman" in psychosis to be the opposite of the attraction toward a woman one finds in neuroses and perversions. He notes that the attraction that the Other woman possesses for the hysteric woman (we have seen this with Sidonie and Dora) shows that the Other woman is not an exclusive element specific to the genital drive of men. Interestingly, Kaltenbeck calls the push-towards-Woman a "clinical belvedere," that is, a vantage viewpoint for both sexes and for all structures (neurosis, perversion, and psychosis) (pp. 9–10).

---

[15] In "On a Question Prior to Any Possible Treatment of Psychosis," Lacan (2006) offers a modified schema R. On the upper left of schema I, in the place of the imaginary phallus, appears transsexualist jouissance. Lacan's formulation of the sinthome offered a new perspective to understand transsexualism as a suppletion, a stand-in for the missing phallic signifier in the Symbolic.

Freud (1919) wrote that "the nucleus of the unconscious (that is to say, the repressed) is in each human being that side of him which belongs to the opposite sex" (p. 200; parenthetical material in the original). As we have seen, for the unconscious of everyone, and regardless of one's sex, the opposite sex is always female. In the same piece, Freud discovered that a recurrent fantasy of feminization that he encountered with neurotic patients displayed a structural character. On the one hand, it represented a feminine attitude: "There can be no doubt that the original fantasy in the case of the girl, 'I am being beaten (i.e., I am loved) by my father,' represents a feminine attitude" (p. 201; parenthetical material in the original). Freud anticipated that this neurotic fantasy, which implied an underlying feminine attitude, was also to be found in psychosis: "I should not be surprised if it were one day possible to prove that the same fantasy is the basis of the delusional litigiousness of paranoia" (p. 194).

Let us insist: The push-towards-Woman has been observed both in men and in women (Kaltenbeck, 1992; Laurent, 1992). This is why Eric Laurent sees it not as a phenomenological category but as a logical concept related to the drive (p. 12). Indeed, Schreber's description of his transformation into a woman conveys a sense of an imposed force, of a drive pulling him into an inevitable sexual metamorphosis. For Laurent (1989), this thrust is how the drive functions in psychosis; it aims at the Woman that all men are lacking (p. 31). This search for Eldorado would be motivated by the urge to find "the woman that does not exist" (Lacan, 1990, p. 60). As Morel (2000a) observes, "The woman only exists in psychosis as a vanishing point of convergence in a delusional perspective, as a point placed in the infinite" (p. 226).

Whereas the push-towards-Woman can account for Schreber's case, Henri's case, and many other cases of male-to-female transsexuals, can it account for cases of female-to-male transsexualism? Here, opinions are divided: Catherine Millot (1981) is inconclusive about female-to-male transsexuals and stresses, like Moustapha Safouan (1974), the psychotic element in transsexualism. According to research on transsexualism in the Department of Psychoanalysis at the University of Paris VIII, male-to-female transsexualism cannot be considered equivalent to female-to-male transsexualism because the relationship to the father is structurally different (Brousse, 2003, p. 83). Geneviève Morel (2000a), who has explored in some detail the types of feminine positioning that are expressed in the pousse-à-la-femme, argues that the push-towards-Woman applies to transsexuals of both sexes.

PUSH-TOWARDS-WOMAN AND SEXUATION

In Lacan's sexuation (1998b) formulas (p. 78), the symbolic phallus requires the correlate of a barred Woman. If the name of the father is foreclosed, the Woman exists as a delusional substitute, equivalent to the exception of the primal father. The Woman functions as an ideal image of the body and as an empty envelope that produces jouissance, a jouissance beyond the phallus, the jouissance of the Other.[16] The Woman becomes a solution to the problem of the real of jouissance, to the problem of a jouissance that—like trauma—resists any imaginary or symbolic assimilation. Thus, Lacan (2006) wrote that, because Schreber was "unable to be the phallus the mother is missing, there remained the solution of being the woman that men are missing" (p. 472). This led Catherine Millot (1990), who followed the thread of "the" Woman, to argue that all transsexuals are psychotic. Given this structure,

> the transsexual symptom appears to function as a substitution of the Name-of-the-Father inasmuch as the transsexual aims to incarnate the Woman. Not *one* woman in the sense of "not-all," implying that no one could claim to represent All women—the transsexual position consists of wanting to be All, all woman, more woman than all woman, and representing them all. (p. 42; italics in the original)

As I have suggested, my general thesis is somewhat different and at least more nuanced. Some revealing nuances are provided by trans people themselves.

BEING THE WOMAN WHO DOES NOT EXIST

American drag queen RuPaul is very aware of the difference between impersonating *a* woman or Woman. He once said, "I do not impersonate females! How many women do you know who wear seven-inch heels, four-foot wigs, and skintight dresses?" He added, "I don't dress like a woman; I dress like a drag queen!" He impersonates "the" Woman. The crucial role played by the mythical Woman for some transsexuals calls up a case that I supervised of the treatment of a presurgical male who was transitioning to female. Victoria was tall, attractive, and seductive; she insisted

---

[16] J.-C. Maleval (1996), exploring what he called the psychotic "dislocation of jouissance," clearly distinguished phallic jouissance from jouissance of the Other:

> The jouissance of the Other is not regulated by the law of the signifier, in a manner that it finds its satisfaction in objects that are not separated from the subject. In Freudian terms, this would be a pre-genital jouissance, this is to say that it is not subjected to the primacy of the phallus. This jouissance is crazy, enigmatic, outside the symbolic; it is centered in the subject's body and on its organs. … The foreclosure of the Name-of-the-Father implies the absence of a limit in regards to jouissance, a limit established by the loss of a primal object. The psychotic subject finds himself invaded by the jouissance of the Other, his body becomes the site of various diverse phenomena, pleasant and painful, voluptuous and anxiety provoking. (pp. 119–120)

that she knew how to give sexual pleasure to any man—she had what it took for that. She could guarantee it: No man could be dissatisfied with her. Victoria was sure she could offer pleasure to every man in the world. For Victoria, access to universal jouissance was just a problem of time—in the end, she would give pleasure to all men.

Not just by her good looks, but in her ability to provide jouissance to men, Victoria felt that there was no other creature more woman than herself. One may conclude that Victoria was positioned as the woman with a capital W, occupying a position equivalent to what in Lacan's (1998b) formulas of sexuation is the father's function, a function that inscribes the universal quantifier for All $\forall$. Victoria is not like other women, and she could provide jouissance to all men, assuming a position of an exception (she positions herself as the one subject who is not subjected to the phallic law of castration, she constitutes an outside of the set). And yet, Victoria, paradoxically, supports the set (every universal needs an exception to prove the rule).

Victoria's case evinces a particular relation to the body: As an 8-year-old boy, she was raped by a relative. She experienced this violent attack against her body with extreme detachment that might remind us of Lacan's (2005) reading of Joyce's particular link to the body. Victoria felt as if her body was some sort of envelope divested of libidinal value. In the transsexual artificiality of an embodiment of the Woman, Victoria remade and reclaimed her body in all its imaginary narcissistic value. With proficient makeup, carefully chosen clothes, and silicone implants, she made of her transformation into the Woman, her creative sinthome. She would quip: "Women envy my body. But I made it. I worked on it."

Victoria seems to confirm Millot's (1990) thesis, which is that Woman as a founding exception can function as a sort of Name-of-the-Father (pp. 36–46). Here Woman can amount to a myth similar to that of the father in Freud's (1912–1913) analysis of the primal horde of "Totem and Taboo." According to the myth, all the sons accept and abide by the law in contrast to the "primal father"; he only stands out as the exception to the law and has access to unlimited jouissance. This exception to the law secures it. This excluded position can be occupied by a tyrant, Woman, a lawless mother, and so on. Victoria sees herself not as a woman among other women, but as Woman, and as such appears as both a limit and a substitute for the paternal function while granting access to unlimited jouissance.

Both the father of the primal horde and Woman are a mythical starting point of unbridled fullness whose "primordial repression" constitutes the symbolic order. Millot (1990) was the first to introduce the idea that the transsexual symptom can have a structural function analogous to that assigned by Lacan to Joyce's writing. However, I disagree with her generalized diagnosis of psychosis. In the same way that one cannot talk about psychosis but only of a psychotic structure with Joyce, a structure such that, without the sinthome of writing, Joyce could have become psychotic. One should not talk of psychosis in transsexuality but only of a psychotic structure.

I AM THE OTHER OF SEX

To return to my original example, one can speculate that Lacan did not recommend Henri's sex change because he guessed that Henri was not so eager to fulfill his wish. As we saw, his request functioned only insofar as it could be maintained as the unrealized pursuit of a chimera. If it had been realized, there was a chance of a psychotic breakdown. Henri's symptom was constructed around the pursuit of an imaginary feminization (there was, however, a real manifestation of jouissance in his body in the voluptuous bliss of his daydreaming fantasies) and as a symbolic reference. His pursuit had to be postponed to an ideal point in the future and projected in an aspiration of himself as the only woman, the exception, "the" woman who would be able to join someone of the opposite sex. Following Lacan's recommendation against surgery in this case, we may argue that Henri did not require an actual realization (that is, in the real of the body) for the transformation to be operative. Hence, I would argue that to assess a request for a sex change it is essential to identify the therapeutic effectiveness of the existing symptoms.

For both Henri and Michel H., Lacan did not recommend sex change surgery. In the case of Michel H., it was because he was a cross-dresser who would lose the source of his jouissance and whose sex change would trap him even more in the torments brought about by the push-towards-Woman. Unlike Schreber, who was first tortured by the transsexual delusion but eventually came to terms with his feminization, we see in Michel H.'s poem that he experienced the push-towards-Woman as a humiliating agony leading to his own death. As Morel (2000a) observed, drugs, alcohol, writing, dance, mathematics, and even psychoanalysis can reknot for some time the registers of Real, Imaginary, and Symbolic—they become a sinthome, a supplement for the Name-of-the-Father (p. 217). This provides a creative solution to the problem of sexuation; however, the push-towards-Woman does not always work as a sinthome.

Henri's case is not too far from Schreber's since for both the push-towards-Woman had a stabilizing effect independent of the need for an actual realization. With David Reimer, discussed in Chapter 7, we encountered someone who was actually "pushed to become a woman" by all the medical technologies and yet who could work under the phallic premise. Even without a penis, he would build a male sexual identity while moving to the right side of sexuation formulas, where he reached a love that was not entirely subjected to the phallus.

Henri and Michel H. both possessed a penis, but the possession alone did not guarantee an inscription within the phallic order. Despite the real presence of the organ, Michel and Henri render pathetic evidence of their non-inscription on the phallic order. Even their names functioned as false names requiring a supplementary act of self-nomination. Similarly, when David Reimer acquired a new name in his transition back to male, he requested that his parents make the final choice for him, replaying what usually happens when a baby is born. It is also worth mentioning that when the boy who was raised as a girl learned the truth of his incredible life, the very first question he asked his father was, "What was my name?" This reveals the importance of the name because it determines a more lasting sense of the body.

In a striking turn of events, as we saw, the authorities declared Henri a girl at birth, and he was named Anne-Henriette. Until the age of 16, Henri's family treated him as a girl, even when they seem to have known that he had male genitalia. He was at ease being a "she" until, all of a sudden, his father forced him to become a man. The father's violence compelled Henri to become what he felt he was not, whereas Michel behaved as if he had what women lacked. Michel was a man dressed like a woman, and he was the phallus and had it. David, who did not have a penis, could nevertheless be inscribed in the phallic order, proving that even when nobody had it or was it, there did not exist any subject who was not subjected to the phallic premise. David's case provides evidence that the unconscious sexual positioning does not depend on organ attribution. David may have identified as a man but unconsciously positioned himself on the female side in terms of the logic of the sexuation grid. He was on the side that indicates the inevitable inscription of the law of sexual difference, a law that is not all subjected to the phallus.

Primeau was a "sexual mutant," masculine and feminine all in one. He was subjugated by the voices in his head, struggling to anchor a shattering jouissance. Henri presented a transsexual jouissance that was sustained by the chimera of one day becoming Woman. Michel H. embodied phallic femininity and experienced jouissance with an organ that was veiled in feminine undergarments. David used phallic emblems as a masquerade to ensure his sexual positioning, a positioning that suggested that he was subjected to the phallic premise, whereas he was not all subjected to it. David, Michel H., and Henri are cases that we can provisionally classify as of neurosis, perversion, and psychosis, respectively. This would prove that transsexualism is not necessarily or uniquely a psychotic phenomenon, and that "transgender" is not in itself a pathological category.

As Lacan (2006) remarked in his discussion of Schreber, the uncertainty about one's sex is a common feature of hysteria (p. 456). For transsexuals, it is the hysteric question that is taken for an answer. The next chapter thus explores sexual identity in clinical cases of hysteria to see whether the varied permutations of the question around which hysteria is structured have been affected by transgender discourse.

Chapter 9

Hysteria and transsexualism

Beyond pink and blue, dolls and cars, and playing house and roughhousing, one wonders, how does a child begin to identify unconsciously as a girl or a boy? The imaginary identification promoted by gender theory is insufficient to account for the unconscious dimension of sexuality. The subject's sexual identity does not depend on an identification with an image (which would fall under the category of performativity) but on a symbolic position (thus closer to performance) that is related to what psychoanalysts call *phallus*— the tool to negotiate the Real that eludes us. The phallus is an obstacle. It is nothing other than a failed answer to the conundrum of sexual difference. This difference cannot be fully grasped (it is just speculation constructed on the real of the impossibility of a sexual rapport). Situating oneself as a man, or a woman, is a complex process, directly connected with the symbolization of the law and castration. The transgender phenomenon proves that there is nothing natural that would direct us to the opposite sex. Sexual identity is a secondary nature. Since the unconscious has no representation of masculinity or femininity, we cannot speak with certainty in terms of sexual identity of being a man or a woman, but only of an assurance, a happy uncertainty.

In his later seminars, Lacan introduced the idea of identification with a symptom as a possible supplement for the nonrapport. Accordingly, sexual positioning could become symptomatic variations: a *sinthome*-she or a *sinthome*-he. The sinthome is a creation that is not trying to "make up" for the disharmony between the sexes; it is a creation that "makes do" around the disjunction. For this reason, Verhaeghe (2009) says that relationships work when the emphasis is not placed on the chimera of overcoming the disharmony between the sexes but on the freedom granted by a creation built around differences. Thus, lovers often feel the need to invent their own language, giving each other a new name (p. 99). What I am proposing is an alternative to the usual psychoanalytic treatment of transgenderism. Transgender activism and scholarship have been wary of psychoanalysis, with good reasons. Psychoanalysis has a history of heteronormatization and pathologization of nonnormative sexualities. My perspective follows

Lacan's later theory of the sinthome to rethink sexual difference. This theory is a departure from the classical Freudian theory of the Oedipus complex and even from Lacan's first formulations that insisted on the Symbolic and the father. It departs as well from a second period in Lacan's work when he would put the emphasis on the theory of fantasy and the object cause of desire. As we have seen, Lacan modified his whole position a last time in the mid-1970s when he elaborated a new conception of sexuality, just before discussing Joyce's writings. Lacan discovered then a new paradigm and a new relation to the body, which is very helpful in advancing the understanding of transgenderism.

Clinical work shows that some breakdowns occur precisely when the unconscious identifications that produced a sexual positioning fall. I have a vivid memory of one patient in crisis who stormed into the barrio's clinic one afternoon shouting that her sons had been transformed into dogs. She yelled that she would not have minded seeing her sons being turned into *patos* ("ducks" but also Puerto Rican slang for gays), but she wept because they had become *perros* ("dogs"). Her crisis exposed her innovative strategy for coming up with an answer to the enigma of sexual difference. Pato and perro introduced opposing pairs, a principle of order, a set of norms comparable to the order of the phallus as a mark of difference between signifiers. Her delusional elaboration, articulated at the top of her lungs in the crowded waiting room, was an improvised invention, an emergency patch responding to the impossible of sexual difference.

THE PHALLUS AS CONSCIENTIOUS OBJECTION

I briefly discuss one of my cases, that of Sergei, to show the role of the phallus and of identifications. Sergei was an artist for whom the identifications that had sustained him in a male position until his early 20s suddenly failed. He had successfully auditioned for a very important job. After several nights of insomnia, finally an idea came to him: He had the conviction that he was going to become a woman. Such a surprising realization would trigger the most extreme anxiety. Tormented but resigned to what he experienced as an inescapable destiny, Sergei acted on his fantasies of emasculation and had sex with a man. He found the experience revolting, and his anxiety increased even more.

The precise moment at which his feminizing delusion appeared was revealing. Sergei experienced this "push-towards-Woman" at a special juncture in his life, when he was about to compete with his father professionally. Sergei's father enjoyed a brilliant international career and was reputed in the same discipline as his son. Sergei's fantasy of becoming a woman, which caused him intense psychic pain, was in fact a response to an excessive jouissance, an excess that he could not symbolize. The shocking irruption of the fantasy was Sergei's way of resolving an impossible situation: It aimed at compensating for the insufficiency of previous identifications that could no longer sustain him at a moment when he was to compete decisively with his father. Sergei was acting out in the Real his need to adopt a passive position toward his father by receiving help, support, and endorsement, a position that he equated with femininity. The rejection of actual sex with a man expressed a masculine protest and implied a tentative phallic inscription.

Sergei's family background was atypical. Not unlike Freud's Hans, he had been called "little Sergei" in his family. Whenever he compared himself to his father, he felt belittled. While an important figure in the world, his father had been placed in a degraded position by Sergei's mother. Through her, it was the whole position of being a *man* that was questioned. The answer to the question, "Am I a man?" a question that was haunting Sergei, was becoming more and more like an obscure riddle. He had been raised in a town whose name, in his native language, is a transliteration of the slang word for gay male. This city, by the way, had been made famous as a result of the artistic achievements of Sergei's father. Sergei had left his native city at a very early age, with encouragements from family members, who all insisted that he would do well because he was already a "man." Then, Sergei had moved to another city to pursue more intense studies with a leading figure in his field, at first, accompanied by his mother, who had to leave behind the rest of the family. Finding it hard to adapt to the new city, his mother became depressed; she missed her husband and family; at the time, the father was having extramarital affairs. Sergei and his mother developed a semi-incestuous bond: The mother was totally devoted to her son's career; they shared a bed, and she had increasingly exhibitionist behavior, often going naked around the house. Eventually, the father came to fetch his wife. The mother was torn between her prodigious son, her successful husband from whom she felt estranged, and her other children left at home. She chose to return home. Sergei stayed alone and continued studying and progressing. Eventually, he got a big career break when he was awarded a scholarship that gave him the opportunity to study in the United States.

Yet, his choices in life appeared limited, overdetermined by a talent that could not be wasted. He had not yet reached adolescence, but to appease their separation, his mother claimed that "he was already a man," that he was mature well beyond his years, hence strong enough to be in New York without her. Then, Sergei arrived in *Man*hattan, where he studied in the prestigious conservatory *Man*nes College of Music. He later continued his studies in the *Man*hattan School of Music. However, the signifier "man" also referred to a degraded place, at least according to his mother. There was, however, an option left, which was to join the other side, namely, the side of women. Sergei started failing in school and eventually left New York to move back to the town from which his father's family came, which was not where his father and family lived. There, he was mentored by a woman who shared a first name with his mother and, most importantly, with the woman who later became his wife.

MAN, WOMAN, HUSBAND

Sergei's question about his sex was a recurrent obsession, oppressive and anguishing. During our treatment, he decided to get married in what initially looked like an impetuous decision. This marriage, however, allowed him to assume a sexual position not fully as man but rather as "husband." Paradoxically, while his father enjoyed continuous professional success, he was looked down at by the mother, who later divorced him "for being a womanizer." "I believed everything my mother said and forgot my father," Sergei said. "I had to take sides and chose my mother's." His mother professed to despise men, especially Sergei's father, who was, according to her, "a great artist, a bad husband, and a horrible man." On the other hand, she was totally devoted to her talented son. Thus, Sergei appeared caught in a double bind. His virility was sustained by his mother's adoration for his being a boy (which made him her favorite) and was contrasted with the negative regard his mother had for men. Not only was his father seen as a horrible man, but also being a man was seen as a horrible fate. "Women were better than men," his mother proclaimed.

Sergei's belief that he was going to become a woman was assuaged by a nomination. He and his father had the same name. Sergei complained that he was often confused with his father, something that he experienced as a mixed blessing. When he decided to get married, to distinguish himself from his father, he hyphenated his last name and added his wife's maiden name to his. Soon after, the certainty of an eventual transformation into a woman subsided: He was no longer sure that it would happen, and the fantasy of emasculation was transformed. It went from being the certainty of an inescapable destiny to being the fear of a contingency. The space for uncertainty opened.

The "artistic name" that Sergei created to be able to make a name for himself and end the confusion with his father acted as a supplement that provisionally made up for the deficiencies in the Name-of-the-Father and inscribed a first trait of difference in the genealogy. His given name contradicted the nominative function: He felt that it did not qualify him as unique and individualized for his Other. Sergei added a last name that was also a first male name. This "middle name" that he "borrowed" from his wife was the first trait of difference between him and his father. This name functioned more in an imaginary than in a symbolic manner due to the role it played in his identity as a husband who takes his wife's name. The wife had the name that she had received from her father, another distinguished man who played an important role for the patient as an idealized yet "fallen" father; this devoted father had sacrificed his own life to promote his daughter's career. Sergei's solution was precarious, but it allowed him to find an outcome facing the riddle of sexuation.

Sergei's sudden push-towards-Woman can be explained as a solution for someone who is excluded from the phallic function. Both he and his father were exceptional figures, but the father's fame had transformed his last name into a name that, like a brand, became a trademark that he owned and could not transmit to his son. The Name-of-the-Father as a name appeared foreclosed. Usually, in neurosis the place of exception is relegated to the phallic function corresponding to the father. For Sergei, however, the father was actually someone "exceptional," not as a father who is subjected to the law he represents, rather as an "exception" to the rule. Because he was the exception from the law, he could nevertheless sustain the universality of the law. As Lacan's formulas of sexuation explain, Sergei's father was placed in a position equivalent to the exception of the primal father ($\exists X \overline{\Phi X}$). Sergei was supposed to become like his father, a destiny that he was reluctant to follow. Becoming a man like him implied also becoming a horrible man; therefore he could not fully accept his father's double-edged virile gift. Hence, only by becoming Woman would he find a solution to the problem, even though it was a solution that tortured him. In the end, being a husband turned into his sinthome as he was a husband who remained very dependent on his wife and on the heritage of the father of her name. Generalizing from similar cases, Juliet Mitchell (2001) reflected on a possible widespread "normal" trend: the absence of the castration complex in men whose heterosexuality is negotiated not via castration but by identifying with the woman they love.[1]

REPARATORY SYMPTOMS

Sergei was responding to an invasion of jouissance that caused him severe anxiety. Taking his wife's name as a supplement to his was a way of introducing something of the Other in the space of a jouissance that was unbearable to him. Sergei's case also proves that certain symptoms are comparable to an emergency repair kit, in this case by lending a spare name just when the Name-of-the-Father faltered. His symptomatic solution made up for the deficiencies in the Name-of-the-Father, albeit provisionally. The extreme anxiety Sergei experienced when he was overwhelmed by the conviction

---

[1] See Mitchell's (2001) discussion of Limentani's (1989) case, "The Limits of Heterosexuality: The Vagina-Man."

that he was going to become a woman was, however, a sort of masculine protest in the face of a destiny that he felt was unavoidable; this anxiety inscribed some sort of sexual difference. Schreber initially experienced his transformation into God's bride with protestation, and later he accepted it but not without reaching occasional states of bliss. Feminization was a fate that had a pacifying effect; the push-towards-Woman was a solution that transformed Schreber into God's object *a*. All along, Sergei refused the idea of becoming a woman. His rejection was a way to inscribe a first trait of difference, a limit, some sort of phallic function. Creatively, Sergei found a form of sexual positioning neither as woman nor as man, but rather as a husband. Always prone to speculations, Sergei had evolved a complex theory about the huge benefits of having adopted his wife's last name. This solution, nevertheless, might fail should they decide to have children as this would imply his assuming a position as a father, an event that might bring up again questions about his sexual positioning. So far, he seems to have found an acceptable compromise.

WORST BIRTH DEFECT

As we see, identifications can stabilize a sexual positioning. This was true of Hera, a Puerto Rican male-to-female transsexual. After having watched a television program on transsexualism in children, which presented young "trans kids" (aged 6 to 16) as being born in the wrong body and caught up in a basic "birth defect," she quoted the slogan when she stated to me that the worst birth defect for a woman was to be born with a penis and a pair of testicles. Hera added that she "did not ask to be born that way," as she was pondering whether one could ask how one "is born." Hera's openness and permeability to popular culture references called up a "borrowed" code to which she related in an almost mimetic manner, as if between her and the Other there was hardly no difference.

Her absolute certainty of being a woman trapped in a man's body, however, stabilized her sexuation. Since childhood, Hera had had a feminine imaginary identification; she knew all along that her round body shape and the fact that she looked exactly like her mother confirmed that she was not a boy but a girl, and that eventually she would become a woman like her mother.[2] Hera's given first name was also her mother's, a name that could be used for boys and girls. Raised as a boy, Hera dutifully followed the family's expectations by going to military school, graduating with honors, and marrying her high school sweetheart, Lisette. Lisette and Hera had

---

[2] Please note that I use the feminine pronoun to refer to Hera because that is how she asked us to refer to her in our work. In the cases I discuss here, I use the pronoun with which patients identify.

three children. During their 7-year marriage, Lisette tolerated Hera's crossdressing because, as Hera told me, Lisette assumed that cross-dressers were heterosexual. Hera would say that in their sexual relations, she imagined that she was the woman being penetrated, or she imagined them as two lesbian lovers.

Lisette and Hera separated because Hera felt trapped in a lie and wanted to "take the whole package," by which she meant living as woman full time and starting the process of "complete" transformation to female. During the divorce from her wife, a bitter dispute over child support payments ensued, and Hera was questioned in her role "as father of the children." She admitted that the children had lost their father but argued that they now had two mothers, an argument that Lisette found infuriating. Prior to the divorce, Hera had found in her wife's femininity a realization of the push-towards-Woman of which the wife was a feminine mirror image. But, the wife's demands concerning Hera's role as father, therefore as man, could not be tolerated. They finally divorced. Soon after their separation, two policemen holding a court order showed up at her job, and Hera was taken to the police station for a few hours to clarify a dispute over unpaid child support, an event that precipitated a psychotic breakdown. Already in the process of transitioning from male to female, Hera then experienced a psychotic breakdown caused by what Lacan would call an "irruption of *One-Father*."

The brief questioning at the police station had catastrophic effects for Hera. She left her job, moved back to her parents' home, and literally went underground, living in a basement, where she remained in constant fear, believing that she would be killed if she went out. Her parents brought her to treatment. Even though she had lived as a woman for over a decade, only recently did she consider sex change surgery. She had hesitations whose foundations were revealed in a slip of the tongue when once she said: "I want to make it happy," whereas she had intended to say: "I want to make it happen." Thus, her reliance on a sex change surgery as a key to happiness, together with her preoccupation with her genitalia as an obstacle that, if eliminated, would grant happiness, betrayed an unshakable belief in a limitless jouissance. Although Hera had other very pressing problems—health problems, unemployment, estrangement from friends and family—she focused only on her sex reassignment as a unique and overreaching problem. Her equating "surgery happy" with "surgery happen" suggested a jouissance that was not imaginary or symbolic, but real. Hera's identification was a certainly a sinthome: She still wanted to become a woman who would transcend gender, who would be an outside sex. Once more, her positioning can be interpreted along the lines of Lacan's (1998b) formulas of sexuation (p. 78).

Hera identified with a limitless enjoyment and imagined a perfect jouissance beyond subjective division. Hera's nostalgia for the previous identifications that sustained her, knotting the three registers of Real, Imaginary, and Symbolic, is revealed by her longing for "the person I used to be before I was ashamed at my job, taken unjustly to jail for unpaid child support. I have never been the same ever since." Although the issue was clarified eventually, the deadly aspect of that nonsymbolized jouissance, all too real, emerged in her comment: "That day I stopped thinking about life, I started thinking about death." Jouissance acquired such deadly potential because it was unbarred jouissance; it was the perfect enjoyment that is the prerogative both of the Woman who does not exist and of the father of the primal horde: Both are mythical figures occupying a position outside the law because they are unbarred, noncastrated.

AT-LEAST-ONE WHO SAYS NO TO CASTRATION

Both Sergei and Hera had fathers who were comparable to Schreber's: They had been pioneers in their fields (Sergei's father was an internationally known figure, and Hera's father was a political leader). Both were placed as an exception for which the Woman was the equivalent of the exempted "at-least-one" who says no to the law of castration. The Woman and the primal father of the horde represent two forms of jouissance not subjected to castration, that is, an impossibly real jouissance (beyond the phallus, that is, outside sex, outside division, and outside castration, as negotiation with lack) with which Hera and Sergei identified. Hera's demand for sex reassignment involved a surgical castration that would make real the female side of the sexuation formulas. It is an absolute law that admits no exceptions.

In Hera's case, the phallus is not taken as a signifier but is confused with the real organ, the lower left-side formula $\forall X \; \Phi X$ ("All are subject to the phallic premise") is interpreted not metaphorically but in its real connotations, and it becomes an absolute that one finds on women's upper right side: $\overline{\forall X} \; \overline{\Phi X}$ ("There does not exist any X that does not fall under the phallic function of castration"). In other words, if castration functions as an absolute without exception, it is as if Hera was saying: "If there is no jouissance without castration, then to put a limit to the jouissance I experience as unbarred, I need a real castration."

While Hera's demand in the treatment was tainted by a certain duplicity since she knew that she must convince me of her right to become a woman (as a "mental health" practitioner, I might have to write the official letter of endorsement required for surgery), her knowledge was nevertheless marked by certainty. It was something that came close to Hegel's absolute knowledge: She knew that she was different, had always been different, and needed to see this difference acknowledged. This explained the tinge of paranoia in her anxiety: She was alone against all the others. The modalities of this difference were underpinned by the logics of sexual difference.

Unlike Hera, who knew all along that she was not like other people and eventually believed with absolute certainty that she was a woman born with testicles and a penis, other analysands present a question about their sexuality that never finds a clear and definite answer. For those analysands, the problem lies in accepting a measure of dissatisfaction and living with the contingency brought about by uncertainty.

Woman is the Other sex for both men and women: "A man serves here as a relay so that a woman becomes this Other to herself, as she is to him" (Lacan, 2006, p. 616). We may make better sense of this assertion and assess the implications if we keep in mind Lacan's formulas of sexuation. According to his formulas, the woman's inscription in the symbolic system can be summed up by stating that not all of a woman is determined by the phallic function. Something in woman rejects the phallic function while at the same time being subjected to it. In terms of the phallic function, a woman is nonetheless within the symbolic order, albeit in a less "complete," "whole" manner than a man. One logical consequence of the difference between the sexes is that men and women will be alienated by language in radically different ways since woman is the Other sex for a woman as she is for a man. This being-the-Other for herself has revealing implications for our understanding of the subsequent cases that I present.

As we have seen more than once, Lacan's notion of sexual difference presented in his formulas of sexuation is not reducible to either anatomy or gender. The word *sexuality* etymologically implies a cut and therefore a difference. The noun comes from the Latin *differentia* and shares its roots with "to differ" or "to postpone"; this etymology sends us back to the Latin *dis* and *ferre* and to the Greek *pherin*, both meaning "to carry." "Difference" entails both a spatial and a temporal dimension. Geneviève Morel (2000c) evoked the temporal aspect of sexual difference when she outlined three temporal registers of sexuation (pp. 30–37). There is a first register of sexuation in the reality of anatomy, that is, in a mythically "natural" difference. The second register is the register of sexual discourse, and it is here that "anatomy" is interpreted according to values of difference brought about by the signifier. The third temporal register consists of sexuation proper, not the binary of phallic versus not phallic, which would suggest a sexual rapport, but two modalities of being: one in which the subject in relationship to the other sex is fully caught in the phallic function (when one is a man) and another in which the subject in relation to the other sex is not all caught up in the phallic function (therefore when one is a woman).

During the second phase of sexuation, the phallic universal is imposed on the perception of bodies and determines from then on whether the body is that of a boy or a girl. Morel (2000c) noted that this had been described by Lacan (1971) as the source of a "common error." The error consists of projecting onto the real of the body a small anatomical difference that is purely symbolic, that is just a signifier, and taking it for the real organ. Seeing the small anatomical difference between boys and girls as a real organ, that place in the body becomes a zone to add or subtract. The work of analysis is to rectify this error, which starts in a symbolic place and slides onto the real of the flesh. This is accomplished by retracing the displacement that has forced the real to pass through the defiles of language. Rejected signifiers like "you are a boy" or "you are a girl" symbolize a modality of jouissance. If they are erroneously transformed into master signifiers of the discourse on sex, then the phallus is no longer a signifier but also a signified. The paradox is that this logic, rather than freeing the subject from the phallus, makes of the phallus a real condition. The demand of the extraction of an organ can be the demand of the extraction of a signifier that has become all too real.

THE APORIA OF SEX

This calls up one of my female-to-male transsexual analysands, whom I call Lou. At the age of 4, Lou was made aware by her father that she was not a boy as she had believed so far, but a girl. First, she thought that her father was mistaken, and that even if he was right and she was now a girl, she would grow up and become a boy later. Eventually, she accepted that she might be a girl and remain one; thus, she acknowledged that there were anatomical differences between males and females. She elaborated that she had to be a girl because she was missing an organ, an organ that she hoped she would eventually grow. Lou took the phallus as a real object, not just as speculation, but as something directly linked to anatomy. As a child, she thought that one day the "error" was going to be corrected. Challenged by her father's adamant disagreement on gender issues, she concluded that even if she was not yet a boy, she would become one, unlike her mother, who had chosen to become a woman.

Lou's wish to defer her difference took the unexpected turn of sending back to her mother her own maternity: She decided to wait a little before the "top" surgery (mastectomy) that she fixed at a certain date, but it happened that it would take place just 9 months later. Like Sidonie's, Lou's hysteria apparently worked in relation to the mother. This time, it was to give birth to her own body via an imaginary transformation that could put the father at some distance since her surgery was something that the mother openly supported and of which her father quietly disapproved. Lou's rejection of her body's female characteristics echo Sidonie's renunciation of her femininity, a renunciation that we can interpret as acting out the mother's own hatred of femininity. Indeed, Lou's mother had had a first child, a boy who was born prematurely and died a few days after the delivery. Lou had identified with this dead child by becoming the boy that was but could not be.

The wish to correct the "error of nature" is often observed in transsexual practices; it is the refusal to accept a sexual discourse that is built on an error, that of taking the phallus for a signifier of sexual difference. As we have ascertained, the phallic criterion only accounts for one sex. And, when this sexual discourse is foreclosed, the error is no longer symbolic, it becomes nature's error and has then to be repaired in the Real. Often, the demand for a sex change is meant to rectify this error in the Symbolic register by correcting the error in the real of the body. Hera denounced the error of nature as a birth defect: She was born a woman with a penis and testicles, and she needed the sex reassignment surgery to correct what she considered as a freak anatomical occurrence. The paradox is that human sexuality is always defective, always erroneous because the phallic order is a classification system based on an organ taken for a signifying instrument.

In this context, the clinical example of Ari is helpful. Ari is a biological female who has had "top" surgery (breasts removed) and takes testosterone. Ari is manipulating his/her body to transform it into a surface with an undecided readability: What s/he wants is to pass as neither male nor female, thus rejecting altogether the phallus as a signifier of difference. If, according to phallic signification, we write two sexes with one signifier, Lou denounces the aporia of sex by refusing to be seen as either. If the phallus is just a parasite, if it is just the conjunction of an organ and the function of language (speech), Ari elevates "the limp little piece of prick" (Lacan, 2005, p. 15) to the status of art and supplements it, transforming physical appearance into the art of divination.

It is true that the phallus, often confused with the limp little prick, is not much more than a signified of jouissance that sexual discourse transforms into a signifier. The phallus refers only to phallic jouissance; other forms of nonphallic jouissance exist and can be experienced, although they remain outside signification. Schreber and Sergei had access to a certain phallic signified, but since the phallic signifier was foreclosed, they could not inscribe jouissance within the phallic function. Schreber eventually achieved an inscription of jouissance by way of the push-towards-Woman. Also by way of the push-towards-Woman, Sergei inscribed sexual difference under the signifier "husband." Their "masculine protest" (Adler, 1938) in the face of feminization had introduced phallic meaning to signify sexual difference.

SEX AND DIFFERENCE

We need to stress both the temporal and spatial aspects of the word *difference*, a double feature that I have mentioned and that has been analyzed at length by Jacques Derrida (1982, pp. 1–27). Unlike English, the French language has maintained the sense of both "differ" and "defer" in one verb: *différer*. The double meaning of difference—temporal (to postpone, to delay) and the nonidentical, which underlines the importance of repetition subordinated to space—has a central clinical significance. We have surveyed the temporal dimension as condensed in Morel's synthesis. The spatial dimension, which is perhaps less visible, produces clinical effects through what Lacan and others have called a "holophrase," a term to which I return and that marks the spatial collapsing of two or more signifiers into one.

Since becoming a woman and wondering what a woman is are essentially different things, the new modality of the question about sexual identity ("Am I straight or bisexual?") means that because one does not become a woman, it is possible to ask the question. A hysteric like Dora trying to make a choice about sexual positioning and who wonders, "What is a woman?" would be considered by Lacan (1993) as "attempting to symbolize the female organ as such." Lacan continued: "The identification with the man, bearer of the penis, is for her on this occasion a means of approaching this definition that escapes her. She literally uses the penis as an imaginary instrument for apprehending what she hasn't succeeded in symbolizing" (p. 178). Hysterics have one thing in common: they have reached the Oedipal crisis without being able to overcome it at the level of the symbolic (Lacan, 1994, p. 139). This means that hysterics have not fully assumed castration and have not fully assumed their sexual positioning.

In my clinical experience, I have found that those analysands who posed the question of sexual identity in terms of "Am I straight or bisexual?" had assumed subjective castration but had yet to attain the type of jouissance reached by "the inverted scale of the Law of desire" (Lacan, 2006, p. 324), a jouissance that can only be reached only after dealing with sexual difference. In analytic practice, we might render the Other as the Other Sex, keeping in mind that, in terms of hysteria, the unconscious fantasy is something constrained not by the Other but by the sinthome. Thus, I discuss the case of Linda, who experienced bulimia as a strategy that allowed her to do without the Other (sex), in other words, to slam the door on the phallic order. She called up for me Freud's little Hans who, when he had discovered that his whole being was attached to the penis, the *Wiwimacher* or "wee-weemaker," then attempted to break away from a doomed union. He tried to attach himself to some Other's body or to something else. Hans managed to move on to another object to escape a primary but fatal bond. In the process, he developed a phobia to horses. This course of action has parallels in the evolution of the little girl, who also finds her way out of the bond to the mother by creating a symptom, a phobia, or bulimia, as with Linda. Her case presents a good example of a symptom produced by a failure at the crucial moment of the subjective constitution that Lacan calls "separation."

Linda, an African American woman, initially came to see me complaining of severe problems with her mother. Before meeting with her mother, she needed to be coached by friends to rehearse her performance well. Linda had moved to Philadelphia just to be close to her mother. In the first session,

Linda told me that she had spent her childhood moving constantly between homes and cities. Linda recalls years in a constant transition between new places, half-furnished homes, schools, and friends. She described always feeling like an outsider, unable to fit in the context. This is how she came to ask the usual question: "Am I straight or bisexual?"

Linda appeared unlike the classic hysteric who is supported in her armature by the love for the father—and who makes her armor out of that love—or also quite far from the paradigmatic obsessional who sustains the proud gaze of the mother in his arrogant parade. Linda seemed not to have found in the primordial Other a place as an object *a*. She arrived in the consultation room having spent the previous years bouncing back and forth from her mother's home to her father's, moving from her aunts' place to her maternal grandmother's house, being kicked out of every place she was at, home or school, lost without a clear sense of direction.

I wondered how she managed to keep a sense of direction, how she could avoid being lost when she behaved if she had nothing to lose and when the Other seemed capable of "losing" her without any remorse. For her, the question "What am I for the Other?" was a burning enigma that could not be easily answered; she could not find in the Other an interval between signifiers, a lack in which she could find an object with which she would identify.

ALIENATION AND SEPARATION

Lacan (1981) introduced the terms *alienation* and *separation* as two operations fundamental to the constitution of the subject (pp. 203–215). The human offspring is born into the verbal world in a state of total dependence on the Other that Freud described as helplessness (*Hilflosigkeit*). This extreme dependence on an other, Freud (1895) notes, is the basis for human communication and moral values (p. 326). The biological incompleteness and insufficiency of the newborn makes the newborn bound to an other, creating a tie that is both ontological and existential. The required response and codification of the Other transforms needs into demands.

Alienation derives from the structural division of the speaking subject. As "speaking beings" subjected to language, we are split by our entry to the symbolic register. This splitting concerns a choice between meaning that is produced by the signifier and is found in the Other and the being of the subject. Lacan (1981) gave the example of a robber who asks: "Your money or your life!" a choice that is clearly impossible (p. 212). Similarly, by choosing meaning, the being of the subject disappears. This is the phenomenon described by Ernest Jones as *aphanisis*. But, if the subject chooses being, he or she may fall into nonmeaning. Such a structural alienation places the subject between a rock and a hard place—the rock of pure being without sense or meaning, presumably an unbearable state, or the loss of being for the sake of meaning. Of course, the dichotomy applies to sexual identity. If a subject chooses being, that is being a man or being a woman, the meaning of that choice is lost. If meaning is chosen, then being appears excluded. This constitutive alienation finds its best expression in the hysterical question about sexual identity, a question that gives poignancy to the splitting of the subject.

The subject thereby becomes aware of the desire of the Other, but cannot yet experience it as desire and instead presents itself in all its impenetrable mystery as a lack. "In the intervals of the discourse of the Other, there emerges in the experience of the child something that is radically mappable, namely, *He is saying this to me, but what does he want?*" (Lacan, 1981, p. 214). The subject experiences it as a question: "The Other is saying this to me, but what does she want?" (Lacan, 1981, p. 212). The subject answers with the production of a lack of her own, the most convenient one being to offer herself as a lack, that is, to offer her own disappearance as an active test of what it is that comes from the Other. Lacan sees in this interaction between child and adult the seed of most eating disorders.

While alienation relates to a division within the subject and to the opposition between meaning and being, separation is tied to a very specific lack, a lack that needs to be recognized in the Other. Separation means the recognition of a gap both in the Other and within the subject. It is a splitting of the phallic object that acknowledges a limit. There, the subject perceives the lack in the Other with which she or he may identify as an object. If the lost object is to be found in the subject, the question becomes: "Can she (the Other) lose me?" This triggers the fantasy of one's own death or disappearance; it often occurs in cases of anorexia, when the subject follows the course of the death drive to produce the lack in the Other. The child seeks out the space in the (m)Other where she is lacking to be the object of her desire. Altogether, separation and alienation are necessary steps in subjective constitution. I have found analysands who had undergone the first step of alienation, which implied a refusal of jouissance, but whose castration had not been fully accomplished, so that their jouissance was not regulated by the pacifying effects of separation.

TO GIVE UP SOME JOUISSANCE

Contrary to a commonsensical assumption that a given person is bad because she or he is perceived as "castrating," psychoanalysis stresses the other side of this view: While castration has it costs, it provides important benefits for the subject and ultimately allows desire to exist. "Castration," as Bruce Fink (1997) defines it, "has to do with the fact that at a certain point, we are required to give up some jouissance" (p. 99).

In this context, we can remember how young children play games of hiding. Their only purpose seems to verify whether they may lack for the Other. Are they noticed as missing? One can see the great joy children experience in the game when they are looked for and found; thus, they become aware that they can be missed by the Other. What is indeed devastating is when a child is hiding and no one notices that he or she is missing. Linda recalled with vivid detail instances when her mother forgot her—once, on a trip to the supermarket when her mother took off with her older brother and left her behind. She also remembered occasions when her mother forgot to pick her up from kindergarten. The important element here is not so much the incident itself but the fact that she remembers so poignantly the feeling of desolation and abandonment.

Let us recall that in alienation the subject disappears (which is aphanisis) under the weight of the Other's signifiers. But in a second stage, when responding to the Other's demand, the subject will find in the intervals of the signifying chain a place where he or she can come into being. It is as if Linda was asking: "What do you want? Can you lose me? Can I be the object of your lack?" The devastating answer would be: "You do not make me lacking, you do not represent my lack, I do not miss you." It is crucial that the Other offers this interval, this lack, this "nothing," to locate there an object with which the subject will identify. The subject operates with her own loss and only then will she invent a phantasmatic mask that covers the first moment of alienation. In that case, the subject will move from disappearing to being lost.

The passage from disappearing object to lost object is necessary: It allows subjects to mourn what they were before for the Other. This can be summed up in clinical work as an elaboration of mourning in which one finds the matrix for subsequent mourning (here, the phallus plays its role as a currency base, becoming the tool that allows the metonymic displacement). I would argue that for Linda this very matrix was failing. Her life was an endless chain of responses, seemingly accidental ones that were vain attempts to inscribe a loss not yet symbolized. Lacan (2004) stated that we mourn people whose lack we had embodied (p. 166). In the work of mourning, we make the other lacking to represent their lack. Only then can we mourn the one whose desire we caused. Since love is "to give what one does not have," as Lacan repeats regularly, it is when we face the loss of the love object that what we do not have comes back to us. Mourning entails a signifying reorganization that attempts to border the hole left in the Real by the disappearance of the object. Then, and only then, can the subject restart the process of desire.

THE OBJECT CAUSE OF DESIRE

Linda's bulimia was an attempt to create a lack in her mother, a lack that was inscribed retroactively. If there was something her mother lacked, then her mother could want something outside herself to satisfy her lack, something with which Linda could identify. This object is called object *a*, an object that commemorates a loss and a lack and defines human sexuality as *a*sexual. We can define the human economy of desire as mediated by the object *a*. Paradoxically, the object *a*, even though it is the cause of sexual desire, is not sexual in itself. This is of special interest in transgender issues because the object *a* usually takes the form of something that may or may not be gendered.

Linda's strategy to find her mother's lack was the following: First, she filled it up by bingeing, and then she purged it, she "emptied." Thus, she carved out a distance between herself and the threatening desire of her mother, a desire that she had experienced as that which would "shut down everything around me." In a slightly different context, dealing with cases of addiction, Nestor Braunstein (1992/2005) discussed methods by which subjects subtract themselves from the process of symbolic exchange. This permits a kind of experimental connection with jouissance that produces a short circuit in the relation to the Other's desire (p. 263). This strategy is quite different from that of the sinthome in which the subject does not refuse the lack of the Other but builds creatively on it.

DESIRE AND ITS REJECTION

Eating disorders, like anorexia, are linked to desire and to its rejection. "It is the child who is most lovingly fed who refuses food and employs his refusal as if it were a desire (anorexia nervosa)" (Lacan, 2006, p. 524). Anorexia is a strategy of separation from the Other when the Other's demand suffocates lack, hence preventing desire. In anorexia, nothing is taken as an object when food smothers the possibility of hunger. For Linda, "feeling empty" made up for desire. "Ultimately, by refusing to satisfy the mother's demand, isn't the child requiring the mother to have a desire outside of him, because that is the pathway to desire that he lacks?" (p. 524).

For Linda, bulimia operated as a regulatory strategy whose aim was to invent a subject facing the failure in the paternal function. To understand why Linda, who had been "most lovingly fed," still "refuses food and employs her refusal as if it were a desire," we need to know more about her relationship to her mother. This was a mother who always insisted: "We are two minds but one soul. We will always be alike." While this statement suggests an identification of mother with daughter, it left Linda clueless regarding what she was for her mother: Was she a clone? Could she really count as a separate object? Perhaps she was not separate? In fact, her mother treated her as an extension of her body, not even a privileged one. This mother fits the image introduced by Lacan (1991a) that compares the mother's desire to an open crocodile mouth inside which a child is trapped

(p. 121). In this allegory of the devouring Other, the only limit to maternal cannibalism is the Name-of-the-Father. The Name plays the role of the stick that prevents the mouth from closing.

HOLOPHRASED

Linda's situation was not a case of psychosis—the Name-of-the-Father was operating—yet, initially, her neurosis was not one of transference. A second step was still missing; it is what we may call the passage from disappearance to loss, which is the condition for the establishment of transference neurosis. In other words, the interval between the main signifier and unconscious knowledge (that is between S1 and S2, in Lacan's terminology) was "solidified" but not clearly established. Such a situation corresponds to what Lacan (1981) described as "holophrased" (p. 237). Lacan borrows the term from linguistics, in which holophrase refers to the earliest stage in a child's language acquisition: A one-word utterance is used to express meaning that, in more mature speech, would normally be developed into a more complex grammatical structure such as a phrase or sentence. The term *holophrase* functions as a verb in Lacan's neologism (Stevens, 1986, p. 71). The holophrase can be found operating in clinical manifestations such as psychosomatic disorders, mental retardation, and psychosis. This solidification in the matheme S1 → S2 relates to the topology of alienation and separation, that is, to the rapport of the subject to the field of the Other and to the lack in the Other.

Linda's illness consisted of being unable to place the lack in the Other and then in herself. For the feminine sexual economy, not having the phallus can be a condition to embody it or receive it from the other. Linda's whole being was consumed with trying to appropriate the phallus. She wanted to appear as the one having the phallus, but she could not trust the Other's love for her because to trust that love she needed to find a lack in the Other that she would represent. For instance, she said that her parents were very much in love when she was born, so in love and absorbed in themselves that she felt they could not really care for her; they nevertheless divorced before she was 4 years old. Her mother described her as having been a very independent baby and a mature child. According to her mother, Linda was so autonomous neither parent tried to play or engage in any way with her. If bulimia is a way to eat the Other, Linda wanted to eat the Other's lack or to create it by being it.

For Linda, separation became a more difficult issue when the union itself was questioned. Her mother claimed that Linda was weaned because she physically kicked her out at age 5 months. According to her mother, baby Linda actually pushed her away. Since the mother was allegedly wounded in the accident, she was forced to send Linda to a day care center, drastically separating from her. The Other seemed unable to oscillate between a measure of presence and absence. Here, absence could not give its security to presence—presence was overwhelming and absence devastating.

SUFFERING IN THE REAL OF THE BODY

For Linda, neither repression nor the return of the repressed seemed to be available. There were no formations of the unconscious, only pure suffering in the real of the body by way of psychosomatic illnesses. Linda had suffered from asthma as long as she could recall and complained that she felt unable to breathe or was "*smothered*," as she would say. This happened when her mother was around, and the situation would become intolerable. Her mother was unable to comfort her and lashed out at her for being sick. Nonetheless, all her history suggests that Linda had an alliance with her mother in an atmosphere of intense loyalty. However, at age 13, she was "thrown out" of her mother's home and sent to another state to live with her father. Linda responded by acting out, using drugs, being sexually active, sneaking out of the house, and getting drunk. She complained that her parents were absent, "always at work," although in fact her mother had abandoned a promising career as a dance performer to stay home and raise the kids. Apparently, the mother would say that her children had been an impediment to her artistic career, and yet she claimed that her children were not a mistake, although they seem to have been a disappointment.

ZONE OF ACTING OUT

Linda's adolescent acting out took place in a situation described as neglect. I read her acting out as located in a particular zone of relation, one that Lacan (2006) calls "zone of acting out" (pp. 327–333). Here, I want to make use once more of Lacan's notion of acting out (a subject's performance of a scene for the gaze of the Other, as a scene that tries to inscribe an object *a*) and of passage to the act (as an attempt to restore the subject who has been barred from the scene by the presence of an object). Since the passage to the act functions as a last resource against anxiety, we can see that Linda's acting out is a way of finding in the Other the path to desire while still regulating jouissance.

Actually, Linda's whole being was trapped in a zone of acting out. She was at the level of pure performance. Her sexuality was in a zone of acting out, as opposed to sexualities in the zone of passage to the act, like the cases of Sergei and Hera, which eventually found stabilization by way of a sinthome. Linda tried to assume her sexual identity from a field of holophrase and through her analysis managed to occupy a different position, moving away from the vortex of jouissance in which she was trapped.

ANXIETY NEVER DECEIVES

When her mother remarried, Linda became very oppositional with her stepdad. Her mother felt that she could not control her and then sent Linda, who was still a teenager, to live with her dad. The mother "let her fall," dropped her, or we could even say dumped her, and responded to the daughter's acting out with a parallel passage to the act. The explanation given by Linda's mother was that since her father had been a drug user and an alcoholic subsequently in recovery, he would know how to handle Linda. To better grasp the dynamics at play here, we need to remember that Lacan departed from Freud when he affirmed that anxiety was not without an object (Lancan, 2004; 2007, p. 147). He was talking about the specific status of object *a*, which precisely allows for such a formulation. If we keep in mind that anxiety appears when the object *a* is revealed, we may define a passage to the act as the result of an encounter with *a*, that is, an encounter not filtered by desire, deprived of the cover of the fantasy. What causes anxiety is the fear of vanishing in the face of the certainty of the jouissance attributed to the Other. Lacan establishes a clear distinction between acting out and passage to the act. While both are strategies deployed against anxiety, in the acting out the subject remains in the scene, whereas in the passage to the act the subject leaves the scene altogether. The acting out is addressed to the Other, while the passage to the act is a flight from the Other into the dimension of the Real; it is an exit from the symbolic network, a dissolution of the social bond. The passage to the act is not a message addressed to anyone but rather it implies a disintegration of the subject who, for a moment, becomes a pure object *a*, a leftover of signification.

APHANISIS

On her arrival at her father's home, which he shared with his elderly parents (Linda's grandparents), Linda made a choice that positioned her on her father's side, a choice that she experienced as losing her mother. Linda developed severe bulimia and lost exactly 39 pounds—which was her mother's age at the time of the separation. She had created in her body the lack that she could not locate in the Other. If Linda obsessively counted her lost pounds, she seemed not to count (or lack) for the Other, and as a consequence her responses would all be played out in the field of the Real. If love is to give what one does not have, Linda gave to that "nothing" the value of an object. Her bulimia was not a signifier relating to another signifier that she could interrogate. Her description of her bulimic episodes calls up a state of aphanisis; then, she disappeared as a subject, as I gather from the poignant description of what happened to her when she binged.

Linda, exiled to her dad's home, arrived searching for a father; yet, the mother already placed him in a degraded position—they were two addicts who would understand each other. She felt abandoned by her mother and punished for her identification with her father. In her new setting, she found her dad remarried and living with his wife and their twin daughters. Her dad was wrapped in a semireligious discourse about the dangers of alcoholism and quite detached from her. It was then that Linda immediately developed bulimia. Nobody seemed to notice. Her acting out continued; because of her behavior, her father kicked her out. Then, she was sent to live with her maternal grandmother; again, she managed to be "kicked out." While living with her grandmother, she fell in love with a boy. She now admits that she was so eager to be with him that she ended up forcing him to reject her. She became aware that she got "a kick out" of rejection, which echoes the episode of her mother describing how baby Linda kicked her out and forced a separation.

The master signifier contained in "kicks" and "kicked out" had served as a guideline to Linda; it functioned as a petrified signifier that would put together accidental life choices. She would obtain jouissance and reach the status of a sexual being when she could be defined as the one who was kicked out by the person she loved. Expelled from school, she was sent back to her mother, who was still very angry and once more rejected her. This was her pyrrhic victory: She became an unsolvable problem for her mother, thus forcing her to acknowledge some lack at the expense of risking her very being.

BULIMIA IN THE LOGIC OF JOUISSANCE

To understand this case, we have to move from the plane of identifications to that of the logic of her jouissance, from her mother's phallic jouissance to an imitation of the Other jouissance. As we have seen, Linda's mother appeared as a big open mouth, the mouth of an unsatisfied mother ready to devour her. This devouring image is for Lacan one of the elementary forms of phobic presentations and can give an answer to the enigma of the desire of the Other. I believe that this image played an important role in her bulimia. Linda was herself cannibalistic, like a baby who cannibalizes her mother. But, it was the unmitigated cannibalism of her mother that prevented her from modulating her own. When she binged, she would pick up those foods that can be reduced to the notion of "junk food" or "bad food." They were chosen because when vomited they would produce a homogeneous mass of milk, cereals, and cookies. This global mass that she threw up was made up of her and her mother, a dejected object *a* that in a repeated passage to the act was dropped, while also eliminating her as a subject from the scene.

Bulimia appeared then as a resisting symptom in Linda's analysis. During her work with me, she was able to stop bingeing and throwing up, and her asthma became less severe, but she still exhibited phobic features in intimate relationships. Linda used bulimia as a way to elude the traumatic reality of failing desires: Caught up between an alcoholic father and a phallic mother, she could not locate a desire that would signify her sexuality. Bulimia dissociated feelings from her body. For instance, if her boyfriend would do something she did not like, she would binge and throw up, then no longer feel the pain. The remorse for having done something worse than him would make her feel no longer entitled to anger. This sudden letting go of anger from her body was achieved by a reduction of her body to pure waste, which calls up the situation of the saint: The saint puts a distance between the world and himself by becoming rubbish, trash, pure refuse. Linda could then forgive all evil since in those moments she felt she was beyond suffering. These features call up a pattern that had interested Lacan in his reading of Joyce as sinthome.

Her bulimia was an instance of extreme phallic jouissance that she described as looking at herself from an exterior point of view, which she did to "feel nothing" or "to have a lack of feeling." This resisting symptom introduced a "nothing." The nothing was a lack, as one speaks of having a lack of feeling. It was also an object that she could have to create further lack. This allowed me to understand how the exclusionary jouissance of the Other remained a powerful force. This force prevented her from having access to her mother's desire, a desire that remained enigmatic. The refractory bulimia suggested a prevalence of the oral stage. She needed to throw up in order not to be eaten, not be devoured by the Other. However, this representation of an open mouth was the devouring open hole left in the Other by the introduction of the castration complex. Often, a phobia appears as a variation of the phallic signification that compensates for a failure in the paternal metaphor, whereas bulimia can be understood as turning one's back to phallic signification. Her phobic features had the function of introducing phallic signification; they helped her open the way to find the other's lack and the remainder of phallic signification—the object *a*.

PHALLIC DOMINATION

Given her mother's phallic power and her father's weakness, Linda found a creative solution in an attempt at approximating an Other jouissance, the jouissance of the right-hand side in the formula of sexuation. In that sense, her bingeing excess was a parody of the mystic's negative illumination. It was to fail, of course, but indicated a desire to be beyond the phallus. In an ironic echo of this doomed endeavor to escape the phallic domination, Linda's job at the time of her entrance in analysis consisted of testing impotence in a medical research unit by photographing and measuring penile erections.

However crucial men were in Linda's universe, they did not register as true holders of the phallus. Obviously, her mother was at ease in a quasi-phallic position. That Linda was always hiding her achievements revealed that she needed to feel she was "like a failure" herself so she would not compete with a mother experienced as a terrifying opponent. Since her mother had failed to open the way to a discourse beyond herself that would point toward desire, Linda preferred to see herself as a failure rather than confront her own hatred. She experienced this hatred as coming from the Other and as completely lethal. Her bulimia attempted to cut a hole, to create a lack in her mother's jouissance.

The Other sex was not complete, but when she was throwing up, Linda was swallowed by a jouissance beyond castration. Linda could not find in her mother's discourse room for a father for whom she was searching. She needed to hold on to her jouissance to make sure that rejection was guaranteed, so that the enigma of sexual difference could remain solvable on the mother's side. Her fantasy glossed over the fact that the Other of desire is effaced behind the Other of the demand. In analysis, she had in fact addressed the enigma of sexual difference, which brought her back to the fact that she needed first to believe that the Other desired her, even when that desire remained opaque for her. Her asthma was caused by situations of loss brought about by extreme and unbearable sadness. Unable to feel sad, unable to let go, she remained in a melancholic state in which she felt betrayed by the Other—since the Other desired without her.

Linda had, like many hysterics, a "fallen" father. Her mother knew no boundaries, no limitations, and lived out the fantasy of an ideal absence of castration; one could say that she was a mother who represented the side for "men" to the left in the formulas of sexuation since she was fully defined by the phallic function. The mother talked too much, treated her daughter as a partner, and seemed not to have fully accepted castration. In fact, her mother controlled Linda as if she was her own law, which calls up the primal father who exists outside symbolic castration. In Freudian theory, the father of the primal horde and the phallic mother are both conceived as all enjoying and lacking nothing. In Lacanian theory, the Woman and the *père-jouissant* (not the symbolic father but a father who enjoys without limit or inhibition; a tyrant) occupy this position of plenitude beyond division. Because these figures possess or embody the phallus in the form of unlimited jouissance, they seem beyond gender in the usual sense; thus, they appear not to be subjected to sexual division.

A LITTLE BIT OF FREEDOM

Linda made a lot of progress during analysis. Entering transference, she ended up accepting castration as a way of accessing desire rather than sacrificing herself to the Other's jouissance. She reached what Lacan calls that "little bit of freedom" promised by analysis and managed to break up the trap of her paradoxical jouissance. This trap was an ultimate defense against desire. She was able to admit that the Other desires, without asking her to embody the deadly primal cause of this desire. This happened when she could disengage herself from a fantasy by reducing it to simple family history. An indication of Linda's evolution can be seen in the development of her career choice. Soon after she started her analysis, she took a new job as an administrative assistant. In her free time, she started to take an interest in cooking. She liked to prepare homemade ice cream, arguing that cream was a dairy product that is close to the body and never completely keeps its shape unless frozen. Then, she moved on to baking. At the same time, she took a part-time job in a restaurant kitchen. She began experimenting with pastry cooking. She did not hesitate to waste her products. The recipes she chose would be those with the most challenging processes, the most expensive, and the hardest to produce. She somehow needed to bake things that would need to be immediately destroyed if the outcome was a failure, but when a pastry project was successful, she found herself not knowing what to do with it. Then, she hastily gave pastries away to friends, as if needing to get rid of her production.

Eventually, she found a way of making her interests more profitable and stable while apprenticing with a famous pastry chef. After several failures in projects of monumental proportions, she discovered chocolate and with it a new relation to her work and her body. By then, she had finished training in a culinary arts school and discovered that her medium was the key. Measuring ingredients, blending cocoa beans, progressing from pralines to chocolate mousse, combining creamy and crunchy, snap and subtlety, turning cocoa into sublime bonbons, Linda found the wonders of chocolate sculpture. Her artisanal chocolates became highly successful and launched her career. Using vintage techniques that repositioned her in both maternal and paternal lineages, she perfected her chocolate making skills. Before long, she was offering limited quantities of her creations to local markets. The chocolates sold very well, and soon Linda started her own company. Her favorites were the chocolates on which she would inscribe words. In psychoanalytic terms, she had managed to inscribe something on the wide expanse of the mother's body, as Freud (1926) would say.³ She also was revisiting issues about her body that her bulimia negotiated. She was extracting the object *a* as an objectal remainder, cut away from the body—an object that she grinded, cooked, melt, solidified, wrapped in beautiful boxes, signed, and sold. Linda had found a creative way to her sinthome.

A MOTHER'S UNBOUND DESIRE

Perry is an Asian American woman who started her analysis 2 years after finishing her undergraduate studies. In the early stages of her career as a playwright, she complained of depression. Her main uncertainties were centered on her anxiety around the question: "Am I straight or bisexual?" Perry is the daughter of very successful Asian American lawyers who moved to the United States after the Korean War. According to the family romance, the mother was the successful parent who had established herself in a prominent position by fighting against sex discrimination in her firm, with such success that she set up the basis for equal opportunity for other women in her profession. Her father, on the other hand, had an equal share of success but appeared in a melancholic position, drinking himself to oblivion every night after work. As her myth of origin, Perry was told that she was conceived against her father's will. He did not want to have children, but like a naughty Queen Jocasta seducing King Laius, Perry's mother stopped taking the contraceptive pill without telling her husband and thus became pregnant without her husband's awareness. The way the analysand related this seemed to suggest that her mother wanted to make a baby without the intervention of a father. What did not appear in this configuration was that when the father learned about the pregnancy, he welcomed the news with great joy and received his child with intense affection. Perry felt all along that her father had a great devotion for her. This devotion was often perceived by the mother as a threat, perhaps as a threat to the fantasy of the conception of a baby on her own, without the intervention of a man or, perhaps, a penis.

Perry worked in her analysis on her initial question, "Am I bisexual or heterosexual?" which gave room to the exploration of the terror she experienced (and of the phobic defenses that consequently she built) in facing a maternal desire that could not be stopped by the evanescent desire of a

---

³ "As soon as writing, which entails making a liquid flow out of a tube on to a piece of white paper, assumes the significance of copulation, or as soon as walking becomes a symbolic substitute for treading upon the body of mother earth, both writing and walking are stopped because they represent the performance of a forbidden sexual act. The ego renounces these functions, which are within its sphere, in order not to have to undertake fresh measures of repression—in order to avoid a conflict with the id" (Freud, 1926, pp. 89–90).

melancholic father. Her mother felt entitled to "jokingly" grope her daughter, arguing that sexualized physical affection was "natural" and claiming that she desired her daughter so much that she ignored the need to ask whether that desire for a child was shared with her husband.

Perry began her analysis while she was in a relationship with a much older man who took care of her like a doting mother, but all the while she entertained fantasies of having sex with women. The hysterical question gave way to concerns expressed by a hystericized body: She suffered inexplicable muscle pains and was afraid of having multiple sclerosis, which she referred to as MS. Her doubts about her sexual identity were made explicit when MS emerged in associations as the title used with the last name or full name of a woman without any reference to a woman's marital status. This other meaning of MS led to a questioning of her own position as a desiring subject, which made her feel more at ease in her place as object of desire. The MS was caused by the apparent excess of the big Other's crushing desire, that is, the damage caused by a mother who appeared to the analysand as occupying the role of the Woman. Her mother appeared as noncastrated in front of a fading father, whom Perry adored and who seemed to prefer his daughter over his wife.

During her childhood, Perry and her father would often take vacations together, leaving her mother at home since Perry's mother was always worried about taking time off from work, anguished about meeting the required billable hours at the law firm, a concern that her father did not seem to share. As an adolescent, on many occasions, Perry would accompany her dad to Christmas parties, dinners with clients, and other social activities in which the "significant other" was expected to join. The Freudian Oedipal fiction was seemingly realized. This Oedipal dialectic, however, made of Perry an imaginary hostage. She was a captive of her mother's supposed omnipotence. The mother was providing Perry with a supply of jouissance that was hard to let go. Her parents' apparent disconnection nevertheless introduced a dimension of lack. But, Perry could not identify with the object capable of filling the lack in the Other. If there was anything her mother wanted, it was a mystery to Perry. She was caught in a contradiction in which she perceived (and bitterly resented) her mother's flaws, all the while being fully committed to the idea that her mother was self-sufficient and the sole legislator of the order of desire. This contradiction bracketed the issue of sexual difference for Perry.

I observed a similarity with Linda's situation, a constellation also seen in other cases of women who found themselves caught up between the "straight" and "bisexual" models. These women had a strong, phallic mother who took them as a confidante, a fading/fallen father, and several phobic features. For Julie, another patient with a similar configuration, the question "Am I straight or bisexual?" arose specifically as a stopper in the wake of the fears brought up by a marriage proposal.

BREAKING WITH THE FEMININE

Julie had consulted by complaining of depression. Julie was a "b" girl, a "breaker," that is a female break dance dancer, a dance usually reserved for "Boys" and recommended neither for the feminine in style nor for the female body. B was also the first letter of her last name, which contains an anagram of break. Julie had a very sick father. When Julie was born, both parents were at the hospital. While her mother was there for the cesarean section that brought her into the world, her dad was admitted for the third of 10 successive brain cancer operations. Julie's dad was a Navy veteran who fought in Vietnam and whose body was actually broken (as a consequence of the war, he suffered severe arthritis). After his numerous surgeries, her father had been left literally broken: blind, disabled, and living on the limited pension of an early retirement. Meanwhile, Julie spun on her head, thus defying gravity and the gravity of her father's condition. Her mother remarried and divorced. The men in her life were not constant, but she had found in Julie a stable companion, a confidante, and expected her to take care of her siblings. Julie described her mother as "man enough to be a woman," a very strong woman who managed to succeed in a profession traditionally reserved for men (she managed a construction company). Julie also thought that her mother behaved sexually like a man-predator.

For Julie, dancing was clearly a sublimation of her love for her father. This Freudian sublimation of the drives suggests what Lacan calls the Other jouissance. "Breaking" started in the streets of New York in the mid-1970s, and the original context for showing off some skill was the battle, in which rival crews battled for supremacy. Most breaking competitions now center on the battle. Each crew sends out one member at a time for a predetermined series of rounds, with judges deciding the winner of each battle. The moves are challenging and look as if they could break the body. Judges look for a number of things but primarily focus on style and power. The best b-boys and b-girls successfully combine both elements. The element of battle is significant since the dance was born in clubs to allow gangs to fight without getting in too much trouble; aggression became an art form.

PHALLUS AS CONTINGENCY

Let us sum up the common elements in the constellation outlined. In the cases sketched, with Linda, Julie, and Perry, we have a fallen father. Their love for their fathers suggested a virile identification with an impotent, fallen father. Apparently, their mothers knew no boundaries and lived out the fantasy of an ideal noncastration (as we saw, they stood on the left side, the side of "Men" in the formulas of sexuation, as they were defined by the phallic function). The three patients have mothers who said too much and took their daughters as partners. They controlled the lives of their daughters, behaving as if they were their own law, which calls up the primal father who stands outside symbolic castration. Their phobic features suggested an unconscious strategy of making up for the deficiencies in the Name-of-the-Father.

In these three analyses, the analysands moved toward a position where the phallic function was a possibility but not a necessity. They thus assumed a position that was less disharmonic in respect to their own sex and thus to the Other sex. Eventually, they moved from accessing the signifier of their desire via a masculine mother since the mothers seemed placed on the male side of sexuation, reaching something more undefined or indefinite in relation to the phallic function. They shifted from an imaginary level of sexual identity (their ego identifications with one or both parents that determined the question "Am I straight or bisexual?") and finally assumed their feminine structure. They had situated themselves at the level of desire and were thus capable of dealing with a jouissance defined by the parameters of the Other jouissance.

Let us better present the paradox. How can an analysand who defines herself in terms of a man (in terms of the phallus, by way of the man who may have it) realize the potential of the Other as Other sex? She is described by Lacan (1998) as *hommosexual* (conflating *homme* [man] and homosexual) (pp. 84–86); she has access to desire in our culture through a man who will tell her who she is; being identified with him, she will love men and pretend to be one herself, with even her desire following a masculine fantasy. Nonetheless, since a woman is "not-all," and therefore less wholly alienated by the phallic function, her not being completely determined by the phallus explains why Lacan asserts that women cannot be "perfect hysterics" (Soler, 2000, p. 193). Indeed, Lacan (1971–1972, class of March 3, 1972) reserves that "perfection" for men when he calls "Socrates, the perfect hysteric" and "Hegel, the most sublime of the hysterics" (2007, p. 35). His idea is that a hysteric woman as not-all cannot be "all" hysteric.

THE MYSTERY OF THE SPEAKING BODY

The last three cases still remain within the structure of hysteria. Hysteria is here defined by a certain question about sexual positioning. By contrast, the transsexual patients we discussed do not pose this question. Their whole being is built around the answer to the question. They believe that they know what they are—a man or a woman trapped in the wrong body—and their main problem will be finding ways of rectifying the error. In hysteria, the libidinal elasticity of the body as organism is tested to its limit (Lacan,

2006, p. 719). Hysterical identifications are always partial, whereas the identification with the sinthome is total. The hysterical question is thus inexhaustible: "Am I a man or a woman?" has to remain a frustrated query. On the other hand, the sinthome produces a complete structural adequation that encompasses the whole body. The consequence is that, as Harari (2002) put it, "the hysteric is clearly torn asunder; while the 'sinthomatic,' although not tranquil, is often without the surging anxiety that afflicts the former" (p. 233).

Language and the body do not get along. Language dissects the human body by producing rests. These leftovers cause desire. This is how Lacan (1990) put it: The psychoanalytic subject "thinks as a consequence of the fact that a structure, that of language—the word implies it—a structure carves up his body, a structure that has nothing to do with anatomy. Witness the hysteric" (p. 6). In Chapter 3, we have seen that for hysteric symptoms, the anatomy at stake is not that of nerves and muscles but an imaginary anatomy that follows language. The disconnect between the real of the body and language is a gap that not only harbors our discontent but also allows for desire to exist. Language carves out privileged erotic zones, draws maps of symptoms. Even if we do as much cutting, tattooing, hormone pumping, dieting, exercising, reducing, or augmenting as we can afford, the body will never find in language a harmonious home. If language alienates the body, it is with language that one can cure it; this is why psychoanalysis is talk therapy.

The body is a sexual body on which the symbolic networks make an inscription; therefore, we can talk of "new sexualities" that have nothing to do with anatomy as they are witnessed by the hysteric. The hysteric is worn out by the unconscious question, "Am I straight or bisexual?" which is a permutation of "Am I a man? Am I a woman?" With hysteric analysands, their essential question is never answered with certainty. They may take an answer, but not all of it. Thus, it looks as if transsexual patients have taken the hysteric question for an answer. As we have seen, the cases of transsexual delusion I have described are very different from those of hysteria, but one may identify elements of sinthome in their bodily transformations. Before deciding whether these are psychotic, it may help to bring them closer to the pure form of the question, "What is a woman?" Is this question answered in advance, for a male-to-female transsexual, when she claims that she is a woman trapped in a male's body?

The transsexual subject may appear protected from the imaginary and symptomatic conjectures the hysteric is endlessly making around her sexual identity. I will argue that in what I provisionally call push-towards-writing, a movement or passion that is often observed in transsexuals, the body finds its anchor in the sea of language. Many people who feel trapped in the wrong gender do experience the drive to write, to produce a text that narrates their experience, offering a testimony to their stories of transformation. It is in the writing of the sex change memoir that a final bodily transformation takes place, when the body is written. This is what I address in the next chapter.

Chapter 10

Writing the *sinthome*
The transsexual body as a written body

Why do so many transsexuals write memoirs? Jay Prosser (1998) tackled this question in an original manner by noting that even long before any book was published, for transsexuals, there had been a founding autobiographical act, an act of recounting triggered by an institutional request or demand. Usually, the demand originates

> in the clinician's office where in order to be diagnosed as transsexual s/he must recount a transsexual autobiography. The story of a strong, early, and persistent transgendered identification is required by the clinical authorities, the psychiatrists, psychologists, and psychotherapists who traditionally function as gatekeepers to the means of transsexual "conversion." Whether s/he publishes an autobiography or not, then, every transsexual, as transsexual, is originally an autobiographer. Narrative is also a kind of second skin: the story the transsexual must weave around the body in order that his body may be read. (p. 101)

Despite the accuracy of the observation, Prosser's quotation may end with the wrong verb. Since most transsexual persons use the verb *read* to say "guess somebody's anatomical identity," which often entails "not to pass," one might be tempted to say then that transsexuals write both to be read and not to be read.

Deirdre McCloskey (1999), a renowned economist and historian who transitioned from male to female in her mid-50s, offers in her memoir *Crossing* a good example of this peculiar use of *read* while expressing the pain and pathos involved in "being read":

> Kate invited Deirdre to her house. ... The two women took her husband and her husband's father to a Thai restaurant for Father's Day, a feminine duty, Deirdre observed, with Kate wrapping presents and organizing ceremonies for her men. Deirdre couldn't tell if the men read her, which merely showed that they were courteous, because they

must have. Kate's father-in-law asked Deirdre how it felt to be such a tall woman.

At the airport ... was late and her makeup was slipping. The clerk laughed at her and called her sir. ... The flight was fourteen hours. ... The young woman in her row was pleasant and didn't seem to read her, despite Deirdre croaks and stuttering from tiredness. ... After a week of unusual amount of being read, which I cannot understand, I had one of my rare middle-of-the-night anxiety attacks. Nothing pathological, just waking up too early and being unable to go back to sleep while thoughts tumbled. Is the genital surgery healing right? Am I just too tall? Will the face lift work? Can I ever get the voice right?

... In time, in time. The facial operations and slow effects of hormones, and morning and evening applications of Estée Lauder products by the half gallon, finally left her unread. Two years later she had stopped testing for passing. Almost. (pp. 194, 204, 205)

Max Wolf Valerio (2006), an American Indian/Latino poet, writer, and performer who transitioned from feminist lesbian woman to heterosexual man, chronicled in detail the first 5 years of his hormonal and social transformation from female to male. To his chagrin, he discovered that taking testosterone left him with an incipient receding hairline. Besides some trepidation about his sudden interest in watching hair transplant TV infomercials, Valerio welcomed this change as a potential cue for people to read him as male (p. 324). Helen Boyd (2007), who, as she put it, lost her husband to another woman when he became the other woman (her husband, a cross-dressing heterosexual man, decided to consider sex reassignment surgery), wrote in *She's Not the Man I Married: My Life With a Transgender Husband*: "It is almost impossible for [her husband] Betty to present as a feminine male because her femininity means that she is often read as a woman" (p. 85). Valerio and Boyd use *read* differently, perhaps to convey that gender is a matter of interpretation, that gender is always a representation to be decoded. These two diverging uses of *reading* for gender presentation, one as not passing and the other as a call for interpretation, are both encompassed by Lacan's concept of the letter, writing, and nomination. The paradoxical transsexual reading would send us once more to Lacan's later developments condensed under the equivocal word *sinthome*. The sinthome is a self-created fiction that allows one to live. It also represents a concluding chapter in Lacan's theory of the subject.

We have seen that Lacan modified his position in the mid-1970s when he elaborated a new conception of sexuality just as he was discussing Joyce's writings to reach a new concept of sexuality and the body. One important aspect of the symptom as sinthome is that Lacan defined it as artifice, emphasizing art's creative aspect. The sinthome is above all a creation, an invention, which suggests that by writing one can reknot the main determinants of one's psychic life. Lacan's innovation with the sinthome that derives directly from an engagement with Joyce's writing brings about a new complication of the notion of authorship. Indeed, on the one hand Joyce became a writer to make a name for himself, but on the other hand he aspired to create a universal language, hence implying a collective agency. My thesis is that a similar tension between the demand for singular recognition and universal agency can be observed in transsexuals, more precisely when they write.

NOVELS OF FORMATION OR NOVEL OF THE ARTIST

In 2005, Jonathan Ames authored a well-received anthology of transsexual memoirs. Ames aptly summed up the structure of sex change autobiographies as a three-act saga: "first act: gender-dysphoria childhood; second act: the move to the big city and the transformation … [third act] the sex change" (p. xii). For Ames, this is the basic outline of all transsexual memoirs: "A boy or a girl very early on in life feels terribly uncomfortable in his or her gender role, and there is a sense that some terrible mistake has occurred, that he or she was meant to be the other sex" (p. xii). This is why Ames finds that transsexual autobiographies follow the structure of a canonical literary genre, the *Bildungsroman,* which he describes as "the coming-of-age-novel" (p. xxi). Ames notes that following the Bildungsroman blueprint, transsexual memoirs observe a progression in which the main characters, now aware of the "error of nature," see family and society as trying to reform them. Often, the protagonists also struggle internally, taking great pains in trying to repress their drive to become the opposite sex.

Eventually, our heroes leave their hometown and venture into the outside world, and they often end up in a big city. It is in this new context that they begin to masquerade as the other sex, perhaps only privately and eventually more publicly. With time, the disguise and perfected ability to pass become more and more permanent and successful, particularly in the second part of the 20th century with the increased availability of hormone treatments and surgical technologies to manipulate the body. Ablations and implants as well as the climactic sex reassignment surgery will finally allow the memoir's protagonist to reclaim a place of self-acceptance and peace. Ames emphasizes the literary and sociological significance of these memoirs; their appeal should be universal insofar as they deal with questions that haunt everyone, such as "Who am I?" and "What am I?"

Ames' description of transsexual memoirs as Bildungsroman or a novel of formation is slightly misleading since transsexual memoirs could be described more accurately as novels of the artist, in a subgenre known as the *Künstlerroman.* There may not be such a huge difference between the two genres; however, this nuance is important for psychoanalytically influenced ears. On the one hand, one would have a formation (*Bildung*) of the unconscious, which means that unconscious phenomena are made visible in transsexual symptoms, while on the other hand one would come closer to art, hence to Lacan's analysis of Joyce when he presents his writing, his art as a sinthome.

One cannot discuss sex change memoirs without making reference to the medical ideology that brought about sex change development. Prosser, a trans man himself, disagrees with a constructivist view that had been put forward by Hausman, who sees transsexual memoir as entirely shaped by medical technology. Prosser (1998) remarks that in most sex change narratives, the relation of authorship and authorization between clinicians and transsexuals is mobile, dynamic, and therefore highly complex (p. 9). If published sex change memoirs are second versions of a first transsexual autobiography told in the doctor's office, it does not necessarily mean that they have been constructed by medical discourse. This does not contradict the fact that autobiographical reports to clinical experts have to conform to the constraints of a genre. Hence, published or unpublished transsexual autobiographers will follow the formal constraints of the genre quite systematically.

Like Prosser, Hausman (1995) observed that the transsexual population is a well-read group and for strategic reasons (p. 143). To successfully obtain the medical treatments requested, the story of transsexuality has to match an officially sanctioned etiology. Indeed, the account has to be convincing: The very telling of the "right" story can confer legitimacy to the sex change demand. The autobiographical narratives of successful transsexuals include detailed inside information; they are written by those who have managed to maneuver adroitly the strict guidelines of sex change protocols. Thus, most memoirs become self-help how-to manuals. Some autobiographies are so aware of this function that they include ample lists of useful information: telephone numbers of plastic surgeons, names of endocrinologists, and compilations of support networks, advocacy groups, and so on. While the autobiographies offer the transsexual reader an authorizing membership in a group and a sense of identity, the clinical autobiographical narrative also teaches them to conform to preestablished parameters defining an official history that tends to erase their own subjectivity. The modalities in which the transsexual story gets constructed offer us a privileged mode of entry into the prevailing discourses on transsexualism.

As we have seen, these discourses have found a starting point in notions of bisexuality. When I examined the evolution of the concept of bisexuality, I pointed out that the notion of physical bisexuality played a significant role in the development of the discourse of transsexuality. Ulrich, Hirschfield, Steinach, Fliess, and Weininger all supported a model of physical bisexuality. Sex was biological and resulted in a combination of masculine and feminine traits. Sex, gender, and sexuality were conflated in a continuum between man and woman. Proportion was the key.

DEFINING TRANSSEXUALISM

Harry Benjamin, who in 1953 became Christine Jorgensen's endocrinologist in the United States, supported the idea of a physical bisexuality. In a letter to Hamburger, the doctor who had treated Jorgensen in Denmark, Benjamin asked if he had detected in Jorgensen's body any ovarian tissue or "hypertrophic or hypersensitive feminizing tissue in her adrenals" (Meyerowitz, 2002/2004, p. 102). In his first article on transsexualism, "Transvestism and Transsexualism," published later that same year, Benjamin no longer referred to "feminizing" "ovarian" tissue, but wrote about the "infinite diversity of the male-female scale." Benjamin was paraphrasing Steinach's theory of bisexuality: "It is well known that sex is never hundred per cent 'male' or 'female.' It is a blend of complex variety of male-female components." And for the causality, physiology prevailed: The "more or less pronounced irregularities in genetic and endocrine development" resulted in "'intersexes' of varying character, degree, and intensity" (p. 102). Benjamin subscribed to biological bisexuality, thus assuming that transsexuals were intersex. The Danish doctor who had operated on Jorgensen had a speculative model that male-to-female transsexuals had a female anatomy and male (XY) chromosomes.

Benjamin believed in anatomical bisexuality, and in that sense, his trajectory seems parallel to that of Charcot in his search for an organic origin of hysteria. Benjamin could not let go of a biological concept to account for the etiology of transsexualism, despite the fact that he could not find any bodily confirmation for transsexualism. Even if he failed to detect any specific glandular or genetic factor in transsexualism, he would not subscribe to the theory of a psychological origin. Benjamin had borrowed Ulrich's formula of a female soul trapped in a male body, all the while looking for answers in the body, not in the soul: "the soma, that is to say the genetic and/or endocrine constitution … has to provide a 'fertile soil' on which the 'basic conflict' must grow in order to become the respective neurosis" (Hausman, 1995, p. 122). Despite the use of the term *neurosis*, both Benjamin (1954) and the Danish team discouraged any psychoanalytic or psychotherapeutic intervention. They even saw these as "a waste of time" (p. 228). As Hamburger's team put it, "it is impossible to make a genuine transvestite [transsexual] wish to have his mentality altered by means of psychotherapy" (Hamburger et al., 1953, pp. 392–393). Benjamin considered psychotherapy and psychoanalysis useless. His objection was that if they could not cure transsexualism, they could not explain it either. Meyerowitz (2002/2004) observed that Benjamin and Hamburger emphasized the biological aspect of transsexualism, which explained for them the failure of psychotherapy in treating the condition and justified a surgical intervention (p. 103).

Thus, "genuine" transsexuals were considered suitable cases for surgical and hormonal treatments. Benjamin (2006) called them "somato-psychic transsexualists" (p. 49); his early examples focused primarily on male to female transsexuals. This is how he likes to describe them, "A patient like that has every right to be accepted as a woman and lead a woman's life. Blind prejudice alone would deny her this right to which her own nature, science and humanity entitle her" (Hausman, 1995, p. 123). Benjamin stated that while "the sexual life of the feminized male may be lively," it was "largely non-genital, His (or rather her) libido is 'cerebral.' It can be aroused and gratified by the fact of 'being a woman'" (p. 123). Initially, Benjamin, Hamburger, and colleagues did not think that vaginoplasty was needed since it was assumed that it was not part of the patient's demand. Hausman (1995) remarks that in the early years of transsexualism, any suggestion that "he" wanted a vagina would have challenged the sanctioned etiology of the disorder and put at risk the very acceptance of the surgery.

Transsexualism was initially presented as having little to do with sexual desire (it did not concern "sex" but sexual identity). Benjamin (1954) had also drawn a clear distinction; he claimed that transvestites derived pleasure from their genitals, whereas transsexuals were disgusted by them. Consequently, transvestites, as a rule, wanted to be left alone, while transsexuals would always seek medical aid (p. 220).

BAFFLED

At the time, transsexualism was seen as an issue of medicalized sexual identity and not of sexual orientation (Hausman, 1995, p. 227). This orientation toward identity seemed to leave out sexuality altogether. For example, Christine Jorgensen's vaginoplasty was not part of her initial surgeries in Denmark; she waited 2 years to have the operation in the United States (pp. 234–236). Jorgensen (1967/2000) wrote her autobiography to increase public understanding of transsexualism. Jorgensen's sex change story had thrust her into the spotlight as an international media sensation; she managed her notoriety quite well, carefully crafting her public image as a restrained, sophisticated, respectable woman. The memoir has been, and continues to be, a central reference on transsexualism for laypeople and professionals alike.

In her memoir, Christine Jorgensen (1967/2000) positioned herself as a pioneer who had a message to deliver. The message needed to reach a wide audience. Perhaps to maintain her respectability, her book presentation was prudish—in it, one cannot find any trace of sexuality and intimacy. Unlike the sex change narratives after the 1970s, all of which exhibit in graphic detail the pain and pathos of the transition, Jorgensen said very little about the surgeries: "I had no wish to share its details with the rest of the world, any more than a complete hysterectomy would be advertised by another woman" (p. 236). What she described was told briefly and in strict medical terms: The first "operation, termed a 'penectomy' meant removal of the immature organs" (p. 125). Her dry style furthers the idea that the subject matter is entirely clinical: "I was scheduled for surgery, for my problem had always seemed to me a wholly medical one" (p. 126). Her account of her third surgery, a vaginoplasty, was also written in a dry medical style, also in stark contrast with the narrative style of the memoir. "With skin grafts taken from the upper thighs, plastic surgery constructed a vaginal canal and external female genitalia. It was a completely successful procedure" (p. 235). In conclusion, one may say that her sex reassignment was a medical event that excluded any subjectivity and potentially troubling expression of desire.

The consequence is that one may well agree with Pat Califia (1997/2003) that Christine Jorgensen's memoir is quite "dull" (p. 26). Susan Stryker (2000) reiterates that for someone who cast a spell over wide audiences, who knew how to play the media, the memoir "sometimes makes for admittedly dull reading," and that it purposefully tries to present a dignified story. Sections of it read like a roll call of famous people with whom Jorgensen lunched, lists of the wonderful clubs in which she performed, never forgetting to mention the amazing outfits that she wore on each occasion (p. x). Its well-mannered, conventional style conveys that the book is about the extraordinary life story of an otherwise normal, ordinary woman. The woman who made global headlines like "Ex GI Becomes Blonde Beauty" or "What's a Woman? City Bureau Baffled by Chris Jorgensen" was intent on proving her respectability as an antidote to her universal mediatization as the first global transsexual celebrity. She never identified as a transsexual or mentioned other transsexuals in the memoir. Christine Jorgensen (1967/2000) comes across as a conventional woman who happens to have an unusual medical problem. Fundamentally, she claimed, she was "the object of one of Nature's caprices" (pp. xiv–xv) when she merely wanted to blend in. However, her photographs show contrasting images of a sexy, lively, glamorous woman attuned with her nightclub performer persona and celebrity status.

Perhaps Jorgensen understated herself because the heroes in her memoir are her doctors; after the sex reassignment, she was so grateful that she took a feminized version of the first name of Dr. Hamburger, the main doctor who treated her, and called herself Christine. And, even though Jorgensen wrote her memoir in 1967, she used the by-then outdated terminology of Steinach's glandular physical bisexuality to account for her condition. She reported Dr. Hamburger's speculation that her case was caused by the chemistry of her cells. If she grew up to be a boy, inwardly she remained a woman because her brain cells were female (p. 92). The hormonal treatment was meant to suppress the male components (p. 93). Steinach would appreciate the irony that on learning the good news that she was allowed to start hormonal treatment, she wrote "Just refer to me as guinea pig 0000" (p. 93).

In the second part of the 20th century, a new discourse about transsexualism emerged, and the key for the new direction was given by Sandor Rado, a psychoanalyst who surveyed in 1940 "the actual status of the idea of bisexuality in the biological field." Rado (1956) concluded that "the old speculative notion of bisexuality [was] in the process of withering away" (p. 142). He summed up his examination of biological bisexuality by declaring that "there is not such a thing as bisexuality either in man or in any other of the higher vertebrates" (p. 145). Rado urged the scientific community to make a shift: "It is imperative to supplant the deceptive concept of bisexuality with a psychological theory based on firmer foundations. ... It is a scientific obligation" (p. 149). And, Benjamin obliged.

In 1954, Benjamin opened a symposium organized by the *American Journal of Psychotherapy* with a paper whose title, "Transvestism and Transsexualism as Psycho-somatic and Somato-Psychic Syndrome," spell out the distinction Benjamin was establishing between the transvestite (psychosomatic) and transsexual (somato-psychic) phenomena. Physical bisexuality was again the point of departure. Benjamin (1954) wrote: "Organically, sex is always a mixture of male and female components," but suggested that mild cases (transvestism) could be "principally psychogenic," while for true "transsexualists" "a still greater degree of constitutional femininity, perhaps due to a chromosomal sex disturbance, must be assumed" (pp. 228–229). For severe cases, Benjamin reiterated that therapy was of no use. He was also not naïve, admitting that for a male-to-female transsexual, surgery "may not always solve [the transsexual's] problem. His feminization craving may never end" (pp. 228–229). He also warned against performing sex reassignment on patients with psychosis or who were in danger of suicide or self-mutilation. Benjamin had a negative bias against psychotherapy and psychoanalysis but created a protocol for sex change in which psychiatrists were given the power to determine who were the potential candidates for surgery; psychiatrists had the final word on the treatment decision but no say on the diagnosis. As Hausman (1995) observed, this illustrates the ambivalent relation between psychiatry and clinical endocrinology in the treatment of transsexualism (p. 124).

Christine Jorgensen defined her condition on physiological grounds, using the old glandular vocabulary of intersex; her true identity resided deep in her tissues. However, in the 1940s the discourse of transsexualism was starting to treat the body as determined by the mind's identifications. For two decades, physicians working with intersex patients were already using the notion of "psychological sex" separate from the biological sex (Meyerowitz, 2002/2004, p. 112). But it was with John Money's new vocabulary of gender in the 1950s that the idea of an "environmental" psychological sex was introduced. As we discussed, the gender–sex divide is a historical development due to the development of sex change medical technology (Hausman, 1995). Prior to the introduction of "gender" in 20th-century discourse as a signifier of "social sex," "sex" was a signifier encoding both biological and social categories (p. 75). As we have seen, the concept of psychosocial gender identity had been invented by John Money in the 1950s and had crucial ideological consequences.

Prosser (1998) objects to Hausman's attribution of unequivocal ideological power to medicine, which places transsexuals as "the dupes of gender" (p. 8), by which he meant that they were duped into believing in a core gender identity. To further the discussion, I analyze a famous case that suggests that some transsexuals could dupe their doctors as well. This case illustrates the extent to which dominant discourses model the way in which the sex change demand is formulated. This example is of interest because it took place at a very special moment in time, when the model of biological bisexuality was giving way to the notion of "gender" seen as gender identity or gender separated from the body.

A UNIQUE TYPE OF A MOST RARE DISORDER

In 1958, Agnes was evaluated at the UCLA (University of California at Los Angeles) Medical Center by a team of doctors, including Robert Stoller (Stoller, Garfinkel, & Rosen, 1960). She was seeking reassignment genital surgery. She was a 19-year-old, white "woman, but with male genitalia" (p. 379). Agnes had been raised as a boy, but during puberty she had developed breasts. At the time, she was living as a woman. Medical tests showed that she was genetically XY and had neither uterus nor ovaries; her chromosomes and glands were male. They detected, however, high levels of estrogen. Agnes was considered an atypical case of intersex, and in 1959, a team of surgeons removed her testicles and penis and constructed labia and a vagina.

Her case was baffling and became an exemplary case study of a rare form of intersex. Stoller and his team speculated that Agnes had a lesion that may have atrophied her testicles, increasing the estrogen production that made her breasts grow and propelling the "biological force" underlying her gender choice (Schwabe, Solomon, Stoller, & Burnham, 1962, p. 844). The anatomical anomaly explained why the "core identity was female" for someone who as a child had been "a normal-appearing boy" and, most importantly, as an adult was declared "genetically male" (Stoller, 1964, p. 255).

Five years after the surgery, Agnes confessed to Stoller that she had been taking estrogen since age 12, something that she had all along denied. At the time, Agnes's mother was recovering from a hysterectomy and had been placed briefly on hormone replacement therapy. Agnes would steal her mother's hormones and by lying to the pharmacist, she continued filling prescriptions on her own. While on estrogen, she developed the physical features that fooled the doctors. The reasons why her case was so convincing reveal the bias and prejudices of the examining team. They trusted her "natural," feminine appearance because "[s]he was tall, slim, with a very female shape. Her measurements were 38–25–38. She had long, fine, dark-blonde hair, a young face with pretty features, a peaches-and-cream complexion, no facial hair, subtly plucked eyebrows, and no makeup except for lipstick." Agnes was convincing because "there was nothing garish or exhibitionistic in her attire, nor was there a hint of poor taste … as is seen so frequently in transvestites" (Garfinkel, 1967/2006, p. 60). Thus, Agnes was not a "caricature," and she did not have any of the "hostility … seen in transvestites and transsexualists." "It was not possible," they gathered, "for any of the observers, including those who knew her anatomic state, to identify her as anything but a young woman" (Stoller et al., 1960, p. 380). Some were misled by her feminine breasts, which one of the doctors privately described as "very beautiful—well stacked" (Meyerowitz, 2002/2004, p. 160). Stoller (1968b) publically retracted his theories about this case, which toppled his belief in a biological force behind gender identity. He admitted that Agnes "is not the example of a 'biological force' that … influences gender identity. … Rather she is a transsexual" (p. 136). The lesson was not lost on either the doctors or the patients seeking a sex change. Was she duping the doctors or simply redefining the medical narrative of transsexuality?

SECOND-WAVE AND THIRD-WAVE SEX CHANGE MEMOIRS

Renée Richards's autobiography of sex change, *Second Serve* (1983), and the sequel, *No Way Renée* (2007), belong to the second-wave model of autobiographies under the aegis of the model of psychic gender detachable from the materiality of the body. Richards's (1983) first memoir has a strong psychological bias and reads like an exemplary case story. The opening quotation is by psychiatrist Karl Menninger and sets the tone of the narrative describing the psychic elements leading to the transsexual "physical make up and sexual psychology" (p. 5). The author's account takes the clinical angle of the introspective psychiatrist building her case material:

> If I sat down to write a case history of an imaginary transsexual, I could not come up with a more provocative set of circumstances than that of my childhood. … My early life is strewn with unsubtle touches that beg to be seen as reasons for my sexual confusion. (p. 5)

The classic psychoanalytic style of the case presentation is meant to prove that her gender trouble is psychological. One finds all the predictable features in the recipe for trauma: dramatic birth, an absent father, a mother with a tortured relation to her own father, who died in a botched surgery at which Renée's mother assisted. The cold and distant mother would only be tender and sensually affectionate with her son early in the morning while getting dressed in front of her son, but otherwise withdrew into a critical and dictatorial detachment from him, imposing tyrannical demands, administering enemas, and preferring to see her son dressed in girls' clothes. "I was told to be a boy. ... But, when I was a girl Mommy loved me" (p. 16). The tomboyish older sister named Michael [sic] would dress her younger brother with her clothes and engage in sexual games, making his penis disappear and victoriously declaring: "See you're not a little boy, you are a girl" (p. 13). In sum, the premise of the memoir is faithful to the constraints of the core gender identity psychological model with one interesting additional psychological twist—the author presents her story as a case of double personality: The successful, handsome, Ivy League educated, athletic eye surgeon, married to a beautiful woman and father of a son, had within himself another person—a woman. The female side of him struggled to emerge from his body while being chastised by the male personality, but eventually Richard became Renée.

A psychoanalytic vocabulary also permeates *Emergence,* the memoir of Mario Martino (1977), which the jacket copy advertised as "the only complete autobiography of a woman who has become a man." It had a foreword by Harry Benjamin, who endorsed this "highly important book, *Emergence* will clarify the minds of female transsexuals and their families, and help them find themselves and their position in life" (p. ix). Martino, a nurse, also played the dual role of subject of study and clinical authority using psychoanalytic jargon, which generates some humorous self-awareness. Evoking his contempt for the father's repressive violence and his adoration for the mother, Martino comments: "A bit of Oedipus, you think?" (p. 28).

Second-wave autobiographies follow the model of core gender identity. They want to confirm the usual transsexual plot of a psychological evolution: They begin with a failure to identify with the gender assigned at birth and move to the realization that the self is trapped in the body of the opposite sex, finally culminating with the decision to transition and the transition itself. Formulaically, the body is remade to align itself with the psychological gender.

Along with today's second-wave model in which bisexuality is anchored in the body itself and coupled with an inner sense of gender identification, a third wave of style of memoirs has emerged. One early example of the emergence of the new style is *Transgender Warriors: Making History From Joan of Arc to RuPaul.* Leslie Feinberg (1996) constructed a proud cross-cultural history of centuries of transgenderism, narrated as a memoir—the autobiography is a combination of historical information, bits of gender theory, and personal views. We now see a new narrative style that adds to the usual components of the memoir, elements of political tracts claiming transgender rights and providing concrete advice.[1] Some of the memoirs are more fragmentary and do not follow the usual teleology. A notable example is Kate Bornstein's (1994) *Gender Outlaw: On Men, Women, and the Rest of Us*. This memoir breaks with the teleological sweep or the continuous movement that used to be typical of earlier sex change memoirs. Bornstein's story shifts back and forth in time, and the plot is conveyed in a freely associative manner as it attempts to offer a model of transsexual identity beyond the man–woman binary:

> My identity as a transsexual lesbian whose female lover is becoming a man is manifested in my fashion statement; both my identity and fashion are based on collage. You know—a little bit from here, a little bit from there? Sort of a cut-and-paste thing. And that is the style of this book. It's a transgender style, I suppose. (p. 3)

The hedonistic undertone signals a different approach to gender trouble that does not exclude humor or bypass the pleasure of writing.

FADE TO NORMAL

Bornstein is enacting what Sandy Stone (1991) recommends when she wants transsexuals to live up to their ideologies. Stone argues that the installation of an "official transsexual history" needed to obtain surgical and hormonal sex change treatment has produced a situation in which the potential for the "intertextuality" of transsexual subjectivity is erased:

> The highest purpose of the transsexual is to erase him/herself, to fade into the "normal" population as soon as possible. Part of this process is known as constructing a plausible story—learning to lie effectively about one's past. ... Authentic experience is replaced by a particular kind of story, one that supports the old constructed positions. (p. 295)

A transsexual who suppresses the ambiguities and complexities of lived experience for the sake of normality is thus not very different from the patient who comes to see an analyst because the plausible story no longer efficiently lies about the past; in both cases, a symptom is endowed with

---

[1] See Finney Boylan (2003), Green (2004), Khosla (2006), Valerio (2006), and Zander (2003).

the potential to start the analytic process. Yet, even when the transsexual narrative repeats the old clichés, one cannot downplay the tremendous impact that the discovery of a sex change memoir has had for many transsexuals. Almost all the sex change memoirs include a moment in which the author recounts reading another sex-change memoir. Often revelatory, the encounter with this type of text proves to be a defining moment anchoring the subject in the realization of an identity.

LIVES ALTERED BY THE PRINTED WORD

Memoirs of sex change are not only numerous but also often have an impressive, life-transforming effect on the future transsexuals who happen to read them—the experience of reading other people's memoirs becomes a turning point in their evolution. For example, in her autobiography *Conundrum*, the writer Jan Morris (1986) recounts with poignant details the charged emotions that accompanied her discovery of a dusty 1933 volume of *Man Into Woman: An Authentic Record of a Change of Sex* in a bookstore in the Welsh town of Ludlow (p. 45). Morris, then in her 20s, felt forever changed when the book provided a confirmation that there were other people with a similar predicament. *Man Into Woman*, an autobiography written under the pseudonym of Niels Hoyer, tells the story of the first recorded case of sex change. Einar Wegener was a Danish painter who had been married but felt he was a woman trapped in a man's body. Wegener consulted many doctors, including a close friend of Eugen Steinach. According to the bisexuality theories of the time, Wegener's treatment consisted of the removal of testicles under the supervision of pioneer sexologist Hirschfield; this was followed by an ovarian transplant to stimulate the feminine side to help Lili Elbe to come into being. Lili Elbe died a year later, during one of several surgeries, possibly a vaginoplasty or even a uterus transplant. Morris found the memoir extremely sad, and yet it gave her hope. She was not alone.

Renée Richards (1983) recalls that reading *Man Into Woman* had a much more propitiatory effect in her previous life as Dr. Richard Raskind than her earlier discovery in the bookshelves of her mother's office (she was a psychiatrist) of the classic Krafft-Ebbing's *Psychopatia Sexualis* (pp. 54–55). The young Raskind was torn between two sides of her persona, the female side as Renée, a heterosexual woman, and the male part as Richard (Dick), a heterosexual man. At age 16, she was fascinated and horrified when reading the massive 19th-century compendium of sexual aberrations, *Psychopatia Sexualis*. Yet, Raskind found very little identificatory comfort in what she dismissed as mere stories of "lunatics." Furthermore, the book made her fear that she was crazy. Discovering the story of Einar Wegener 2 years later was a lucky breakthrough: "I had hit the jack pot" (p. 55). Not only had she found that it was acceptable to have the personality of a woman trapped in a man's body, there was also a radical solution available. For her male side, the book had dire consequences, but for Renée it was the beginning of hope as it confirmed that there was a reason to exist.

Nancy Hunt (1978), a male-to-female transsexual and former *Chicago Tribune* award-winning journalist, describes the life-transforming effect that reading a first person account of sex reassignment had on her:

> I can remember only once when my life has been altered by the printed word. That was upon reading an article in the *New York Times Magazine* on March 17, 1974. ... It described the transition from man into woman of an English journalist now known as Jan Morris. (p. 137)

Reading Morris's (1986) memoir *Conundrum* was more than an inspiration for Hunt—it became a role model to emulate. "Morris had faced this dilemma and solved it, and given the courage and the resolution, so could I. Morris had taken hormones and so could I. ... Morris had gone to Dr. Harry Benjamin in New York, starting down the road that would end up in the operating table, and I could do that too" (pp. 139–140). Two days after reading the article, Nancy Hunt wrote to Benjamin, knowing that she "had crossed a river and would never go back" (p. 141).

The encounter with the text is a completely transformative experience that reveals a truth up to then unknown, but that once acknowledged, starts a process that is unstoppable. Max Valerio (2006) was browsing in bookstore, a usual pastime, and found on top of a stack, in the table of remaindered bargain books and for $2.50, *Female-to-Male Transsexualism*, by Leslie Lothstein. Perplexed, Valerio looked at the book jacket and asked himself: "What is this? A book about—female to male transsexuals? What if ... I am a transsexual?" (p. 77). He was transfixed by the book and the discovery, gripped by a fascinated, uneasy excitement. Valerio experienced awe and horror along with a sense of irreversible destiny: "I was beginning to enter the crossroads—the place of raw, unmitigated energy" (p. 77).

Similarly, Dhillon Khosla (2006), a lesbian lawyer in the San Francisco area, also a singer and songwriter in his spare time, had been for 28 years living as a woman. Suddenly, he discovered the truth of his gender in an epiphany, when reading interviews of female-to-male transsexuals in a 1994 article of the *New Yorker*:

> And as I read the things these men said ... [f]lashes of recognition went off in my mind, arranging themselves like the pieces of a puzzle. ... The relief, however, was short-lived. Next came the tough question: Now that I knew the truth, what was I going to do about it?" (pp. 4–5)

Soon after reading the article, Khosla found himself attending a monthly meeting for female-to-male transsexuals.

In a similar way, for Jayne County (1995), a well-known New York rock-and-roll female impersonator, tells us in her memoir that it was reading an autobiography, this time of the transsexual Canary Conn, that provided the revelation about her true gender and gave her a new sense of identity and purpose: "I decided that I had a transsexual identity." County concluded that she was already female and chose to "go the whole way and have a sex change" (p. 99).

In all these examples, the individual, private encounter with the printed word had an illuminating effect, setting into motion a series of events that forever changed the lives of the readers. This huge potential of the letter has not been neglected by organizations such as the Foundation for Gender Education; they sell all manner of books about transsexualism and transvestism and use transsexual autobiographies as the mainstay of their educative outreach. While it is true that the autobiographical texts institute a certain discursive hegemony with their repetitive patterns, I want to stress that such formulaic narratives have a transformative effect on those who read them and feel saved by the printed word. Sandy Stone (1991) highlighted the importance of reading and related it to writing in what she claimed is "the essence of transsexualism":

> I could not ask a transsexual for anything more unconceivable than to forgo passing, to be consciously "read," to read oneself aloud, and by this troubling and productive reading to begin to write oneself into the discourses by which one has been written—in effect, then to become a (look out—dare I say it again?) a post-transsexual. (p. 299)

The first memoirs were written not to be read, by authors who meant to pass. The new posttranssexualism aims at being read, that is at coming to terms with a certain failure in passing, which should have a liberating effect: an effect of writing. This writing on the body is not identical to a Butlerian position of masquerade but approaches Lacanian notions of the letter as sinthome.

NARRATIVE TRANSITIONS

There are unavoidable tensions in transsexual autobiographies. If the aim of the autobiography is to document the transition, for instance, to show how somebody born a man becomes a woman, the purpose of the transsexual's travelogue is in contradiction with the common transsexual's claim that: "I was woman all along, but happened to be in the wrong body." Prosser (1998) contends that this tension between transformation and continuity in the self is inherent to the autobiographical genre (p. 119). However, often the motivation for the transition is to accomplish a sex change that will not leave vestiges of the former sex on the body. If the transsexual wants a complete transformation to pass as a member of the new sex, the autobiography defeats this purpose. By making public the account of the steps of the transition, very often documented with photographs, the autobiography somehow exposes the decoy. And yet, by publishing the account, the transsexual who does not want to be read as a transsexual but rather wants to pass as normal will become publicly recognized as a transsexual.

Prosser (1998) emphasizes this paradox and highlights the fact that while there may be sex changes accomplished by surgery and hormones, the somatic transformation is not sufficient. Writing autobiographies of sex change generates transitional moments that are "more in keeping with the flow of the story to cohere the transsexual subject." In this case, indeed, the narrative "enacts its own transitions" (p. 123). It is therefore on this last stage of the transition, that is on the narrative transition itself, that I want to focus. It is a transition that takes places in and through writing, at a moment when the autography seems to recapture the body, thus anchoring it through a textual embodiment.

THE BODY AS WRITTEN

Sexual difference is neither just the body (as biological substrata) nor the psychic introjections of the social performance of gender (a socially constructed role). Neither the perspective of biological essentialism nor that of social constructivism have been able to solve the problem of unconscious sexual difference. Since sexual difference is neither sex nor gender, sex needs to be symbolized, and gender needs to be embodied.

I argue that sex change memoirs are a narrative form with a specific function for the subjectivity of their authors—they help embody sexual difference. In some cases, transsexual memoirs can function as a process of self-invention for their authors. Moreover, sex change memoirs provide an excellent testing ground for Lacan's theory of the sinthome. Even though we know that the psychoanalytic perspective on sexual difference implies that it is not a question of anatomy but rather of its consequences, we have noted that a majority of transsexuals struggle to conform rigidly to the normative demands of a sexual identity in contradiction with their anatomical sex. While they engage in technologically assisted manipulations of their bodies, their torment seems to be the result of the limits imposed by an anatomy experienced as a tragic destiny.

There is a paradoxical literalization of what psychoanalysis calls *castration* in some sex change practices. This is illustrated in a gripping passage of Martino's (1977) memoir of a "painful life to live, a painful life to write" (p. xi). Martino describes a second phalloplasty that seemed to fail; the first one was unsuccessful, and the neopenis had to be surgically excised. As the tip of his new penis became black, rotted away, and necrotized, he had to sit in water every night to slowly cut away dead tissue. He comments ironically: "Talk about castration complex! Psychologically this cutting was almost impossible for me, yet it has to be done" (p. 262). Mario broke away from the increasing distress about the inadequate results of surgery when he came to the realization that even if he wanted "a perfect phallus" he had to accept the impossibility of the wish. "So today I'm happy with what I have: a respectable phallus—three fourths perfect" (p. 263). The phallus is a prosthesis, even then an incomplete one, three fourths perfect. This demonstrates that what psychoanalysis calls "phallus" is not an object but an instance to symbolize the drives, or fundamentally a signifier.

Feminist and deconstructive critiques of the Lacanian concept of phallus have neglected Lacan's main innovation on the question of sexuality. This is an aspect that Tim Dean emphasizes when he called our attention to Lacan's logic of the object *petit a* and saw in it a breakthrough that offers a nonnormative understanding of sexuality. Dean (2000) observes that "it is not so important that the phallus may be a penis, or in Judith Butler's reading, a dildo, as it is a giant red herring" (p. 14). The phallus is clearly a misleading clue comparable to the use of smoked herrings to mislead hounds following a trail. To pun somewhat on the phrase, I would like to suggest that the phallus is less a red herring than a "read" herring—in fact, like gender, it is subject to interpretation, and it will always be read like a text.

Since sexual difference is real and resists symbolization, it creates a symptom, but this symptom is something that cannot be rectified or cured; it is nevertheless something with which every subject must come to terms. In Lacan's (1976/1977, 1977, 2005) later formulation of the sinthome, the idea of the symptom acquired a new meaning. The sinthome is a purified symptom, it remains beyond symbolic representation and exists outside the unconscious structured as language. In this sense, the sinthome is closer to the Real. Lacan reached the final conclusion that there is no subject without a sinthome. Lacan's contention that there is no sexual relation entails that there is no normal relation, and therefore that any relationship between partners is a *sinthomatic* one.[2]

---

[2] The sinthome is a self-created artifice that re-knots the registers of Real, Symbolic, and Imaginary into a particular sexual rapport: "On the level of the sinthome, there is a relationship where there is a sinthome" (Lacan 1976/1977, p. 20). There is a rapport, but the lack of the sexual relation is maintained.

SCHREBER, PIONEER TRANSSEXUAL MEMOIRIST

Revisiting the case of Schreber will be useful here as he was one of the first successful memoir writers. One might even say that Schreber's *Memoirs of My Mental Illness* (2000) is the prototype of the whole genre. Schreber was to Freud what Joyce is to Lacan: Both are writers who need a text to deposit a truth about the experience of jouissance such that it exceeds all limits. Jouissance underpins the creation of a sinthome by which text and body are held together. Lacan claimed that Joyce had been saved from psychosis by writing. Similarly, Schreber was freed from the mental asylum by his memoirs. Even if Lacan tends to treat Joyce's entire oeuvre as a memoir in a questionable biographical reading that verges on psychobiography, I argue that this approach to Joyce's work as a memoir serves above all to emphasize its function as sinthome.

Some 20 years after a seminar that dealt with Schreber's transsexual psychosis, Lacan turned his attention to Joyce. As we have seen, Lacan focused on a passage of *A Portrait of the Artist as a Young Man*, when Stephen remembers a moment of rage at his schoolmates and describes experiencing both his anger and his body as suddenly falling away like the peel of a ripe fruit. In this passage, Lacan catches a very particular body, a body that can fall from itself, similar to a wrapping that cannot hold fully its contents. To explain this slipping of the body, Lacan (2005) used the expression "to let fall" (*laissez-tomber*) (p. 150).

We may recall that in previous chapters this phrase of Lacan's was used in connection with Sidonie's suicide attempt, when the young woman threw herself on the rails of a trolley underpass. Thus, Sidonie could let herself fall (laissez-tomber) after she had fallen from her father's field of vision, and her adored lady, feeling spited, had "dumped her" (Lacan, 2004). Sidonie's fall was a desperate attempt to salvage a lost situation; she identified with the fallen object and fell with it, out of the scene while restructuring it. After Sidonie's suicide attempt, we may remember, the lady, who up to that moment had been quite distant, was moved by such a gesture of devotion and paid more attention to the young woman; her parents also became less restrictive.

In Joyce's Stephen Dedalus, something else happens in the body, something falls like a soft, ripe fruit peel. This reveals for Lacan (2005) a particular mode of relation to one's own body:

> So then what meaning are we to give to what Joyce bears witness to? He bears witness not simply to his relation to his own body but, as it were, to the psychology of this relation. After all, psychology is nothing other than the confused image we have of our own body. But this confused image is not without a component of affects, since we call them this way. In imagining this psychical relationship, there is something in the psyche that is affected, that reacts, that is not detached, which

> is unlike Joyce's experience, after [Stephen] had been beaten by four or five school friends. In Joyce, something simply goes away, shed away like the skin of a fruit.
>
> It is rather striking that there should be people who have no affect in response to the bodily violence they have undergone. The situation is ambiguous. Perhaps it gave him some pleasure, since masochism is never to be ruled out with Joyce. ... What is most remarkable is the metaphor he employs—the detaching of something like a fruit skin. This one time, he did not enjoy it, he had a reaction of disgust. Here is something that is psychologically valid. This disgust concerns his own body. It is like someone who puts a parenthesis, who drives away the bad memory.
>
> Having a relation to one's own body as foreign is a possibility, which is expressed by the verb "to have" that we use for the body: one *has* one own's body, one is not one's body in any degree. This is what makes people believe in the soul, after which there's no reason to stop, we end up thinking we have a soul to crown it all. But here, the form of the *letting fall* (*laisser tomber* [italics in the French text]) of the relation to one's own body is entirely suspect for a psychoanalyst, since the idea of oneself as body has a certain weight. This is what is called the *ego* [italics in the French text]. (pp. 149–150)

Like a bad memory, the beating is not repressed but rather slips, falls away, until it loses its determining power. Once the peel has come away, Stephen views his body as foreign, relates to it with disgust. This disgust, which is a common affect that one finds marking the way most sex change memoir authors relate to the pretransition body, is in fact a reparation. The ego recaptures the fallen peel, and the body becomes disgusting, an internal foreign land.

Like a foreigner resident who applies for citizenship and becomes a naturalized national, the lost body can be recuperated via writing. Lacan (2005) contends that writing itself can hold the body. I argue that in many cases it is not enough to undergo corporeal reconstruction. First of all, transsexuals often change their names and even their birth certificates after the material transformation of the body in sex reassignment. The change that takes place is at the level of the flesh, hence in a realm that is close to the Real but is not sufficient. There is first a change in the flesh, then the artifice of writing is necessary before a full embodiment is accomplished.

INCORPORATIONS

Sex change narratives describe all the painful stages through which the narrator has gone while breaking free from a body that is experienced as foreign. Transsexuals claim that they are members of the opposite sex: "A female spirit trapped in a male body," for example, is a most common trope. In many memoirs of sex change, the body has a specific status. The body can be a rigid constraint; it can be seen as an exterior that oppresses the interior in which the real being, the true self, is trapped, locked. This image of the body as cage or prison is a recurrent theme in sex change autobiographical narratives, as noted by Tamsin Wilton (2000). Often, sex change appears as the only possible escape from the confines of excessive jouissance: "I was trapped inside a living chamber of horrors" (Griggs, 1998, p. 88). Lewins (1995) expanded this notion: "In the case of transsexuals locked inside a prison of flesh and blood, there is a constant ache for emancipation" (p. 14). Morris (1986) reiterates the same idea: "If I were trapped in that cage again nothing would keep me from my goal" (p. 169). In sex change narratives, people can have a self that stands in opposition to their body.

Many transsexuals have a peculiar, truncated relation to their bodies, and I will try to show that in the transsexual "artifice" one may find, on certain occasions, a creative sinthome. It takes the form of an answer that helps reclaim the body and regulate jouissance. Let us explore this contention with Deirdre McCloskey's (1999) *Crossing*. Here, it is important to stress the function of writing as modifying the materiality of the body and therefore impacting a point of view. Deirdre was born a male and had cross-dressed since puberty. At 52, after 30 years of marriage and two grown children, Deirdre realized that she not only wanted to become a woman, but also had been a woman all along. Here is what McCloskey called "an epiphany": "On the twentieth day of August 1995 a little after noon the dam broke and the water of his life swirled out onto the plain. He knew himself. Herself. That's it, she said: I am a woman" (p. 51). At age 54, Donald changed into Deirdre.

Donald cross-dressed for the first time at age 11. The memory of the event remained clear. He was in bed sick. His mother was downstairs in the kitchen taking care of his new baby sister:

> [Donald] was having the first wet dream of maleness. Oddly his dreams were of femaleness, of having it, of being. Upstairs in the bathroom he took a pair of his mother panties from the laundry basket, put them on, and found a rush of sexual pleasure—not joyous, or satisfying, merely There. It was a mild ache, pleasant and alluring, mixing memory and desire: the women half dressed in Filene's [store], the little ballerinas, his mother. There was nothing of male lust in it except the outcome. It was not curiosity about what lay underneath women's clothing. It was curiosity about being. (pp. 5–6)

This is not a case of fetishism (in fetishism, the feminine clothes would be the substitute for the mother's phallus the child believed in and is unwilling to give up). Donald took his mother's panties and put them on, experiencing intense jouissance ("wet dream of maleness"), while trying to deal with sexual difference ("dreams of femaleness, of having it, of being"). If we replace in this description the word *femaleness* for *phallus*, then, his account becomes "his dreams were of [the phallus], of having it, of being." It is clear that Donald's memory is about the dissymmetry in the phallic function, a dissymmetry that creates the opposition that Freud summed up as "having" and "not having." It becomes, in the Lacanian reading, "having" and "being": Man has the phallus and woman has not, but because of this, she can embody it, thus "be" the phallus.

Donald was thus grappling with the relation of the subject to the phallus, a relation evoked by Lacan (2006) as "a relation between the subject and the phallus that forms without regard to the anatomical distinction between the sexes and that it is thus especially difficult to interpret in the case of women and with respect to women" (p. 576). Donald concluded that "it was curiosity about being," which sums up his sexual positioning and shows that he was identified with being the phallus.

We have seen how painful it was for Deirdre (McCloskey, 1999) to be read as a transsexual; a nose job, a facelift, make-up classes, a voice operation, a collection of wigs—all these were aimed at transforming herself in a way that would be unreadable. Similarly, Lacan (1998b) described Joyce's work as "unreadable" because "the signifier stuffs the signified" (p. 37). When a transsexual body is read, is it a body that is reduced to a letter? Is Deirdre's desire to pass, not to be read, a way of rejecting the letter as an effect of discourse? Or when Deirdre is read, has her distraught feeling of inadequacy something to do with readability, as if a sexual relation that can neither be written nor be read had become legible?

Crossing (McCloskey, 1999) is a sex change memoir that faithfully follows the requirements of the genre: The boy was already a girl. That transsexual narrative already plotted in the body, however, acquires coherence in the body through the narrative. The autobiographical narrative changes the subject of the narrative, boy becomes girl, or vice versa, its narrative composes the "I." Let us note that *Crossing* is written in the third person when telling the stories of Donald and Deirdre, with an intermediate stage as a cross-dressing Dee. All along, the narrative is punctuated by occasional comments in bold and in the first person singular, in the voice of Deirdre. This voice-over progressively inscribes Deirdre as the story's hero, finally allowing her to "hear the good news of forgiveness, the duty to offer, and the grace to receive" (p. xvi). McCloskey goes from fearing being "read like a book, detected in the wrong gender" (p. 29), aware that "testing for being read is paranoid style of life" (p. 45), to writing a book to "live as a woman, without notice or comment" (p. 254).

Although McCloskey's memoir sounds credible, the effect of her writing lacks the opacity, the enigmatic quality that one finds in Schreber or Joyce and that makes of their texts a sinthome. Finally, one can say that Deirdre McCloskey was no longer torn by crossing (which could suggest deciphering, inventing, or undoing meaning) because she was too thrilled by her ability to pass.

MALE OR FEMALE?

Deirdre's happiness thus depended on being recognized as a woman, blending in, passing. The ability of transsexuals to pass relies on others who sanction the gender they present; this confirmation is often a primary concern. Freud (1932/1933) remarked that the first assessment one makes on meeting a person on the street is the question: "Male or female?" Most of the time, this distinction is made instantaneously, without any information about the person's exact genital configuration. Every day, we make multiple gender attributions that are not based on the genitals, but on other makers of gender differences like clothing, manners, behavior, and style. If we look at body markers, often it is the face that plays the most important role in gender attribution. To be very blunt, I reiterate that in most social interactions, we recognize each other by our faces rather than by how our genitals look.

In narratives of sex change, it is often the transformation of the face that plays as important a role as the genital modification. Max Valerio (2006) had been taking testosterone for some time when he met with an old friend, Jan, who used to be male and had not seen Max since he started his transition. Max and Jan have this exchange:

> Jan keeps looking at my face and body, slightly stunned, taking me in. She is registering all the little and large changes. The shape of my eyes, the cut of my jaw, how it's gotten squarer, the muscles in my arms, the width of my neck, my nose that's grown stronger, particularly at the bridge. All the subtle characteristics that make a person look either like a man or a woman.
>
> "You really look like a man," she says, wide-eyed, shaking her head in wonder.
>
> "You really look like a woman," I reply, smiling a broad smile now. … "It's a though a film has been peeled off your face. Now you're here, the real you that was underneath is revealed." (p. 315)

Similarly, the face as site of sexual identity plays an important role in Dhillon Khosla's (2006) transition from woman to man. His memoir opens with a dream: He tries to open a door, the handle turns, but the door does not open; he pushes and pushes, and finally is able to make the door open a few inches. He peers into the other side and sees his own face staring back (p. 3). This dream that Khosla had at age 19 when he was still a woman is presented in the memoir as a prophetic, transparent metaphor. When Khosla describes the attendants at a first meeting for female-to-male transsexuals, the face is what makes the gender performance believable. Of those who failed to pass as males, "some had facial hair but female-shaped faces beneath it; others had androgynous faces but pear-shaped bodies" (p. 8). At the end of one of those meetings, Dhillon Khosla met Jack, whose transition had started after reading the same *New Yorker* article that Khosla was given. Reading also had a life-transforming effect on Jack. The very next day after discovering the *New Yorker* essay, Jack had started pursuing a mastectomy and soon after began taking testosterone. During their friendly chat, when Jack asked Dhillon if he wanted to be referred to as "he," the latter was hesitant:

> Looking at his face, an undeniable male face, I found myself wavering. So far, I had been undecided about male hormones. And so, to justify my position, I said to Jack, "When I look in the mirror, I can sometimes see a pretty boy." He responded with, "When I look in the mirror, I see a man." ... His response hit home: it made me realize that that he didn't have to do any manipulations in his mind when he saw his reflection, while I was trying to convince myself into seeing what I felt inside. I'm not sure I can explain it, but I know that the part of me that thought that I could simply carry my true identity inside my own mind fell apart while looking at his face. (p. 10)

When Dhillon decided to start his transition and had to meet with a therapist to get one of the two referral letters for the reassignment surgery, the face again was a marker of gender:

> When Dr. Singleton opened the door, my mind was still imprinted with the image of a man from the voice I'd heard on the phone. And that image was not immediately dispelled on first sight.
> Although the doctor had long hair and was wearing a dress, her facial structure and her lumbering walk had strong remnants of the masculine. As we entered her office, I wondered how she could be happy. She must constantly confront people who see her as male. (p. 136)

What stands out in all these examples is that if the surgery allows the body to change, it is the autobiography that gives the author its true face. Prosser (1998) observed that mirror scenes constitute a convention of transsexual autobiography. Yet, the tinkering cannot just be explained by basic notions of the Lacanian "mirror stage." This is a slippage to which Prosser was not immune when he wrote: "Like Narcissus captured by the sight of his reflection, the transsexual autobiography neither fully merges with nor moves away from the image of the changed self" (p. 131). In fact, the writing of the memoir is not about narcissism in the classical sense; it is rather the ego scriptor who reconstitutes the ideal image of the self via writing.

Psychologically, something supports the body as image. Lacan (2005) calls it the self, or the self as body, the body as image—*that* falls (p. 150). What can be retrieved from this fall, via the agency of writing, is the ego. In the example taken from *A Portrait of the Artist*, we have seen that Stephen dropped his relationship to his body. After the beating, his body was experienced as something weightless, which fell like the peel of a fruit. Lacan ascribes to the ego the support of the body as image; what supports the relation to one's body as image is something one cannot see in the mirror. With Joyce, Lacan discovers that the ego scriptor can restore the subject's relation to the body. Writing helps incarnate the ego. This is why many sex change memoirs are also transition diaries. The function of writing as corrector of the relationship with one's body is well illustrated by Erica Zander (2003), who transitioned from male to female at the age of 48. Zander concludes her 350-page trans activist memoir and postoperative diary by implying that writing the book was also part of her transition:

> Did I wait too long? ... Considering all those years I tried to get to grips with my situation. ... I had to do it, and I would do it again—there was just no other way out for me. Also, having written some twelve hundred pages over the years, trying to sort out my impossible feelings, I guess I had to write this book as well. And if it helps only one transsexual man or woman make the right decision without wasting years of time and energy on unproductive worries, this is a lovely bonus. (pp. 342–343)

FACE AS PRESENTATION OF THE SELF

What distinguishes most transsexual memoirs attempting to shape a new face for their authors is that they follow a paradoxical movement in which an inscription (which in Lacanian terms partakes of the Real or the Symbolic) restores the fallen Imaginary of an ego. In these memoirs, one can only have a mirror image once it has been written. Hence, the inscription allows for the restored visual image to form. The face that is constructed is therefore structural and could call up the phenomenological approach of Levinas (1969/1985), who defines ethics as the rapport of two faces (p. 85).

What distinguishes transsexuals, however, is that the almost infinite distance between one face and the other will be crossed by one single person. This has been well observed by Jamison Green (2004), author of another transsexual memoir. He formulated the idea quite compellingly when he wrote: "No one can tell exactly what will happen to any particular body when *any* hormone is administered. No one can predict, as pre-adolescents, what we will look like when we grow up, and neither can we know precisely what cross-sex hormones will do to our bodies" (p. 90; italics in the original). The sex change decision entails a plunge into the unknown for the transformation keeps a part of mystery, and no transsexual can hope to appear the same but different, as when Marcel Duchamp painted Mona Lisa with a beard, to suggest that she may have been a man, and then presented an exact copy of the original as being "Mona Lisa shaved." This uncertainty led Green to an extended meditation on visibility:

> What makes a man a man? His penis? His beard? His receding hairline? His lack of breasts? His sense of himself as a man? Some men have no beard, some have no penis, some never lose their hair, some have breasts; all have a sense of themselves as men, Transsexual men are also men. Transsexual men are men who have lived in female bodies. ... The crux of the matter of gender for *anyone* is their own visibility and sufficient external confirmation of their gender identity; thus, if a person is comfortable with her or his gender-body congruity or incongruity, and their gender is confirmed by the people around them whom they value, they will feel "seen" and validated by others. Until I changed my body I always had to struggle to be visible. That's not the case for every transperson; it was the case for me. (pp. 186–187; italics in the original)

In a slightly different key but with a similar pathos, Leslie Feinberg's autobiographical novel (Feinberg is a transsexual), *Stone Butch Blues* (1993), presents us with the confusion that Jess Goldberg, a working class masculine woman who underwent surgery and lived as a man but eventually decided to stay in-between sexes. S/he came to the decision to stop taking testosterone when hir face no longer confirmed hir self:

> What I saw reflected in the mirror was not a man, but I couldn't recognize the he-she. My face no longer revealed the contrasts of my gender. I could see my passing self, but even I could no longer see the more complicated me beneath my surface. ... I hadn't just believed that passing would hide me. I hoped that it would allow me to express the part of myself that didn't seem to be woman. I didn't get to explore being a he-she though. I simply became a he—a man without a past.
> Who was I now—woman or man? (pp. 221–222)

The writing of the memoir can bring the author home to the body transformed. This is how Max Valerio (2006) describes it:

I don't look like a teenager any longer, but clearly like an adult man. Fully grown. I've arrived. ... My jaw is more defined and square, the muscles in my face are set into a tender expression. Men's facial muscles show more because they just generally have less fat in their bodies, and the muscles tend to be larger.

It's gotten to the point that if I tell someone I once was a woman, they don't believe me. (p. 325)

Valerio became an embodied, not merely textual body, an author with a face, a subject with a possible relation to his body.

THE TIN DRUM

Is subjectivity just an effect of signification? Is the body purely imaginary? I explore a last example to argue that the new face that is produced in sex change memoirs is not of the order of the Imaginary but of the sinthome, closer to the register of the Real. In the well-known and often-quoted *Conundrum* (1974/1986), Jan Morris presented her "escape from maleness into womanhood" as a journey with "some higher origin or meaning," adding: "I equate it with the idea of soul, or self, and I think of it not just as a sexual enigma, but as a quest for unity" (pp. 9–10). By "unity," Morris implied that she would be able to become one with the truth of her sexuality, a truth confirmed by a childhood memory: "I have had no doubt about my gender since that moment of self-realization beneath the piano [when she realized that she was born in the wrong body]. Nothing in the world would make me abandon my gender concealed from everyone though it remained; but my body, my organs, my paraphernalia, seemed to me much less sacrosanct, and far less interesting too" (pp. 25–26). Morris was certain that "gender" was opposed to "body," "organs," "paraphernalia." This was because, as with most memoirists, Morris had been trapped in "sexual incongruity" (p. 172): "I was born with the wrong body, being feminine my gender but male my sex, and I could achieve completeness only when the one was adjusted to the other" (p. 26), she writes. Interestingly, Morris distinguished "feeling like a woman" from "having the body of a woman." She concludes: "Male and female are sex, masculine and feminine are gender, and though the conceptions overlap, they are far from synonymous" (p. 25).

Kenneth Paradis (2006) pointed out the political implications of Morris's (1974/1986) carefully constructed argument: "By locating the truth of sex in the experiencing self rather than in the reproductive anatomy, the body becomes an object of subjective agency that can legitimately be altered" (p. 157). With this strategy, Morris was aware that she was anticipating a trend. "Could it be that I am merely a symptom of the times, a forerunner perhaps of a race in which sexes would be blended amoeba-like into one? The world was contracting fast ... might not mankind discard its sexual divisions too?" (p. 42). Beyond these futuristic fantasies, Morris admitted that she was not simply looking for a sex change but for the realization of her self: "That my inchoate yearnings, both born from wind and sunshine, music and imagination—that my conundrum might simply be a matter of penis or vagina, testicle or womb, seems to me still a contradiction in terms, for it concerned not my apparatus, but my *self*" (pp. 21–22; italics in the original). Morris' quest was for a state of unity that was experienced as completion, making her body whole. "I had myself long seen in my quest some veiled spiritual purpose, as though I was pursuing a Grail or grasping Oneness" (p. 105). Morris felt trapped between a self/spirit that was mythically and essentially female and a constraining male anatomy; as a solution, she longed for the One. To make sense of how her feminine self, alienated in her male body, eventually manages to achieve unity via a genital ablation, hormones, and transsexual autobiography, one needs to explore the idiosyncrasies of Morris's peculiar relationship to her body.

Morris (1974/1986) wrote that in her previous life as a man,

> though I resented my body, I did not dislike it. I rather admired it, as it happened. It might not be the body beautiful, but it was lean and sinewy, never ran to fat and worked like a machine of quality, responding exuberantly to a touch of the throttle or the long haul home. (p. 79)

Morris's male body was "a marvelous thing to inhabit" (p. 82). But by her mid-30s, after the birth of Morris's daughter Virginia, she developed a bitter self-repugnance: "I began to detest the body that had served me so loyally" (p. 89). Morris became exiled from her body, which she experienced as an exterior One with which she tried to reconcile. "And so I asked myself, in mercy, or in common sense, if I cannot alter the conviction to fit the body, should we not in certain circumstances, alter the body to fit the conviction? ... To alter the body! To match my sex to my gender at last and a make whole of me" (p. 49). "All I wanted was liberation, or reconciliation—to live as myself, to clothe myself in a more proper body, and achieve Identity at last." Morris solution to the dilemma was "to adapt my body from a male conformation to a female, and I would shift my public role altogether, from the role of a man to the role of a woman" (p. 104). In Casablanca, Morris underwent sex reassignment surgery with Dr. B. "I had a new body. Now when I looked down at myself I no longer seem a hybrid or a chimera: I was all of a piece. ... I felt above all deliciously *clean*. ... I was made, by my own lights, normal" (p. 141; italics in the original). The sex change operation triggered a normalization that affected the body and the spirit: "My body seemed to be growing more complex, more quivering in its responses, but my spirit felt simpler" (p. 107).

WRITING AS A RESPONSE TO THE INVOKING DRIVE

Of her previous life as James, Jan explains: "I was a writer. Full as I was of more recondite certainties, I have always been sure of that too. I never for a moment doubted my vocation" (Morris, 1974/1986, p. 67). In writing about her writing, Morris describes her style as if it was already revealing an essential, traditional femininity, "the quick emotionalism, the hovering tear, the heart-on-sleeve, the touch of schmaltz" (p. 133). Or again: "I often detected in myself a taste for the flamboyant ... often a compensation for uncertainty" (p. 132). Feeling that s/he has been a writer since early childhood, Morris condenses this posture in a hedonist mode: "Creating to please my senses was certainly my own literary method" (p. 95).

More deeply though, writing had been an attempt to make body and spirit cohere, less to please her senses than as an effort to find a strategy capable of regulating excess jouissance. This was achieved by way of an artifice, of a supplement (in the same way, there was the sex change but also writing about it) that allowed for an incarnation of what before had only been experienced in the Real. This Real corresponds to what is enacted in mystical phenomena or realized in psychosis: It is founded on the impossibility of sexual equivalence or rapport, which was at root the "sexual incongruity" experienced by Morris (1974/1986).

When Prosser (1998) talks about "transsexual mirror stages," he quotes Morris's (1974/1986) mirror scene in *Conundrum*, minutes before going to the operating room for a sex change in Morocco. Already anaesthetized, pubic hair shaven and disinfected, Morris staggers while going "to say good bye to myself in the mirror. We would never meet again, and I wanted to give the other self a long last look in the eye, and a wink for luck." The person who writes will emerge "alive and well, and sex-changed in Casablanca. ... I had a new body" (pp. 140–141). This scene is not only a transitional moment in Morris's transsexual trajectory but also the most crucial point in the transsexual narrative. As Prosser (1998) comments, this is when the "me" written about in the biography and the "I" that writes become one; they had been "so far separated by sex" and now are "fused into a singly sexed autobiographical subject, an integral 'I'" (p. 100). Here is the place where I see the function of Lacan's ego as scriptor.

It is indeed the writing of the memoir that allowed Morris to "embody" her body. By the same token, the sex reassignment surgery reknotted the Imaginary, the Real and the Symbolic. Morris (1974/1986) woke up ecstatic from the surgery despite the sharp pain: "I found myself, in fact, astonishingly happy" (p. 140). The Moroccan surgeon who performed her sex change seemed aware of what was at stake in Morris's ordeal; during the postoperative examination, Dr. B. commented in a mix of French and heavily accented English nicely rendered in Morris's transcription: "*Très, très bon*, you could nevair get surgery like this in England—you see, now you would be able to *write*" (p. 142; italics in the original).

Now being able to write, Jan Morris (1974/1986) constructed with *Conundrum* a text that gives credibility to her being a woman. Thus, the memoir comes full circle. It opens with "I was three years old when I realized that I have been born in the wrong body and should really be a girl. I remember the moment well, it is the earliest memory of my life" (p. 3). And Morris concludes "it is only in writing this book that I have delved so deeply into my emotions" (p. 169); it was also through writing that Morris completed the evolution toward a solution to the conundrum of her existence. The book closes with

> if I stand back and look at myself dispassionately, as I looked at myself that night in the mirror in Casablanca—If I consider my story in detachment I sometimes seem, a figure of a fable or allegory. ... I see myself not as a man or woman, self or other, fragment or whole, but only as a wondering child with the cat beneath the Bluthner [piano]. (p. 174)

This is the vignette with which the autobiography begins and ends. It keeps acquiring new meaning through writing. The letter may be the same, but it reads differently. Now, being-able-to-do-with, Morris has acquired *savoir faire*, know-how. Finally a One has been achieved through Morris's singular sinthomatic identification, and it testifies to the power of transformation contained in writing.

Sex change memoirs are meant to be read, to be interpreted. They beg for deciphering. They are as often symptoms as sinthome*s*. Does this mean that they are great literature? Perhaps not, at least not always, but they all aspire to the most essential function of literature. They are love letters to others or to oneself that somehow inscribe sexual difference. Writing a sex change memoir aims not just at passing from one side to the other. Since this type of writing engages directly with castration, it negotiates with the Real, as anyone who writes will know, but more poignantly or dangerously so for the transsexuals when they write.

In some cases, writing about one's transsexual transformation is of the order of the sinthome; there are many cases when the transformation achieved a reknotting of the three registers of the Real, Symbolic, and Imaginary. Then, the sinthome shapes the singularity of an "art," a *techne* that reknotted a workable consistency for the subject; this movement can best be evoked by saying that it moves the subject from a certain contingency to absolute necessity. Thus, Morris (1974/1986) describes her trajectory as inevitable, predestined, as if the sex change had always been bound to happen:

> I do not for a moment regret the act of change. I could see no other way, and it has made me happy. ... Sex has its reasons too, but I suspect the only transsexuals who can achieve happiness are those ... to whom it is not primarily a sexual dilemma at all—who offer no rational purpose to their compulsions, even to themselves, but are simply driven blindly and helplessly. ... We are the most resolute. Nothing will stop us, no fear of ridicule or poverty, no threat of isolation, not even the prospect of death itself. (pp. 168–169)

One can see why her sinthome was necessary: It was necessity itself. A sinthome is what does not cease to be written. In Morris' case, the sinthome has produced less a "woman" than a "woman of letters."

Conclusion

"Male and female created He them; and blessed them, and called their name Adam, in the day when they were created" (Genesis 5:2). Male and female, two positions, but only one name: Adam? Madam? Or, as the old palindrome has it: "Madam, I'm Adam"? Now, it seems, His creation can be if not surgically enhanced, at least hormonally supplemented—besides, it looks as if everyone may have done it, not just transgender people, but really everyone. From baseball players to your aging neighbor, everyone seems ready (re)made.

We may be entering a postsexual era. In the time of digital connection, of Photoshop and airbrushing, we are all becoming copies of a copy. Or at least our ideals are. Take a look at various global celebrities. Women who look like lanky boys with oversized breasts, remade men who appear so made up that they come across as feminine: clones of clones. Is sexual difference disappearing?

If this is the case, there is still one neurosis that is solely constructed around issues of sexual difference: hysteria. Every time a contemporary hysteric poses a question about sexual positioning or identifies with the opposite sex, the subject is simultaneously revealing, masking, and challenging the precariousness of the whole process of sexuation. We have clearly gone beyond the essentialist postulations of many psychoanalytic schools that give priority to the reproductive organs as organizers of a so-called healthy and mature sexuality. They ascribe to anatomy the role of normalizer in a type of sexuality that is focused on the genitals and on a single prescribed act. This normalizing role has been challenged by transsexual discourse and practices.

For Lacanian psychoanalysis, as we have seen, sexual desire and jouissance do not have predetermined objects but multiple possibilities for desire with no discernible relation to gender. Freud already extended the scope of sexuality to the entire body: "any part of the skin and any sense-organ—probably, indeed, *any* organ—can function as an erotogenic zone" (Freud, 1905, p. 233; italics in the original). Furthermore, human sexuality is marked by a logic of discordance. Indeed, we have dealt more than once with Lacan's model of sexuation and have seen that it identifies "man" and "woman" as positions according to inscriptions in language; ultimately, they correspond not to two genders but to different modes of jouissance. These two sides are heterogeneous and not complementary: The model of sexual difference elaborated by Lacanian theory proposes a mode of being that is not all subjected to the phallic premise and not all determined by castration.

A clinical practice that follows the contours delineated by these formulas of sexuation presents us with several paradoxes. To make clinical sense of the formulas, one should always link them with the concept of the sinthome—this has been my theoretical gamble. The sinthome directs us to the singularity of a quasi-artistic production that aims at reknotting a body whose consistency is never given, while the formulas of sexuation help us think sexual difference without the rock of the phallus. The transsexual transformation may be, in certain cases, of the order of the sinthome. In those cases, indeed, the transformation achieves a reknotting of the three registers of the Real, Symbolic, and Imaginary.

That is to say that transgenderism should not be systematically defined as pathology. If transgenderism is not pathological, then a sex change should not be considered either a treatment or a cure. Some transsexual discourses and practices are significant insofar as they inscribe sexual difference without the usual reference to the phallus. In that sense, they are close to psychoanalysis. To unleash the potential of the questions brought about by transgender discourses and practices, the questions need to remain open.

In the United States, there is a trend toward what I have called the democratizing of transgenderism, which corresponds to the increasing publicity given to transgenderism. One might even speak of a "transgeneralization," by which I mean a generalization of transgenderist ideologies and practices. The admittedly marginal figure of the transsexual seems to promise a new utopia for the 21st century. To be sure, it is not outside the tenets of liberal democracy to assert that one's freedom should include the right to choose one's gender while claiming ownership of one's body. Such a right, however, should not reduce one's body to a malleable commodity. The media attention given to transgenderism suggests that the battle in the 20th century for sexual equality has turned into a battle for the control of one's sexual body. A new modality of the 19th century hysteric's questioning of sexual identity has crucial implications for our current understanding of subjectivity, especially considering the premium placed on identity by contemporary U.S. society.

I have tried to explore what it means to sustain the analytic promise, to operate with the analyst's desire for pure difference in today's cultural context. More precisely, this is accomplished by supporting an ethics of difference in a supposedly egalitarian society. My contention is that when sexual choice is democratized, universalized, or forcibly inscribed under a logic of all, thus excluding the not-all, or Other sex, then choice is not truly democratic and ultimately denies the intractability of the real of sexual difference. Often, one witnesses the return of the repressed divide as racial identity (as I have seen in Philadelphia, transgender institutions are de facto racially segregated—there are three main clinics serving the transgender population: one serves a predominantly white group, the other is catering to African Americans, the third is for Latinos; Asian transsexuals have formed their separate group but do not have their own clinic). I have presented a description of the U.S. cultural context in which transgenderism is celebrated in keeping with the tenets of liberalism—one should be free and have the right to choose. This ideology permeates clinical presentations by modifying the formulation of the hysterical question about sexual identity as it is affected by a postfeminist discourse that produces the transsexual phenomenon.

Gender is not a core like Stoller argued, with his construction of "core gender identity," but rather a peel, more like the skin that can fall from a ripe fruit as we saw Joyce use it in a famous metaphor. Using that view, gender is outside, foreign, and in that sense, one may look for it not in the depths of the psyche or the deep tissues but projected on the surface. However, when psychoanalysis deals with sexual difference it is neither with sex, as a biological substratum, nor gender, as a sociocultural construct.

Gender needs to be embodied, and sex needs to be symbolized. This is the main lesson of psychoanalysis, even if the process always fails and thus leaves a nonsymbolized, disembodied leftover, which Lacan called the Real.

The unconscious reveals that there is no stable sexual identity, only sinthomatic identities. Man and woman are alienating positions that are regulated by a cunning phallic order. One can remain trapped in hysterical identifications that serve the master while still looking for a new guarantee or a totalizing Other. But, there is another option: to reinvent one's sexuality by identifying with one's sinthome. Quite ill-equipped, speaking subjects have to assume a sexual positioning, oriented only by the psychic representatives of the consequences of sexuality, because at its most basic, sexuality is represented in the psyche by the relation of the subject to something other than sexuality itself—death.

Sexual reproduction relates to the fact that the living being subjected to sex falls under the blow of individual death. A sexed living being is no longer immortal. Sex represents a portion of death for the living being (Lacan, 1981, p. 205). In fact, the unconscious cannot symbolize sexual difference any more than it can represent death to itself. For the unconscious, death is a matter of belief. Sex and death are what we cannot look in the face—they are a reality we find it impossible to confront, that we cannot represent, about which we know nothing. Death is real. Death is related to the type of reproduction we call sexual.

If death is a matter of belief for the unconscious, paradoxically, it is a belief that makes life bearable. Is the fantasy that one can change one's gender on demand the continuation of an old dream of immortality? Let us not forget that Steinach, the pioneer of sex change operations, had managed to convince Freud that he had a cure for mortality. However, as Beckett (1965/1970) aptly put it while referring to Proust's narrator, one should heed to his belief that "our life is a succession of Paradises successively denied, and that the only true Paradise is the paradise that has been lost, and that death will cure many of the desire for immortality" (p. 26).

References

Abelson, J. et al. (2006). Factors associated with "feeling suicidal." *Journal of Homosexuality, 51*(1), 59–80.
Abraham, H., & Freud, E. (Eds.). (1965). *A psychoanalytic dialogue: The letters of Sigmund Freud and Karl Abraham*. New York: Basic Books.
Acocella, J. (1999). *Creating hysteria: Women and multiple personality disorder*. San Francisco: Jossey-Bass.
Adler, A. (1938). *Social interest: A challenge to mankind*. London: Faber & Faber.
Aflalo-Lebovits, A. (1984). Sur le cas de la jeune homosexuelle. *Analytica Revue, 35*, 23–42.
Agamben, G. (2005). *State of exception* (K. Attel, trans.). Chicago and London: The University of Chicago Press.
Al-Arabiya TV. (2005, July 2). *Iran: Have a sex change on us* [Television broadcast]. Retrieved March 30, 2009, from www.youtube.com/watch?v=Pt9oZlOU5UE
Alby, J. M. (1956). *Contributions à l'étude du transsexualismme*. Paris: DEA.
Allouch, J. (2002). Freud embringué dans l'homosexualité féminine. *Cliniques méditerranéennes, 65*, 105–130.
Allouch, J. (2004). *Ombre de ton chien: Discours psychanalytique, discours lesbien*. Paris: Epel.
American Academy of Pediatrics, Committee on Genetics, Section on Endocrinology, Section on Urology. (2000). Evaluation of the newborn with developmental anomalies of the external genitalia. *Pediatrics, 106*(1), 138–142.
American Psychiatric Association. (2000). *Diagnostic and statistical manual of mental disorders* (4th ed., text rev.). Washington, DC: Author.
Ames, J. (Ed.). (2005). *Sexual metamorphosis: An anthology of transsexual memoirs*. New York: Vintage Books.
André, S. (1999). *What does a woman want?* (S. Fairfield, Trans.). New York: Other Press.
André, J., Lanouzière, J., & Richard, F. (1999). *Problématiques de l'hystérie*. Paris: Dunod.
Angelides, S. (2001). *A history of bisexuality*. Chicago: University of Chicago Press.
Angier, N. (1997, March 14). Sexual identity not pliable after all. *New York Times*, Section A, p. 1.

Anzieu, D. (2004 [1973, 2000]). La bisexualité dans l'auto-analyse de Freud. In J. B. Pontalis (Ed.), *Bisexualité et difference des sexes* (pp. 275–296). Paris: Gallimard.
Arnold, A., Xu J., Grisham, W., Chen X., Kim, Y., & Itoh, Y. (2004). Minireview: Sex chromosomes and brain sexual differentiation. *Endocrinology, 145*(3), 1057–1062. Retrieved September 8, 2009 from http://endo.endojournals.org
Aubry, J. (1983). *Enfance abandonnée*. Paris: Métailié.
Baglivi, G. (1723). *The practice of physick, reduc'd to the ancient way of observations, containing a just parallel between the wisdom of the ancients and the hypothesis of modern physicians*. London: Midwinter, Linton, Strahan.
Barossa, J. (2001). *Hysteria*. London: Icon Books.
Bartlett, N., Vasey, P., & Bukowski, W. (2000, December). Is gender identity disorder in children a mental disorder? *Sex Roles: A Journal of Research*. Retrieved March 30, 2009, from http://findarticles.com/p/articles/mi_m2294/is_2000_Dec/ai_75959827
Baudrillard, J. (2002). *Screened out*. London: Verso.
Baumgardner, J. (2007). *Look both ways: Bisexual politics*. New York: Farrar, Straus & Giroux.
Be-All Chicago. (2009). Home page. Retrieved March 30, 2009, from http://www.be-all.org/
Beatie, T. (2008, June 19). Labor of love. *The Advocate*. Retrieved March 30, 2009 from http://www.advocate.com/article.aspx?id=43981
Beckett, S. (1965/1970). *Proust and three dialogues with Georges Duthiut*. London: Calder.
Benjamin, H. (1945). Eugen Steinach, 1861–1944: A life of research. *Scientific Monthly, 61*, 427–442.
Benjamin, H. (1953). Transvestism and transsexualism. *International Journal of Sexology, 7*, 12–14.
Benjamin, H. (1954). Transvestism and transsexualism as psycho-somatic and somato-psychic syndromes. *American Journal of Psychotherapy, 8*(2), 219–230.
Benjamin, H. (1966). *The transsexual phenomenon*. New York: Julian Press.
Benjamin, H. (2006). Transsexualism and transvestism as psycho-somatic and somato-psychic syndromes. In S. Stryker & S. White (Eds.), *The transgender studies reader* (pp. 45–52). New York: Routledge.
Bercherie, P. (1983). *Génese des concepts freudiens*. Paris: Navarin.
Bernheim, H. (1913). *L'hystérie*. Paris: Doin.
Bernheim, H. (1917). *Automatisme et suggestion*. Paris: Alcan.
Bernheimer, C., & Kanahe, C., (Eds.). (1985/1990). *In Dora's case: Freud, hysteria, feminism*. New York: Columbia University Press.
Bernstein, F. (2004, March 7). On campus rethinking biology 101. *New York Times*, Style section.
Blair Bell, W. (1915). Hermaphroditism. *Liverpool Medico-Surgical Journal, 35*, 272–292.
Bleizer, J. (1994). *Ventroloquized bodies: Narratives of hysteria in nineteenth-century France*. Ithaca, NY: Cornell University Press.
Blévis, M. (2004). La mère de la "jeune homosexuelle" mise à nu par ses célibataires, même. *Les Lettres de la S.P.F., 12*, 93–107.
Bloom, A. (2002). *Normal: Transsexual CEOs, crossdressing cops, and hermaphrodites with attitude*. New York: Vintage Books.

Bolin, A. (1993). Transcending and transgendering: Male-to-female transsexuals, dichotomy and diversity. In G. Herdt (Ed.), *Third sex, third gender: Beyond sexual dimorphism in culture and history* (pp. 447–486). Cambridge, MA: MIT Press.
Bolin, A. (1997). Transforming transvestism and transsexualism: Polarity, politics, and gender. In Bullough, B., Bullough, V., & Elias, J. (Eds.), *Gender blending: Transvestism (cross-dressing), gender heresy, androgyny, religion and the cross-dresser, transgender healthcare, free expression, sex change surgery, who loves transvestites, the law and the transsexual* (pp. 25–32). Amherst, NY: Prometheus Books.
Bornstein, K. (1994). *Gender outlaw: On men, women, and the rest of us*. New York: Vintage Books.
Bornstein, K. (1998). *My gender workbook: How to become a real man, a real woman, the real you, or something else entirely*. New York: Routledge.
Boss, J. M. (1979). Seventeenth-century transformation of the hysteric affection, and Sydenham's Baconian medicine. *Psychological Medicine, 9*, 221–234.
Boyd, H. (2007). *She's not the man I married: Life with a transgender husband*. Emeryville, CA: Seal Press.
Brabant, E., Falseder, E., & Giamperi-Deutsch, P. (Eds.). (1992). *The correspondence of Sigmund Freud and Sándor Ferenczi, Vol. 1: 1908–1914*. Cambridge, MA: Belknap Press of Harvard University.
Bradley, S., Oliver, D., Chernick, A. B., & Zucker, K. J. (1998). Experiment of nurture: Ablatio penis at 2 months, sex reassignment at 7 months, and a psychosexual follow-up in young adulthood. *Pediatrics, 102*(1). Retrieved March 3, 2007, from http://pediatrics.aappublications.org/cgi/content/abstract/102/1/e9
Braunstein, N. (1992/2005). *La jouissance*. Paris: Eres.
Breger, L. (2000). *Freud: Darkness in the midst of vision*. New York: Wiley.
Brill, S., & Pepper, R. (2008). *Transgender child: A handbook for families and professionals*. San Francisco: Cleis Press.
Brome, V. (1984). *Freud and his disciples: The struggle for supremacy*. London: Caliban.
Bronfen, E. (1998). *The knotted subject: Hysteria and its discontents*. Princeton, NJ: Princeton University Press.
Brooks, P. (1993). *Body work: Objects of desire in modern narrative*. Cambridge, MA: Harvard University Press.
Brousse, M.-H. (2003). The-push-to-the-woman: A universal in psychosis? *Psychoanalytical notebooks: Sexuation and sexuality: Review of the London society of the new Lacanian school, 11*, 79–98.
Bruno, R. (1997). Devotees, pretenders and wannabes: Two cases of factitious disability disorder. *Sexuality and Disability, 15*(4), 243–260.
Burgess, C. (1999). Internal and external stress factors associated with the identity development of transgendered youth. *Journal of Gay and Lesbian Social Services, 10*(3/4), 35–47.
Butler, J. (1988). Performative acts and gender constitution: An essay in phenomenology and Feminist theory. *Theatre Journal, 40*(4), 519–531.
Butler, J. (1990). *Gender trouble: Feminism and the subversion of identity*. New York: Routledge.
Butler, J. (1993). *Bodies that matter: On the discursive limits of "sex."* New York: Routledge.

Butler, J. (1997). Melancholy gender/ Refused identification. In *The psychic life of power: Theories in subjection* (pp. 132–150). Stanford, CA: Stanford University Press.
Butler, J. (2004). *Undoing gender*. New York: Routledge.
Califia, P. (1997/2003). *Sex changes: The politics of transgenderism*. San Francisco: Cleis Press.
Castel, P.-H. (2003). *La métamorphose impensable: Essai sur le transsexualisme et l'identité personnelle*. Paris: Gallimard.
Cauldwell, D. O. (1947). *Effects of castration on men and women*. Girard, KS: Haldeman-Julius.
Cauldwell, D. O. (1949). Psychopathia transexualis. *Sexology, 16,* 274–280.
Cauldwell, D. O. (1950). *Questions and answers on the sex life and sexual problems of trans-sexuals*. Girard, KS: Haldeman-Julius.
Cauldwell, D. O. (1951). *Sex transmutation—Can one's sex be changed?* Girard, KS: Haldeman-Julius.
CBS Evening News. (2005, May 2). *Iran: Nose job capital of world women lining up in record numbers for cosmetic surgery* [Television broadcast]. Retrieved September 14, 2009 from http://www.cbsnews.com
Charcot, J. M. (1877). *Lectures on the diseases of the nervous system* (G. Gigerson, Trans.). London: New Sydenham Society.
Chauvelot, D. (1995). *L'hystérie vous salue bien!: Sexe et violence dans l'inconscient*. Paris: Denoël.
Chiland, C. (2003). *Transsexualism: Illusion and reality* (P. Slotkin, Trans.). Middletown, CT: Wesleyan University Press.
Chodoff, P. (1982). Hysteria and women. *American Journal of Psychiatry, 139,* 545–551.
Colapinto, J. (2000). *As nature made him: The boy who was raised as a girl*. New York: Harper Perennial.
Cole, C. M., O'Boyle, M., Emory, L., & Meyer, W. (1997). Comorbidity of gender dysphoria and other major psychiatric diagnoses. *Archives of Sexual Behavior, 26*(1), 13–26.
Conn, C. (1974). Canary: The story of a transsexual. Los Angeles: Nash Publishing.
Corbett, K. (2001). More life: Centrality and marginality in human development. *Psychoanalytic Dialogues, 11,* 313–335.
Corners, G. (1923). *Rejuvenation: How Steinach makes people young*. New York: Seltzer.
Cottet, S. (2000). Four preliminary questions to a renewal of the clinic. *Psychoanalytical Notebooks 4, Psychiatry and Psychoanalysis*. Retrieved March 30, 2009, from http://www.londonsociety-nls.org.uk
County, J. (1995). *Man enough to be a woman: The autobiography of Jane County*. New York and London: Serpent's Tail.
Cromwell, J. (1999). *Transmen and FTMs: Identities, bodies, genders, and sexualities*. Urbana: University of Illinois Press.
Cullen, W. (1781). Of the hysteria or the hysteric disease. In *First lines of the practice of physic* (pp. 98–115). Edinburgh: William Creech.
Currah, P., Juang, R., & Price Minter, S. (Eds.). Introduction. In *Transgender rights* (pp. xiii–xxiv). Minneapolis, MN: University of Minnesota Press.

Curtis, V. A. (2007). Dirt, disgust and disease: A natural history of hygiene. *Journal of Epidemiology and Community Health, 61*, 660–664.

Dalery, J. R., & de Villard, F. (1981). The role of hormones in the sex differentiation of the central nervous system in animal and man: Critical study. *Annales médico-psychologiques, 139*(7), 721–740.

David, C. (1992/1997). *La bisexualité psychique*. Paris: Payot & Rivages.

David-Ménard, M. (2004). L'exaltation d'une jeune fille et ses enjeux pour la psychanalyse: qu'est-ce que la psychogenèse? *Les Lettres de la S.P.F., 12*, 65–75.

Dean, T. (2000). *Beyond sexuality*. Chicago: University of Chicago Press.

De Lauretis, T. (1987). *Technologies of gender: Essays on theory, film and fiction*. Bloomington: Indiana University Press.

Delavenay, E. (1987). Lawrence, Otto Weininger and "rather raw philosophy." In C. Heywood (Ed.), *D. H. Lawrence: New studies* (pp. 137–157). London: Macmillan.

Delay, J. M. (1956). *La jeunesse d' André Gide* (Vol. 1). Paris: Gallimard.

Delay, J. M. (1957). *La jeunesse d' André Gide* (Vol. 2). Paris: Gallimard.

Delay, J. M., Deniker, P., Volmat, R., & Alby, J. M. (1956). Une demande de changement de sexe: Le trans-sexualisme. *L' Encéphale: Journal de neurologie, de psychiatrie et de médicine psychosomatique, 45*(1), 41–80.

Derrida, J. (1982). *Margins of philosophy* (A. Bass, Trans.). New York: Harverster Press.

De Sutter, P., Kira, K., Verschoor, A., & Hotimsky, A. (2002). The desire to have children and the preservation of fertility in transsexual women: A survey. *The International Journal of Transgenderism, 6*(3).

Devor, A. (1994). Transsexualism, dissociation, and child abuse: An initial discussion based on nonclinical data. *Journal of Psychology and Human Sexuality, 6*(3), 49–72.

Devor, H. (1997). *FTM: Female-to-male transsexuals in society*. Bloomington: Indiana University Press.

Diamantis, I. (2004). La prudence de la chair: Homosexualité et phobie. *Les Lettres de la S.P.F., 12*, 51–64.

Diamond, M. (1965). A critical evaluation of the ontology of human behavior. *The Quarterly Review of Biology, 40*(2), 147–175.

Diamond, M., & Sigmundson, H. K. (1997). Sex reassignment at birth: Long-term review and clinical implications. *Archives of Pediatric and Adolescents Medicine, 151*(3), 289–304. Retrieved on October 7, 2009 from http://www.hawaii.edu/PCSS/biblio/articles/1961to1999/1997-sex-reassignment.html

Dixon, L. (1995). *Perilous chastity: Women and illness in pre-enlightenment art and medicine*. Ithaca, NY: Cornell University Press.

Domurat Dreger, A. (1998). *Hermaphrodites and the medical invention of sex*. Cambridge, MA: Harvard University Press.

Domurat Dreger, A. (1999). *Intersex in the age of ethics*. Hagerston, MD: University Publishing Group.

Donahoe, P. K., & Hendren, W. H. (1976). Evaluation of the newborn with ambiguous genitalia. *Pediatric Clinics of North America, 23*, 361–370.

Donahoe, P. K., Powell, D. M., & Lee, M. M. (1991). Clinical management of intersex abnormalities. *Current Problems in Surgery, 28*(8), 513–570.

Drescher, J. (2001). That obscure subject of desire: Freud's female homosexual revisited: Review. *Journal of the American Psychoanalytic Association, 49*, 1447–1450.

Eissler, K. (1971). *Talent and genius: The fictitious case of Tausk contra Freud.* New York: Quadrangle Books.

Ekins, R. (2005). Science, politics and clinical intervention: Harry Benjamin, transsexualism and the problem of heteronormativity. *Sexualities, 8*(3), 306–328.

Elliott, C. (2000). A new way to be mad. *The Atlantic.* Retrieved July 28, 2007, from http://www.theatlantic.com/doc/prem/200012/madness

Elliot, C. (2003, July 3). Costing an arm and a leg: The victims of a growing mental disorder are obsessed with amputation. *Slate.* Retrieved March 30, 2009, from http://www.slate.com/id/2085402/

Ellis, H. (1942). *Sexual inversion.* New York: Random House.

Epstein, J., & Straub, K. (Eds.). (1991). Introduction, In *Body guards: The cultural politics of gender ambiguity* (pp. 1–28). New York: Routledge.

Falzeder, E., Brabant, E., Giampieri-Deutsch, P., & Hoffer, P. (Eds.). (2000). *The correspondence of Sigmund Freud and Sándor Ferenczi: Volume 3, 1920–1933.* Cambridge, MA: Belknap Press of Harvard University.

Fathi, N. (2004, August 2). As repression lift, more Iranians change their sex. *New York Times.* Retrieved from http://www.nytimes.com

Fausto-Sterling, A. (1999). *Sexing the body: Gender politics and the construction of sexuality.* New York: Basic Books.

Fédida, P. (1973/2000/2004). D'une essentielle dissymétrie dans la psychanalyse. In J. Pontalis (Ed.), *Bisexualité et différence des sexes* (pp. 237–249). Paris: Gallimard.

Feinberg, L. (1993). *Stone butch blues: A novel.* New York: Firebrand.

Feinberg, L. (1996). *Transgender warriors: Making history from Joan of Arc to RuPaul.* Boston: Beacon Press.

Feltzine, F. (1995). Clinique de l'homosexualité féminine. *La lettre mensuelle, 136*, 18–20.

Finney Boylan, J. (2003). *She's not there: A life in two genders.* New York: Broadway Books.

Fink, B. (1997). *The Lacanian subject: Between language and jouissance.* Princeton, NJ: Princeton University Press.

First, M. (2004). Desire for amputation of a limb: Paraphilia, psychosis, or a new type of identity disorder. *Psychological Medicine, 34*, 1–10.

Fliess, W. (1987). Masculin et féminin in *La déclaration de sexe. Littoral, 23/24*, 63–72. (Original work published 1897)

Fliess, W. (1906). *In eigener Sache: Gegen Otto Weininger und Hermann Swoboda.* Berlin: Goldschmidt.

Fliess, W. (1918). Sexualität und Symmetrie. *Zeitschrift für Sexualwissenschaft, 5*(8/9), 249–294.

Fliess, W. (1923). *Der Ablauf des Lebens: Grundlegung zur exakten Biologie.* Leipzig: Deuticke. (Original work published 1906)

Fliess, W. (1977). *Les relations entre les nez et les organes génitaux de la femme: Présentées selon leur significations biologiques.* Paris: Editions du Seuil. (Original work published 1897)

Foucault, M. (1975). *The birth of the clinic: An archeology of the medical perception* (A. M. Sheridan Smith, Trans.). New York: Vintage Books.
Foucault, M. (1979). *Discipline and punish*. New York: Random House.
Foucault, M. (1980). Introduction. In *Herculine Barbin: Being the recently discovered memoirs of a nineteenth-century French hermaphrodite* (R. McDougall, Trans.) pp. vii–xvii. New York: Pantheon Books.
Freud, E. (Ed.). (1960). *Letters of Sigmund Freud* (T. Stern & J. Stern., Trans.). New York: Basic Books.
Freud, S. (1888/1893). Some points for a comparative study of organic and hysterical motor paralysis. In J. Strachey (Ed. & Trans.), *The standard edition of the complete psychological works of Sigmund Freud* (Vol. 1, pp. 155–172). London: Hogarth Press.
Freud, S. (1893). Charcot. In J. Strachey (Ed. & Trans.), *The standard edition of the complete psychological works of Sigmund Freud* (Vol. 3, pp. 7–23). London: Hogarth Press.
Freud, S. (1895). Project for a scientific psychology. In J. Strachey (Ed. & Trans.), *The standard edition of the complete psychological works of Sigmund Freud* (Vol. 1, pp. 281–391). London: Hogarth Press.
Freud, S. (1900). The interpretation of dreams. In J. Strachey (Ed. & Trans.), *The standard edition of the complete psychological works of Sigmund Freud* (Vols. 4 & 5). London: Hogarth Press.
Freud, S. (1901/1905).Fragment of an analysis of a case of hysteria. In J. Strachey (Ed. & Trans.), *The standard edition of the complete psychological works of Sigmund Freud* (Vol. 7, pp. 1–122). London: Hogarth Press.
Freud, S. (1905). Three essays on the theory of sexuality. In J. Strachey (Ed. & Trans.), *The standard edition of the complete psychological works of Sigmund Freud* (Vol. 7, pp. 123–246). London: Hogarth Press.
Freud, S. (1908). Hysterical fantasies and their relation to bisexuality. In J. Strachey (Ed. & Trans.), *The standard edition of the complete psychological works of Sigmund Freud* (Vol. 9, pp. 155–166). London: Hogarth Press.
Freud, S. (1909). Analysis of a phobia in a five-year-old boy. In J. Strachey (Ed. & Trans.), *The standard edition of the complete psychological works of Sigmund Freud* (Vol. 10, pp. 5–147). London: Hogarth Press.
Freud, S. (1911). Psychoanalytic notes on an autobiographical account of a case of paranoia (dementia paranoides): The case of Schreber. In J. Strachey (Ed. & Trans.), *The standard edition of the complete psychological works of Sigmund Freud* (Vol. 12, pp. 1–82). London: Hogarth Press.
Freud, S. (1912). On the universal tendency to debasement in the sphere of love. In J. Strachey (Ed. & Trans.), *The standard edition of the complete psychological works of Sigmund Freud* (Vol. 11, pp. 177–190). London: Hogarth Press.
Freud, S. (1912–1913). Totem and taboo: Some points of agreement between the mental lives of savages and neurotics. In J. Strachey (Ed. & Trans.), *The standard edition of the complete psychological works of Sigmund Freud* (Vol. 13, pp. vii–162). London: Hogarth Press.
Freud, S. (1914). Remembering, repeating and working through (Further recommendations in the technique of psychoanalysis). In J. Strachey (Ed. & Trans.), *The standard edition of the complete psychological works of Sigmund Freud* (Vol. 12, pp. 147–148). London: Hogarth Press.

Freud, S. (1917). Mourning and melancholia. In J. Strachey (Ed. & Trans.), *The standard edition of the complete psychological works of Sigmund Freud* (Vol. 14, pp. 237–258). London: Hogarth Press.

Freud, S. (1919). "A child is being beaten": A contribution to the study of the origin of sexual perversions. In J. Strachey (Ed. & Trans.), *The standard edition of the complete psychological works of Sigmund Freud* (Vol. 17, pp. 175–204). London: Hogarth Press.

Freud, S. (1920). The psychogenesis of a case of homosexuality in a woman. In J. Strachey (Ed. & Trans.), *The standard edition of the complete psychological works of Sigmund Freud* (Vol. 18, pp. 145–172). London: Hogarth Press.

Freud, S. (1923a). The ego and the id. In J. Strachey (Ed. & Trans.), *The standard edition of the complete psychological works of Sigmund Freud* (Vol. 19, pp. 1–66). London: Hogarth Press.

Freud, S. (1923b). The infantile sexual organization: An interpolation into the theory of sexuality. In J. Strachey (Ed. & Trans.), *The standard edition of the complete psychological works of Sigmund Freud* (Vol. 19, pp. 141–148). London: Hogarth Press.

Freud, S. (1924). The dissolution of the Oedipus complex. In J. Strachey (Ed. & Trans.), *The standard edition of the complete psychological works of Sigmund Freud* (Vol. 19, pp. 171–180). London: Hogarth Press.

Freud, S. (1925). Some psychical consequences of the anatomical distinction between the sexes. In J. Strachey (Ed. & Trans.), *The standard edition of the complete psychological works of Sigmund Freud* (Vol. 19, pp. 243–258). London: Hogarth Press.

Freud, S. (1926). Inhibitions, symptoms, and anxiety. In J. Strachey (Ed. & Trans.), *The standard edition of the complete psychological works of Sigmund Freud* (Vol. 20, pp. 75–166). London: Hogarth Press.

Freud, S. (1927). Fetishism. In J. Strachey (Ed. & Trans.), *The standard edition of the complete psychological works of Sigmund Freud* (Vol. 21, pp. 152–157). London: Hogarth Press.

Freud, S. (1929/1930). Civilization and its discontents. In J. Strachey (Ed. & Trans.), *The standard edition of the complete psychological works of Sigmund Freud* (Vol. 21, pp. 57–146). London: Hogarth Press.

Freud, S. (1931). Female sexuality. In J. Strachey (Ed. & Trans.), *The standard edition of the complete psychological works of Sigmund Freud* (Vol. 21, pp. 221–244). London: Hogarth Press.

Freud, S. (1932/1933). New introductory lectures on psychoanalysis, Lecture 34: Femininity. In J. Strachey (Ed. & Trans.), *The standard edition of the complete psychological works of Sigmund Freud* (Vol. 22, pp. 112–135). London: Hogarth Press.

Freud, S. (1937). Analysis terminable and interminable. In J. Strachey (Ed. & Trans.), *The standard edition of the complete psychological works of Sigmund Freud* (Vol. 23, pp. 209–254). London: Hogarth Press.

Freud, S. (1954). *The origins of psychoanalysis. Letters to Wilhelm Fliess, drafts and notes: 1887–1902*. M. Bonaparte, A. Freud, & E. Kris (Eds.). New York: Basic Books.

Freud, S. (1959). *On the history of the psychoanalytic movement*. New York: Basic Books. (Original work published 1914)

Freud, S. (2003). *The psychopathology of everyday life* (A. Bell, Trans.). New York: Penguin Books. (Original work published 1901)
Freud, S., & Breuer, J. (1895). On the psychical mechanism of hysterical phenomena: Preliminary communication. In J. Strachey (Ed. & Trans.), *The standard edition of the complete psychological works of Sigmund Freud* (Vol. 2, pp. 3–17). London: Hogarth Press.
Freud, S., & Weiss, E. (1975). *Lettres sur la pratique analytique*. Paris: Privat.
Frignet, H. (2000). *Le transsexualisme*. Paris: Declée de Brouwer.
Furth, G., & Smith, R. (2002). *Amputee identity disorder: Information, questions, answers, and recommendations about self-demand amputation*. Bloomington, IN: 1st Books Library.
Fuss, D. (1993). Fallen women: Identification, desire, and "a case of homosexuality in a woman." In M. Warner (Ed.), *Fear of a queer planet: Queer politics and social theory* (pp. 42–68). Minneapolis: University of Minnesota Press.
Fuss, D. (1995). Fallen women: "The psychogenesis of a case of homosexuality in a woman." In *Identification papers: Readings on psychoanalysis, sexuality, and culture* (pp. 57–82). New York: Routledge.
Fuss, D. (1999). Fallen Women: "The psychogenesis of a case of homosexuality in a woman." In R. Lesser & E. Schoenberg (Eds.), *That obscure subject of desire: Freud's female homosexual revisited* (pp. 54–75). New York: Routledge.
Gaines, R. (1993). Cross-gender behavior and gender conflict in sexually abused girls. *Journal of the American Academy of Child and Adolescent Psychiatry, 32*(5), 940–947.
Galen of Pergamon. (1976). *De locis affectis* (R. Siegel & S. Karger, Trans.). New York and Basel: Karger.
Garfinkel, H. (2006). Passing and the managed achievement of sex status in an "interesexed" person. In S. Stryker & S. Whittle (Eds.), *The transgender studies reader* (pp. 58–93). New York: Routledge. (Original work published 1967)
Gay, P. (1983). *The education of the senses: Vol. I: The bourgeois experience: Victoria to Freud*. London: Oxford University Press.
Gay, P. (1989). *Freud: A life for our time*. New York: Anchor Books.
Gherovici, P. (2003). *The Puerto Rican syndrome*. New York: Other Press.
Gilbert, M. (Director) (2003). *Whole* [Motion picture]. St. Paul, MN: Frozen Feet Films.
Gindele, T. (2003a). Annexe chapitre 1. In I. Rieder & D. Voigt (Eds.), *Sidonie Csillag: Homosexuelle chez Freud, lesbienne dans le siècle* (pp. 40–43). Paris: Epel.
Gindele, T. (2003b). Postface: Freud, Lacan, Sidonie. In I. Rieder & D. Voigt (Eds.), *Sidonie Csillag: Homosexuelle chez Freud, lesbienne dans le siècle* (pp. 395–400). Paris: Epel.
Goldner, V. (1999). Backcover blurb. In R. Lesser & E. Schoenberg (Eds.), *That obscure subject of desire: Freud's female homosexual revisited*. New York: Routledge.
Gordene Mackenzie, O. (1994). *Transgender nation*. Bowling Green, OH: Bowling Green University Popular Press.
Gourevitch, D. (1984). *Le mal d'être femme: La femme et la médecine dans la Rome antique*. Paris: Société d'édition "Les Belles Lettres."
Green, J. (2004). *Becoming a visible man*. Nashville, TN: Vanderbilt University Press.

Grigg, R. (1987). Freud's problem of identification. *Newsletter of the Freudian Field*, 1(1), 14–17.
Grigg, R. (1989). Metaphor and metonymy. *Newsletter of the Freudian Field*, 3(1/2), 58–79.
Grigg, R. (1999). From the mechanism of psychosis to the universal condition of the symptom: On foreclosure. In D. Nobus (Ed.), *Key concepts of Lacanian psychoanalysis* (pp. 48–74). New York: Other Press.
Griggs, C. (1998). *S/HE: Changing sex and changing clothes (dress, body, culture)*. Oxford, UK: Berg.
Grosz, E. (1994). *Volatile bodies: Toward a corporeal feminism*. Bloomington: Indiana University Press.
Gueguen, P.-G. (1994). Mademoiselle Vinteuil et la jeune homosexuelle. *Pas Tant*, 31, 30–35.
Haeberle, E. (1985). The transatlantic commuter: An interview with Harry Benjamin (b. January 12, 1885) on the occasion of his 100th birthday. *Sexualmedizin*, 14. Retrieved September 5, 2009 from http://www2.hu-berlin.de/sexology/gesund/archiv/trans_b5.htm
Halperin, D. (1995). *Saint-Foucault*. New York: Oxford University Press.
Hamburger, C., Stürup, G., & Dahl-Iversen, E. (1953). Transvestism: Hormonal psychiatric and surgical treatment. *Journal of the American Medical Association*, 15, 391–396.
Hamilton, E., & Cairns, H. (Eds.). (1963/1973). *The collected dialogues of Plato*. Princeton, NJ: Princeton University Press.
Harari, R. (2001). *Lacan's seminar on anxiety: An introduction*. New York: Other Press.
Harari, R. (2002). *How James Joyce made his name: A reading of the final Lacan* (L. Thuston, Trans.). New York: Other Press.
Harris, A. (1999). Gender as contradiction. In R. Lesser & E. Schoenberg (Eds.), *That obscure subject of desire: Freud's female homosexual revisited* (pp. 156–179). New York: Routledge.
Harrison, F. (2005, January 5). *Iran's sex change operations* [Television broadcast]. BBC News. Retrieved March 30, 2009, from www.news.bbc.co.uk/2/hi/programmes/newsnight/4115535.stm
Harrus Revédi, G. (1997). *L' Hystérie*. Paris: Presses Universitaires de France.
Harry Benjamin Gender Dysphoria Association (HBGDA). (1998). *The standards of care for gender identity disorders, fifth version*. Retrieved from http://www.tc.umn.edu/~colem001/hbigda/hstndrd.htm
Hartmann, L., Schaid, D., Woods, J., Crotty, T., Myers, J., Arnold, P., Petty, P. et al. (1999). Efficacy of bilateral prophylactic mastectomy in women with a family history of breast cancer. *The New England Journal of Medicine*, 340, 77–84.
Hausman, B. (1995). *Changing sex: Transsexualism, technology, and the idea of gender*. Durham, NC: Duke University Press.
Hausman, B. (2001). Recent transgender theory (review essay). *Feminist Studies*, 27(2), 465–490.
Hausman, K. (2003). Controversy continues to grow over *DSM's* GID diagnosis. *Psychiatric News*, 38(14), 25.
Herrn, R. (1995). On the history of the biological theories of homosexuality. *Journal of Homosexuality*, 28(1/2), 31–56.

Hirschfeld, M. (1918). Sexuelle Zwischenstufen. *Sexualpathologie*. Bonn: Marcus & Webers.
Hirschfeld, M. (1923). Die intersexuale Konstitution. *Jahrblatt für sexuelle Zwischenstufen, 23,* 3–27.
Hirschfeld, M. (1936). *Le sexe inconnu.* Paris: Editions Montaigne.
Hirschfeld, M. (1956). *Sexual anomalies.* New York: Emerson Books
Hoebecke, P. (2001, October). *Obtaining rigidity in "total phalloplasty": Experience in 30 patients.* Paper presented at the XVII Harry Benjamin International Gender Dysphoria Association Symposium, Galveston, TX.
Hoyer, N. (1933). *Man into woman: An authentic record of a change of sex.* New York: Dutton & Co.
Hubert, H. (2001). L'énigme transsexuelle. In F. Sauvagnat (Ed.), *Divisions subjectives et personnalités multiples.* Paris: Presses Universitaires de Rennes.
Hulshoff Pol, H., Cohen-Kettenis, P., Van Haren, N., Peper, J., Brans, R., Cahn, W., et al. (2006). Changing your sex changes your brain: Influences of testosterone and estrogen on adult human brain structure. *European Journal of endocrinology/European Federation of Endocrine Societies, 155,* 107–114.
Hunt, N. (1978). *Mirror image: The odyssey of a male-to-female transsexual.* New York: Holt, Rinehart, & Winston.
Intersex Society of North America (ISNA). http://www.isna.org
Irigaray, L. (1985a). *This sex which is not one* (C. Porter, Trans.). Ithaca, NY: Cornell University Press.
Irigaray, L. (1985b). *Speculum of the other woman* (G. Gill, Trans.). Ithaca, NY: Cornell University Press.
Israël, L. (1979). *L'hystérique, le sexe et le médecin.* Paris: Masson.
Janet, P. (1965). *The major symptoms of hysteria, lecture I: The problem of hysteria.* New York: Hafner. (Original work published 1929)
Jones, E. (1953). *The life and work of Sigmund Freud, Vol. I: The formative years and the great discoveries, 1856–1900.* New York: Basic Books.
Jones, E. (1955). *The life and work of Sigmund Freud, Vol. II: 1901–1919: Years of maturity.* New York: Basic Books.
Jorden, E. (1603). *A briefe discourse of a disease called the suffocation of the mother. Written upon occasion which hath beene of late taken thereby, to suspect possession of an evil spirit, or some such supernaturall power, wherein is declared that divers strange actions and passions of the body of man, which in the common opinion are imputed to the Divell, have their true natural causes and do accompany this disease.* London: Windet.
Jorgensen, C. (2000). *Christine Jorgensen: A personal autobiography.* San Francisco: Cleis Press. (Original work published 1967)
Journées d'études de L'Association Freudienne Internationale. (2002). *Le cas de la jeune homosexuelle vu par Lacan et Freud.* Paris: Édition de l'Association Freudienne Internationale.
Joyce, J. (1992). *A portrait of the artist as a young man.* New York: Penguin.
Kaltenbeck, F. (1992). Le 'pousse-à-la-femme,' un belvédère clinique. *La Lettre Mensuelle de L'Ecole de la Cause Freudienne 112: L'Autre sexe,* 9–10.
Kao, A. (n.d.). *The difficult appendage.* American Medical Association Virtual Mentor, Promoting the Ethics and Professionalism of Tomorrow's Physicians. Retrieved July 28, 2007, from http://www.amaassn.org/ama/pub/category/3063.html

Katz, J. N. (1995/2007). *The invention of heterosexuality*. Chicago: University of Chicago Press.
Kessler, S. (1990). The medical construction of gender: Case management of intersexed infants. *Signs: Journal of Women in Culture and Society, 16*(1), 3–26.
Kessler, S. (1998). *Lessons from the intersexed*. New Brunswick, NJ: Rutgers University Press.
Khosla, D. (2006). *Both sides now: One man's journey through womanhood*. New York: Tarcher/Penguin
King, H. (1993). Once upon a text. In S. Gilman, H. King, R. Porter, G. S. Rousseau, & E. Showalter (Eds.), *Hysteria beyond Freud* (pp. 3–90). Berkeley: University of California Press.
King, H. (1998). *Hippocrates women: Reading the female body in ancient Greece*. New York: Routledge.
Kinsey, A. (1953). *Sexual behavior in the human female*. Philadelphia: Saunders.
Kinsey, A., Pomeroy, W., & Martin, C. (1948). *Sexual behavior in the human male*. Philadelphia: Saunders.
Klein, R. (2003). The birth of gender. *Psychoanalytical Notebooks: Sexuation and Sexuality, A Review of the London Society of the New Lacanian School, 11*, 51–60.
Knickmeyer, R. C., & Baron-Cohen, S. (2006). Fetal testosterone and sex differences in typical social development and in autism. *Journal of Child Neurology, 21*(10), 825–845.
Kofman, S. (1985). *The enigma of woman in Freud's writing* (C. Porter, Trans.). Ithaca, NY: Cornell University Press.
Kososfky Sedgwick, E. (1993). How to bring your kids up gay: The war on effeminate boys. In M. Warner (Ed.). *Fear of a queer planet: Queer politics and social theory* (pp. 69–81). Minneapolis: University of Minnesota Press.
Krafft-Ebing, R. (1886/1965). *Psychopathia sexualis*. New York: Putnam's Sons.
Kris, E. (1977). Introduction (E. Mosbacher & J. Strachey, Trans). In M. Bonaparte, A. Freud, & E. Kris (Eds.), *The origins of psychoanalysis, letters of Wilhelm Fliess, drafts, and notes: 1887–1902*. New York: Basic Books. (Original work published 1954)
Lacan, J. (1957–1958/2006). On a question prior to any possible treatment of psychosis. In *Ecrits: The first complete edition in English* (B. Fink, Trans.) (pp. 445–448). New York: Norton.
Lacan, J. (1966/1967). Psychanalyse et médecine. *Lettres de l'école freudienne I*, pp. 34–61.
Lacan, J. (1971–1972). *Le Séminaire XIX ... ou pire. Le savoir du psychanalyst*, unpublished.
Lacan, J. (1973). L'étourdit, *Scilicet, 4*, 5–52.
Lacan, J. (1976/1977). Le séminaire: Livre XXIII: Le sinthome. *Ornicar? 10*, 3–24.
Lacan, J. (1977). Le séminaire XXIV, L'insu que sait de l'une bévue, s'aile a mourre, *Ornicar? 11/12*, 6–7.
Lacan, J. (1979). On transmission. *Lettres de l'École, 25*(2), 219–220.
Lacan, J. (1981). *The four fundamental concepts of psychoanalysis: The seminar of Jacques Lacan, Book 11* (J. A. Miller, Ed., & A. Sheridan, Trans.). New York: Norton.

Lacan, J. (1986). Présentation des mémoires du Président Schreber en traduction française. *Ornicar?* 38, 5–10.
Lacan, J. (1989). Science and truth (B. Fink, Trans.). *Newsletter of the Freudian Field*, 3(1/2), 4–29.
Lacan, J. (1990). *Television: A challenge to the psychoanalytic establishment*. New York: Norton.
Lacan, J. (1991a) *Le séminaire de Jacques Lacan: Livre VIII: Le transfert 1960–1961*. Paris: Seuil.
Lacan, J. (1991b). *Le séminaire: livre XVII: L'envers de la psychanalyse*. Paris: Seuil.
Lacan, J. (1992). *The seminar of Jacques Lacan: Book VII. The ethics of psychoanalysis 1959–1960* (J. A. Miller, Ed. & D. Porter, Trans.). New York: Norton.
Lacan, J. (1993). *The seminar of Jacques Lacan: Book III: The psychoses 1955–1956* (J. A. Miller, Ed., & R. Grigg, Trans.). New York: Norton.
Lacan, J. (1994). *Le séminaire: Livre IV: La relation d'Objet, 1956–1957* (J. A. Miller, Ed.). Paris: Seuil.
Lacan, J. (1996). Entretien avec Michel H. In M. Czermak & H. Frignet (Eds.), *Sur l'identité sexuelle: A propos du transsexualisme* (pp. 311–353). Paris: Editions de l'association Freudienne Internationale.
Lacan, J. (1998a). *Le séminaire: Livre V: Les formations de l' inconscient,1957–1958* (J. A. Miller, Ed.). Paris: Seuil.
Lacan, J. (1998b). *The seminar of Jacques Lacan: Book XX. On the limits of love and knowledge, 1972–1973* (J. A. Miller, Ed. & B. Fink, Trans.). New York: Norton.
Lacan, J. (2001). *Autres écrits*. Paris: Seuil.
Lacan, J. (2004). *Le séminaire: Livre X: L'Angoisse* (J. A. Miller, Ed.). Paris: Seuil.
Lacan, J. (2005). *Le séminaire: Livre XXIII: Le sinthome 1975–1976* (J. A. Miller, Ed.). Paris: Seuil.
Lacan, J. (2006). *Ecrits: The first complete edition in English* (B. Fink, Trans.). New York: Norton.
Lacan, J. (2007). *The seminar of Jacques Lacan: Book XVII: The other side of psychoanalysis* (J. A. Miller, Ed., & R. Grigg, Trans.). New York: Norton.
Lane, C. (2007). *Shyness: How normal behavior became a sickness*. New Haven, CT: Yale University Press.
Laqueur, T. (1990). *Making sex: Body and gender from the Greeks to Freud*. Cambridge, MA: Harvard University Press.
Laurent, E. (1989). Límites en las psicosis. In *Estabilizaciones en las psicosis*. Buenos Aires: Manantial.
Laurent, E. (1992). Lettre à la lettre mensuelle in *La Lettre Mensuelle*. Ecole de la Cause Freudienne, 114, 12.
Lebrun, J.-P. (1997/1999). *Un monde sans limite: Essais pour une clinique psychanalytique du social*. Paris: Eres.
Le Gaufey, G. (1987). L'hypothèse de la bisexualité chez Freud. *Littoral, 23/24*, 59.
Lehmann-Haupt, C. (1985, April 4). Books of the times [Review of the book *The Complete Letters of Sigmund Freud to Wilhelm Fliess 1887–1904*, J. Moussaiedd-Mason, Ed., & Trans.]. *New York Times*. Retrieved from http://www.nytimes.com
Leigh Brown, P. (2006, December 2). Supporting boys or girls when the line isn't clear. *New York Times*.

Le Rider, J. (1982). *Le cas Otto Weininger: Racines de l'antiféminisme et de l'antisémitisme*. Paris: PUF.
Lesser, R., & Schoenberg, E. (Eds.). (1999). *That obscure subject of desire: Freud's female homosexual revisited*. New York: Routledge.
LeVay, S. (1991a). A difference in hypothalamic structure between heterosexual and homosexual men. *Science, 253*, 1034–1037.
LeVay, S. (1991b). *The sexual brain*. Cambridge, MA: MIT Press.
LeVay, S. (1997). *Queer science: The use and abuse of research into homosexuality*. Cambridge, MA: MIT Press.
Levinas, E. (1969/1985). *Totality and infinity: An essay on exteriority*. A. Lingis (Trans.). Pittsburgh: Duquesne University Press.
Lew, R. (1994a). La malédiction sur le sexe. In M. Scheidhauer (Ed.), *Une question incontournable: La bisexualité (Fliess-Freud-Weininger)* (pp. 91–95). Paris: Lysimaque.
Lew, R. (1994b). Preface. In M. Scheidhauer (Ed.), *Une question incontournable: La bisexualité (Fliess-Freud-Weininger)* (pp. 5–7). Paris: Lysimaque.
Lewins, F. (1995). *Transsexualism in transsexuals*. Melbourne: Macmillan.
Lichtenberg Etinger, B. (2002). Weaving a trans-subjective tress of the matrixial *sinthome*. In L. Thurston (Ed.), *Reinventing the symptom: Essays on the final Lacan* (pp. 83–109). New York: Other Press.
Limentani, A. (1995). *Between Freud and Klein*. New York: Free Association Books.
Lothstein, L. (1983). *Female-to-male transsexualism: Historical, clinical, and theoretical issues*. Boston, London, Melbourne, and Henley: Routledge & Kegan Paul.
Lowenfeld, H. (1968). Hysteria: The history of a disease [Book review]. *International Journal of Psycho-Analysis, 49*, 101–103.
Lueck, T. (2007, July 29). To serve, protect, and mind their manners. *New York Times*. Retrieved September 14, 2009 from http://www.nytimes.com
Lynn, D., & Vaillant, G. (1998). Anonymity, neutrality and confidentiality in the actual methods of Sigmund Freud: A review of 43 cases, 1907–1939. *American Journal of Psychiatry, 155*, 163–171.
MacDonald, M. (Ed.). (1991). *Witchcraft and hysteria in Elizabethan London: Edward Jorden and the Mary Glover case*. London: Routledge.
Mahieu, E. (2004). *El empuje a la mujer: Formas, transformaciones y estructura*. Cordoba, Argentina: El espejo Ediciones.
Mahoney, P. (1979). Friendship and its discontents. *Contemporary Psychoanalysis, 15*(1), 98–105.
Maines, R. (1999). *The technology of orgasm: "Hysteria" the vibrator, and women's sexual satisfaction*. Baltimore: Johns Hopkins University Press.
Major, R. (1995/1996). Lacan as psychiatrist or: Comment ne pas être fou. *Journal of European Psychoanalysis, 2*. Retrieved Match 7, 2007, from http://www.psychomedia.it/jep/pages/number2.htm
Maleval, J.-C. (1996). Logique du délire. In *Collection médecine et psychothérapie*. Paris: Masson.
Malleus Maleficarum (M. Summers, Trans.). (1951). London: Pushkin Press. (Original work published 1494)
Mannoni, O. (2003). "I know well, but all the same ... " In M. Rothenberg, D. Foster, & S. Žižek (Eds.), Perversion and the social relation (pp. 68–92). Durham and London: Duke University Press.

Marantz Henig, R. (2005, March 22). At war with their bodies, they seek to sever limbs. *New York Times*. Retrieved September 3, 2009 from http://www.nytimes.com
Marc, C. (1840). *De la folie, considérée dans ses rapports avec les questions médico-judiciaires*. Paris: Baillière.
Martino, M. (1977). *Emergence: A transsexual autobiography*. New York: Crown.
McCloskey, D. (1999). *Crossing: A memoir*. Chicago: University of Chicago Press.
McGowan, T. (2004). *The end of dissatisfaction: Jacques Lacan and the emerging society of enjoyment*. Albany, NY: State University of New York Press.
McGuire, W. (Ed.). (1994). *The Freud/Jung letters*. Princeton, NJ: Princeton University Press. (Original work published 1974)
Melman, C. (1984). *Nouvelles études sur L'hystérie*. Paris: Denoël.
Mercader, P. (1994). *L'illusion transsexuelle*. Paris: L'Harmattan.
Merskey, H. (1985). Hysteria: The history of a disease: Ilza Veith. *British Journal of Psychiatry, 147*, 576–579.
Meyerowitz, J. (2002/2004). *How sex changed: A history of transsexuality in the United States*. Cambridge, MA: Harvard University Press.
Micale, M. (1989). Hysteria and its historiography: A review of past and present writings, II. *History of Science, 27*, 331.
Micale, M. (1995). *Approaching hysteria: Disease and its interpretations*. Princeton, NJ: Princeton University Press.
Millett, K. (1970). *Sexual politics*. New York: Doubleday.
Millot, C. (1981). Un cas de transsexualisme féminin. *Ornicar 22/23*, 167–176.
Millot, C. (1990). *Horsexe: Essays on transsexualism* (K. Hylton, Trans.). New York: Autonomedia.
Mitchell, J. (2000). *Mad men and medusas: Reclaiming hysteria*. New York: Basic Books.
Mitchell, J. (2001). Sexuality, psychoanalysis, and social changes. In A. Molino & C. Ware (Eds.), *Where id was: Challenging normalization in psychoanalysis* (pp. 96–108). New York: Continuum.
Mitchell, J., & Rose, J. (Eds.). (1985). *Feminine sexuality: Jacques Lacan and the École Freudienne*. London: Macmillan.
Mitchinson, W. (1986). Hysteria and insanity in women—A nineteenth-century perspective. *Journal of Canadian Studies, 21*, 87–105.
Money, J. (1952). *Hermaphroditism: An inquiry into the nature of a human paradox*. Unpublished doctoral dissertation, Harvard University, Cambridge, MA.
Money, J. (1961a). Components of eroticism in man: The hormones in relation to sexual morphology and sexual desire. *Journal of Nervous and Mental Diseases, 132*, 239–248.
Money, J. (1961b). Sex hormones and other variables in human eroticism. In W. C. Young (Ed.), *Sex and internal secretions* (pp. 1383–1400). Baltimore: Williams & Wilkins.
Money, J. (1973). Gender role, gender identity, core gender identity: Usage and definition of terms. *Journal of American Academy of Psychoanalysis, 1*, 397–402.
Money, J. (1975). Ablatio penis: Normal male infant sex-reassigned as a girl. *Archives of Sexual Behavior, 4*, 65–71.

Money, J. (1990). Androgyne becomes bisexual in sexological theory: Plato to Freud and neuroscience. *Journal of the American Academy of Psychoanalysis, 18*, 392–413.
Money, J., & Ehrhardt, A. (1996a). *Man and woman, boy and girl*. Northvale, NJ: Aronson.
Money, J., & Ehrhardt, A. (1996b). *Man and woman, boy and girl: The differentiation and dimorphism of gender identity from conception to maturity.* Baltimore: Johns Hopkins Press. (Original work published 1972)
Money, J., Hampson, G., & Hampson, J. (1955). An examination of some basic sexual concepts: The evidence of human hermaphroditism. *Bulletin of Johns Hopkins Hospital, 97*, 301–319.
Money, J., Jobaris, R., & Furth, G. (1977). Apotemnophilia: Two cases of self-demand amputation as a paraphilia. *Journal of Sex Research, 13*, 115–125.
Money, J., & Musaph, H. (1977). *Handbook of sexology*. New York and Amsterdam: Excerpta Medica.
Money, J., & Tucker, P. (1975). *Sexual signatures: On being a man or a woman*. Boston: Little Brown.
Morel, G. (2000a). *Ambigüedades sexuales: Sexuación y psicosis*. Buenos Aires: Manantial.
Morel, G. (2000b). Le pousse-à-la-femme: Problématique. In *Figures de pousse-à-la-femme: Cercle Franco-Hellénique de Paris de L'École Européenne de Psychanalyse* unpublished seminar.
Morel, G. (2000c). Psychoanalytical anatomy. In R. Salecl (Ed.), *Sexuation* (pp. 30–37). Durham, NC: Duke University Press.
Morris, J. (1986). *Conundrum*. New York: Holt. (Original work published 1974)
Moussaieff-Masson, J. (1985). *The complete letters of Sigmund Freud to Wilhelm Fliess 1887–1904*. Cambridge, MA: Belknap Press of Harvard University.
Muram, D., & Dewhurst, J. (1984). Inheritance of intersex disorders. *Canadian Medical Association Journal, 130*(2), 121–125.
Nasio, J.-D. (1998). *Hysteria from Freud to Lacan: The splendid child of psychoanalysis*. New York: Other Press.
Naversen Geraghty, L. (2007, August 2). I am not a crab: When wrinkles lie. *New York Times*. Retrieved September 14, 2009 from http://www.nytimes.com
Newman, K., Randolph, J., & Anderson, K. (1992). The surgical management of infants and children with ambiguous genitalia: Lessons learned from 25 years. *Annals of Surgery, 215*(6), 644–653.
Newton, E. (1979/1972). *Mother camp: Female impersonators in America*. Chicago: University of Chicago Press.
Parnell, P., & Richardson, J. (2005). *And Tango makes three*. New York: Simon & Schuster.
Payne, J. F. (1900). *Thomas Sydenham*. New York: Longman, Green.
Pfaefflin, F. (1997). Sex reassignment, Harry Benjamin, and some European roots. *The International Journal of Transgenderism, 1*(2). Retrieved September 5, 2009 from http://www.symposion.com/ijt/ijtc0202.htm
Pfeiffer, E. (Ed.). (1972). *Sigmund Freud and Lou Andreas-Salomé letters*. New York: Harcourt, Brace & Jovanovich.
Pfennig, R. (1906). *W. Fliess and seine Nachentdecker O. Weininger und H. Swoboda*. Berlin: Goldsmith.

Plato. Gill, C. (Ed. and Trans.) (1999). *The symposium*. New York: Penguin Putnam.
Pommier, G. (2000). Existe-t-il une distribution logique des homosexualités? *La Clinique Lacanienne 4: Les Homosexualités*, 73–99.
Pontalis, J. B. (Ed.) (1973). *Bisexualité et différence des sexes*. Paris: Gallimard.
Porge, E. (1994). *Vol d'idées? Wilhelm Fliess, son plagiat et Freud*. Paris: Denoël.
Porter, R. (1993). The body and the mind, the doctor and the patient: Negotiating hysteria. In S. Gilman, H. King, R. Porter, G. S. Rousseau, & E. Showalter (Eds.), *Hysteria beyond Freud* (pp. 225–285). Berkeley: University of California Press.
Porter, R., & Rousseau, G. S. (1993). Introduction: The destinies of hysteria. In S. Gilman, H. King, R. Porter, G. S. Rousseau, & E. Showalter (Eds.), *Hysteria beyond Freud* (pp. vii–xxiv). Berkeley: University of California Press.
Prosser, J. (1998). *Second skins: The body narratives of transsexuality*. New York: Columbia University Press.
Quart, A. (2008, March 16). When boys will be girls. *New York Times Magazine*. Retrieved September 5, 2009 from http://www.nytimes.com
Queller, J. (2008). *Pretty is what changes: Impossible choices, the breast cancer gene and how I defied my destiny*. New York: Spiegel & Grau.
Quinet, A. (1988). Schreber's Other. In D. Allison, M. Prado de Olivera, & A. Weiss (Eds.), *Psychosis and sexual identity: Toward a post-analytic view of Schreber's case* (pp. 30–42). Albany: State University of New York.
Rabant, C. (1992). *Inventer le réel: Le déni entre perversion et psychose*. Paris: Denoël.
Rado, S. (1956). *Psychoanalysis of behavior: The collected papers of Sandor Rado*. New York: Grune & Stratton.
Reischel, J. (2006, May 30). See Tom be Jane: The country's youngest transgender child is ready for school. But is school ready for her? *Village Voice*. Retrieved on September 5, 2009 from http://www.villagevoice.com/2006-05-30/news/see-tom-jane/
Reischel, J. (2007, June 20–26). Queer in the crib: Born gay, the dawn of the very young queer. *Village Voice*.
Revédi, G. (1997). *L'hystérie*. Paris: Presses Universitaires de France.
Rich, A. (1972). The ninth symphony of Beethoven understood at last as sexual message. In *The fact of a doorframe: Poems selected and new: 1950–1984*. New York: Norton.
Rich, A. (1986). Compulsory heterosexuality and the lesbian continuum. *Blood, bread, and poetry: Selected prose, 1979–1985*. New York: Norton.
Richards, R. (1983). *Second serve*. New York: Stein & Day.
Richards, R. (2007). *No way Renée: The second half of my notorious life*. New York: Simon & Schuster.
Rieder, I., & Voigt, D. (2003). *Sidonie Csillag: Homosexuelle chez Freud, lesbienne dans le siècle*. Paris: Epel.
Riese, W. (1958). The history of the term and conception of neurosis in pre-Freudian origins of psychoanalysis in science and psychoanalysis (p. 66, footnote). In J. Masserman (Ed.) *Science and psychoanalysis* (pp. 29–72). New York: Grune & Stratton.
Roazen, P. (1968). *Freud: Political and social thought*. New York: Knopf.

Romano, T. (2007, June 20–26). Bye, bye, boobies: Fundraising parties for trans surgery are all the rage. *Village Voice*.

Rosario, V. (2004). The biology of gender and the construction of sex? *GLQ: A Journal of Lesbian and Gay Studies, 10*(2), 280–287.

Rottneck, M. (1999). *Sissies and tomboys: Gender nonconformity and homosexual childhood*. New York: New York University Press.

Roudinesco, E. (1997). *Jacques Lacan* (B. Bray, Trans.). New York: Columbia University Press.

Rousseau, G. S. (1993). "A strange pathology": Hysteria in the early modern world 1500–1800. In S. Gilman, H. King, R. Porter, G. S. Rousseau, & E. Showalter (Eds.), *Hysteria beyond Freud* (pp. 91–221). Berkeley: University of California Press.

Roy, A. (Ed.) (1982). *Hysteria*. New York: Wiley.

Ryan, C., & Futterman, D. (1998). *Lesbian and gay youth: Care and counseling*. New York: Columbia University Press.

Safouan, M. (1974). Contribution à la psychanalyse du transsexualisme. *Scilicet, 4*, 137–159. Republished in Le Champ Freudien (1974) Etudessur l'Oedipe, pp. 74–97. Paris: Seuil.

Salecl, R. (2004a). *On anxiety*. New York: Routledge.

Salecl, R. (Ed.). (2004b). *Sexuation*. Durham, NC: Duke University Press.

Salecl, R. (2006, February 16). Who am I for myself? Anxiety and the tyranny of choice. Retrieved September 5, 2009 from http://slought.org/content/11318/

Salecl, R. (2007). Analysis in times of tyranny of choice. In *The Ethics of Psychoanalytic Treatment* (pp. 219–239). Paris: Formations Cliniques du Champ Lacanien.

Scheidhauer, M. (Ed.). (1994). *Une question incontournable: La bisexualité (Fliess-Freud-Weininger)*. Paris: Lysimaque.

Schneiderman, S. (Ed.). (1980). *Returning to Freud: Clinical psychoanalysis in the school of Lacan*. New Haven, CT: Yale University Press.

Schreber, D. P. (2000). *Memoirs of my nervous illness*. New York: New York Review of Books. Original work published 1903.

Schur, M. (1972). *Freud: Living and dying*. New York: International Universities Press.

Schwabe, A., Solomon, D., Stoller, R., & Burnham, J. P. (1962). Pubertal feminization in a genetic male with testicular atrophy and normal urinary gonadotropin. *Journal of Clinical Endocrinology and Metabolism, 22*, 8, 839–845.

Sciolino, E. (2000, September 22). Iran's well-covered women remodel a part that shows. *New York Times*. Retrieved September 14, 2009 from http://www.nytimes.com

Sengoopta, C. (1996).The unknown Weininger: Science, philosophy, and cultural politics in fin-de-siècle Vienna. *Central European History, 29*, 453–493.

Sengoopta, C. (1998). Glandular politics: Experimental biology, clinical medicine, and homosexual emancipation in fin-de-siècle Central Europe. *Isis, 89*(3), 445–473.

Sengoopta, C. (2000a). The modern ovary: Constructions, meanings, uses. *History of Science, 38*, 425–488.

Sengoopta, C. (2000b). *Otto Weininger: Sex, science, and self in Imperial Vienna*. Chicago: University of Chicago Press.

Sengoopta, C. (2000c). Tales from the Vienna labs: the Eugene Steinach-Harry Benjamin correspondence. *New York Academy of Medicine*, 2, 2–7.
Sengoopta, C. (2003). "Dr Steinach coming to make old young": Sex glands, vasectomy and the quest for rejuvenation in the roaring twenties. *Endeavour*, 27, 122–126.
Shapiro, J. (1991). Transsexualism: Reflexions on the persistence of gender and the mutability of sex. In J. Epstein & K. Straub (Eds.), *Body guards: The cultural politics of gender ambiguities* (pp. 248–279). New York: Routledge.
Shepherdson, C. (2000). *Vital signs: Nature, culture, psychoanalysis*. New York: Routledge.
Shorter, E. (1994, June 17). The reinvention of hysteria. *New York Times Literary Supplement*.
Showalter, E. (1993). Hysteria, feminism, and gender. In S. Gilman, H. King, R. Porter, G. S. Rousseau, & B. Showalter (Eds.), *Hysteria beyond Freud* (pp. 286–344). Berkeley: University of California Press.
Showalter, E. (1997). *Hystories: Hysterical epidemics and modern culture*. New York: Columbia University Press.
Skuse, D. (2006). Sexual dimorphism in cognition and behaviour: The role of X-linked genes. *European Journal of Endocrinology / European Federation of Endocrine Societies*, 155, S99–S106.
Slater, E. (1982). What is hysteria? In A. Roy (Ed.), *Hysteria* (pp. 37–40). New York: John Wiley.
Sloan, D., & De Landri, C. (Producers). (2007, April 27). My secret self: A story of transgender children. In *20/20*. New York: ABC.
Smiley, L. (2007, July 11). Boy/girl interrupted. *San Francisco Weekly*. Retrieved September 8, 2009 from http://www.sfweekly.com/2007-07-11/news/girl-boy-interrupted/
Smith-Rosenberg, C. (1985). *Disorderly conduct: Visions of gender in Victorian America*. New York: Knopf.
Soler, C. (2000). *La maldición sobre el sexo*. Buenos Aires: Editorial Manantial.
Spitz, R. (1945). Hospitalism: An inquiry into the genesis of psychiatric conditions in early childhood. *The Psychoanalytic Study of the Child*, 1, 53–74.
Spitz, R. (1966). *The first year of life: A psychological study of normal and deviant object relations*. New York: International Universities Press.
Stack, C. (2001). Dirty talk: Response to that obscure subject of desire: Freud's female homosexual revisited. *Gender and Psychoanalysis*, 6, 85–89.
Stack, M. (2005, January 30). Iran bans being gay, but allows sex change. *The Seattle Times*.
Steinach, E. (1912). Willkürliche Umwandlung von Säugetiermännchen in Tiere mit ausgeprägt weiblichen Geschlechtscharacteren und weiblicher Psyche [Arbitrary transformation of male mammals into animals with pronounced female sex characters and feminine psyche]. *Pflügers Archiv*, 144, 71–108.
Steinach, E. (1913a). Pubertätsdrüsen und Zwitterbildung. *Archiv für Entwicklungsmechanik*, 42, 307–332.
Steinach, E. (1913b). Feminierung von Männchen und Maskulierung von Weibchen [Feminization of males and masculization of females]. *Zentralblatt für Physiologie*, 27, 717–723.
Steinach, E. (1916). Pubertätsdrüsen und Zwitterbildung [Puberty glands and hermaphroditism]. *Archiv für Entwicklungsmechanismus*, 42, 307–332.

Steinach, E. (1920). Künstliche und natürliche Zitterdrüsen und ihre analogen Wirkungen: Drei Mitteilungen. *Archiv für Entwicklungsmechanismus der Organismen, 46*, 12–37.

Steinach, E. (1940). *Sex and life: Forty years of biological and medical experiments*. New York: Viking Press.

Stevens, A. (1986). *Remarques sur l'usage du terme holophrase dans l'enseignement de Jacques Lacan* (DEA). Unpublished manuscript.

Stevens, J. M. (1975). Gynaecology from ancient Egypt: The papyrus Kahun: A translation of the oldest treatise on gynaecology that has survived the ancient world. *The Medical Journal of Australia, 21*, 949–952.

Stoller, R. (1964). A contribution to the study of gender identity. *Journal of the American Medical Association, 45*, 220–226.

Stoller, R. (1968a). A further contribution to the study of gender identity. *International Journal of Psychoanalysis, 49*.

Stoller, R. (1968b). *Sex and gender: On the development of masculinity and femininity*. New York: Science House.

Stoller, R. (1975). Bisexuality: The 'bedrock' of masculinity and femininity. In *The Transsexual Experiment, Volume Two of Sex and Gender* (pp. 7–18). London: Hogarth Press.

Stoller, R. (1985). *Presentations of gender*. New Haven, CT: Yale University Press.

Stoller, R., Garfinkel, H., & Rosen, A. (1960). Passing and the maintenance of sexual identification in an intersexed patient. *Archives of General Psychiatry, 2*, 379–384.

Stone, S. (1991). The *Empire* strikes back: A posttranssexual manifesto. In J. Epstein & K. Straub (Eds.), *Body guards: The cultural politics of gender ambiguity* (pp. 280–304). New York: Routledge.

Strachey, J. (1962). Editor's Note. In J. Strachey (Ed., & Trans.), *Freud: Three essays on the theory of sexuality* (pp. xi–xiii). New York: Basic Books.

Stryker, S. (2000). Introduction. In *Christine Jorgensen, A Personal Autobiography* (pp. v–xiii). San Francisco: Cleis Press.

Stryker, S., & Whittle, S. (2006). *The transgender studies reader*. New York: Routledge.

Sulloway, F. (1979). *Freud: Biologist of the mind*. New York: Basic Books.

Swoboda, H. (1906). *Die gemeinnützige Forschung und der eigennützige Forscher: Antworten auf die von Wilhelm Fließ erhobenen Beschuldigungen*. Vienna: Braümiller.

Sydenham, T. (1848). *Epistolary dissertation 1681/82: The works of Thomas Syndenham, M.D.* London: Sydenham Society.

Syndenham, T. (1850). *The works of Thomas Syndenham* (2 vols.). London: Sydenham Society.

Telegraph.co.uk (2009, March 21). Man to become first in world to give birth to twins. Retrived September 3, 2009 from http://www.telegraph.co.uk/news/worldnews/europe/spain/5027071/man-to-become-first-in-world-to-give-birth-to-twins.html

TFFGS (Transgender Family and Friends Support Network) of the PFLAG (Parents and Friends of Gay and Lesbians). Medical Abuse of GLBT Youth. Retrieved from http://www.critpath.org/pflag-talk/gid.htm.

Thullier, J. (1999). *The ten years that changed the face of mental illness*. Malden, MA: Blackwell Science.
Trebay, G. (2008, June 22). He's pregnant. You're speechless. *New York Times*, Fashion & Style section, p. 1.
Trillat, E. (1986). *Histoire de l'hystérie*. Paris: Seghers.
Tucker, D. (Director). (2005). *Transamerica* [Motion picture]. Solena Beach, CA: Genius Productions.
Valentine, D. (2007). *Imagining transgender: An ethnography of the category*. Durham, NC: Duke University Press.
Valerio, M. (2006). *The testosterone files: My hormonal and social transformation from female to male*. Emeriville, CA: Seal Press.
Veith, I. (1965). *Hysteria: The history of a disease*. Chicago: University of Chicago Press.
Verhaeghe, P. (1997/1999). *Does the woman exist? From Freud's hysteric to Lacan's feminine* (M. du Ry, Trans.). New York: Other Press.
Verhaeghe, P. (2009). *New studies of old villains: A radical consideration of the Oedipus complex*. New York: Other Press.
Von Mahldsdof. (1995). *I am my own wife: The true story of Charlote von Mahlsdorf*. San Francisco: Cleis Press.
Wajeman, G. (1982). *Le maître et l'hystérique*. Paris: Navarin.
Walder, J. (2007, February 1). At home with Renée Richards: The lady regrets. *New York Times*. Retrieved September 5, 2009 from http://www.nytimes.com
Warner, M. (Ed.) (1993). *Fear of a queer planet: Queer politics and social theory*. Minneapolis, MN: University of Minnesota Press.
Weinenger, O. (1903). *Geschlecht und Charakter: Eine prinzipielle Untersuchung*. Vienna: Leipzig.
Weinenger, O. (2005). *Sex and character: An investigation of fundamental principles* (D. Steuer & L. Marcus, Eds., L. Löb, Trans.). Bloomington: Indiana University Press. (Original work published 1903)
Weiss, E. (1970). *Sigmund Freud as a consultant: Recollections of a pioneer in psychoanalysis*. New York: Intercontinental Medical Book.
Westphal, K. F. O. (1869). Die conträre Sexualempfindung. *Archiv für Psychiatrie und Nervenkrankheiten, 2*, 73–108.
Whytt, R. (1767). *Observations on the nature, causes, and cure of those disorders which have been commonly called nervous, hypochondriac, or hysteric: To which are prefixed some remarks on the sympathy of the nerves*. Edinburgh: Balfour.
Willis, T. (1684). *Essay of the pathology of the brain and nervous stock: In which convulsive diseases are treated of*. London: Dring.
Wilton, T. (2000). Out/performing our selves: Sex, gender and Cartesian dualism. *Sexualities, 3*(2), 237–254.
Young, H. (1924). Preliminary report of a case of mixed sex: An apparent male with a testis in scrotum on right side; Ovary, tube, and uterus in inguinal canal on left side. *Bulletin of the John Hopkins Hospital, 35*, 167.
Zander, E. (2003). *Transactions*. Stockholm: Periscop Förlag.

Index

A

Abelson, Jeanne, 36
Abraham, Felix, 157
Abraham, Karl, 69
Acocella, Joan, 5
Acting out, 66, 69, 101, 117, 118, 119, 122, 202, 203
Adler, Alfred, 195
Aflalo-Lebovits, Agnès, 94
Agamben, Giorgio, 4
Al-Arabiya TV, 3
Alby, Jean-Marc, 156, 165
Alienation, 60, 197–199, 201
Almada, Nadia, 6
Allouch, Jean, 93
American Academy of Pediatrics, 19
American Psychiatric Association, 10, 15, 25
Ames, Jonathan, 217
André, Jacques 53n
André, Serge 73, 105
Androgyny, 137, 138
Angelides, Steven, 72
Angier, Natalie, 86, 137, 141
Anorexia, 16, 198, 200
Anzieu, Didier, 73
Aphanisis, 197, 203–204
Apotemnophilia, 15, 16
Aristophanes, 138, 139
Aristotle, 57
Arnold, Arthur, 138
Augustine, St., 44
Aubry, Jenny, 104

B

Baglivi, Georgio, 46
Barossa, Julia, 53n
Bartlett, Nancy, 27
Baudrillard, Jean, 8
Baumgardner, Jennifer, 38
Be-All convention, 7–8
Beatie, Thomas, xi, 12
Beckett, Samuel, 248
Bell, Blair, William, 31
Benjamin, Henry, 15, 28, 29, 33, 34, 79, 80n, 81, 82, 83, 87, 88, 89, 151, 219, 222, 225, 228
Bercherie, Paul, 45
Bernheim, Hippolyte, 51
Bernheimer, Charles, 53n
Bernstein, Fred A., 23, 37
Bisexuality
    anatomical, 219
    chasm between sexes, 75–76
    defining, 74
    embryos, in, 84, 85, 86
    Fliessian-Weiningerian theory of, 84
    Freud's description of, 72–73
    gender debate, importance to, 137
    hysteria, relationship between, 92–93
    importance of, 71
    Jorgenson case as extreme case, 88
    Oedipus complex, link between, 77
    problematical nature of, according to Freud, 73–74
    psychic, 88–89
    theory of, birth of, 63, 65, 66, 67, 70, 71–72
    transsexuality, relationship between, 218, 225–226
    universal disposition of, 74, 75
Bleizer, Janet, 53n, 54

Blévis, Marcianne, 124
Bloom, Amy, 34
Body dysmorphic disorder, 16, 17
Body integrity identity disorder (BIID), 15, 16–17, 19
Bolin, Anne, 32, 81
Bornstein, Kate, 8, 226
Boss, Jeffrey M., 54
Boyd, Helen, 216
Boylan, Jennifer Finney. *See* Finney Boylan, Jennifer
Brabant, Eva, 70
Bradley, Susan, 133
Braunstein, Nestor, 127, 200
Breger, Louis, 70
Breasts
    libidinal importance of, 14
    mastectomy, 11, 23
    preoccupation with, 13
Brill, Stephanie, 10
Brome, Vincent, 68n
Bronfen, Elisabeth, 53n
Brooks, Peter, 48
Brousse, Marie-Hélène, 176, 177, 179
Bruce/Brenda case. *See* Reimer, David, case of
Bruno, Richard, 16
Bulimia, 17, 199–200, 201, 204–205
Burgess, Christian, 36
Bush, George W., 4
Butler, Judith, xi, 4–5, 39, 72, 109, 110, 11, 113, 114–115, 116–117, 119, 120, 129, 136, 141–144, 147, 231

C

Califia, Pat, 33, 221
Castel, Pierre-Henri, 156, 164
Castration, 14, 19, 20, 21, 59, 76, 77, 79, 80, 81, 82, 97, 98, 103, 104, 106, 110, 112, 123, 124, 125, 126, 127, 128, 145, 164, 173, 175, 181, 185, 189, 192, 196, 198, 243
Cauldwell, David, 28
CBS Evening News, 41
Charcot, Jean-Martin, 50–51, 52, 55, 65, 92, 219
Chase, Cheryl, 136
Chauvelot, Diane, 53n
Chiland, Colette, 2

Chodoff, Paul, 50
Christianity, influence of perception of virtue, 44
Colapinto, John, 131, 133, 134, 135, 136, 145, 146, 148
Cole, Collier M., 36n
Conn, Canary, 229
Corbett, Ken, 115
Corners, George F., 83
Coronado, Ruben Noe, 17–18
Cottet, Serge, 164n
County, Jayne, 229
Cross-dressing, 234. *See also* Drag
Csonka, Margarethe, 93 (*see also* Scillag, Sidonie)
Cullen, William, 47
Currah, Paisley, 25
Curtis, Valerie, 56n

D

Dalery, Jean, 138
David, Christian, 73
David-Ménard, Monique, 107n
De Lauretis, Teresa, 30
De Marcis, Marie, 62
Dean, Tim, 11, 33, 116, 231
Death, 247–248
Delavenay, Emile, 83n
Delay, Jean, 155, 156, 159, 163
Demand, 20, 21, 106, 107, 119, 128, 154, 159, 173, 192, 194, 195, 197, 199, 206, 215, 217
Democracy, 3, 4, 8, 246
Democratizing, 1, 4, 23–40
Derrida, Jacques, 195
Devor, Aaron, 36n
Devor, Holly, 36n
Diamantis, Irene, 107
Diamond, Milton, 86, 134, 135, 136, 137, 140, 141, 143, 144, 145
Dorumat, Dreger, Alice, 18, 19, 31, 135, 145
Donahoe, Patricia, 19, 135
Drag, 4–5, 180–182
Drescher, Jack, 108
Duchamp, Marcel, 239
Duval, Jacques, 62

E

Ego, 120

Ehhardt, Anke, 147
Eissler, Kurt, 69
Ekins, Richard, 34
Electra complex, 77
Elliot, Carl, 15, 16
Ellis, Havelock, 86
Epstein, Julia, 30
Exogamic exchanges, 96

F

Factitious disability disorder, 16
Falzeder, Ernst, 79n
Fathi, Nazila, 3
Fausto-Sterling, Anne, 18, 19, 34, 39, 83n, 84, 135n, 140
Fédida, Pierre, 71, 73
Feinberg, Leslie, 28, 32, 225, 239
Feltzine, Francis, 107
Female impersonation (drag), gender theory, influence on, 4–5
Femininity, 110–111
　classical Greece, in, 41–42
　hysteria, association with, 48
　psychoanalytical definition, 74
　Schreber, involvement in case of, 174–175
　sex and gender, as separate from, 126
　Sidonie's rejection of, 128
Ferenczi, Sándor, 69–70
Fetishism, *versus* cross-dressing, 234–235
Finney Boylan, Jennifer, 2, 11n, 27, 226n
First, Michael, 15n, 16, 17
Fliess, William, 65, 66, 67, 68, 69, 70, 71, 75, 83, 88, 89, 140, 218
Foucault, Michel, 4, 6, 56, 60, 144
Freud, Anna, 93
Freud, Sigmund, 13, 14
　bisexuality, theory of, 63, 65, 66, 67, 68, 70, 71–72, 73–74
　cancer, 79
　career, early, 65
　castration complex, 20–21, 81
　Darwinism, 86
　discussions of own failures, 151–152
　dominant sex, concept of, 76
　Dora, case of, 91–92, 93–94, 96, 97–99, 100–101, 106, 118
　enigmatic quality of women, belief in, 75
　helplessness, concept of, 197
　homosexual drive, theories of, 70
　homosexuality, unconscious, 176
　hypnosis, 51–52
　hysteria, concepts of, 51, 53–54, 91–92, 99–102 (*see also* Hysteria)
　melancholy, thoughts on, 119
　normal *versus* abnormal sexuality, 47
　Oedipus complex (*see* Oedipus complex)
　paranoia, theory of, 69
　parental influence on homosexuality, theories on, 107
　plagiarism, accusations of, 67, 68, 69, 72
　psychoanalysis, 51–52, 53–54
　self-analysis, 66
　sexuality, origins of theories of, 65–66
　sexuality, riddle of, 76–77
　Sidonie case (*see* Scillag, Sidonie)
　Steinach procedure, received, 79–80
　unconscious, 43
Frignet, Henry, 163
Furth, Gregg, 15–16
Fuss, Diana, 102–103, 105–106, 107–109, 117, 119, 120

G

Gaines, Richard, 36
Galen of Pergamon, 43–44, 58, 59
Garfinkel, Harold, 223, 224
Gay, Peter, 67, 79
Gender. *See also* Gender identity disorder (GID)
　assumptions regarding, 2
　binary nature of, 113–114
　brain regions, role of, 137–138
　choice, as, 1
　defining, 24, 147
　embodiment, 247
　genetics, 136–137, 144
　grammar of, 113–114
　gravitational pushes, 117–118
　hypothalamus, role of, 137
　identification, 24

identity (*see* Gender identity)
  infancy, in, 58–59, 115–116
  metaphysics of, 83
  nature *versus* nurture debate, 136
  neutrality, 116
  norms, 13
  one, concept of, 58–61
  performance, concept of, 114–115
  preoccupation with, 13–14
  psychosexual bias, 136
  roles, 142, 147
  semantics/word choices, 23–24
  social constructs, *61,* 136, 147
  technology, relationship between, 30–31
  Western concepts of, 30
  word, history of the, 30, 31–32
Gender identity, 36–38
  anatomy, relationship to, 143–144
  continuum of, 89
  defining, 147
  invention of concept, 88–89
  nondiscrimination policies at colleges and universities, 37–38
  origins of concept, 62
Gender identity disorder (GID), 9
  body integrity identity disorder, compared to, 17
  controversy over diagnosis, 25, 26
  diagnosis, of transgendered persons, 25
  Diagnostic and Statistical Manual of Mental Disorders, inclusion in, 25–26
  indicators in children, 26
  standard of care, 33–34
Gender performativity, 4–5
Gender reassignment surgery. *See also* specific transsexuals
  costs, 2–3
  experiments, Steinach's, 78, 79, 80–82
  frequency of, 35
  intersex, 140
  neovagina, 57
  protocols, 6–7, 31, 135
  Reimer, David, case of (*see* Reimer, David, case of)
Geter, Andre, 3
Gherovici, Patricia, 42, 55
Gilbert, Melody, 20

Gindele, Thomas, 101
Goethe, Johann Wolfgang von, 66
Goldberg, Jess, 239
Goldner, Virginia, 102
Goldschmidt, Robert, 148
Green, Jamison, 226n, 238–239
Grief work, *(Trauerarbeit),* 119
Grigg, Russell, 99n, 108n, 174
Griggs, Claudine, 234
Grosz, Elizabeth, 31

H

Haeberle, Erwin, 80n, 87
Haeckel, Ernst, 86–87
Halperin, David, 115
Hamburger, Christian, 29, 88, 219, 220, 221
Harari, Roberto, 119, 167, 172, 212
Harrison, Frances, 4
Harris, Adrienne, 100
Harrus Revédi, Gisèle, 53n
Harry Benjamin Association, 34
Hartmann, Lynn, 11
Hate crimes, transitioning early as preventive measure, 10
Hausman, Bernice, 30, 31, 62, 148, 218, 220, 222, 223
Hausman, Ken, 26
Henri, case of, 182, 183
  belief in self as female, 157–158
  cryptorchidism, 157
  dresses and attire, 157
  fantasies, 161–162
  father's role, 163
  hospitalization, 156–157
  Lacan's treatment of, 158–159
  libido, 159
  overview, 155–156
  passiveness, 162
  push-towards-Woman, 177
  romantic interests, 157
  sex change, longing for, 160–162
  subjectification of sex, 162
  therapy, 158
Hera, case of, 190–192, 193
Hermaphrodites, 78, 148. *See also* Intersexuality
  psychology of, 142–145
  sexual reassignment of, 18
  Steinach's theory of, 84
  theories of, 84

Herrn, Rainer, 84
Herophilus, 58
Heterosexual matrix, 110
Hippocrates, 59
  corpus, 43, 46, 48, 53, 54
Hirschfield, Magnus, 28, 68, 77, 78, 81, 84, 85, 86, 157, 218, 227
Hoebecke, Piet, 57
Holophrase, 201–202
Homophobia, 34
Homosexuality. See also Bisexuality
  biology of, 86–87
  cultural struggles, 110
  desire, 108, 109
  Dora, case of, 91–92
  erotic bonds to mother, 110
  female, 103, 109–110, 123–124, 125
  Fuss's analysis of, 102–104
  parental bonds, 104–105
  persecution of, 85–86
  persecution of, in Iran, 3
  Steinach's "cure," 84–85, 140
  Steinach's theory of, 84
  unconscious, 176
  undercurrent of, according to Freud, 70, 71
Hospitalism, 104
Hoyer, Niels, 227
Hunt, Nancy, 228
Hubert, Hervé, 159
Hulshoff Pol, Hilleke, 137
Hunt, Nancy, 228
Hypnosis
  hysteria, associated with, 51–53
Hysteria, 13, 28–29
  anatomy, associated with, 50–51, 52, 54
  bisexuality, link to, 92–93
  classical Greek thoughts on, 41–42
  commonalities, 196
  defining, 55–56
  description of, 42
  devil, association with the, 44–45
  Dora, case of, 91–92
  female sexuality, associated with, 47
  femininity, associated with, 48
  Freud's errors regarding, 99–102
  Galenic treatment for, 46
  gender divide of, 48–50
  Hippocratic corpus, in, 43, 46, 48, 53, 54
  history of word usage, 41
  hypnosis, associated with, 51–53
  illness, perception as, 45–47
  Julie, case of, 210
  Linda, case of, 196–197, 199, 201–202, 203–204, 206, 207, 208
  masculine, 92
  medical care of, 45–46
  Perry, case of, 208–209
  persecution of women, associated with, 44–45
  phallus, role of, 98–99
  Plato's prescription for, 42
  Roman prescriptions for, 43–44
  sexual identity, relationship between, 245–246
  sexual positioning, 211–212
  sexual uncertainty, relationship between, 92
  subjectivity of, 60, 62–63
  symbolic elements of sexual body, 212–213
  symptoms, 42, 52–53, 55, 56–57
  transsexuals, in, 183–184
  witches, association with the, 44

I

Incest
  homosexuality, link to theories of, 123–124
  Lacan's ideas regarding, 104
Intersex Society of America, 135n, 136
Intersexuality, 18
  Agnes, case of, 223–224
  genitalia issues, 19–20
  medical decisions, modern, 19
  origin of term, 148
  Reimer, David, case of (see Reimer, David, case of)
  sexual reassignment, 20
  sociocultural conventions regarding, 19–20
Irigaray, Luce, 76, 113, 114
Israël, Lucien, 56n

J

Janet, Pierre, 52

Joan of Arc, 28
Joan/John case. *See* Reimer, David, case of
John Money Gender Identity Institute, 131, 133, 141. *See also* Money, John
Jones, Ernest, 71, 123, 197
Jones, Howard, 131–132
Jorden, Edward, 45
Jorgensen, Christina, 29, 88, 148, 163, 219, 220, 221, 222
Jouissance, 127, 161, 164–165, 170, 176–177, 177, 189, 198–199, 203, 234
Joyce, James, 152–153, 172, 181, 182, 205, 216, 217, 232–233, 235, 236, 238, 247
Jung, Carl, 70, 77

K

Kahun Papyrus, 41
Kaltenbeck, Franz, 178, 179
Kao, Audiey, 16
Katz, Jonathan N., 86
Kessler, Suzanne, 19, 136
Khomeini, Ayatollah, 3
Khosla, Dhillon, 226n, 228–229, 236–237
King, Helen, 53, 54, 55, 57, 59, 60, 62
Kinsey report
  bisexuality statistics, 29
Kinsey, Alfred, 87, 88
Kinship, 96
Klein, Richard, 143n
Knickmeyer, Rebecca, 138n
Kofman, Sarah, 75n
Krafft-Ebing, Richard, 28, 71n, 80, 86, 227
Kraus, Karl, 68
Kris, Ernst, 67

L

Lacan, Jacques, 149
  bisexuality, theories on, 92, 93
  Corinne, case of, 173
  Freud, differences with, 123
  Henri, case of, 156, 165, 167, 168, 169
  identification, concept of, 185
  mirror stage, 237, 238

mothers, theories of, 200–201
paranoia, interest in, 109
phallus *versus* penis, 59
punishment-fulfillment theories, 95–96
sexual difference, 75
sexuation, 76, 77, 125–129, 193, 246
sinthome, 152, 153, 154, 169, 178n, 186, 216, 217
Symbolic sex, 61
  Woman, 180–182
Lacanian psychosis, 169
Lack
  as logical limit, 20
  of rapport between the sexes, 140
  of symmetry between man and woman, 49, 198
  real, 160, 163
Lane, Christopher, 26n
Laqueur, Thomas, 57, 58, 59, 60, 61, 62, 116, 161
Lasègue, Charles, 55
Latency phase, 123
Laurent, Eric, 179
Lebrun, Jean-Pierre, 7
Le Gaufey, Guy, 69
Lehmann-Haupt, Christopher, 70
Leigh Brown, Patricia, 35
Lepois, Charles, 45
Le Rider, Jacques, 83n
Lesbian, gay, bisexual, transgender (LGBT), 34
Lesbianism, 9
  Freud's interest in, 93
Lesser, Ronnie, 93, 102n
LeVay, Simon, 86, 138
Lévi-Strauss, Claude, kinship theories, 96
Levinas, Emmanuel, 238
Lew, René, 69, 75
Lewins, Frank, 234
Libido, 14
Lichtenberg Etinger, Bracha, 153
Limentani, Adam, 189n
Little Hans, 14
Lothstein, Leslie, 228
Lowenfeld, Henry, 53
Lueck, Thomas, 35
Lupron, 9, 10
Lynn, David, 109

M

MacDonald, Michael, 45
Mackenzie, Olga G., 34
Mahieu, Eduardo, 175
Mahoney, Patrick, 68n
Maines, Rachel, 43, 44n, 48, 49
Major, René, 156n
Maleval, Jean-Claude, 180n
Malleus Maleficarum, 44
Mandeville, Bernard de, 55
Mannoni, Octave, 14
Marantz Henig, Robin, 15, 16, 17
Marc, Charles, 165
Martino, Mario, 225, 231
Masculinity, psychoanalytical definition, 74
McCloskey, Deirdre, 215, 234–235, 236
McGowan, Todd, 8
McGuire, William, 70
McHugh. Paul, 10
Melancholy, 119
Melman, Charles, 53n, 56n
Menninger, Karl, 224
Mentally ill, historical treatment of, 47
Mercader, Patricia, 161
Merskey, Harold, 53n
Meyerowitz, Joanne, 29, 33, 76, 219
Micale, Mark, 48, 53, 55
Michel H. case, 169–174, 182, 183
Millett, Kate, 136
Millot, Catherine, 6, 7, 11, 12, 81, 178, 179, 180, 181
Mirror stage, 159, 160, 237–238
Mitch, case of, 12–15
Mitchell, Juliet, 53n, 189
Mitchinson, Wendy, 50
Money, John, 10, 15, 16, 18, 30, 31–32, 131, 133, 135, 136, 138, 139, 140, 141, 142, 143, 144, 147, 148, 149, 222, 223. *See also* Reimer, David, case of
Morel, Geneviève, 104, 164, 165, 179, 182, 193, 196
Morris, Jan, 227, 228, 234, 240–242, 243–244
Mother, as Oedipal rival, 121
Mourning, 119, 120
Moussaieff-Masson, Jeffrey, 68n
Muram, David, 19

N

Name-of-the-Father, 173–174, 188, 189, 201
Nasio, Juan David, 92
Naversen Geraghty, Laurel, 15
Newman, Kurt, 19
Newton, Esther, 4, 5, 39
Numantius, Numa, 85

O

Object *a*, 101, 102, 116, 118, 119, 122, 186, 190, 197, 200, 202, 203, 205, 208, 231
Oedipus complex, 76, 77–78, 95, 97–98, 104–105, 108, 121, 177
Omnisexual, 38
One-Father, 176, 191
Outside sex, 11–12

P

Paranoia, 109
Paraphilia, 15, 17
Parmenides, 138
Parnell, Peter, 13
Patriarchy, intolerance in, 15
Passage à l'acte, (passage to the act), 117, 118, 119, 202, 203
Payne, Joseph F., 45
Penectomy, 221
Pfaefflin, Friedemann, 78, 79n
Pfenning, Richard, 67
Phallus
   actual, 113
   contingency, as, 210–211
   domination by, 205–207
   female sexual economy, 201
   paternal, 106
   role of in identification, 186–188
   Sergei, case of, 186–188
   signification, 164–165
   symbolic, 19–21, 98, 105–106
   transsexualism, role in, 163–164
   unit of exchange, as, 145–147
Pinel, Phillipe, 47
Plato, 138
Pommier, Gérard, 123, 124
Porge, Eric, 68n
Porter, Roy, 60

Pregnant men, 12, 17–18
Primal horde, 127, 181
Primeau, Gérard
  background, 167
  hospitalization, 166
  imposed speech, 166–167
  self-assessment as transexual, 167–168
  sexuality as choice, 168–169
Prince, Virginia, 32–33
Prosser, Jay, 2, 215, 218, 223, 229, 230, 237, 242
Psychoanalysis. *See also* Freud, Sigmund
  desire, issues of, 116
  heterosexism in, 116, 185
  historicism of, 61
  invention of, 66
  sex and gender issues in, 116
Puerto Rican syndrome, 42, 55
Pumping parties, 2
Push-towards-Woman, 174
  feminization, fantasy of, 178–179
  Michel H's relation to, 182
  Michel H. case, 173
  Oedipal phenomenon, *versus*, 177–178
  overview, 174–175
  Schreber's transformation, in context of, 175–176, 177
  Sergei, case of, 186–188, 189, 195
  sexuation, relationship to, 179–180

Q

Quart, Alissa, 38, 39
Queer theory, 93, 115
Queller, Jessica, 11
Quinet, Antonio, 161

R

Rabant, Claude, 162
Rado, Sandor, 222
Raskind, Richard, 227–228
Regression, 103–104, 105, 108, 109, 110, 119, 120, 160
Reimer, David, case of
  awakening sense of something being wrong, 132–133
  coital exercises/abuse, 133
  death by suicide, 147
  estrogen therapy, 132
  impact of psychosexual theory, 140
  marriage, 146
  overview, 131–132
  psychiatric care, 134–135
  push-towards-Woman, 182–183
  rejection of all feminine things, 133
  reversion to male, 134
  sexuality, medical community's involvement in, 141
  suicide attempts, 134, 145
  Time coverage of, 135–136
  tomboyishness, 133
  unhappiness, 141–142
  vaginal surgery, 134
Reischel, Julia, 34, 35
Rich, Adrienne, 9, 110
Richards, Renée, 6, 28, 174, 175, 224–225, 227
Rieder, Ines, 93
Riese, Walther, 47
Roazen, Paul, 69
Romano, Tricia, 35
Rottneck, Matthew, 36n
Rosette, Mademoiselle, 165
Roudinesco, Elisabeth, 109
Rousseau, G.S, 60
Roux, Willhelm, 81–82
Roy, Alec, 53n
RuPaul, 180
Rush, Benjamin, 47
Ryan, Caitlin, 36n

S

Safouan, Moustapha, 164, 179
Salecl, Renata, 6, 7
Schaefer, Leah, 34
Scheidhauer, Marcel, 68n
Schreber, Daniel Paul, 154–155, 158–159, 160, 161, 162, 163, 164, 165, 174, 175, 176, 177, 178, 179, 180, 195, 232–233
Schur, Max, 73n
Schwave, Arthur, 223
Scillag, Emma, 124–125
Scillag, Sidonie, 93–94, 95–97, 99–100, 102–105, 107, 116–117, 118, 121–123, 124–125, 128, 151, 152, 153–154
Sedgwick, Eve Kosofsky, 12, 27

Sengoopta, Chandak, 66n, 78, 79, 81n, 82, 83, 84, 85n
Separation, 196, 197, 200, 201
Sex drive, 143
Sex transmutationist, 28
Sexual identity. *See also* Gender identity
  anatomy, realities of, 231
  assumptions regarding, 1
  choice, free, 7, 168–169
  Freud's theories on development of, 120–121
  gender parody, relationship between, 114
  infants, "sexing" of, 5
  medicalization of choice, 6
  psychoanalytic perspective, 5
  Reimer, David, in, 182–183 (*see also* Reimer, David, case of)
  secondary nature, as, 185, 193
  societal shifts, 8–9
Sexual liberation, 8
Sexuality
  chemical theories of, 81
  primordial disposition toward, 87
  spectrum of, 62–63
  Ulrich's theory of, 87
Sexuation formulas, 126–129, 179–180, 189, 191, 192, 210–211, 246
Shapiro, Judith, 34
Shepherdson, Charles, 1, 6–7, 61
Shorter, Edward, 56
Showalter, Elaine, 48
Sigmundson, Keith, 134, 136, 147
Sinthome, xii, 152, 153, 154, 160, 163, 167, 168, 178, 181, 182, 185, 186, 189, 191, 196, 200, 205, 208, 212, 216, 217, 218, 229, 231, 232, 234, 243–244, 246, 247
Slater, Eliot, 48
Smiley, Lauren, 9, 10
Smith, Robert, 16
Smith-Rosenberg, Carroll, 50
Sodomy laws, 86
Soler, Colette, 211
Spitz, Renée, 104
Stack, Megan, 3
Steinach, Eugen, 28, 73, 77, 78, 79, 80, 81, 82, 83, 84, 85, 87, 88, 89, 139, 140, 218, 219, 221, 227, 248

Stoller, Robert, 32, 73, 113, 147, 161, 174, 175, 223–224, 247
Stone, Sandy, 226, 229
Stryker, Susan, 221
Sublimation, 210
Suicide
  Reimer, David, case of (*see* Reimer, David, case of)
  Sidonie, attempts by, 96–97, 116–117, 153–154
  transgendered persons, among, 36
Sulloway, Frank, 67, 73, 83n
Superego, 77
Swoboda, Hermann, 66, 67, 68, 69
Sydenham, Thomas, 42, 45, 46, 47, 55

T

Thullier, Jean, 157
Transable, 17
Transamerica, 21, 57
Transference, 73, 100, 119, 122, 123, 152, 201, 207
Transgender Family and Friends Support Network, 34
Transgender Law Center, 10
Transgenderism
  APA diagnosis of, 26
  children with, 9, 10
  complexity of, 29–30
  difficulties of transgendered persons, 38–40
  health problems of transgender persons, 36
  ideological alliances, 33
  media fascination with, 35–36
  radical edge to term, 32–33
  sexual practice *versus* identity, 33
  word origins and usage, 32–33
  word, history of, 25
Transitioning
  childhood, during, 10
  defining, 25
  difficulties associated with, 38–40
  enormity of, 2
  narratives of, 229–230
Transsexualism
  assumptions regarding, 1
  biological aspects of, 219–220
  complexities of, 226–227
  defining, 219–220
  endocrinology, 81, 82, 222

error of nature discourse, 165–166
female to male, 194–195
film, exploration in, 21
gender reassignment surgery (see
   Gender reassignment surgery)
Genuine, use of term, 220
Henri, case of (see Henri, case of)
Hera, case of (see Hera, case of)
icons of, 28
identity issues, 36–38
male-to-female, 32
memoirs by, 36, 215–216, 220–221,
   224–226, 227–228, 233–236
   (see also specific transsexual
   memoirists)
Michel H. case of, 169–174
narrative transitions, 229–230
origins of terminology, 28, 29
phallus, role of, 163–164
population statistics, 34, 35
religious framework of, 4
Steinach's contributions to, 80–81
   (see also Steinach, Eugen)
support of, in Iran, 3–4
therapeutic, view of reassignment
   as, 4
transitioning (see transitioning)
treatment protocols, 34
trivialization of, 2
visibility of, modern, 3–5
Transvestite
   origin of term, 2
Trebay, Guy, 12
Trillat, Etienne, 50n

U

Ulrichs, Karl Heinrich, 85–86, 87, 219

Unisexuality, 84
Urning, 86
Uterus, historical view of, 41–42

V

Vaginoplasty, 220, 221
Valentine, David, 29
Valerio, Max Wolf, 216, 226n, 228,
   236, 239–240
Veith, Ilza, 44n, 54, 55, 62
Verhaeghe, Paul, 48, 61, 185
Victoria (drag), 180–181

W

Wajeman, Gérard, 55, 56n
Weininger, Otto, 66, 67, 68, 69, 76,
   80, 83, 84, 218
Weiss, Edoardo, 94
Westphal, Karl, 86
Whytt, Robert, 46, 47, 55
Willis, Thomas, 45, 46
Wilton, Tamsin, 234
Women's colleges, as places of
   transformation, 39
Woodward, Luke, 23

Y

Young, Hugh, 18

Z

Zander, Erica, 226n, 238
Zeus, 139

The twelfth Figure, of the Womb

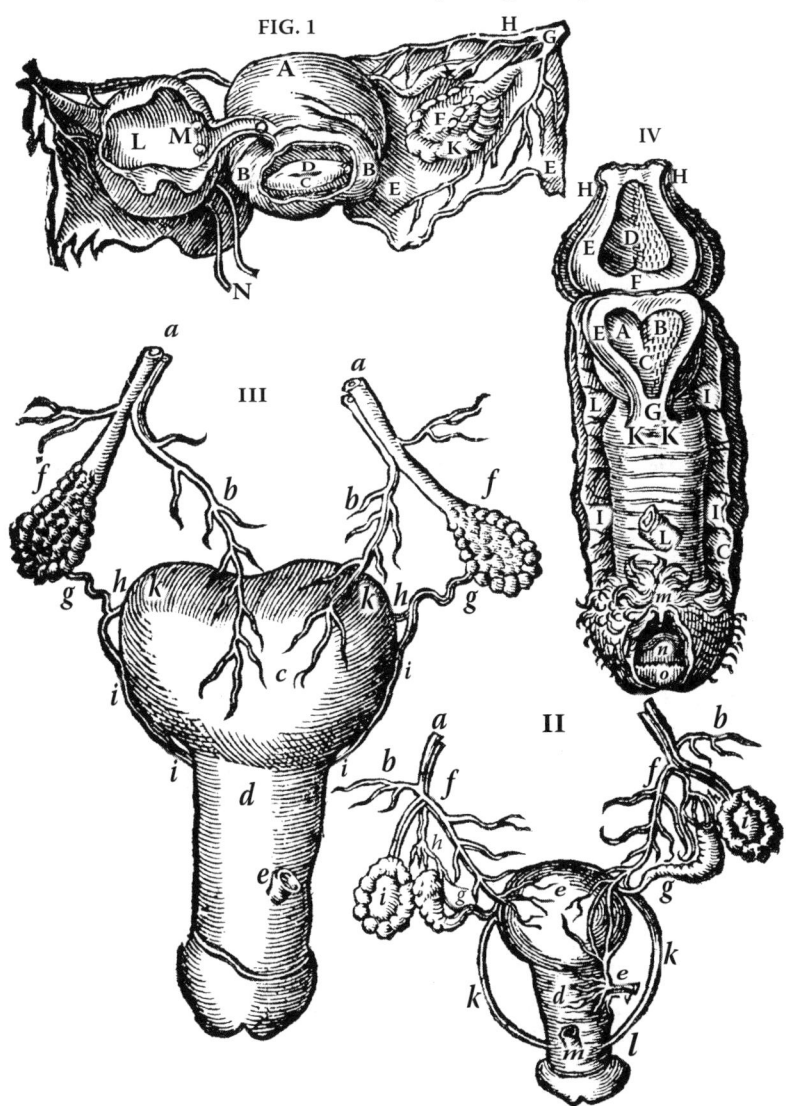

Figure 1 Ambroise Paré's (1510–1590) representations of the female organs of generation as penis-like vaginas and uteri. Reproduced from Ambroise Paré, *The Workes of That Famous Chirurgion Ambrose Parey, trans. out of the Latine and compared with the French* by Thomas Johnson. London: Cotes & Du-gard, 1649, p. 31. Courtesy Library of the College of Physicians of Philadelphia.

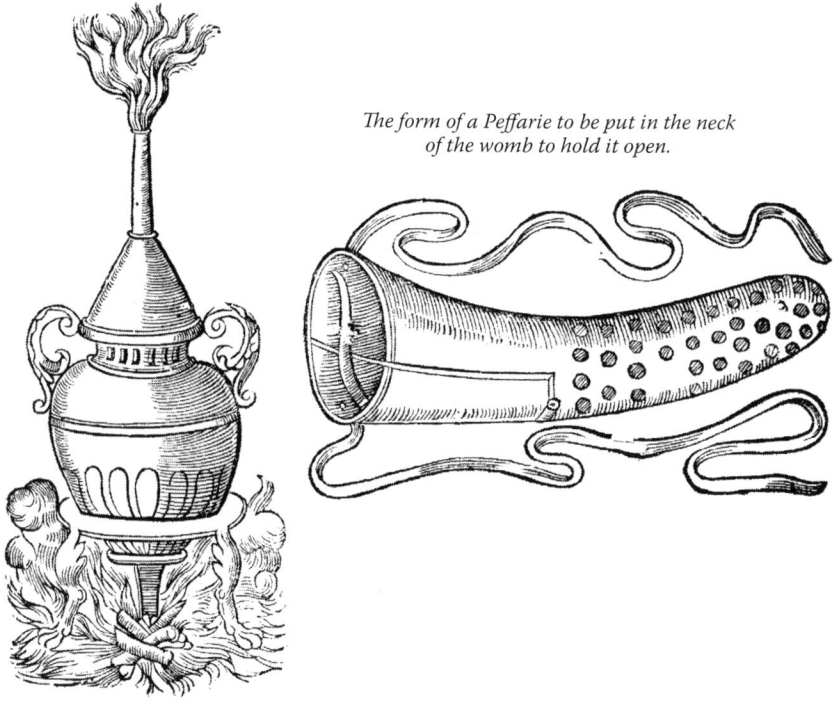

Figure 2 Ambroise Paré's contraptions for the treatment of hysteria. Left: Fumigation machine. Right: Pessary for cervical insertion. The holes are designed to spread fumes into the uterus. Reproduced from Ambroise Paré, *The Workes of That Famous Chirurgion Ambrose Parey, trans. out of the Latine and compared with the French* by Thomas Johnson. London: Cotes & Du-gard, 1649, p. 635. Courtesy Library of the College of Physicians of Philadelphia.

Planche XXIX

HYSTERO-EPILEPSIE

CONTRACTURE

Figure 3 Charcot's hysteria was spectacle—photograph in contracture stage of hysteroepilepsy of Augustine, celebrated hysteric patient of the Salpêtrière Hospital and surrealist muse. Reproduced from *Iconographie photographique de la Salpêtrière, Service de J. M. Charcot* (Vol. 2), by Désiré Magloire Bourneville and Paul Régnard. Paris: Bureau du Progrès medical/Delahaye and Lecrosnier, 1878. Courtesy Library of the College of Physicians of Philadelphia.

Figure 4 Early 1900s tango scene. On a Buenos Aires sidewalk, men drink, dance tango, and listen to a *bandoneón*. Anonymous photographer. 1907(?). Source: Archivo General de la Nación.

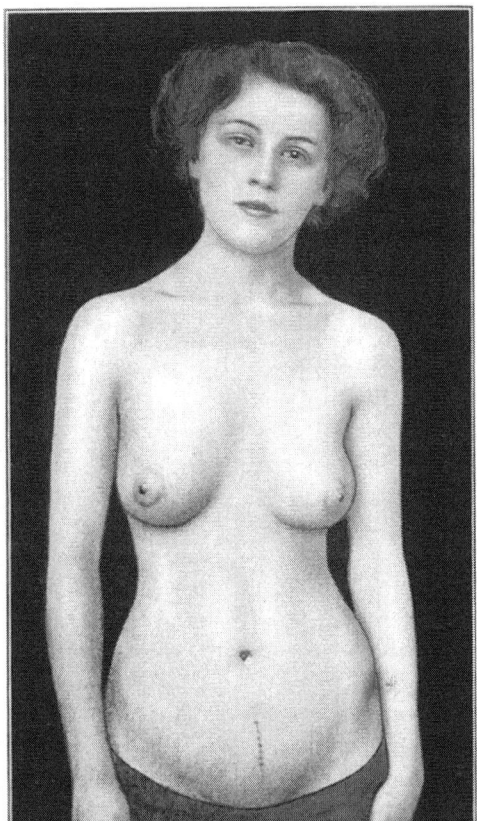

Photograph of a male partial tubular hermaphrodite, showing the complete development of feminine secondary characteristics.

Figure 5 While the caption reads "photograph of a male," today this case would be classified as intersex (androgen insensitivity syndrome or AIS; a XY so-called male but without receptors for testosterone; fetuses develop feminine characteristics). The scar testifies to exploratory surgery to determine gender. Intersex patient of Dr. Russell Andrew (1910s). Reproduced from William Blair Bell, *The Sex Complex* (2nd ed.), New York: Wood, 1921. Courtesy Library of the College of Physicians of Philadelphia.

EUGEN STEINACH, 1861–1944

Figure 6 Eugen Steinach (1861–1944), Viennese physicist and innovator who performed the first sex change surgeries by gland transplants and isolated the "sex hormones." Courtesy The Kinsey Institute for Research in Sex, Gender, and Reproduction.

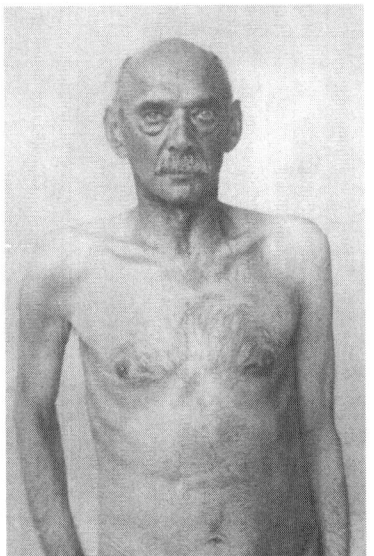 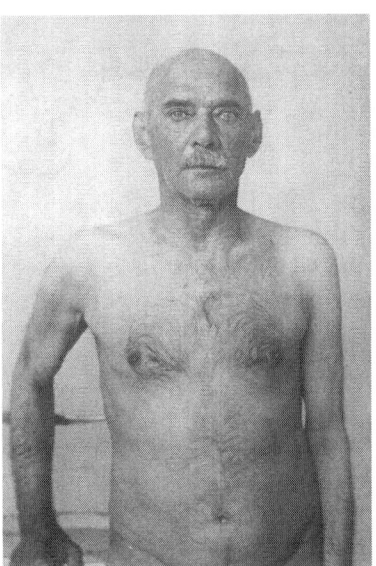

Figure 7 Man who underwent the "Steinach operation," a vasoligature that promised rejuvenation. Left: Before the operation. Right: After the operation. Steinach used these pictures as proof of an improved, more youthful appearance attained by the surgery. Courtesy The Kinsey Institute for Research in Sex, Gender, and Reproduction.

Feminization series (guinea-pigs). *Left to right*: normal brother, feminized brother, normal sister, castrated brother.

Figure 8 By 1912, Steinach had succeeded in changing the sex of guinea pigs by transplantation of sex glands. The female guinea pig is usually half the size of the male. The point is that castration is not sufficient to change appearance; only implanted ovaries or testicles produce a visible modification and change in sexual behavior. Reproduced from Eugen Steinach, *Sex and Life: Forty Years of Biological and Medical Experiments*, New York: Viking Press, 1940. Courtesy Library of the College of Physicians of Philadelphia.

Figure 9 By a coincidence, in 1952 the term *hysteria* disappeared from American psychiatric texts, and a medical team led by Christian Hamburger performed the first globally publicized surgical sex change on Christine Jorgensen. *New York Daily News*, L. P., December 1, 1952. Reprinted with permission. Courtesy The Kinsey Institute for Research in Sex, Gender, and Reproduction.

When Christine arrived in Denmark, she was a handsome man named George.

The feminizing effect of the first operation is obvious in this photograph taken in 1951.

This recent portrait of Christine shows her dramatic transformation from man to woman.

Figure 10 Christine Jorgensen's (1926–1989) transformation from man to woman. Courtesy The Kinsey Institute for Research in Sex, Gender, and Reproduction.

Figure 11 Christine Jorgensen capitalized on her celebrity status by becoming a nightclub entertainer. *Daily Mirror*, May 21, 1954. Courtesy The Kinsey Institute for Research in Sex, Gender, and Reproduction.

Figure 12 Harry Benjamin (1885–1986), German-born endocrinologist, the first doctor in the United States specializing in transsexualism. Photo by William Dellenback. Courtesy The Kinsey Institute for Research in Sex, Gender, and Reproduction.

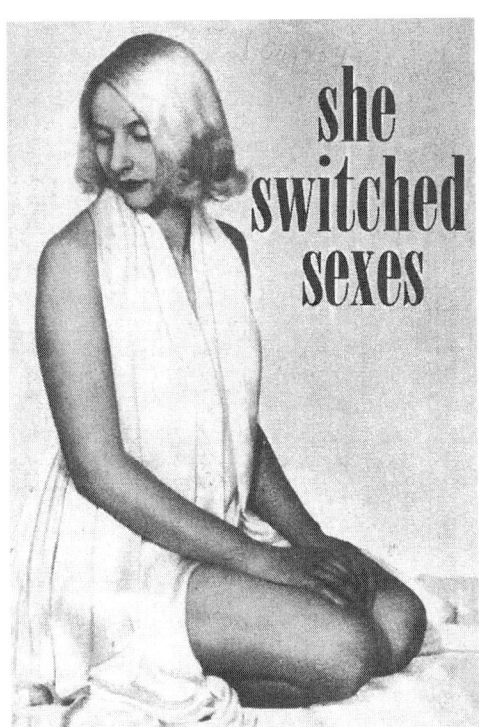

Figure 13 In the 1950s, popular media kept on publicizing sex changes, like this 1954 article about a female-to-male transition, subtitled "Transformation: From Shapely Blond to Sinewy Male Made Kim Happy." *Brief,* August 1954. Courtesy The Kinsey Institute for Research in Sex, Gender, and Reproduction.

Stripper Hedy Jo Star's Amazing Story

I CHANGED MY SEX FROM MAN TO WOMAN

(As Told To Don JACKSON)

Suppose tomorrow, by some improbable stroke of fate, you where given the opportunity to decide whether you wished to remain as you are or change your sex, would you draw back in revulsion or would you grab at the chance?

Have you ever envied the lot of the opposite sex, felt the life to be easier, more exciting or better suited to your temperament?

Though I was born a man, I have always envied women and practically ever since I was knee high to a grasshopper, I've wanted to be a woman.

The natural desire in me was to be a woman because I acted and thought like one.

Such a desire in me did not constitute an impulse of the moment or a deep-seated psychological aspect of homosexuality.

From my own experience it is equally ridiculous to declare the assumption of somewhat manly traits by women a show of Lesbianism.

Though the double standard still prevails, emancipation and freedom of expression have made both adopt some habits in common.

Girl athletes, executives and public officials that are accepted as a matter of course today, would have been considered highly abnormal a few years ago.

By the same token, male designers, hairdressers and interior decorators at one time were looked upon with suspicion.

However, it would only be fair to state that divergency from the "normal" can and does exist.

Sometimes it finds expression in harmless masquerades, and at others in outright acts considered contrary to law.

Take myself, for instance. I was born in Oklahoma as a male, and christened Carl Rollins Hammonds. "Hedy Jo Star" is my stage name. My father died several years ago. My mother is Bertha Hammonds and she lives at 1522 Westwood St., Oklahoma City. Any reader of MIDNIGHT wishing to write to me can do so to this address. Or you can reach me at 177 North State St., Suite 412, Chicago, Ill.

I have to give a few of these facts to explain a little of my birth and earlier days.

If you were to ask my mother 'today' what she thinks of my sex change into a woman, she would answer you, "It should have been done many years ago!"

For the first 18 years of my life I lived as a boy, but I acted and thought as a girl. Even my anatomy was that of a male.

Hedy Jo Star as a baby, as a boy and as a man.

Then I decided that instead of being what I called myself half-man and half-woman, I decided to go all the way and have surgery performed on me to transform me physically and entirely into a woman.

The daily papers carry accounts of men who have attempted to live their lives as women, and even women who have gone so far as to marry one of their own sex.

Generally, these individuals have long fought and finally lost out in their battle to pursue the life which society decrees proper for one of their own sex.

The attempt, for an individual whose tendencies are definitely homosexual to pursue a normal existence can be torturous to an extreme.

He is a psychological misfit, trying vainly to conform to an almost impossible situation.

Though I am definitely not a homosexual—or have ever been—it was because of this that I decided to place my whole existence in the hands of surgery to make my transformation complete.

I guess you could say that I was an enoist.

The enoist's greatest difficulty comes from attempting to cope with his particular divergence in a world which rarely understands him.

The manifestations of his state often create erroneous impressions.

Actually, an enoist seldom, if ever, has an urge towards his own sex. His peculiarity, if it may be termed that, springs from his genuine admiration of the opposite sex and expresses itself in his desire to embrace some of the qualities of that sex.

An enoist is generally an aesthetic person who considers purely masculine pursuits slightly coarse and looks with favor upon the delicacy and beauty of feminine life.

This does not mean that every cultured man is an enoist, but it does follow that because of his sensitive nature the average enoist is inclined to be of a cultured bend.

Another type who must be seriously considered is the transvestite whose greatest delight is to don feminine garb.

I have met up with plenty of these individuals.

This type may also be completely impervious to the charms of his own sex and never dream of making an advance in such a direction.

Nevertheless, he is apt to encounter difficulty with those who interpret his masquerade as an out-and-out expression of homosexuality and condemn it as such.

It is hard for those who consider themselves normal to understand the motivation behind such a seemingly unorthodox action.

Yet, top ranking experts of sexual behaviour will readily admit that the borderline between "normal" and what may constitute a perversion is very thin, indeed.

The reason for such an abnormality is far more often mental than physical. Generally, the men and women who hunger to live the life of the opposite sex exhibit no anatomical differences from others of their sex.

In outward appearance they are fine physical specimens. The fires of satisfaction which burn beneath the surface have been fanned into flame because of a variety of reasons.

For a number of years I was active in show business —always as a woman, even though my body was that of a male.

During this period I used special latex rubber busts which were created exclusively for me.

They were very realistic and never questioned by anyone.

I had been consulting various specialists and surgeons and they examined me from my head to my toes. I went through exhaustive tests in New York's Park East Hospital and as well as in the famed John Hopkins Hospital.

My male busts were changed to female by a new "bust plastic" process recently invented. My surgeon was Dr. Elsie La Roe, one of the world's foremost plastic surgeons.

Every part of my anatomy was operated on. My male organs were changed to that of the female, complete in every respect.

I have all the medical evidence to corroborate this.

As a male my measurements were: chest, 38; waist, 29; hips, 34½.

After my sex operation these became: bust, 42; waist, 26; hips, 38.

I was told that in very rare cases do surgeons actually suggest a complete sex transference to insure a happier life.

I have conclusively proven that sex is mutable.

Even as people laugh at the antics of female impersonators, unhappy people struggle with their grave problem of adjustment to their sex, or a change over into another.

The ramifications of the issue are tremendous, and the critics of such an idea are legion.

Hedy Jo Star as a woman after the operation.

I Had To Correct Nature's Mistake

Figure 14 Hedy Jo Star was a famous male-to-female stripper who gave a serialized first-person account of her transition under the general heading of "I Changed My Sex." This became the title of her autobiographical memoir. In the 1960s, she had a regular column dispensing advice on sexual issues. *Midnight*, October 29, 1962. Courtesy The Kinsey Institute for Research in Sex, Gender, and Reproduction.

Figure 15 Serialized memoir of the most famous of French *travesti*, performer Coccinelle. Jacqueline-Charlotte Dufresnoy (1931–2006) became an international media sensation and an inspiration since her debut as a transgender showgirl in 1953. *Confidential*, July 24, 1963. Courtesy The Kinsey Institute for Research in Sex, Gender, and Reproduction.

Figure 16 In the 1960s, the popular media would regularly give accounts of successful sex changes like this one portraying fashion model April Ashley. Courtesy The Kinsey Institute for Research in Sex, Gender, and Reproduction.

Figure 17 In 1966, the African American magazine *Sepia* documented "the first Negro sex-change" from man to woman of nurse and jazz vocalist Delisa Newton (born 1934). *Sepia*, April 1966. Courtesy The Kinsey Institute for Research in Sex, Gender, and Reproduction.

Figure 18 John Money (1921–2006), psychologist and sex researcher and key figure in creating the John Hopkins University Gender Identity Clinic in 1966, the first university medical center for sex reassignment surgery. Photo by William Dellenback. Courtesy The Kinsey Institute for Research in Sex, Gender, and Reproduction.

Figure 19 Luke Woodward (center), a transgender student at Brown University. Wood has been an advocate for a better environment for other transgender students. Photograph by George Ruhe/Enelysion; originally published March 7, 2004 in the *New York Times*. Courtesy of George Ruhe.

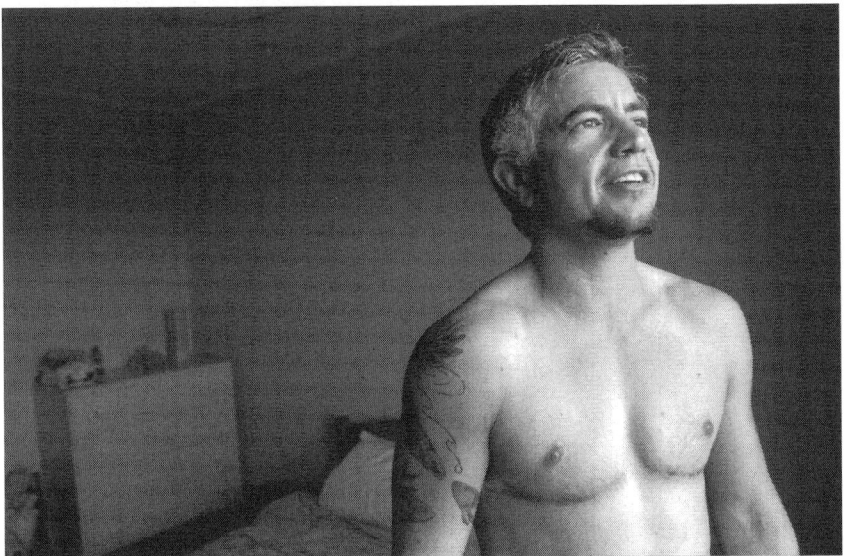

Figure 20 Shane Caya, an attorney, displays his mastectomy scars in *The New York Times*. Photograph by Darcy Padilla; originally published August 20, 2006 in the *New York Times*. Courtesy of Darcy Padilla.

Figure 21 Jenny Finney Boylan, acclaimed author and professor of English. Photograph by James Bowdoin. Courtesy Jenny Finney Boylan.

Figure 22 Nina Poon, transgender woman, makeup artist, and illustrator. Poon has been seen in the apparel publicity campaign "We All Walk in Different Shoes." Photograph by Nina Poon. Courtesy Nina Poon.

Figure 23 Stu Rasmussen, mayor of Silverton, Oregon, reelected in 2008, is the first openly transgender mayor in the United States. Photograph by Lisa Kereszi. Originally published in *Details Magazine*. Courtesy of Lisa Kereszi.

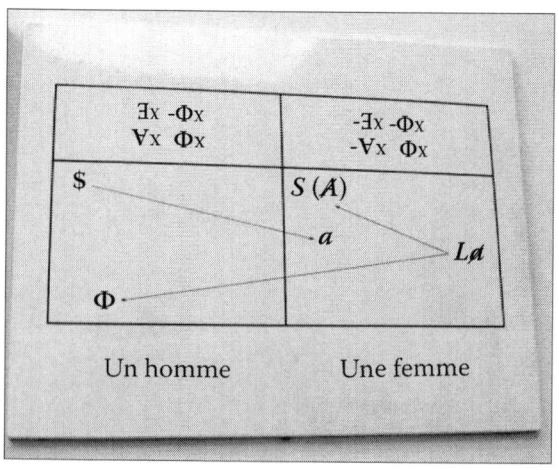

Figure 24 Rendering of Lacan's sexuation formulas. Photograph by the author. Private collection.

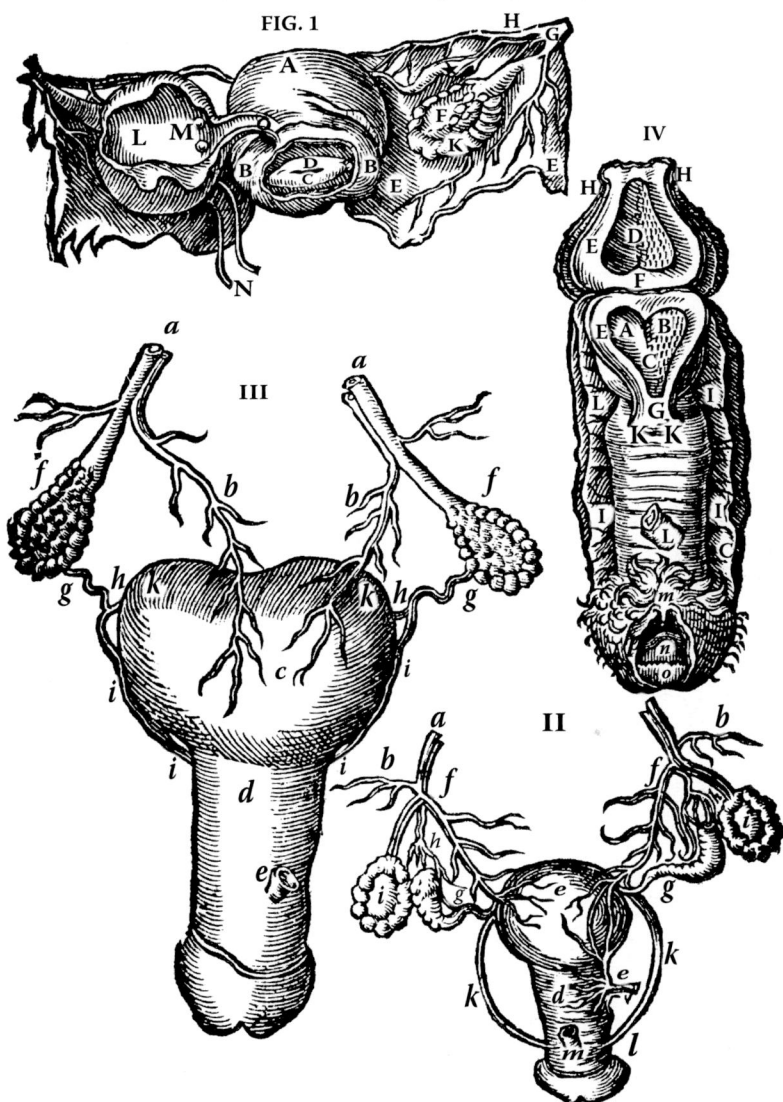

Figure 1 Ambroise Paré's (1510–1590) representations of the female organs of generation as penis-like vaginas and uteri. Reproduced from Ambroise Paré, *The Workes of That Famous Chirurgion Ambrose Parey, trans. out of the Latine and compared with the French* by Thomas Johnson. London: Cotes & Du-gard, 1649, p. 31. Courtesy Library of the College of Physicians of Philadelphia.

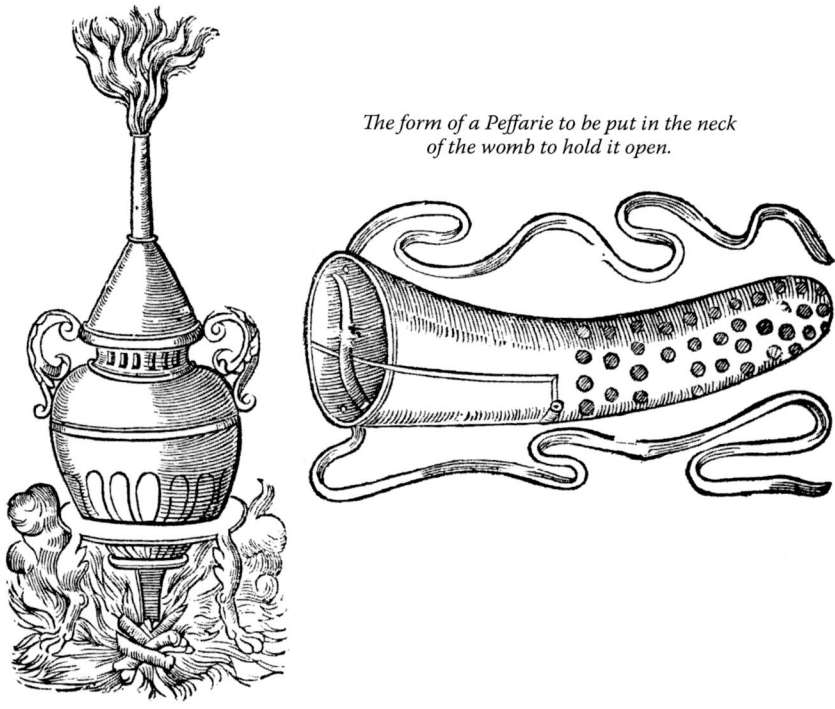

Figure 2 Ambroise Paré's contraptions for the treatment of hysteria. Left: Fumigation machine. Right: Pessary for cervical insertion. The holes are designed to spread fumes into the uterus. Reproduced from Ambroise Paré, *The Workes of That Famous Chirurgion Ambrose Parey, trans. out of the Latine and compared with the French* by Thomas Johnson. London: Cotes & Du-gard, 1649, p. 635. Courtesy Library of the College of Physicians of Philadelphia.

Planche XXIX

HYSTERO-EPILEPSIE

CONTRACTURE

Figure 3 Charcot's hysteria was spectacle—photograph in contracture stage of hysteroepilepsy of Augustine, celebrated hysteric patient of the Salpêtrière Hospital and surrealist muse. Reproduced from *Iconographie photographique de la Salpêtrière, Service de J. M. Charcot* (Vol. 2), by Désiré Magloire Bourneville and Paul Régnard. Paris: Bureau du Progrès medical/Delahaye and Lecrosnier, 1878. Courtesy Library of the College of Physicians of Philadelphia.

Figure 4 Early 1900s tango scene. On a Buenos Aires sidewalk, men drink, dance tango, and listen to a *bandoneón*. Anonymous photographer. 1907(?). Source: Archivo General de la Nación.

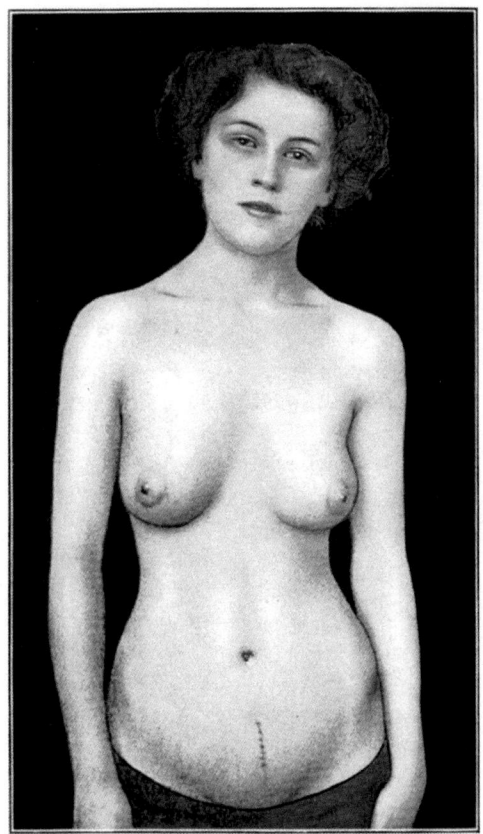

Photograph of a male partial tubular hermaphrodite, showing the complete development of feminine secondary characteristics.

Figure 5 While the caption reads "photograph of a male," today this case would be classified as intersex (androgen insensitivity syndrome or AIS; a XY so-called male but without receptors for testosterone; fetuses develop feminine characteristics). The scar testifies to exploratory surgery to determine gender. Intersex patient of Dr. Russell Andrew (1910s). Reproduced from William Blair Bell, *The Sex Complex* (2nd ed.), New York: Wood, 1921. Courtesy Library of the College of Physicians of Philadelphia.

EUGEN STEINACH, 1861–1944

Figure 6 Eugen Steinach (1861–1944), Viennese physicist and innovator who performed the first sex change surgeries by gland transplants and isolated the "sex hormones." Courtesy The Kinsey Institute for Research in Sex, Gender, and Reproduction.

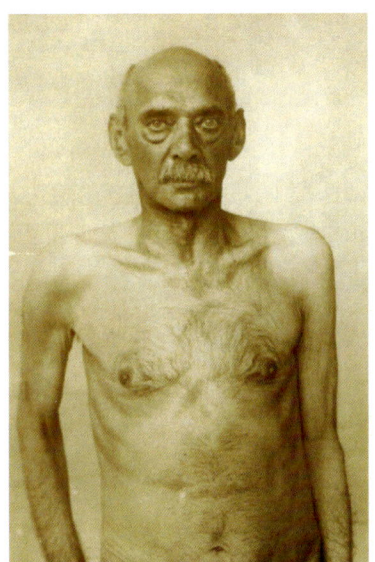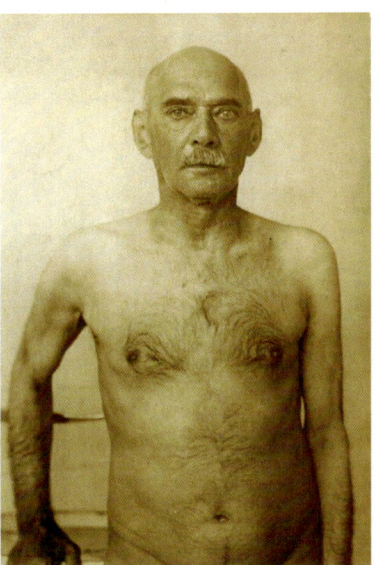

Figure 7 Man who underwent the "Steinach operation," a vasoligature that promised rejuvenation. Left: Before the operation. Right: After the operation. Steinach used these pictures as proof of an improved, more youthful appearance attained by the surgery. Courtesy The Kinsey Institute for Research in Sex, Gender, and Reproduction.

Feminization series (guinea-pigs). *Left to right*: normal brother, feminized brother, normal sister, castrated brother.

Figure 8 By 1912, Steinach had succeeded in changing the sex of guinea pigs by transplantation of sex glands. The female guinea pig is usually half the size of the male. The point is that castration is not sufficient to change appearance; only implanted ovaries or testicles produce a visible modification and change in sexual behavior. Reproduced from Eugen Steinach, *Sex and Life: Forty Years of Biological and Medical Experiments,* New York: Viking Press, 1940. Courtesy Library of the College of Physicians of Philadelphia.

Figure 9 By a coincidence, in 1952 the term *hysteria* disappeared from American psychiatric texts, and a medical team led by Christian Hamburger performed the first globally publicized surgical sex change on Christine Jorgensen. *New York Daily News, L. P.*, December 1, 1952. Reprinted with permission. Courtesy The Kinsey Institute for Research in Sex, Gender, and Reproduction.

When Christine arrived in Denmark, she was a handsome man named George.

The feminizing effect of the first operation is obvious in this photograph taken in 1951.

This recent portrait of Christine shows her dramatic transformation from man to woman.

Figure 10 Christine Jorgensen's (1926–1989) transformation from man to woman. Courtesy The Kinsey Institute for Research in Sex, Gender, and Reproduction.

Figure 11 Christine Jorgensen capitalized on her celebrity status by becoming a nightclub entertainer. *Daily Mirror*, May 21, 1954. Courtesy The Kinsey Institute for Research in Sex, Gender, and Reproduction.

Figure 12 Harry Benjamin (1885–1986), German-born endocrinologist, the first doctor in the United States specializing in transsexualism. Photo by William Dellenback. Courtesy The Kinsey Institute for Research in Sex, Gender, and Reproduction.

Figure 13 In the 1950s, popular media kept on publicizing sex changes, like this 1954 article about a female-to-male transition, subtitled "Transformation: From Shapely Blond to Sinewy Male Made Kim Happy." *Brief*, August 1954. Courtesy The Kinsey Institute for Research in Sex, Gender, and Reproduction.

Stripper Hedy Jo Star's Amazing Story

I CHANGED MY SEX FROM MAN TO WOMAN

(As Told To Don JACKSON)

Suppose tomorrow, by some improbable stroke of fate, you were given the opportunity to decide whether you wished to remain as you are or change your sex, would you draw back in revulsion or would you grab at the chance?

Have you ever envied the lot of the opposite sex, felt the life to be easier, more exciting or better suited to your temperament?

Though I was born a man, I have always envied women and practically ever since I was knee high to a grasshopper, I've wanted to be a woman.

The natural desire in me was to be a woman because I acted and thought like one.

Such a desire in me did not constitute an impulse of the moment or a deep-seated psychological aspect of homosexuality.

From my own experience it is equally ridiculous to declare the assumption of somewhat manly traits by women a show of Lesbianism.

Though the double standard still prevails, emancipation and freedom of expression have made both adopt some habits in common.

Girl athletes, executives and public officials that are accepted as a matter of course today, would have been considered highly abnormal a few years ago.

By the same token, male designers, hairdressers and interior decorators at one time were looked upon with suspicion.

However, it would only be fair to state that divergency from the "normal" can and does exist.

Sometimes it finds expression in harmless masquerades, and at others in outright acts considered contrary to law.

Take myself, for instance. I was born in Oklahoma as a male, and christened Carl Rollins Hammonds. "Redy Jo Star" is my stage name. My father died several years ago. My mother is Bertha Hammonds and she lives at 1522 Westwood St., Oklahoma City. Any reader of MIDNIGHT wishing to write to me can do so to this address. Or you can reach me at 177 North State St., Suite 412, Chicago, Ill.

I have to give a few of these facts to explain a little of my birth and earlier days.

If you were to ask my mother today what she thinks of my sex change into a woman, she would answer you, "It should have been done many years ago."

For the first 18 years of my life I lived as a boy, but I acted and thought as a girl. Even my anatomy was that of a male.

Hedy Jo Star as a baby, as a boy and as a man.

Then I decided that instead of being what I called myself half-man and half-woman, I decided to go all the way and have surgery performed on me to transform me physically and entirely into a woman.

The daily papers carry accounts of men who have attempted to live their lives as women, and even women who have gone so as far as to marry one of their own sex.

Generally, these individuals have long fought and finally lost out in their battle to pursue the life which society decrees proper for one of their own sex.

The attempt, for an individual whose tendencies are definitely homosexual to pursue a normal existence can be tortuorous to an extreme.

He is a psychological misfit, trying vainly to conform to an almost impossible situation.

Though I am definitely not a homosexual—or have ever been—it was because of this that I decided to place my whole existence in the hands of surgery to make my transformation complete.

I guess you could say that I was an enoist.

The enoist's greatest difficulty comes from attempting to cope with his particular divergence in a world which rarely understands him.

The manifestations of his state often create erroneous impressions.

Actually, an enoist seldom, if ever, has an urge toward his own sex. His peculiarity, if it may be termed that, springs from his genuine admiration of the opposite sex and expresses itself in his desire to embrace some of the qualities of that sex.

An enoist is generally an aesthetic person who considers purely masculine pursuits slightly coarse and looks with favor upon the delicacy and beauty of feminine life.

This does not mean that every cultured man is an enoist, but it does follow that because of his sensitive nature the average enoist is inclined to be of a cultured bend.

Another type who must be seriously considered is the transvestite whose greatest delight is to don feminine garb.

I have met up with plenty of these individuals.

This type may also be completely impervious to the charms of his own sex and never dream of making an advance in such a direction.

Nevertheless, he is apt to encounter difficulty with those who interpret his masquerade as an out-and-out expression of homosexuality and condemn it as such.

It is hard for those who consider themselves normal to understand the motivation behind such a seemingly unorthodox action.

Yet, top ranking experts of sexual behaviour will readily admit that the borderline between "normal" and what may constitute a perversion is very thin, indeed.

The reason for such an abnormality is far more often mental than physical. Generally, the men and women who hunger to live the life of the opposite sex exhibit no anatomical differences from others of their sex.

In outward appearance they are fine physical specimens. The fires of satisfaction which burn beneath the surface have been fanned into flame because of a variety of reasons.

For a number of years I was active in show business —always as a woman, even though my body was that of a male.

During this period I used special latex rubber busts which were created exclusively for me.

They were very realistic and never questioned by anyone.

I had been consulting various specialists and surgeons and they examined me from my head to my toes. I went through exhaustive tests in New York's Park East Hospital and as well as in the famed John Hopkins Hospital.

My male busts were changed to female by a new "bust plastic" process recently invented. My surgeon was Dr. Elsie La Roe, one of the world's foremost plastic surgeons.

Every part of my anatomy was operated on. My male organs were changed to that of the female, complete in every respect.

I have all the medical evidence to corroborate this.

As a male my measurements were: chest, 38; waist, 29; hips, 34½.

After my sex operation these became: bust, 42; waist, 26; hips, 38.

I was told that in very rare cases do surgeons actually suggest a complete sex transference to insure a happier life.

I have conclusively proven that sex is mutable.

Even as people laugh at the antics of female impersonators, unhappy people struggle with their grave problem of adjustment to their sex, or a change over into another.

The ramifications of the issue are tremendous, and the critics of such an idea are legion.

Hedy Jo Star as a woman after the operation.

I Had To Correct Nature's Mistake

Figure 14 Hedy Jo Star was a famous male-to-female stripper who gave a serialized first-person account of her transition under the general heading of "I Changed My Sex." This became the title of her autobiographical memoir. In the 1960s, she had a regular column dispensing advice on sexual issues. *Midnight*, October 29, 1962. Courtesy The Kinsey Institute for Research in Sex, Gender, and Reproduction.

Figure 15 Serialized memoir of the most famous of French *travesti,* performer Coccinelle. Jacqueline-Charlotte Dufresnoy (1931–2006) became an international media sensation and an inspiration since her debut as a transgender showgirl in 1953. *Confidential,* July 24, 1963. Courtesy The Kinsey Institute for Research in Sex, Gender, and Reproduction.

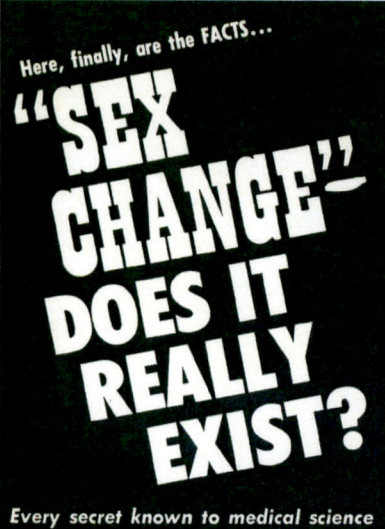

Figure 16 In the 1960s, the popular media would regularly give accounts of successful sex changes like this one portraying fashion model April Ashley. Courtesy The Kinsey Institute for Research in Sex, Gender, and Reproduction.

Figure 17 In 1966, the African American magazine *Sepia* documented "the first Negro sex-change" from man to woman of nurse and jazz vocalist Delisa Newton (born 1934). *Sepia*, April 1966. Courtesy The Kinsey Institute for Research in Sex, Gender, and Reproduction.

Figure 18 John Money (1921–2006), psychologist and sex researcher and key figure in creating the John Hopkins University Gender Identity Clinic in 1966, the first university medical center for sex reassignment surgery. Photo by William Dellenback. Courtesy The Kinsey Institute for Research in Sex, Gender, and Reproduction.

Figure 19 Luke Woodward (center), a transgender student at Brown University. Wood has been an advocate for a better environment for other transgender students. Photograph by George Ruhe/Enelysion; originally published March 7, 2004 in the *New York Times*. Courtesy of George Ruhe.

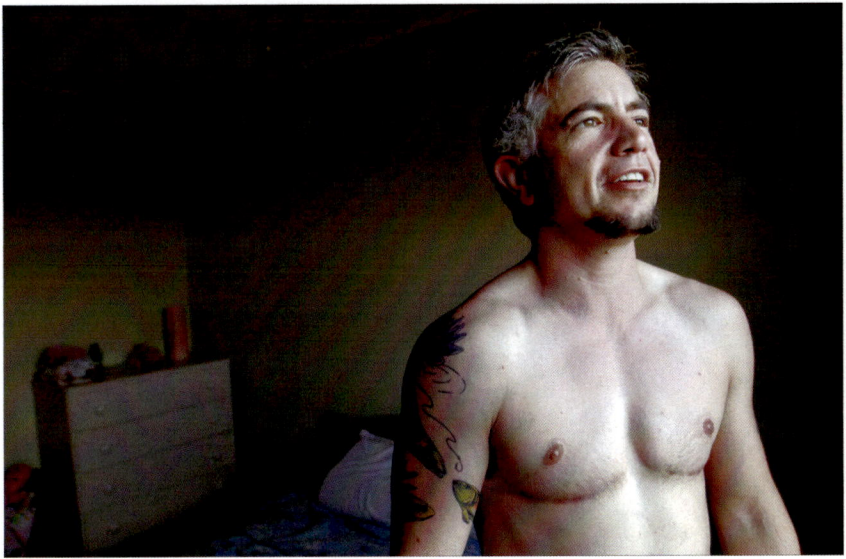

Figure 20 Shane Caya, an attorney, displays his mastectomy scars in *The New York Times*. Photograph by Darcy Padilla; originally published August 20, 2006 in the *New York Times*. Courtesy of Darcy Padilla.

Figure 21 Jenny Finney Boylan, acclaimed author and professor of English. Photograph by James Bowdoin. Courtesy Jenny Finney Boylan.

Figure 22 Nina Poon, transgender woman, makeup artist, and illustrator. Poon has been seen in the apparel publicity campaign "We All Walk in Different Shoes." Photograph by Nina Poon. Courtesy Nina Poon.

Figure 23 Stu Rasmussen, mayor of Silverton, Oregon, reelected in 2008, is the first openly transgender mayor in the United States. Photograph by Lisa Kereszi. Originally published in *Details Magazine*. Courtesy of Lisa Kereszi.

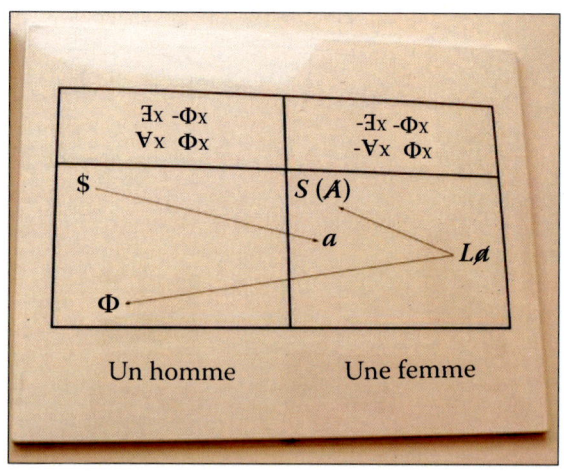

Figure 24 Rendering of Lacan's sexuation formulas. Photograph by the author. Private collection.